ph   n   (4 07

|

The WELFARE *of* NATIONS

The
WELFARE
of
NATIONS

James Bartholomew

Biteback Publishing

First published in Great Britain in 2015 by
Biteback Publishing Ltd
Westminster Tower
3 Albert Embankment
London SE1 7SP
Copyright © James Bartholomew 2015

ISBN 978-1-84954-830-4

A CIP catalogue record for this book is available from the British Library.

Set in Adobe Garamond Pro

Printed and bound in Great Britain by

To...

*the people who really went out of their way to help me with the research for
this book: Jeremy Hosking played the key role of giving me some funding; Meir
Kohn, economics professor at Dartmouth College, regularly sent me links to
articles which could be of use, provided contacts and, just as important, gave
me encouragement; Christian Wignall chauffeured me from one appointment to another in San Francisco and Oakland, patiently waiting for me to
emerge after each one. He also helped with contacts and kindly did restlessly
intelligent research for me on various subjects; J. P. Floru of the Adam Smith
Institute and Philip Booth of the Institute of Economic Affairs both repeatedly
suggested and introduced me to contacts around the world; Leszek Balcerowicz, former deputy Prime Minister of Poland, as well as granting me a
couple of interviews, opened doors for me in Warsaw which otherwise would
have remained shut; Eva Cooper helped me with contacts in various parts of
the world and answered questions about Sweden; Pedro Schwartz arranged
interviews for me in Spain; Janadas Devan, director of the Institute of Policy
Studies in Singapore, set up several days' worth of meetings. To my surprise I
found one them was with the deputy Prime Minister; Lindsay Mitchell, in
New Zealand, organised an extraordinary day for me in and around Welling-
ton, meeting one interesting person after another; and Greg Lindsay, founder
and executive director of the Centre for Independent Studies in Sydney, set up
a programme of meetings for me, gave me a bed for the night and made the
supreme sacrifice of letting me play bad golf at his club.*

Contents

The World Quiz

H ow much do you know about the way the world works? Is Sweden really socialist to the core? Which country is the lone parenting capital of the world? Is America a free-market, capitalist nation with barely any social provision? How does Britain fare in treating breast cancer compared to other countries which do not have a national health service? Which country has the lowest unemployment?

Take the quiz. Write down your answers and see how you score:

1. **What is the average rate of 'functional illiteracy' in the advanced world?**

a) 2 per cent   c) 11 per cent

b) 5 per cent   d) 18 per cent

2. **Which of these countries has the highest proportion of people living alone?**

a) USA   c) Australia

b) Italy   d) Sweden

3. **In early 2014, one of these countries had an unemployment rate of 25.6 per cent and another only 2.8 per cent. Which was which?**

a) Spain   d) Poland

b) Singapore   e) Japan

c) France   f) Switzerland

4. **Which of these countries has the worst five-year survival rate for breast cancer?**

a) USA   c) Netherlands

b) UK   d) Australia

5. What percentage of the elderly living in residential care in England and
Wales says that they wish that they were dead?

    a) 3 per cent   c) 12 per cent

    b) 8 per cent   d) 21 per cent

6. At what age are Polish soldiers and policemen eligible to retire on a pension?

    a) 35   c) 55

    b) 45   d) 65

7. Who said, 'He who does not work shall not eat' (and that only those who
work should be allowed access to consumer goods)?

    a) Adam Smith   c) Margaret Thatcher

    b) Milton Friedman   d) Lenin

8. What is or was 'the rubber room'?

    a) A windowless room with rubber walls for uncontrollable students
    in a Bronx school

    b) A room in a French *mairie* to which records revealing the corrup-
    tion of officials are taken to be destroyed

    c) A place in New York where teachers went during the long-winded
    process of firing them

    d) A rest and recreation room for union officials in Spanish
    companies

9. What was the rate of youth unemployment in Spain in early 2014?

    a) 17 per cent   c) 34 per cent

    b) 23 per cent   d) 54 per cent

10. How many people in the USA received food stamps (2013)?

    a) 3 million   c) 21 million

    b) 12 million   d) 48 million

11. Which country has the highest proportion of 'free' or 'charter' schools?

    a) Australia   c) UK

    b) Sweden   d) USA

12. Which country has the lowest unemployment rate?

a) Switzerland   c) Singapore

b) Sweden   d) USA

13. Between 1987 and 2001, the proportion of social housing in Germany changed. In which way?

a) It more than doubled   c) It increased by a quarter

b) It increased by over a half   d) It more than halved

14. Which country has the highest rate of criminal assaults and threats?

a) Australia   c) USA

b) England and Wales   d) Sweden

15. Which country has the highest number of angioplasty, hip replacement and knee replacement operations per 100,000?

a) France   c) Germany

b) USA   d) Sweden

16. Who said, 'I propose to create a Civilian Conservation Corps to be used in simple work; more important, however, than the material gains will be the moral and spiritual value of such work'?

a) President Hoover

b) President Coolidge

c) President F. D. Roosevelt

d) President Reagan

17. Which country is the world capital of lone parenting (has the highest rate)?

a) Sweden   c) USA

b) Denmark   d) UK

18. Which country spends a massive 29.4 per cent of its government budget paying pensions?

a) Switzerland   c) Italy

b) UK   d) Netherlands

19. The proportion of women over sixty-five without partners who live with one of their children has declined to only 3 per cent in one of these countries but has remained at 61 per cent in another. Which is which?

a) Belgium   d) Denmark

b) Portugal   e) UK

c) France

20. Who suggested that law school training is excessively long and courses should only last two years instead of three?

a) Margaret Thatcher   c) President Obama

b) Milton Friedman   d) Lee Kuan Yew

Answers: 1. d; 2. d;[1] 3. a and b respectively[2] (Japan and Switzerland also had much lower than average unemployment rates); 4. b;[3] 5. d;[4] 6. a; 7. d; 8. c; 9. d;[5] 10. d; 11. b; 12. c; 13. d; 14. b;[6] 15. c[7] (in fact Germany does the most in each of the three categories of operation); 16. c;[8] 17. c;[9] 18. c;[10] 19. d and b respectively;[11] 20. c.[12] Give yourself a point for every correct answer.

How did you score?

1–7 You really need to read this book!

8–14 You are pretty well informed and obviously take an interest in the subject. For you, this book is like getting a free upgrade to first class.

15–22 Impressive. You are an expert. It would be an honour if you would read this book.

Preface

'No! No! No!'

How Lady Thatcher helped to prompt the writing of this book

IN MAY 2006, I WENT to a lunchtime talk at the Institute of Economic Affairs, not far from the Houses of Parliament. After it finished, I was about to leave when, unexpectedly, John Blundell, the then director general, invited me to join others at a reception in a room nearby. It was for Václav Klaus, President of the Czech Republic, who was visiting London at the time. Even more to my surprise, I saw that among the people who had come to see him was Baroness Thatcher.

Suddenly I found myself being introduced to her. John Blundell marched me up to her and instructed me to tell her about the book I had written. Startled, I said that the book – *The Welfare State We're In* – had argued that the modern British welfare state, despite its good intentions, had done a great deal of harm and we would be better off if it had not been created. Straight away she demanded to know what, if that were the case, should be done about it.

I had been asked this question repeatedly when I had given talks about the book. I gave my usual reply: 'Unfortunately I am very doubtful that a democracy would accept the changes that would make things really better. And I do not want to recommend something second best.'

Baroness Thatcher was not having that. She said something like, 'No! No! No! You can't say there is a problem and not come up with a solution! You must suggest an alternative! If you say the welfare state is no good, you must suggest an alternative!'

I resorted to another of my standard answers: 'The research would cost a great deal of time and money in order to arrive at any conclusion worth hearing. And anyway, people find blueprints boring.'

She was impatient with that, too, saying, 'If you can't think of a good way of communicating it, you must *find* a way of communicating it!' or words to that effect. I was like a junior minister getting his marching orders.

I am afraid I still believe that a democracy is unlikely to adapt and stick to an ideal solution. However, after the prompting I got from her and others and after years of a niggling sense that 'surely at least something could be done' I came round to the concept of this book, which is, in part, an attempt to answer Baroness Thatcher's question.

I also wanted to try to assess how welfare states are changing world civilisation. In my research, I have travelled to eleven countries and studied more. I have found that the bare statistics are often misleading. Talking to people on the spot can reveal this, and give rise to insights that no amount of deskbound study could reveal.

Why are so many Swedish people disabled?

The world of welfare from Opheltas to Bismarck to the clever research of Kathryn Edin

I N THE MIDST OF THE greatest economic depression the USA has ever known, thirteen million people are unemployed.[1] More than 5,000 banks have folded. Hundreds of thousands of families have been made homeless after defaulting on loans. Many have gone to shanty towns. At this extraordinary time of national crisis in 1935, President Franklin D. Roosevelt introduces the 'New Deal' – a collection of programmes intended to end the crisis. His advisers have different ideas. They argue with each other. He himself has no great theory but he is a confident man, willing to try things out and see how they go. One thing he is sure of is that he wants men to work. He does not want just to give them money. He is also concerned about overspending.

In June, he bypasses Congress and issues an executive order. He creates one of his lesser-known programmes, the National Youth Administration. The aim is to find work for young people who have left school and cannot get a job. He does not want them to be idle at this formative age.

He signs the order on a Tuesday morning. That same day, an ambitious young man telephones key contacts to put himself forward for the job of administering the programme in his home state of Texas. His speed of reaction and energy get him the job within a month. He becomes the youngest state director of the programme in the country. He is only twenty-seven.

He finds sponsors to provide materials for each project. Housing has to be found for the young participants. Supervisors need to be hired. He brings astonishing energy and determination to the job. He builds a reputation for getting things done. He also creates a political base in his home state from which, as soon as possible, he will be able to run for national office. He travels by car and plane. He is on the phone. He starts work at seven in the morning and goes on until eleven at night. 'You would ask him about the weather and he would start talking about projects,' a friend remarks.

The young man swiftly signs up 350 sponsors. Within six months, he has got 18,000 young people working on parks, constructing buildings and so on. The national director of the programme, Aubrey Williams, says he is the best administrator he has got. Eleanor Roosevelt, the First Lady, wants to meet him.

What is the name of this exceptional young man? Lyndon B. Johnson.

According to one of his biographers, his successful experience as an administrator of the National Youth Administration 'confirmed his belief that in order to meet public goals it was necessary only to pass a good bill and put a good man in charge'.[2] Twenty-eight years later, Lyndon Johnson is President of the USA following the assassination of John F. Kennedy. Ambition still burns fiercely within him. Brought up as a supporter of Roosevelt and a successful administrator of a New Deal programme, the focus of his ambition becomes

President Johnson embarked on 'an unconditional war on poverty'

nothing less than 'an unconditional war on poverty'. Poverty has not been a major issue previously but he makes many speeches in which he urges that the greatness of America is not compatible with the poverty that remains in it. He says this is 'more than a beginning. It is a total commitment by this President and Congress and this nation to pursue victory over the most ancient of mankind's enemies.'

When Johnson makes this speech to Congress in 1964, America has not long before been among the victors of the Second World War both in Europe and against Japan. It has enjoyed fast-growing prosperity. The 'can do' attitude of Americans is famous. Why should the American capacity for doing things not be applied to poverty, too? Johnson goes on, 'If we can bring to the challenges of peace the same determination and strength which has brought us victory in war – then this day and this Congress will have won a more secure and honourable place in the history of the nation and the enduring gratitude of generations of Americans to come'. He believes he is making history. In a speech on the campus of the University of Michigan, he refers to 'the Great Society'. He has used the phrase before but in this speech it is central. It becomes the phrase by which his massive programme of legislation becomes known.

THE FINAL COUNTRY I VISITED for my research was the United States. One day, in Washington DC, I went to talk to an expert on care for the elderly who was based in one of the grand government buildings not far from the Senate. After the meeting, I walked across the street towards the Senate itself – a magnificent building designed in the neo-Classical style and poised on top of a hill. It inspires a feeling of power and order.

Eventually I turned away to set off back to my hotel. As I walked along a featureless, straight street, I saw some people ahead on the pavements on both sides. Some were standing. Others were sitting on a low wall. Some were in groups of two or three. Others were alone.

What they were doing?

As I got closer I realised that most were black. I saw around the corner that still more were waiting – but waiting for what?

I looked at a building on the far side of the road and saw a sign saying 'John L. Young Center for the Homeless'. Were they waiting for accommodation? It seemed strange. The journalist in me wanted to go up to them and ask. I also wanted to take photographs. But I felt I would be intruding on people in unfortunate circumstances. I said nothing and took no photographs. I just wrote down on my notepad: 'very sad sight' and then, 'separate sadness'. They were not chatting with each other. They were each in individual, separate experiences of misfortune.

Seeing them gave me a strong feeling of how important it is to get welfare as right as we can. None of us should insist on his or her political prejudices. We should look at the evidence and try to be honest about it. Too much is at stake to indulge bar-room views.

Half a century ago, the President of this exceptionally rich country proudly decided to wage 'an unconditional war on poverty'. And yet only 500 yards away from the Senate – grand symbol of democracy and power – more than thirty melancholy people are waiting for something in a public, humiliating way.

It so happens that there is nothing new about the paradox of a wealthy country with a large number of welfare dependants. This is exactly what struck Alexis de Tocqueville when he visited England in 1833. He remarked how strange it was that while Britain was pre-eminently rich and successful, it had more paupers than other, poorer countries.

We can see two things combining to produce Johnson's 'war on poverty': the powerful ambition of a man who wants to make his mark and widespread optimism that a government can achieve whatever it sets out to do. With Johnson's determination and experience at dealing with Congress, he gets through a wide range of radical laws.

Lyndon Johnson is one of the founders of the American welfare state. At first sight, he seems a world away from the originator of another welfare state. But let's travel back in time to the late nineteenth century to meet this other one.

Otto von Bismarck is the most powerful man since Napoleon. In contrast to Johnson, he is a conservative and monarchist. He is politically brilliant, dedicated to his cause, and has created modern Germany.

We know quite a lot about his thinking due to a strange circumstance. From time to time, he uses a friendly journalist, Moritz Busch, to plant stories in the newspapers. Unbeknownst to Bismarck, Busch keeps copious notes of his conversations with Bismarck, including the Chancellor's off-the-record remarks.[3]

Otto von Bismarck intended to 'avert a revolution'

On 18 January 1881, Moritz Busch writes to Bismarck, 'reminding him of my readiness to place myself at his disposal' in case he wishes 'to have any matter of importance discussed in the German or English press'. Two days later, Busch receives a letter inviting him to call on Bismarck the following day. So on Friday 21 January 1881, Busch goes to the Chancellor's palace.

Bismarck starts their conversation by remarking to Busch, 'So you have come for material, but there is not much to give you.' Then he remembers something. 'One thing occurs to me, however. I should be very thankful to you if you would discuss my working-class insurance scheme in a friendly spirit.'[4] Bismarck explains his motives with extraordinary frankness: 'a beginning must be made with the task of reconciling the labouring classes with the state. Whoever has a pension assured to him for his old age is much more contented and easier to manage than the man who has no such prospect.' His idea is to make the working classes 'easier to manage', thus enabling him to perpetuate the monarchical rule to which he is devoted.

He frankly admits that this social insurance may cost a lot of money. 'Large sums of money would be required for carrying such schemes into execution, at least a hundred million marks, or more probably two hundred. But I should not frightened by even three hundred millions. Means must be provided to enable the state to act generously towards the poor.' He discusses how money might be raised through the tobacco monopoly. But he tells Busch he 'need not emphasise this point'. Presumably he wants to present the advantages rather than the costs. But the money can be found and he concludes, 'If the sums thus acquired are used for securing the future of our working population, uncertainty as to which is the chief cause of their hatred to the state, we thereby at the same time secure our own future and that is a good investment for our money. We should thus avert a revolution, which might break out fifty or perhaps ten years hence.'[5]

It could not be clearer. Bismarck is a conservative and monarchist. He is introducing social insurance largely for the purpose of foiling a socialist revolution which, he believes, would otherwise take place. The cunning Chancellor is thinking long term, protecting his king and the society he cherishes.

He is soon criticised by some people for introducing what is sometimes called 'state socialism'. To which he replies – in the classic manner of a politician who is a realist, 'It may be state socialism, but it is necessary.'

State welfare did not begin with Bismarck...

GOVERNMENT WELFARE PROGRAMMES DATE BACK to the earliest records of Western civilisation. In part of ancient Greece, laws provided that those who were disabled fighting in war should be 'maintained at the public charge'. This was ordered by Pelsistratus, who ruled in Athens most of the time between 561 and 527 BC. He, it seems, was following a precedent set by Solon, who lived even earlier, from about 638 BC to 558 BC. Solon ordered that the sons of those killed in war should 'be educated and bred up at the public expense'. Polybius in his *Histories* reported that a politician called Opheltas, in the third century BC in Boeotia, a region of Greece, 'was always inventing some plan calculated to benefit the masses for the moment, while perfectly certain to ruin them in the future'.[6]

Under the Romans, the 'dole' of grain was first subsidised at the initiative of Gaius Gracchus in 123 BC. After him, the generosity of the dole went further when Publius Clodius Pulcher, in 57 BC, made it free. This was the ancient equivalent of food stamps. Those entitled to it had a ticket (*tessera*) which could be exchanged every month.

In medieval Europe, the church took the leading role in looking after the poor, aged and disabled. Hospitals, almshouses and schools were founded which received considerable donations from the devout. Some reminders of this survive. In Siena, you can visit the hospital of Santa Maria della Scala, founded eight centuries ago, which stands opposite the famous cathedral. In Ghent, you can visit some of the House of Alijn almshouses that were administered by the church.

But governments – particularly local governments – took an increasing role at the time of the Reformation.

The House of Alijn almhouses in Ghent long pre-date modern welfare states

Leading intellectuals of the day considered how best welfare should be administered. Martin Luther wrote that every town and village should make a register of poor people in need of aid – 'paupers', they were called – because otherwise those who got most money would be 'vagabonds and desperate rogues'. He admitted, 'I have myself of late years been cheated and befooled by such tramps and liars more than I wish to confess.'

In 1525, the town of Ypres devised a system for the 'relief' of paupers which had enormous influence. Under this system, begging was banned. Individual officials were meant to visit the poor in their homes and act like their 'common parents', making sure they had enough to eat and that they went to school or got training for a job or, if they were workshy, obliging them to work. If they refused work, the officials would punish them. The money to pay for this was to be collected through house-to-house collection of alms as well as boxes in churches and bequests. With all this provision of relief in place, Ypres felt able to ban begging.

The system was so controversial that it was brought to the Sorbonne for judgment as to whether or not it was in accordance with the Scriptures, the teaching of the Apostles and the laws of the church. The Sorbonne decided, with provisos, that it was acceptable. The system was described as 'hard but useful … pious and salutary'.[7]

In the nineteenth century, there was also rapid development of mutual aid organisations, provident societies, trade unions, friendly societies and commercial insurance to various extents in different countries. Finally national governments took an increasing role – slowly in the 19th century but with increasing speed in the 20th.[8]

And yet who can be sure what is going on in Bismarck's mind? A few months later, Bismarck invites Busch to visit him again. This time Bismarck refers to social insurance as 'our practical Christianity'.

Busch is surprised. He asks, 'Practical Christianity? Did I right understand Your Serene Highness?'

Bismarck replies, 'Certainly. Compassion, a helping hand in distress. The state, which can raise money with the least trouble, must take the matter in hand. Not as alms, but as a right to maintenance, where not the readiness but the power to work fails.'

So perhaps compassion is a part of his motivation. Or perhaps he is merely rehearsing arguments which will enable him to get the legislation passed, without really believing in them.

Finally we see his remorseless political intelligence, which is always looking well ahead. He declares, 'This question will force its way; it has a future. It is possible that our policy may be reversed at some future time when I am dead; but state socialism will make its way. Whoever takes up this idea again will come to power.'

Bismarck's prediction proves correct. All around the world in the following decades, politicians gain or keep power by espousing what he called 'state socialism'. It is what we now know as the 'welfare state'. It is hard to think of anyone who did their political careers anything but good in the hundred years after Bismarck spoke by espousing the cause of social security.

The politicians who took part in creating modern welfare states like Lyndon Johnson and Otto von Bismarck may appear to have been very different characters with different agendas. But they all had some of the following motives in varying proportions:

1) Compassion for the poor and afflicted.

2) Outrage at the perceived injustice of society.

3) A desire by conservatives or centrists to hold onto power by undercutting the appeal of socialism, which was seen as dangerously damaging.

4) Ambition to gain a prestigious place in history.

5) Belief that poverty could be completely eradicated by governments.

The motives ranged from the cynical to the utopian and – such is human nature – some politicians were motivated by both simultaneously.

So how did it all go? Did Lyndon Johnson win his war on poverty?

There is a bewildering array of welfare programmes in the USA. So let's just take one: food stamps. The number of people in the USA deemed to need government help to get food on the table is more than forty-six million.[9] That is one in every seven.[10] Given that America has been the outstandingly rich and successful large country of the past century, this is an astonishing figure. But even this figure does not include every person in America currently described as being in poverty. Lyndon Johnson's ambition to eradicate poverty appears to have failed – perhaps even to have backfired.

> 'When one crosses the various countries of Europe, one is struck by a very extraordinary and apparently inexplicable sight.
>
> 'The countries appearing to be the most impoverished are those which in reality account for the fewest indigents, and among the peoples most admired for their opulence, one part of the population is obliged to rely on the gifts of the other in order to live.
>
> 'Cross the English countryside and you will think yourself transported into the Eden of modern civilisation ... Now look more closely at the villages; examine the parish registers, and you will discover with indescribable astonishment that one sixth of the inhabitants of this flourishing kingdom live at the expense of public charity.'
>
> Alexis de Tocqueville, *Memoir on Pauperism* (1835)

As the wealth of America has increased, so has the number of people apparently in need of help. The budget devoted to welfare has increased again and again. It now amounts to $523 billion a year.[11] Yet the numbers who need support still grow. What has gone wrong?

Some may be thinking, 'It may have gone wrong in America but America adopted a particularly bad kind of welfare.' In France, more than anywhere perhaps, there is scorn for American economic and social policy. The 'Anglo-Saxon' approach is seen as brutish, grudging and damaging to the harmony of society. There is a great belief in 'solidarity' – a binding together of the classes. In France, welfare is based on compulsory, universal social insurance, not on merely providing a safety net for the poor. Armed with this positive attitude and a different system, have the French succeeded in eliminating poverty and providing employment in a way that has been beyond the Americans?

No. Unemployment has soared from an average of 1.5 per cent in the 1950s to 9.0 per cent in the 1980s and 10.4 per cent in 2014.[13] If the country had decided to increase unemployment as a matter of policy, it could hardly have done better. It has been a major welfare failure. Social spending has correspondingly risen higher and higher as a proportion of GDP, climbing from 12.5 per cent in 1960 to 32.5 per cent in 2010.[14] The number of officially disabled rose by a quarter in the decade leading to 2007.[15]

> In La Rochelle, France, Nicole Liguori started offering subsidised lunches once every two weeks. Diners had to pay €2.50 for the meal. Local supermarkets helped by providing food and donations. Ms Liguori said, 'I was aware of the condition of people I met and chatted to in the street. The retired, the homeless and the unemployed who, in addition to the material miseries, feel profoundly alone.'[12]

What about other countries which have introduced welfare states? What has happened among them?

Back in 1950, the unemployment rate in the member countries of the Organisation of Economic Cooperation and Development (OECD) was just under 4 per cent. But if one goes back further still, to the beginning of the twentieth century, before almost any country had created unemployment insurance benefits, the rate was lower still. There are no overall OECD figures for that time but, in Britain, the rate was a mere 2.5 per cent in 1900. In Germany it was 4.7 per cent in 1903, falling to 2.7 per cent in 1906.[16] Now, since welfare states have been introduced in full measure,

> 'To provide for poor men is harder than men think, considering that it cannot be duly executed without great diligence, study and wisdom.
>
> *Forma subventionis pauperum* – a description of the Ypres system published in 1531.

average OECD unemployment has risen to 8.2 per cent in 2011, moderating to 7.4 per cent in mid-2014. In the European Union, where welfare states are most fully developed, the lowest rate in recent years was 7.0 per cent (2008) and it has subsequently risen to a peak of 10.8 per cent (2013).[17] But the rise in the number of those officially unemployed does not tell the whole story. In some ways, things are even worse. For many countries, 'early retirement' has become a politically convenient disguise for further unemployment. France, Belgium, Austria, Greece and Italy have this type of hidden unemployment. Belgium and Austria both have particularly large gaps between the official retirement age for men of sixty-five and the actual average retirement age of fifty-nine.[18]

One of the most remarkable statistics I came across in my research is that in Poland in 2004, among people aged fifty-five to sixty-four, the proportion that were actually working amounted to only 28 per cent.[19] In other words, the vast majority of people stopped working once they were past fifty-five. Since then, the proportion working has crept up to 37 per cent. But even now there are huge numbers of men and women of working age in Poland who are not working yet who are not officially classed as 'unemployed'. They are the 'hidden unemployed'.

There is also hidden unemployment among people on disability benefits. Of course, some are genuinely disabled. But many are not. There are huge contrasts

The Sun, March 16, 2012. The cartoon appeared after a number of instances of fit people claiming benefits were exposed.

in the numbers who receive disability benefits in different countries. In Japan, 2 per cent of working-age people are officially disabled. In Sweden, more than 10 per cent are.[21] If these figures reflected reality, you would expect, when walking through the streets of Stockholm, to see many people being pushed around in wheelchairs or struggling on crutches. Yet no such spectacle is to be seen.

It is astonishing and, frankly, hard to believe that the rate of disability in one advanced country is five times greater than in another. Conceivably, Japan is refusing to recognise the true disabled condition of some people. But it seems more likely that the cause of the violent contrast is that many people in Sweden are not genuinely disabled but have found that welfare benefits for incapacity are well worth having and can be obtained without too much difficulty. In other words, they are unemployed.

The apparently disabled of Britain have historically been concentrated in areas of high unemployment, again suggesting that going onto disability benefit has been an alternative to going onto unemployment benefit. An analysis of the large numbers on the benefit by a Labour government in the 2000s suggested that a million people on the benefit were capable of work. Around the world, the proportion of people of working age who are apparently too ill to work has risen. In the USA, it doubled from 2.3 per cent in 1989 to 4.6 per cent in 2009.[22] The rise in the numbers claiming disability benefit took place in parallel with the fall in the numbers on the welfare rolls.[23] For many, disability has become an alternative way of obtaining payments without working.

The average proportion on disability benefits in OECD countries is 5 per cent. Let us conservatively guess that the rate of genuine disability in an advanced country is, say, 3 per cent, slightly above Japan's. If that is right, then more than 2 per cent of the working age population of the advanced world is claiming disability benefit without being genuinely disabled. If we add that figure to the official OECD unemployment rate, true unemployment rises to 10.2 per cent. To this should be added the early retirees who are, in reality, other members of the hidden unemployed. That could

Pauline Ford was a poor woman who lived in a mobile home and claimed welfare benefits. She lived frugally. She never went out and didn't smoke or drink. In 2011, she was convicted of fraud because she had not disclosed that she had built up savings of £22,000.

Of course she should have disclosed this under the law. But it is also true that if she had drunk and smoked or if she had bought furniture and gold chains, she would not have had the savings and she would not have committed a crime.

Most people on means-tested benefits in Britain are aware that if they build up savings, they will cease to be entitled to certain benefits. The British welfare state thus discourages saving by the poor.[23]

amount to a further 2 per cent, raising the true unemployment level to over 12 per cent. Even this is unlikely to be the end of the story because it does not capture so-called 'discouraged' workers who are not registered as unemployed.

Such a level of unemployment is unparalleled in human history. It amounts to a worldwide welfare disaster. Instead of Lyndon Johnson winning a war on poverty, he – and other clever, generally well-intentioned leaders around the world – have created systems in which permanent mass unemployment has become normal. While the wealth of the world has increased tremendously over the past thirty years, let alone the past hundred, instead of achieving the economic well-being for all that our ancestors expected, we have mass dependency on hand-outs.

But there is another aspect of this which the world has been even more reluctant to face. In Madrid, I talked to many people about the extraordinarily high unemployment there, which, at the time, had reached 23 per cent of those of working age. One person I spoke to was the Madrid minister of health, Javier Fernández Lasquetty. He stopped for a moment, mid-conversation, and remarked, 'Actually, we don't know what is the level of unemployment. It is a mystery.'

He meant that the government did not know the number of people who were working unofficially – without paying social insurance contributions or taxes. Spain undoubtedly has one of the biggest black economies in Europe. Many lower-paid immigrants from Latin America and Romania especially cannot get jobs at the minimum wage. But many get by on '*chapuzas*' – odd jobs for which they are paid in cash. And it is not just in Spain. Hidden economies are part of many welfare states.

In America, Christopher Jenks, an academic, and his colleagues were puzzled that, in surveys, a lot of families on the lowest incomes said that they were not experiencing material difficulties. Most of these apparently very poor people said they were not going hungry or having their gas or electricity cut off. The academics hired a graduate student, Kathryn Edin, to find out what was going on. She was to interview some of the people they had been questioning. She contacted them but found that they were reluctant to talk openly. She realised that they suspected she was working for the welfare department or some other government agency. So she decided to take a different approach. Instead of interviewing people who had no reason to trust her, she arranged to be introduced by people who already knew and were trusted by welfare recipients. Then, once she had the trust of such people, she interviewed them and also asked them to introduce her to others.

By gaining their trust and interviewing people two or more times, Kathryn Edin – and Laura Lein, who joined her – discovered the answer to the mystery of how women with very low incomes were getting by. The answer was this: they had other sources of cash. Edin and Lein and their colleagues talked to 379 women and found only one who did not have an extra source of income. Except in a minority of cases where the income was officially recognised or declared, the women kept their income secret from government officials. Among those they interviewed who were unemployed and receiving welfare benefits, the average benefits were $565 per month but average spending was 55 per cent more: $876.

There were two main sources of extra money. One was people they knew: family, friends and, more importantly, current boyfriends or absent fathers. Their second source of cash was work. A small amount was officially reported but the vast majority was off the books. A minority of the earnings was so-called 'underground' work such as prostitution and dealing in drugs or stolen goods. The proportion doing work not officially declared was about 39 per cent. That is without including all those doing 'underground' work.

What proportion of welfare mothers gets income from other sources?

Reported work	5%
Unreported work	39%
'Underground' work	8%
TOTAL FROM WORK	**46*%**
Family and friends	46%
Boyfriends	29%
Absent fathers formally	14%
Absent fathers covertly	23%
TOTAL FROM PEOPLE	**77*%**

*Some mothers have more than one kind of extra income.

Source: Kathryn Edin and Laura Lein, *Making Ends Meet* [25]

Because of Edin's remarkable investigation – which I have found is respected on all sides – we know that American single mothers have been keeping a great deal of work secret from the authorities. It seems likely that other groups, such as men, are doing something similar. It also seems probable that something similar is taking place in other countries where no one has yet done such painstaking research.

One point about this that the authors do not labour – but which is implicit – is that the mothers are making ends meet by cheating. The vast majority of the extra income they get should be declared to their welfare officer and result in lower benefits. So cheating is normal. You could even argue that it is part of the system. It is easy to imagine those involved feeling that they would be fools not to do what so many others are doing. They would also be in even greater financial difficulty. Edin and Lein make it crystal clear that the lives of these women are difficult despite the extra money. Fifteen per cent said that they had gone hungry at some point during the previous twelve months despite receiving food stamps. Seventeen per cent reported having had their electricity or gas cut off.

Monthly income of welfare-reliant mothers

Welfare benefits	$565
Earned income tax credits	$3
Reported work	$19
Unreported and 'underground' work	$109
Family, friends, boyfriends and absent fathers	$151
Agency-based support	$37
TOTAL INCOME	**$883**

Source: Edin and Lein, *Making Ends Meet*.[26]

The research by Edin and Lein takes the lid off the world of welfare benefits. It is supported by research commissioned by Peter Lilley, British Secretary of State for Social Security in the 1990s. His staff similarly found that the expenditure of the poorest 10 per cent of people was considerably higher than their apparent income.

The implications of this hidden world of economic activity are strange. We previously found that there is more unemployment that the official figures suggest but, on the other hand, Edin's research tells us that simultaneously there is hidden employment. Edin's work means, among other things, that there is less poverty than the official figures suggest – particularly for countries where benefits are means tested and there is a strong incentive to keep income secret. So the most quoted measure of inequality of income – the Gini coefficient – is unreliable. It exaggerates inequality of incomes, especially in those countries where benefits are mainly means tested.

Amid the confusion, one powerful truth emerges from the clouds bright and clear: many welfare systems around the world have been highly dysfunctional.

- The number of unemployed has dramatically increased.

- More people have become benefit dependent despite these countries becoming much richer.

- A large proportion of people now dependent on welfare or other benefits are lying about their incomes. Lying has been made normal.

- The cost of welfare systems has grown enormously. Welfare expenditure is now larger than all other government expenditure put together in Denmark, Finland, France, Germany, Austria, Italy, New Zealand, Spain and Sweden.[27] The average spend in advanced countries is 22 per cent of GDP.[28]

The situation of the poor has also become worse in other ways, too – ways less susceptible to being weighed up by numbers.

The change in the lives of many of the poor is reflected eloquently by Barack Obama in his book *Dreams from My Father*. Obama worked as a community organiser in Chicago in the late 1980s. He said about the middle-aged, working class, black Americans he met in Roseland, one of the less well-off suburbs: 'On the strength of two incomes, they had paid off house notes and car notes, maybe college educations for their sons or daughters whose graduation pictures filled every mantelpiece.'[29] But he remarked that when his conversations with them turned to the future of the neighbourhood, they 'were marked by another more ominous strain'. People worried about 'the decaying storefronts, the aging church rolls, kids from unknown families who swaggered down the streets – loud congregations of teenage boys, teenage girls feeding potato chips to crying toddlers, the discarded wrappers tumbling down the block – all of it whispered painful truths, told them the progress they'd found was ephemeral, rooted in thin soil; that it might not even last their lifetimes'.

Obama came to think that much poorer people he had known earlier during his time in Indonesia had enjoyed better lives. 'For all that poverty, there remained in their lives a discernible order. The habits of a generation played out every day beneath the bargaining and the noise and the swirling dust. It was the absence of coherence that made a place like Altgeld [an area of public housing in Chicago] so desperate.'

Obama felt that 'something different' was also taking place on the South Side, another part of Chicago. There was 'a change in atmosphere, like the electricity of an approaching storm'. This brought the 'sense shared by adults and youth alike, that some, if not most of our boys were slipping beyond rescue'.

This evocation of how a culture and way of life were changing before his eyes involves more than just unemployment. It brings in other aspects of the welfare state that will be covered later such as parenting, housing, education, saving and behaviour. But the central thing that goes wrong in so many welfare states is that so many people are unemployed. Without jobs, they cannot pay off 'house notes and car notes'. They cannot enjoy normally functioning family structures. They cannot have order in their lives of the sort that even Indonesian slum-dwellers have.

Why is there so much unemployment in so many welfare states? The question needs answering.

2.

Heart of the darkness

Welfare states and unemployment

PHIL STARTED WORKING WHEN HE was seventeen. He got married and had children. It sounds like a pretty normal kind of life. But when he was thirty-two, the business he was working for went bust and he lost his job. He thought he had managed to deal with the crisis when he got a job with another company. But his new employer failed to pay him. Naturally he became extremely worried. He was not the only adult in his home who could earn. He had a wife. But he felt it was his job to bring in the money, to finance the home and provide for his children.

He kept pressing the company to pay him. Instead, it fired him. Naturally his financial worries increased. He tried to get another job but he could not find one. 'I had to pay rent, petrol and get a new school uniform for one of the kids ... I had to go on the social [claim welfare benefits].' The welfare money was useful but it was not enough to keep the family going in the way he was used to. Phil began to think of commit-ting suicide. 'You start thinking 'Is it easier for them if I'm not here? ... If I'm not here she [his wife] would probably get more money for the kids, the bills would die with me, you wouldn't be driving the car and using petrol'.''

Phil's life hung in the balance. He had got to this stage because of losing his job. He felt he was not playing the role in life which he had before. He missed feeling he had a certain status in life and a purpose. His unemployment also led to money worries, which caused arguments with his wife. We know the outline of this true story because Phil was so close to suicide that he contacted the Samaritans, a charity which supports those considering suicide. The Samaritans published his story (obviously changing his name).[1]

Of course, not all people who lose their jobs contemplate suicide. But unemployment is far more depressing than most realise. Some large-scale surveys are conducted on happiness and unhappiness. In the USA, 11.6 per cent of the population declared themselves 'not too happy' in surveys between 1972 and 1994.[2] But when it came to the unemployed, the figure more than doubled to 29.6 per cent. In Europe the rise was from 18.6 per cent to 33.0 per cent. In Europe, people were also asked about their 'life satisfaction'. Among the general population, 4.9 per cent were 'not at all satisfied' but more than two and half times as many of the unemployed – 13.3 per cent – felt the same way. Of course this correlation is likely to be partly due to the unemployed being poorer. But it goes beyond that. An academic study of the figures found that 'being unemployed increases the chance that the respondent declares himself dissatisfied with life, even after holding other things constant that may be expected to be associated with unemployment (e.g. family income, marital separation)'.[3] Moreover, 'the size of the impact is large and similar across countries'.

The unemployed have increased susceptibility to malnutrition, illness and mental stress.[4] They are more likely to have poor self-esteem, leading to depression. Goldsmith, Veum and Darity, using data from the US national Longitudinal Study of Youth, found that being jobless injured self-esteem and fostered feelings of 'externality' and helplessness among youths.[5] The unemployed have lower life expectancy and are indeed more likely to commit suicide.[6]

Why do I mention all this? Because there has been a tendency in recent times to treat mass unemployment as something that does not matter that much. People who, a few decades ago, would have been passionate about attaining 'full employment' have given up the battle cry and now demand 'equality' instead. It seems as though they have given up hope of returning to full employment so they have convinced themselves that it does not matter so much. But unemployment matters a great deal. It causes misery and, of course, it makes people poorer. The need for money to pay for unemployment and welfare benefits also means that others must bear higher taxes so they are poorer, too. We have become accustomed to permanent, mass unemployment and have lost sight of the fact that it is relatively new.

Britain had full employment – less than 4 per cent unemployment – in at least four out of the ten years before the First World War.[7] Germany did slightly better, enjoying full employment for seven of those years. France managed full employment all the way up until the depression of the 1930s.[8] In Germany, there was full employment for twenty-seven years up to 1974.[9] In Australia, the average unemployment rate was a mere 2 per cent between 1950 and 1974.[10]

UK unemployment before the welfare state[11]

Why has unemployment sky-rocketed since those days? Various explanations have been put forward. They include globalisation and changes in the nature of work caused by such things as automation. The underlying idea in both cases is that, in rich countries, the cost of low-skilled people has become too high compared to the cost of using labour from poor countries, where that is feasible, or compared to machines or computers such as automated check-out tills.

It is true that globalisation has meant that much low-value work has been exported. It is also true that machines are doing many jobs that used to be done by people. But if either of these things were the real cause of overall unemployment, you would expect mass unemployment to have appeared in all rich countries. But it hasn't. Unemployment levels in such countries have varied dramatically. You would also expect the highest unemployment to be in the richest countries where labour is most expensive. But that is not the case, either.

Switzerland is one of the richest countries per capita in the world apart from small tax havens and oil-rich states.[12] So here unemployment should be particularly bad. But Switzerland has one of the lowest rates of unemployment in the advanced world. If Switzerland, of all countries, can manage relatively low unemployment in the face of globalisation and the rest, something else must be going on. What? Has it got some special recipe for low unemployment?

I am in Zurich in the offices of the Schweizerische Arbeitgerberverband, an employers' organisation. Everything is modern and practical. Behind a large desk sits Thomas Daum.

'Why has Switzerland got such low unemployment?' I ask him.

His answer is unexpected. 'It is easy to fire people,' he says.

It's a paradox but not a difficult one. His idea is that a company that knows it can fire people is more willing to hire them.

It is far easier to fire people in Switzerland than in France or Spain, Daum says. It is true that, in Switzerland, an employer has to give a reason for making someone redundant but the explanation can simply be that the boss does not get on with him. A company also has to give some warnings but the number is unspecified. Usually it is one, two or three. If a company is found to have fired someone in a way that is not allowed – for being a member of a union, for example – then there is a fine. But even then the employer is not forced to take the worker back, unlike in France or Germany. The Swiss think that effective working depends on mutual trust and confidence, Daum says. When that is destroyed, it is no good continuing.[13]

Unemployment rates of countries with no minimum wage

Italy	12.6%
Finland	8.5%
Sweden	8.2%
OECD average	7.4%
Denmark	6.5%
Iceland	5.4%
Germany	5.2%
Switzerland	4.8%
Norway	3.3%
Singapore	2.0%

Sources: OECD and others.[15]

Of advanced economies which have no national minimum wage, six out of nine have unemployment rates below the OECD average. The advanced country with the lowest unemployment rate in the world has no minimum wage. The country with the lowest unemployment rate in Europe – Norway – has no minimum wage. However, Italy, which also has no national minimum wage, has unemployment well above average. It may be that no national minimum wage (or a low one) is a necessary but not a sufficient condition for really low unemployment. Subsequent to this survey, Germany introduced a national minimum wage.

The idea is that being able to fire people matters is quite striking. But it seems unlikely that this could be the whole story. What other factors might enable Switzerland to have low unemployment?

During my time in Switzerland, I found that it has no national minimum wage. It does have minimum wages for workers from the European Union and in certain individual cantons but there is no general minimum wage.[14]

What about welfare benefits? Could they be a factor? Switzerland, like many continental countries, has an unemployment insurance system. While you are working, you contribute. When you are fired, you get insurance benefits. Unemployment benefit in Switzerland is generous: A single person gets 70 per cent of his or her previous salary, while those who are married or who have children get 80 per cent. These benefits last quite a long time, too. If someone has worked for a company for eighteen months, the unemployment benefit can last up to 400 days. That is the maximum for everyone. But throughout this time, the person must prove every month that he or she is actively looking for a job. He or she must accept the offer of any suitable work.[16] And if the worker fails to get a new job, then, when the benefit runs out, he or she faces a major drop in income. Social assistance is assessed and paid for by the canton or commune – communes being the smallest and most local tier of government.[17] In some parts of Switzerland, local governments expect people to call on members of his or her family for support before claiming help in social assistance.[18]

Switzerland illustrates that it is possible to have relatively high benefits, at least for a while, yet still have low unemployment. But Switzerland is rigorous in demanding that the unemployed seek work. The OECD has said it 'stands out as one of the [member] countries with the strongest search requirements'.[19] And is it also significant that, after the insurance runs out, the social assistance money is far less.

> 'In Switzerland, where unemployment has been around the one per cent mark since the 1950s, each Canton is responsible for the welfare of its inhabitants. Workfare has been in force throughout this period.'
>
> Ralph Howell, *Why Unemployment?*[20]

What about education? Is the schooling a factor in Switzerland's low unemployment? The OECD's survey of educational attainment shows Switzerland is better than average in reading but not dramatically so. So that does not seem to explain it. However, there is one particular feature of education in Switzerland which might be significant.

Still in Zurich, I walk from the city centre across the long bridge that stretches above the river Limmat. I turn right alongside the river and then left up Ausstellungsstrasse. I come to an open patch of ground on the right with a modern building to one side. It is the entrance to the Technische Berufsschule (Technical Vocational School). I go in and am directed to an upper floor where the rector, Dr Ernst Pfister, has his office. Pfister is correct, cordial and a fount of knowledge.

He gives me a tour of the school and, in the course of it, we come to two large rectangular rooms. They contain rows of engines and engine parts and four cars. At least one of the cars has wheels on rollers so that the engine can run with the car in gear. The exhaust pipes are connected to vents so that the gas emissions are safely removed. I am not a car enthusiast but even I can't help finding it rather exciting to see real cars and working engines displayed and ready for use. It is easy to imagine a sixteen-year-old who has not been much interested in academic subjects like algebra or languages suddenly discovering an enthusiasm for learning when brought into contact with these machines.

Every single student at the school works for a company. They are all, effectively, apprentices. They are only admitted to the school once they have obtained a contract with an employer. In fact, most of their time is spent at work. Time at the school varies between one and two days a week.

The system is thus a combination of apprenticeship and vocational training. The schooling is intended to enrich the work and vice versa. The school also provides general education. The course lasts four years and students must successfully reach one level before being allowed onto the next. Companies take a leading role in this system. They hire the students and can request schools to come up with new courses as products and services change.

Is this form of education widespread? Yes. More students go to vocational schools in Switzerland than universities. A purely academic education is reserved for a minority.

This system may make young people more 'job ready' than other ones. A student who has been through one of these courses offers an employer a great deal of knowledge and experience. He or she can be productive straight away. That is quite a contrast with students who have graduated from university in, say, media studies, philosophy or history of art.

The rate of unemployment among younger people should give an indication of whether Swiss vocational training makes a difference. If so, the result is clear. Switzerland has half the youth unemployment rate of the rest of the advanced world.[21] More tellingly still, Switzerland is one of the two countries with the lowest proportion of youth unemployment compared to adult unemployment.[22] In most countries, the youth unemployment rate is two to four times the adult rate. In Switzerland, it is only 70 per cent higher. The other country with a similarly good ratio is Germany. Germany also has a strong emphasis on vocational education.

That is a flavour of how Switzerland, a rich country with low unemployment, manages things. Maybe we should now look at a country which is at the other end of the scale: a less wealthy country which has had a real problem with mass unemployment.

I am in Madrid, climbing the stairs of an elegant but slightly creaky old building. I get to an antique wooden door and soon find myself in the tiny waiting area of a busy office. Felipe Navio González warmly greets me. He is a young entrepreneur who has created a new internet-based business. To me, he looks so young he should still be at college.

He takes me out to a café, buzzing with enthusiasm. His head is full of the things he needs to focus on for his young business: getting customers, using technology and so on. He has created a recruitment website using information from the 'friends' that people have on Facebook. If someone applies through his website for a job at, say, L'Oréal, the company is automatically notified if any of the person's friends already work for the company. So L'Oréal can check out an applicant through someone it already employs. Felipe says this increases the chances that an applicant will be hired.

Many young people are desperately keen to work for his young company. Interns work beyond normal working hours, hoping to impress him and be hired full time. He has to tell them to go home in the evening. But he cannot take many of them into full-time work because, at that point, he has to pay the industry-wide minimum wage established by the union.

The national minimum wage in Spain is low and irrelevant.[23] The important minimum wages are set by negotiation with unions across industries and regions. In Felipe's business, it is €15,000 a year, he says. There is no point trying to employ someone for less than that because even if a new employee agrees to work at a lower rate, once in the job, he or she can report Felipe to the union and he will be in trouble.

'What would be the effect on your ability to grow if there were no minimum wage?' I ask.

'It would be transformational!' he exclaims excitedly. He could employ more people and grow faster.

Milton Friedman on those who advocate a minimum wage

'THERE ARE ALWAYS ... TWO groups of sponsors: there are the well-meaning sponsors and there are the special interests who are using the well-meaning sponsors as front men ... The special interests are, of course, the trade unions ... The do-gooders believe that by passing a law saying that nobody should get less than ... whatever the minimum wage rate is you are helping poor people who need the money. You are doing nothing of the kind. What you are doing is to ensure that people whose skills are not sufficient to justify that kind of a wage will be unemployed. It is no accident that the teenage unemployment rate ... is over twice as high as the overall unemployment rate. It is no accident that that was not always the case until the 1950s when the minimum wage rate was raised very drastically, very quickly. Teenage unemployment was higher than ordinary unemployment because, of course, the teenagers are the ones who are just coming into the labour market … The minimum wage law is most properly described as a law saying that employers must discriminate against people who have low skills … The consequences of minimum wage rates have been almost wholly bad: to increase unemployment and to increase poverty. Moreover the effects have been concentrated on the groups that the do-gooders would most like to help. The people who have been hurt most by minimum wage laws are the blacks. I have often said that the most anti-negro law on the books of this land is the minimum wage rate.'

This is the view of one young businessman. Does the experience of Spain provide any evidence to support it?

Let us look at how the economic crisis around the world in 2008 affected Spain. As it flared up, there was no wage flexibility in Spain. Collective bargaining agreements there have a life of two to three years. At that moment of crisis, demand for labour was going down but the price of labour could not fall. In fact, wage rates went on rising because of the minimum wage deals. It seems likely that the inflexibility of wages contributed to this. Unemployment in Spain rose by more than seven percentage points in a single year. It was a disaster.

'Industry perishes, because it cannot bear the burden laid upon it of short work for high wages. Then the worker suffers from that as well as the entrepreneur.'[24]

Bismarck on fixing [minimum] wages.

Is there anything else in Spain which could be a factor? Here's another possibility: companies are required by law to pay some employees to work on trade union business once the companies have reached a certain size. One can imagine that this could discourage some companies from expanding. After all, the creation of jobs depends on two things: a willing and able employer as well as a willing and able employee.

What about the point that Thomas Daum made in Zurich? Employers are more likely to hire, he claimed, if they can fire employees without too much difficulty. How easy is it to fire employees in Spain? It depends. Long-term employees are extremely difficult to fire. Their removal has to be 'justified' but the special labour courts set up to decide such things have almost always decided that redundancy is *not* justified. Many judges in these courts are former active union members.

Until 2012, the cost of firing someone in an 'unjustified' way was forty-five days of redundancy pay for each year of service. So the longer that someone had worked for a company, the more expensive it was to fire him. The maximum compensation was only reached after twenty-eight years of service. The cost of firing someone then could amount to three and a half years' pay! This makes a huge contrast with Switzerland. Long-term employees of Spain have vastly superior rights. You could say that the unfortunate Swiss workers don't have rights. They only have jobs.[25]

What about the welfare benefits in Spain? Are they so generous that they discourage work? In fact, the benefits in Spain appear similar or perhaps even slightly less generous than those in Switzerland. After four years in a job, you build up an entitlement to two years' unemployment benefit which is worth 70 per cent of your previous wages for six months, falling to 60 per cent for the remaining eighteen months. After that, you are entitled to social assistance which, I am told, is very low and difficult to qualify for unless you are very poor. So far, there seems to be no great contrast.

In Spain, as in Switzerland, you are similarly required to seek work. But here we find a difference: in Spain, a public agency tries to find jobs for the unemployed. It appears to be spectacularly unsuccessful. Only a tiny fraction of hirings – less than 3 per cent – have been done through this agency.[26] In theory you are required to accept one of three jobs offered to you. But you do not have to accept a job over 30 kilometres away. And you do not have to accept it – at least for the first year – if it is not in your normal profession or line of work.[27] In practice, the requirement to seek work does not seem strictly enforced anyway. Felipe tells me that some friends of his were fired and went off for a trip to Brazil for three to six months. They continued to receive unemployment benefit. So, while on the surface the unemployment benefits in Spain seem similar to Switzerland, in practice it seems that Switzerland is far more rigorous in obliging people to seek work.

There is one other possible factor in Spain that seems worth mentioning: the wedge. The 'wedge' is the difference between what it costs a business to employ someone and what that person receives in cash after tax and social security contributions. Spain has a massive wedge. It is so big that Andalucía, a region of Spain, remarks on its website: 'Social security payments can come as quite a shock to those new to the Spanish system.'[28] The site gives an example of an employee whose salary is €1,500 a month. The employer has to pay €600 per

> ## 'Social security payments can come as quite a shock to those new to the Spanish system'
>
> Andalucía.com website

month in social security contributions on the employee's behalf. So the total cost to the employer is actually €2,100 a month. As for the employee, about 6.4 per cent is taken off his or her salary for unemployment insurance. Then income tax is deducted which, after a tax-free personal allowance, would be, for this level of income, 24.75 per cent.[29] So the end result is:

Cost of the employee for the employer:

Wage	€1,500
plus Social insurance	€600
Total cost	**€2,100**

Amount actually received by the employee:

Wage	€1,500
less Unemployment insurance	(€95)
less Income tax	(€208)
Cash received	**€1,197**

The employee receives €1,197 per month but the cost to the employer is over 75 per cent more: €2,100. When I bring the subject up with Felipe, he exclaims, 'For every two people I hire, I could hire a third if it were not for social security! And if I did that, it would cost the government less in unemployment benefit!'

How does the Spanish wedge compare with that of Switzerland? I calculate that, in Geneva, the cost to an employer is about 37 per cent more than what is received by the worker.[30] So the wedge is far smaller than in Spain.

These have been snapshots of how things work in Switzerland and in Spain. We have come across some possible causes of unemployment. But which one – or ones – are the real culprits and which are mere distractions?

Here are the possible causes, one by one:

'Regulations sometimes overlooked in their impact on unemployment are those dealing with occupational licensing. If individuals cannot use their cars as cabs, sell homemade sandwiches on street corners, or move furniture without the appropriate licences, then their job opportunities are limited. Licensing boards are typically controlled by practitioners in the relevant occupations, and these practitioners often use their licensing powers to restrict the number of entrants to their occupations.'

Farell E. Block, *Unemployment: Causes and Cures*[31]

1. Regulations! Regulations! Regulations!

Thomas Daum in Zurich suggested that oppressive rules about firing people cause unemployment. Like other regulations, they increase the cost to a business of hiring someone. But, in theory, this should not cause unemployment. Businesses should simply pay lower wages to compensate. But if a high cost of regulations is combined – as in Spain – with minimum wages, then lower wages are not allowed. So employing people becomes unprofitable. Businesses must close down or set up in another country.[32] It is a combination of the two factors – oppressive regulations and minimum wages – that damages employment.

Why does France have 2.4 times as many companies with forty-nine employees as with fifty employees?[33] A company with fifty or more workers has to submit to a raft of rules and regulations that cost money and time. It must create three worker councils. If it wants to fire workers, it must submit re-structuring plans to these councils. It must introduce profit-sharing. And so on. Companies prefer to stop growing rather than to pay these extra costs. As a result, these companies produce fewer jobs than they would otherwise.

2. The wedge

Similarly, in theory, a big wedge should not cause unemployment. A company should simply pay a lower wage to compensate for the extra costs. But if there is a minimum wage, the lower wage is forbidden. That is when employing people may make no financial sense, leading to unemployment.

Different sizes of wedge

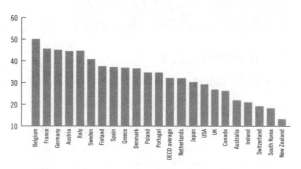

Income tax plus employee and employer contributions less cash benefits for single persons on 67 per cent of average earnings as a percentage of labour costs, 2013, for selected countries. The numbers would be bigger if they were expressed as percentages of the net earnings of the employee. Note that continental European countries account for all of those above the OECD average.

Source: OECD[34]

3. Low-quality education

Wherever I have gone I have been told by those who try to find people jobs that illiteracy makes it more difficult. But again, in theory, illiteracy should not of itself cause unemployment. Less literate people should simply command lower wages. At the beginning of the nineteenth century, most people were illiterate, yet they worked. Switzerland suffers from a significant rate of functional illiteracy – 13.7 per cent. This is not much better than average yet Switzerland has relatively low unemployment.[35] Illiteracy does not necessarily cause unemployment. But if a lower wage is ruled out by a minimum wage, then there will be unemployment.

The minimum wage as a race issue

'Before minimum wage laws were instituted in the 1930s, the black unemployment rate was slightly *lower* than the white unemployment rate in 1930. But then followed the Davis–Bacon Act of 1931, the National Industrial Recovery Act of 1933 and the Fair Labour Standards Act of 1938 – all of which imposed government-mandated minimum wages, either on a particular sector or more broadly … The inflation of the 1940s largely nullified the effect of the Fair Labour Standards Act, until it was amended in 1950 to raise minimum wages to a level that would actually have some effect on current wages. By 1954, black unemployment rates were double those of whites and have continued to be at that level or higher. Those particularly hard hit by the resulting unemployment have been black teenage males.'

Thomas Sowell, *Basic Economics*[36]

4. A minimum wage

The three factors so far mentioned do not cause unemployment by themselves but they lower the wages which an employer can afford to pay. People will probably reluctantly take lower pay unless something stops them. That something can be a minimum wage. It can also be welfare benefits that are more attractive than the lower wage. Welfare benefits can act as a proxy minimum wage. And welfare benefits can be combined with hidden employment to create an even better alternative.

In 2006, David Neumark and William Wascher reviewed more than 100 studies of the effect of minimum wages.[37] They concluded that 'the preponderance of the evidence points to disemployment effects' and that 85 per cent of the most credible studies pointed to negative effects. Most tellingly, they said that the studies which followed the least skilled groups showed especially strong evidence of causing unemployment.

I am suggesting that unemployment is not caused by a minimum wage alone nor by any other factor by itself but by the combination of a significant minimum wage (or proxy minimum wage of easily obtained welfare benefits) with other factors.[39] It is the interplay of factors that can be disastrous, as it has been in

Spain. Unfortunately, many welfare states have fallen foul of this. They have increased the costs of employing people, reduced the cash benefit of working and then, on the other side, they have created high minimum wages or easily obtained welfare benefits. Politicians creating a high minimum wage or high benefits may have looked 'generous' but they have caused mass unemployment and, through this, they have created misery for millions of individuals.

Let's just stop for a moment and consider: if all this is correct, then the permanent mass unemployment we have seen in so many advanced countries is a result of their welfare states. The creation of a 'welfare state' has brought about something wholly opposed to human welfare: unemployment. It is an irony – a tragic irony. The possibility that something as well intentioned, generally, as a welfare state should have caused such a tragedy should surely make us seek ways to make things better. Has any country ever found a way to improve matters when they have gone wrong?

After the Second World War Germany was a star performer. Growth was faster and the people became richer than in nearby France and Britain. But gradually things began to go wrong. Each new high in unemployment was above the previous one. The unification of East and West Germany may have been a political triumph but it created even more unemployment.

In many countries, a great deal of significance is sometimes attached to a particular number. In Germany, people were appalled that unemployment was approaching four million.[42] The level was first breached in 1996 but soon fell back. Relief was only temporary, though, and in 2002 there were nearly 4.1 million unemployed

> would be comforting to [be]lieve that government [ca]n simply decree higher [pa]y for low-wage workers, [wi]thout having to worry about [un]fortunate repercussions, but [th]e preponderance of evidence [in]dicates that labor is not [ex]empt from the basic economic [pri]nciple that artificially high [pr]ices cause surpluses.'
>
> [Tho]mas Sowell, *Basic Economics*[40]

Ian Sharp and Stephanie Fennessy lived together with their ten children receiving some £50,000 a year in welfare benefits.[38] Mrs Fennessy remarked, 'The benefits are being offered to me, so I'd be silly to turn them down.' Benefits can have a similar effect to a minimum wage, preventing people from taking work.

– approaching 10 per cent of the workforce.[43] The human and economic crisis became political.

A scandal in February 2002 added fuel to the fire. The government department responsible for finding jobs for the unemployed was revealed to have been fiddling the numbers. It had 'extensively manipulated its job placement figures'.[44] The department was exposed as untrustworthy and ineffective.

Inreased unemployment of the young

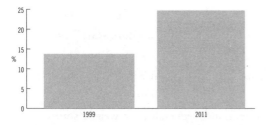

This big rise in the rate of unemployment for unskilled workers in the UK aged sixteen to twenty-four took place when the minimum wage was increased by 13.4 percentage points more than average earnings and more than twice as much as consumer prices.[41]

Gerhard Schröder, the German Chancellor, had to act. He made a telephone call to a trusted friend, Dr Peter Hartz, who was human resources director at Volkswagen. It was an unusual thing to do and Hartz himself remarked later, 'I was actually surprised when I got the call.'[45] Schröder asked Hartz to head a commission to recommend what should be done about the unemployment crisis. The commission's recommendations resulted in four new laws that came into force between 2003 and 2005, known as Hartz I, II, III and IV.

These reforms brought about a change in philosophy. Previously welfare benefits were an entitlement. People were not under any strong pressure to take jobs which did not appeal. Hartz changed that. He put a clear and strong obligation on the unemployed to seek work. He introduced 'Help and Hassle'.[46] The government would help you if you were unemployed. But you had to seek work straight

Dr Peter Hartz: 'I was actually surprised when I got the call.'

away. In fact, you became obliged to notify the agency that you had been made redundant as soon as you were told – before your period of notice ran out. If people did not try to obtain a job seriously or refused a job, their benefits could be temporarily suspended. The burden of proof was transferred to the claimants. If a claimant dropped out of a training programme, his or her benefits could be suspended. People were not allowed to be as choosy about what job they took. They had to take any reasonable job in relation to their qualifications and could be required to travel and even move.

Another change was that private companies were allowed to try to place people in jobs. Evaluation of their performance was based on the results achieved. Training schemes were reformed and people were required to go on them regardless of whether they were on unemployment benefit or means-tested benefits.

The duration of some benefits was reduced and conditions tightened. Previously, an older worker who lost his job could live on benefits for at least two years and eight months. This led to people using this concession as a form of government-financed early retirement. Hartz cut the entitlement period to twelve months or less for most people and eighteen months for older people. It was also made more difficult to qualify for unemployment benefit. You had to have worked for twelve out of the previous twenty-four months instead of twelve out of thirty-six months previously. And once the unemployment benefit ran out, the drop in income when you moved onto social assistance was made considerably bigger.

Two new legal categories of jobs were created: mini- and midi-jobs. These were low-paid, temporary and part-time jobs. If you took a mini-job you were not taxed; you did not have to pay social security

'Sit-down money'

Colloquial phrase for welfare benefits used by native Australians

contributions (nor did your employer); and you could continue to receive your benefits up to a point. In other words, mini-jobs scythed through possible financial disincentives to work. The maximum pay in these mini-jobs was only €400 a month. But you could take more than one. Hartz also loosened restrictions on temporary work and made it somewhat easier for employers to fire workers.[47]

Key elements of the Hartz reforms

1. Welfare recipients were required to seek work.
2. Private companies were used to find work for the unemployed.
3. Work was made to pay better than welfare benefits by removing tax and social insurance payments for mini- and midi-jobs.
4. Restrictions on part-time work were relaxed.
5. It was made easier to fire employees.

The Hartz legislation amounted to a wide-ranging attack on possible discouragements to work both for employers and employees.

Can unemployment insurance survive?

There are two basic kinds of welfare benefits: one based on insurance contributions paid by people in work and the other based on people's needs. Continental Europe mostly has an insurance-based system. But the model has taken a battering. In some countries, such as Sweden and the Netherlands, the amount paid in insurance benefits has been reduced.[48] Also the period of time for which it is payable has been shortened in various countries including Denmark, Sweden, France and the Netherlands.[49]

When insurance benefits run out, people typically go onto means-tested benefits, which are lower and therefore cheaper for governments. But the trend is for more and more people to be on means-tested benefits rather than insurance-based ones.

Will insurance benefits eventually become a mere facade in front of a benefits system which is predominantly based on means-testing? That is what happened in Britain.[50]

Did it work? Not immediately. In early 2006, unemployment was still high and Schröder was voted out of government. But by 2008 the number of unemployed had fallen all the way from over five million down to 3.5 million. Even more impressive was Germany's performance after the financial crisis of that year. Most countries in the Eurozone suffered considerable rises in unemployment lasting four or five years. But unemployment in Germany, after a brief rise, continued to fall. From the peak of over 11 per cent in 2004, it fell to 5.5 per cent in July 2012.

The turnaround in German unemployment ascribed to the Hartz reforms (compared to France and the UK)

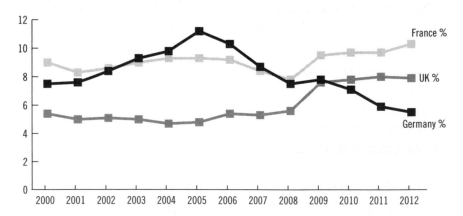

Source: Eurostat[51]

The improvement in youth unemployment was particularly good. While in the vast majority of countries it rose dramatically following the financial crisis,

Germany was one of only four of the thirty-four OECD countries that managed to reduce youth unemployment between December 2007 and July 2012.[52] Germany achieved the lowest figure of them all: 8 per cent. The average for the OECD was 16.1 per cent. In Spain it was an horrendous 52.9 per cent. Germany achieved this turnaround by increasing incentives for people to take jobs and by making it more cost effective for businesses to employ people. To put it another way, Germany dismantled some of the disincentives it had previously created.

The improvement in Germany is well known. But it was not the first time something like this has happened. Something similar took place in the Netherlands previously. In that case, the improvement took longer because, at first, they tried remedies that made no impact. In the 1970s, they tried spending money on public works and subsidising companies in difficulty. The unemployment problem got worse. Only after measures were taken that changed incentives – reducing the minimum wage, reducing welfare benefits and increasing the requirement on people to seek work – did the jobless rate fall.[53]

Oh no! Not Speenhamland again!

In the late eighteenth and early nineteenth century, in a Berkshire village called Speenhamland, wages were subsidised according to people's perceived needs. Employers took advantage of the system and paid lower wages than they would otherwise have done. The taxpayer picked up the bill. The same kind of thing was tried in Germany following the Hartz reforms. Government subsidies were paid to those in work – partly to give them a better standard of living and partly to make sure they were better off working than not working. But employers took advantage by paying workers little, knowing that the government would supplement the wages.

But the fastest and most dramatic transfer of people from welfare benefits to work took place in the USA after President Clinton signed the Personal Responsibility and Work Opportunity Act in 1996. Perhaps the state which became most famous for having success with it was Wisconsin. How did Wisconsin do it?

Activity conditions do succeed in getting people off benefits and into work, but they do it not by giving them the skills and opportunities they were previously lacking, but by making a life on benefits appear less desirable, relative to a life in employment, than it was before. This is the real (but often hidden) purpose of schemes like these and it works, for if you have to engage in "work-like" activities to qualify for benefits, you might as well take a real job and get paid better for doing it.

Peter Saunders, *Re-moralising the Welfare State*[54]

I am in Milwaukee, the biggest city in the state. I walk a few blocks from the faded grandeur of the Hilton Milwaukee City Center hotel to a modest office block. I am greeted by a slight, polite man called David Riemer, who leads me upstairs to his office. Riemer has a few mementoes of President Franklin D. Roosevelt around the room because he is a fan and thinks the President has often been misunderstood.

Riemer is thoughtful and knowledgeable about the history of welfare in the USA. He is also part of it. He tells me how events developed from his point of view. In the early 1990s, the number of welfare dependants in Wisconsin was rising strongly. There was a growing feeling that something should be done. Wisconsin had long and proud traditions both of work and of caring for workers. It was one of the first states to introduce unemployment insurance.

Benefits in Wisconsin were higher than in the neighbouring state of Illinois. It was discovered that people were taking the bus journey across the state boundary, travelling from Chicago to Milwaukee, just to get the higher benefits. Naturally the people of Wisconsin did not want their taxes to be used to provide cash to people some of whom had never even visited the state before.

Tommy Thompson, a Republican, was running for governor and proposed welfare reforms. He won the election and put forward his proposals. But David Riemer, who had thought about this issue more profoundly than most, believed they were just tinkering. The system needed more radical change. In 1993, he attended a picnic party to celebrate the re-election of the Democrat mayor of Milwaukee. Over *hors d'oeuvres* he started talking to Antonio Riley, a Democrat state legislator. Riley agreed with Riemer that the changes being proposed were not sufficiently radical.[55] It was an unusual situation: two Democrats wanted more radical welfare reform than a Republican governor was proposing. Antonio Riley asked Riemer what he could do about the main legislation that was then up for debate, the AFDC (Aid to Families with Dependent Children) programme, mainly received by unemployed single mothers.

'End it!' said Riemer.

Riley asked, 'Can I do that?'

'You are a state legislator. You can introduce any law you want.' Riemer argued that the state should not offer hand-outs for nothing. It should offer work.

Two weeks later, the two men sat down and drafted a bill. The Democrats controlled the state congress so the question was: how would Tommy Thompson, the governor, respond?

Thompson now had two reform bills ready to go: the Republican one and the more radical Democrat one. He was lobbied by many people. One was Riemer himself, who urged the governor to accept the Democrat bill, saying, 'We will support you.'

Thompson went with the Democrat proposal. He vetoed parts of it but the essentials survived. And so, in this strange way, with elements of support from both sides of the American political divide, welfare reform in Wisconsin went through.

Quality of administration matters

"THERE ARE NO JOBS!" THAT is what people told me outside a government "job center" in New York City.

'To check this out, I sent four researchers around the area. They quickly found 40 job openings. Twenty-four were entry-level positions. One restaurant owner told me he would hire 12 people if workers would just apply.

'It made me wonder what my government does in buildings called "job centers". So I asked a college intern, Zoelle Mallenbaum, to find out. Here's what she found.

'"First I went to the Manhattan Jobs Center and asked, 'Can I get help finding a job?' They told me they don't do that. 'We sign people up for food stamps.' I tried another job center. They told me to enrol for unemployment benefits."

'So the "jobs" centers help people get handouts. Neither center suggested people try the 40 job openings in the neighborhood.

'My intern persisted.

'"I explained that I didn't want handouts; I wanted a job. I was told to go to 'Workforce 1', a New York City program. At Workforce 1, the receptionist told me that she couldn't help me since I didn't have a college degree. She directed me to another center in Harlem. In Harlem, I was told that before I could get help, I had to come back for an 8.30 a.m. 'training session'."

'Our government helps you apply for handouts immediately, but forces you through a maze if you want to work.'

John Stossel [56]

What were the key elements? Actually there was only one: work. That is why it was called 'Wisconsin Works' or 'W-2' for short. A vital part of this was breaking down any barriers to work. The reforms went through several versions in the following years. But the original principles are worth recording partly because the publicity given to them helped to make the changes effective. They were posted in welfare administration offices all over the state.[57]

1. For those who can work, only work should pay.

2. W-2 assumes everybody is able to work, or, if not, at least capable of making a contribution to society through work activity within their abilities.

3. Families are society's way of nurturing and protecting children, and all policies

must be judged in light of how well these policies strengthen the responsibility of both parents to care for their children.

4. The benchmark for determining the new system's fairness is by comparison with low-income families who work for a living, not by comparison with those receiving various government benefit packages.

5. There is no entitlement. The W-2 reward system is designed to reinforce behaviour that leads to independence and self-sufficiency.

6. Individuals are part of various communities of people and places. W-2 operates to enhance the way communities support individual efforts to achieve self-sufficiency.

7. The W-2 system provides only as much service as an eligible individual asks for or needs. Many individuals will do much better with just a light touch.

8. W-2's objectives are best achieved by working with the most effective providers and by relying on market and performance mechanisms.

How did these principles work out in practice? How do they work now? I am at the Dane County Job Center on the outskirts of Madison, Wisconsin's capital. I am in a meeting room with tables arranged in a square and myself in the middle of one side. About fourteen administrators from the local office and the state face me from around the square. They range from front-line staff to senior managers.

I put to them a practical problem: 'Imagine a lone mother gets off the bus and comes to this office. She has a baby with her. She says she needs money and somewhere to live. What do you say to her?'

One of the fourteen immediately says that they ask her if she could not stay with her family.

'Imagine she says that her family are 500 miles away in another state and anyway they have rejected her. So where can she sleep tonight?'

They say they would suggest a shelter for the homeless such as one provided by the Salvation Army. But they add that the young woman will soon learn that this shelter is nothing she can settle into. She will only be allowed to stay for ninety days and it will only be available to her during the night time. They don't flinch from saying that housing is hard to get. They tell me that a lot of people live doubled-up in apartments.

The young woman will probably be steered towards the Wisconsin Works programme. On this first day or next, she will attend a one-hour group class with some eight to ten participants to introduce her to how the programme operates. At the end of that she will have five minutes with an adviser and within three days will have an 'intake appointment' which could last between one hour and two and a half hours.

The aim is simple: to discover what stands in the way of this person standing on her own two feet and overcoming it. An individual employability plan is devised. Then the state official and the woman both sign the plan. It is like a contract.

I ask, 'What are the top few obstacles to work that you come across?'

One of the fourteen around the table says, 'A criminal record.' Another says, 'Poor education.' 'Finding transport to get to work,' says a third. That sounds like a reasonable 'top few'. But then someone adds 'housing' and others agree. Another 'common obstacle' is mentioned and then another. In the end I note down nine 'top' obstacles to work:

1. A criminal record

2. Poor education

3. Difficulty getting transport to a job

4. Lack of housing

5. Lack of support from family or friends

6. Mental health problems

7. Poor work history

8. Alcohol and drug use

9. Lack of a work ethic

One classic obstacle is not mentioned: the cost of childcare. That's because it was always a key part of Wisconsin Works that the mother would have help with that. There is a centre where children can be dropped off. The mother pays some of the cost so she still has an incentive to save money if she uses a certified child minder or family members.

If the young mother can't write a CV, she goes on a course to help her to do that. If the problem is the cost of travel to work, she might be sent to a non-profit organisation that arranges shared travel to keep down the cost. The women take part in workshops for a week and get advice on dealing with the usual difficulties. There is a workshop on budgeting, for example. As soon as possible, the lone mother is found work or trains for a specific kind of job.

Various training programmes are available. A common one leads to a qualification as a certified nursing assistant but there are also training courses available in construction and clerical work.

Job-searching at the Dane County Job Center

Once these training courses are completed, the search for a normal commercial job begins. That is the target they are working towards. But those who cannot get such jobs straight away are allocated work provided by the state or by non-profit organisations. This could be in a charity shop or perhaps a warehouse where the state has an arrangement with a commercial employer. In healthcare, there are jobs such as acting as an attendant whose tasks include taking people to appointments within a hospital.

If someone persistently fails to keep the jobs she takes, she has a 'barrier screening' session. I am introduced to a woman who does this barrier screening. She says her job is to find out what the underlying problem is. Sometimes the lone mother finds that just talking about her problems helps her to solve them. Sometimes a problem is not revealed at first because it is embarrassing. It might be the long-term impact of being abused as a child. Some are too ashamed to admit that they are unable to read and that this is what is causing the problem. The interview includes set questions designed to bring out hidden issues like that.

There are three things going on here: one is improving the employability of the woman, a second is helping overcome difficulties and a third is pressing and requiring her to seek work.

> **'Men and women who have bee[n] unemployed for a certain perio[d] should be required as a conditi[on] of continued benefits to attend work or training centre[s]'**
>
> Sir William Beveridge (later Lord Beveridge) in influential report, *Social Insurance And Allied Servi[ces]* (1942). This part of his plan, however, was [not] implement[ed]

Wisconsin Works has been an astonishing success. It brought down the number of lone parents on welfare from 55,000 to 10,000 between 1996 and 2004.[58] The result is all the more astonishing because the numbers had already been brought down from 90,000, probably due to the tightening up of conditions done by Governor Thompson before Wisconsin Works came into effect. The reduction in numbers has been sustained, too.[59] Some have objected that the improvement has come about merely because people who were previously working in the shadow economy are now working on the books. They imply that the difference is insignificant. But, even if it were true to some extent, working 'off the books' means getting welfare cheques and not paying taxes. It amounts to defrauding taxpayers. The more people who do it, the greater that the cost of financing this fraud is for other people. Taxes have to be higher than they otherwise would be. And that, in turn, means that the incentive to cheat is all the greater. It is a vicious circle which divides workers into fraudsters and those they are defrauding. Before these reforms, the long-term trend was of ever-rising numbers of lone mothers on welfare. That trend has been stopped and reversed dramatically in Wisconsin but also in the USA generally. It is a decided improvement.

The US turnaround in single mother welfare dependency

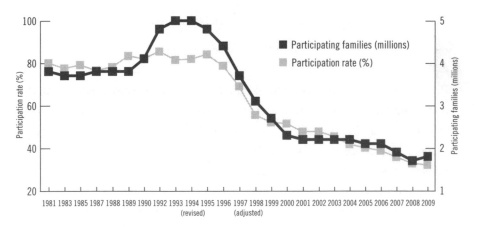

Number and percentage of eligible families, mostly single mothers, participating in the AFDC/TANF Cash Assistance Program.

Source: US Department of Health and Human Services[60]

So it has been a success and yet there is a depressing aspect to reform in Wisconsin and elsewhere in the USA. During my visit, I gradually came to realise that this programme for lone mothers was only one part of a great web of welfare programmes. Success has been achieved with lone mothers – varying from state to state – but meanwhile the number of Americans receiving government hand-outs from another programme, food stamps, has been soaring. The number claiming benefits on the basis that they are disabled has risen, too.

Number of Americans receiving food stamps

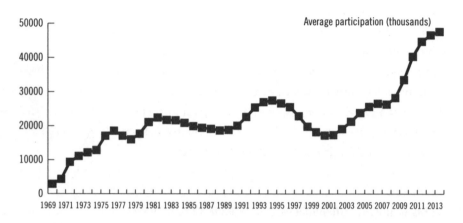

Participation in the Supplementary Nutrition Assistance Program, generally known as 'Food Stamps'.

Source: US Department of Agriculture, Food and Nutrition Service[61]

What is the difference between what has been done with lone mothers and, say, the food stamp programme? There are many differences, no doubt. But one stands out. Food stamps can be obtained without having to turn up every day to do work or training. With some exceptions, the 'workfare' idea has only been applied to lone mothers. Otherwise, the American welfare juggernaut continues to thunder on its way.

The approach Wisconsin took to lone mothers has been radical and successful. But we should remember that America is not the place with the lowest unemployment in the advanced world. Nor is Switzerland, Germany or the Netherlands. The country with the lowest unemployment rate in the advanced world – only 2.0 per cent in early 2014 – is Singapore.[66] What is the approach here? I am in a welfare benefits office in the South East region of Singapore near one of the Mass Rapid Transit stations. The glass front is like that of any of the shops in this shopping centre and the front desk with a receptionist is like that of a hairdresser or clinic. Pamphlets are available from racks on the wall and there are seats where you can wait. It is pleasant and unremarkable – a contrast to the bleak halls for benefit applicants I have seen in some countries.

Soon I meet Stanley Fong, the young general manager. We go to one of the four interview rooms at the rear. I ask him, 'If I were a jobless man who came into this office saying I needed money, what would you say to me?'

He replies that sometimes people are seen immediately but normally an appointment is made. The time set aside for the one-to-one interviews is forty-five minutes to an hour. It covers a lot of ground according to a plan but it is still a conversation.

'Suppose that, at that meeting, I say I need money?'

Fong says straight away I will be asked, 'What are the resources available to you through family and friends?'

This is already different from most other countries. In Singapore, I am not meant to come to the welfare office at all if I can obtain help from my family.

The question is not some meaningless formality, either. If I persist in asking for money, I will have to fill in a form detailing all my income, expenses and savings. I must also list all the members of

As health has improved, the number of people of working age receiving disability benefits has quadrupled

Number (millions)

Number of working-age disability benefit recipients in the USA.[62] The number almost quadrupled over this period while the overall population of the USA rose by only 41 per cent.[63] Since 2003, the number on disability benefits has continued upwards and was approaching seven million in 2012.[64]

The proportion of awards related to infections/parasites, injuries, respiratory ailments, endocrine/nutritional/metabolic problems, the nervous system, neoplasms and circulatory problems has declined.[106] The awards which proportionately increased are those related to mental and musculoskeletal problems. These have gone from 27 per cent to 51.7 per cent of all cases. The same trend has been seen in other countries. These two causes of disability have one thing in common with each other: it is not possible objectively to verify whether someone genuinely suffers from them or not.

my household, their occupations and incomes and confirm that the welfare office can contact other government agencies to share information about my circumstances and those of all other members of my household. I will have to confirm that the other members of my household are aware of this and have agreed to it. In other words, if I am living with my parents and one of them is earning a good wage, there is no way that I will get a cent from the government. The family is expected to provide.

If that hurdle is crossed, I will probably still get no cash or other support unless I agree to conditions and sign up to a plan. The plan will be designed to get me into a job and self-reliance. All help will be temporary. The welfare office's primary aim is to help me get a job.

I will be tested to assess my abilities. If I am illiterate, I will get literacy lessons. I will get help with writing a curriculum vitae. On the basis of my qualifications and physical capabilities, we will agree what other training I might do. I might be sent to an education and training centre to learn skills such as gardening or security. Or we might agree I should train to work in the food or retail business.

As in Wisconsin, the office is trying to discover my barriers to work and lower them. The idea is to make sure that people who get onto the programme get a job and become self-reliant. Although this is like Wisconsin, it is tougher and applies to all benefits, not just those of lone mothers. As the conversation goes on, the phrase that keeps coming into my mind is 'compulsory self-reliance'.

Fong remarks, 'Sometimes there is discomfort on the part of the resident. A lot would rather just have cash. We don't make it straightforward and comfortable for them. We really want self-reliance.'[67]

> **'We have arranged help but in such a way that only those who have no other choice will seek it. This is the opposite of attitudes in the West, where liberals actively encourage people to demand their entitlements with no sense of shame, causing an explosion of welfare costs.'**
>
> Lee Kuan Yew, Prime Minister of Singapore 1959–90[68]

Singapore takes a particularly robust attitude. But there is a further special and unusual aspect of Singapore that might be significant. The tax wedge is much smaller than in other countries. Those on very low wages pay no tax at all. Even those earning well above the median wage only have 4.2 per cent of their income taken in tax.[69] Here is an even more remarkable fact: people pay no social insurance contributions. They pay money into personal savings accounts instead.[70] It is a wholly different system.

So a person's money does not disappear into some government account from which benefits are paid out to others. Money is deducted from their pay but it is invested and attracts interest for that specific individual. The money can be used to provide a pension, to pay for healthcare and to buy a home. People surely feel quite differently about contributions to their own accounts than they would towards social insurance contributions. The more they put in, the wealthier they become. The problem of the wedge and the way it discourages the worker and the employer is largely removed.

Singapore appears like the ultimate welfare state for ensuring minimal unemployment. The regime would probably be too hardline for most democracies to accept. But some of its methods can certainly be copied.

Social insurance is better than means-testing because...[72]

1. Social insurance encourages employment because people must work before they qualify for the benefit.
2. Means-tested benefits can discourage employment when large-scale benefits for people with substantial 'needs' would be withdrawn if the person takes a job.
3. Under means-testing, less money is paid when two parents live together but only one of them works. So it can damage families.
4. Means-testing results in more completely workless households.
5. Means-testing tends to discourage saving.
6. Means-testing incentivises people to lie about their savings.
7. In-work means-tested benefits can be taken advantage of by employers to pay lower wages. They know that the benefits will make up much of the shortfall.

Means-testing is better than social insurance because...

1. Means-testing keeps the cost down in the short term – though not necessarily in the long term.
2. Means-testing keeps social insurance contributions down, increasing net take-home pay and encouraging legitimate work.
3. Means-testing can readily be framed to allow and encourage part-time work.
4. Means-testing can leave those who don't need benefits freer of state interference in their lives.

In purely economic terms, the arguments may seem fairly well balanced. But means-tested benefits have a much greater tendency to damage the behaviour of recipients, discouraging saving, penalising parents who stay together and incentivising lies. So social insurance appears to be preferable. Singapore has succeeded with means-tested benefits but only because these benefits have been minimal and rigorously policed.

There are other possibilities which have not been tried by modern governments. One could copy what has been done in Singapore with regard to pensions and healthcare: requiring people to make savings in a designated account. These savings could be drawn on if a person becomes unemployed. Another possibility would be to require people to take out unemployment and disability insurance but with competing companies and mutual societies. This would bring more choice, competition and innovation. Mutual or friendly societies might also encourage mutual support.

Which is the best kind of government programme for getting the unemployed into work?

Sometimes governments actively to try to get the unemployed into jobs. Efforts to do this are called 'active labour market programmes' in the jargon. Which kind works best?

Alessio Brown and Johannes Koettl looked at tens of studies of the subject.[71] This is what they found:

Not-so-good programmes

Subsidies to companies to retain employees despite a downturn: 'Very cost-ineffective'. Money is wasted keeping people in jobs when many of them would have kept their jobs anyway. The money spent benefits those in jobs without helping the unemployed. The money encourages industries and individuals to delay adapting to changed circumstances.

In-work benefits for low-paid workers such as tax credits and reduced social security payments: Not cost effective. A 'huge' cost is incurred subsidising employment which would have continued anyway. In some cases, employers rather than employees get the financial advantage.

Public works: These can crowd out private employment. They can 'lock in' workers who consequently do not seek long-term employment elsewhere. They are normally focused on low-skilled work and can remove the incentive for people to train and develop their skills. 'The evidence on the ineffectiveness of public works has been widely documented.' However, one study has shown that the closer the public work is to regular work, the better its impact. Sometimes public works are combined with workfare (see below), in which case they may be more useful.

Better programmes

Subsidies to companies to hire new employees: These can give the long-term unemployed experience of the workplace, which makes them more employable. They give employers a chance to try out people who they would not have tried otherwise. They can help the unemployed compete with the employed, making the market more competitive. But money can also be wasted on subsidising people who would have got jobs anyway ('deadweight cost'). Companies might simply hire subsidised people rather than employing those without a subsidy. Overall, such subsidies can, with suitable targeting of beneficiaries, be 'cost effective'. 'Self-employment subsidies are especially effective for the disadvantaged in the labour market, namely young, low-skilled, long term unemployed and inactive workers.'

Training on the job and/or classroom training: Governments spend more on this kind of programme than any other but the results are mixed. On-the-job training is 'particularly effective in comparison to classroom training'. One study found that combining on-the-job training with classroom sessions increased the impact by 30 per cent compared with classroom sessions alone. Tightly targeted training in small programmes has better results. But people are less likely to get work while the training continues.

The best programmes

Workfare and sanctions for not taking work: The threat of having benefits removed if a person does not seek work has a 'strong and significant' effect. One study found that the numbers taking jobs doubled after sanctions were imposed. Denmark had particular success through combining sanctions with tighter conditions for unemployment benefit.

Job search assistance: 'Very cost-effective'. Studies show an increased likelihood of getting a job of between 10 and 30 per cent. It should be 'targeted at workers with low employment probabilities at the beginning of the unemployment spell and at long term workers'. If combined with the threat of sanctions, it can be more effective. The effectiveness may be less during economic downturns.

What this report could not capture was the importance of the quality of the implementation of these programmes. Job search assistance, for example, can vary from the extremely useful to a complete waste of time.

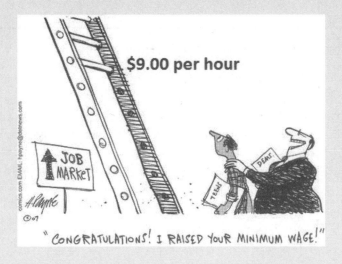

After seeing the experiences of Switzerland, Spain, Germany, Wisconsin and Singapore, the picture seems a lot clearer. For the most part, the permanent mass unemployment of modern times has been caused by welfare states. They have done it by increasing the costs of employing people for business and reducing the net cash benefit of working for employees. These factors have been particularly damaging when combined with a high minimum wage or proxy minimum wage in the form of easily obtained welfare benefits. Some welfare states have also contributed to unemployment through their housing, pensions, labour market and education policies, as we will see.

The permanently high unemployment that has been created has been highly damaging to the happiness of millions of people. It has been a scandal and a tragedy. It has also caused collateral damage that we will come to later, harming civility and honesty, weakening families and, of course, enfeebling economic growth.

The remedies are of two sorts. The first is simply minimising the obstacles to employment described previously: taking away the extra costs imposed on businesses, reducing the tax and social insurance taken from employees and lowering or abolishing minimum wages. There are precedents for all these things including the reduction in the minimum wage in the Netherlands. The second kind of remedy that has been shown to be effective is 'labour activation': requiring people to seek work, subsidising training aimed at actual jobs and removing barriers to work such as illiteracy.

There is no great difficulty identifying such remedies. The difficulty, in our representative democracies, has been for governments and people to face up to them and implement them.

A better benefits system for full employment

Unemployment insurance as the main system supplemented by much less attractive means-tested benefits.

The option of choosing from competing private unemployment insurance schemes.

No minimum wage or, failing that, regional minimum wages.

'Labour activation' policies including helping the unemployed with work-seeking, job-focused training, literacy courses and workfare. Work is the priority.

Private companies, paid by results, to help people get jobs.

Elimination or reduction of things that deter companies from hiring. This includes making it easy to fire employees, minimising employment regulations and removing the right of trade unions to have their staff paid for by companies.

It must be always and clearly financially advantageous for the low-paid to get a job.

3.

In search of the best healthcare system in the world

Rather like looking for the Lost Ark of the Covenant

I AM IN ZURICH RAILWAY station with its magnificent, wide concourse and roof supported by soaring metal arches. Along the sides are some restaurants. At the far end are a newspaper stall and then the platforms. The concourse is bustling with people hurrying to catch their trains. I am going to catch a train, too, but, on my way, a brightly lit temporary stall in the middle of the concourse catches my eye. Some young women are handing out leaflets. I wonder what they are advertising and I take one, but it is in German and I can't read it. Gradually I work it out, nonetheless. It is health insurance. Health insurance, I am discovering, is part of everyone's life in Switzerland.

I pass through this station several times during my stay in Zurich. On one occasion, I take a suburban train to Zug, a provincial town. It is a short journey and I share it with commuters returning from their day's work. I am going to interview Konstantin Beck. The reason I want to talk to him is that I am trying to find a good health-care system — in fact, the best

Temporary stall in Zurich station advertising health insurance

healthcare system in the world. Various conversations I have had back in Britain have led me to think that Swiss healthcare is a candidate and Konstantin Beck knows it intimately because he works for one of the big Swiss health insurance companies.

As the train trundles along, I like to think I already have a moderately good grasp of Swiss healthcare. It is like this: imagine you are a Swiss citizen. You are obliged to buy health insurance. That is the law. But you can choose between different health insurance groups offering a range of policies. Whichever policy you buy will provide at least the minimum, government-specified coverage.

What about the poor who can't afford health insurance? They must buy it, too. They get help with the cost. True, they can't choose the most luxurious policies with private rooms and so on. But they are covered.

What about those with major, existing health problems or the elderly, who, on average, have more medical expenses than the young? Do they have to pay much more? No. Payments are 'equalised'. Insurers are obliged to accept people regardless of their age or health history at the same price. The difference in risks is adjusted in a way that you, the buyer, do not see.

What if you, in a moment of rebellion or forgetfulness, fail to choose an insurer? You will be insured automatically anyway. There is no getting out of it.

So what is supposed to be good about this system? Those who like it admire the way that choice and competition run right through it. First, you choose your insurance organisation so the insurers are competing for your business. They compete with each other partly on price and partly on extras. They need to offer an attractive deal or they will go out of business. Then the insurers, in turn, choose among competing hospitals, clinics, doctors and so on. Some hospitals are private. Some are owned by one of the twenty-six cantons into which Switzerland is divided. All the hospitals need business so they try to offer the best deals to the insurers. There are therefore two layers of competition – one between insurers and the other between healthcare providers like hospitals. Some think this system encourages the best possible service at the lowest possible cost.

My train arrives at Zug. Konstantin Beck is on the platform waiting to greet me. We leave the station and walk to a café nearby.

Beck knows a lot about healthcare systems, not just the Swiss one. I ask whether he thinks the Swiss system is a good one.

'Yes,' he replies.

It is an encouraging start.

He says it is true that newspapers complain about insurance premiums being expensive. But, in many cases, people themselves make the choice to buy the higher-priced policies. Premiums vary a lot. People can pay less if they choose a policy which has a 'gatekeeper'.

What is a 'gatekeeper'?

A general practitioner. A policy with a gatekeeper is cheaper because you are not allowed to go straight to a specialist. You must first go to a general practitioner who will assess your condition and decide whether to send you on to a much more expensive specialist. The system saves money because, in many cases, the general practitioner will decide that he or she can deal with your problem and you do not need to see a specialist at all.

You can also pay less for your policy if you choose 'managed care'. That means you can only go to a limited selection of doctors or hospitals. The most expensive policies allow you to go to any doctor or hospital in Switzerland.

The system as a whole has popular support, says Beck.

'How do you know?' I ask.

Because every now and again, he says, the country has a referendum in which the system is challenged by those who do not like some aspect of it. Consistently the people vote to keep it.

As I come from Britain, with its history of people waiting a long time to be seen by specialists and waiting again to have tests and operations, I ask about waiting lists.

There are virtually none, he says. 'If you want a hip replacement, you might possibly be asked to wait three months. But if it is urgent, it could happen more quickly.'

'How long would you wait for an MRI scan?'

'No more than a few weeks.'

It sounds good. Maybe this is indeed the best healthcare system in the world. But I am obliged to ask him if there is anything wrong with it.

He admits that, yes, there are a few problems. A doctor can send in excessively high bills to the insurance company. Or he may refer patients to hospitals too readily. In both cases, the insurance companies have to pay up. I say nothing but I am thinking that this defect does not sound too terrible.

Could the system be used in other countries, I ask? Does it depend on Swiss efficiency for it to work well? Beck does not comment except to say that the system does depend on claims from the doctors being reliable. You have to be able to 'believe the bills'.

He says that one problem is that the compensation which insurers receive for taking on those with existing health problems is not as accurate as it should be. Insurers still have an incentive to sign up the young and healthy. He says there has been a thirteen-year battle to try to get extra compensation for taking on those who have been in hospital the previous year. This would be a rough and ready adjustment but it would help. As Beck talks, it becomes clear that the system is constantly being adjusted and refined. He says that, yes, Switzerland is improving, step by step. Eventually, he says, the Swiss system can become as good as the Dutch one.

It takes me a moment to digest what he has just said. I have come to Switzerland to hear about the much-praised Swiss system. Up until now, it seems that the news is good and it works well. But now he is saying that – in one respect, at least – the Dutch system is better. It is not often that a Swiss person tells you that another country does something better.

I can't remember whether I already intended to visit the Netherlands. But obviously now I have to.

A few months have passed and I am now in Rotterdam. Frankly, it is not the prettiest town in the Netherlands. It was severely bombed in the Second World War. But a major port and large areas of water give it a light, open feeling. I am visiting Erasmus MC, the third or fourth largest hospital in Europe, serving 4.3 million people – a vast place, currently being rebuilt. The press officer guides me through a labyrinth of corridors to get to the next person I am seeing. Finally she knocks on a door and I am introduced to genial, smiling Dr Eric Sijbrands.

Dr Sijbrands specialises in diabetes. The hospital has a particularly difficult problem with this disease. Rotterdam is a multi-ethnic city and 70 per cent of diabetes outpatients don't speak Dutch. That makes communication difficult but what makes the situation worse is that many patients come from south Asia, Turkey and Morocco, where people tend to have more problems with type II diabetes. Sijbrands tells me they get it when they are younger and thinner than western Europeans. The disease is 'meaner' with them, too.

He tries to get his patients to improve their diets. But it is difficult. He recalls how he once became very depressed about how things were going. He had long experience of trying to persuade patients to change their diets for a year, then for a second year and a third. When he failed to persuade patients to make a significant change after three years, he admits he felt like giving up. He had a feeling that he had 'achieved almost nothing'. He had a few days off and gloomily sat at home wondering, "What am I doing here?'" He wished he could help his patients more effectively.

Dr Sijbrands wrestled with various ideas of what could be done to improve things. He gave up many but persisted with one: the notion of 'diabetes stations'. These would be rooms, not far from where patients live, where they could go and administer tests on themselves. A computer would provide personalised guidance through each test. It would communicate in the patients' own language. They would be able to see for themselves what sort of progress was being made. Any unexpected or worrying results could quickly be flagged up automatically to their doctors.

He went to the innovation department of the hospital and persuaded it to support the idea. Now it is being tried out. These stations are being created around

Rotterdam. One of the initial results has been a 70 per cent reduction in patient visits to the hospital. It turns out that patients like visiting the machines better than visiting the doctors. They are emailed recipe ideas written in their own language and in accordance with their traditional diets.

Eric shows me one of the machines and I do a few tests. I am impressed. This seems to be an innovation which might both save money and treat patients more successfully. It looks like public-spirited healthcare at its best.

From what sort of a system has it emerged? And, even more important, is this really a good system of healthcare?

I go on to see a clutch of doctors and academics in the Netherlands, trying to discover the answers. But it is not easy. I gradually learn that the Dutch do not like to make dramatic statements. Everything is carefully expressed. Hardly anyone is frank and downright. Gradually, though, I manage to work out that there has been a revolution in Dutch healthcare, but one that has taken place in slow motion.[1]

Dr Sijbrands at one of his 'diabetes stations'

The healthcare system used to be very government controlled. But in 1987 a leading businessman called Wisse Dekker wrote a report which argued that it should be open to private competition.[2] This provoked vehement opposition – by Dutch standards. It was blocked. Governments came and went. Some were in favour of the idea and some against. But over a long period of time filled with debate, argument and consensus-building, a government-dominated system gradually allowed in some private competition.

Planning and experimentation took place in the five years from 1995. In the five years after that, some hospitals began using parts of a new system. Different groups all had their say. It was long-winded and complex.

I am used to governments making bold new changes decisively. In one interview in Amsterdam, I fail to hide my feeling that it sounds a roundabout and irksome business. But Tom Groot of VU University replies, 'If we hadn't done this, the current system would not have emerged.' He and several others I talked to in the Netherlands believe the debate and consensus-building led to a better, more securely based system.

So what is it?

At first sight, it seems similar to the Swiss one. Everyone has to be insured and everyone can choose among competing insurers. But there are two areas where systems like this have tricky details to decide upon. One is the amount of compensation paid to the insurers for accepting high-risk patients. That is where Konstantin Beck seemed to think the Dutch were ahead of the Swiss. The other is the amount paid for treatments by the insurers to hospitals and clinics.

The Dutch have had problems with this second issue. Before the 1980s, the government doled out money to hospitals according to the number of beds they had and suchlike. The result was that the hospitals were not very productive and there were waiting lists. They had no incentive to be productive. So the system was changed. Hospitals were paid according to their 'production' – how many operations they did. This encouraged hospitals to do more operations but now they had no incentive to innovate or keep costs down. So that became expensive.

Doctors were then asked to define typical conditions that patients suffer from and specify normal procedures and how much they should cost. This was called a 'diagnostic treatment combination'. The hospitals or specialist clinics would be paid a fixed sum for each diagnostic treatment combination and so would have an incentive to come up with cheaper and better ways to treat patients. Increasingly the insurers could also negotiate with hospitals and clinics over how much they paid for treating certain conditions. This led to an increase in specialist clinics, which make themselves very efficient in a particular treatment – laser eye surgery, for example. Waiting lists came down. But the trouble with this was that there was a huge number of diagnostic treatment combinations, which made the system cumbersome. The next move was drastically to reduce them.[3]

The insurers are increasingly able to negotiate with hospitals and other providers on price and quality. In 2005, they could negotiate some of the terms on which they bought 10 per cent of healthcare provision. In 2012 it was up to 70 per cent.

It sounds as if the system is constantly being refined. It certainly seems much better than in the 1970s.

In the conversations I have, I get the impression that everyone thinks the Dutch system is pretty good. But no one is openly enthusiastic about it. So is it good or not?

I ask another academic, Professor Erik Schut of Erasmus University in Rotterdam, which system he thinks is the best in the world. He is reluctant to make an outright judgement. He is only willing to indicate a relatively favourable view of the Dutch and German systems. That is it. It is a curious business. I came to the Netherlands with the idea that it might have an even better system than the Swiss. Yet when I come here, many of the experts are surprisingly equivocal about it.

One evening, near the end of my stay, I have supper with a personal contact

– someone who has nothing to do with healthcare except, of course, for being a patient now and again. We meet in the Dauphine Café-Restaurant, a bustling place in Amsterdam, and I ask him, almost incidentally, what his experience is of Dutch healthcare. He becomes quite agitated talking about it.

'You ring up the doctor and you can't speak to him! Instead you speak to a receptionist who asks you lots of questions. But you might not want to discuss your case with a receptionist. To get to see the doctor soon you have to be pushy. The pushy get through. The meek must wait.' His description of general practitioners makes it sound as though the 'gatekeepers' – through which it is normal to go in the Netherlands – have gates with rusty old hinges, which they are reluctant to open.

What about the hospitals? There are still waiting lists for operations, my contact exclaims. People go to Germany or Belgium if they want to get treated quickly. The French system, which he knows about because his wife is French, is much better because there are no gatekeepers and the general practitioners come to see you in your own home. They won't do that in Holland.

This is only anecdotal. Perhaps it is exaggerated or out of date. But the conversation reminds me of something a senior doctor said earlier in my visit. He was a German working in the Netherlands – obviously in a particularly good position to compare the two systems. What did he think?

At first he gave me what sounded like a balanced judgement in the Dutch style. He told me the Dutch system is structured, centralised and evidence-based. There are gatekeepers and it is cheaper. The German system is good but it is expensive.

Then he leaned forward confidentially: 'Don't write this down,' he smiled. 'But I still have my German health insurance.'

It was a telling moment. The Dutch system has its virtues, no doubt. It is fashioned and continually refined by highly intelligent, serious, public-spirited people. But when it comes to the crunch, some people, at least, prefer a less controlled system that costs more but offers faster service and more freedom for the individual. The German system is complex and varied. It has compulsory insurance but a key element is that patients can choose whichever general practitioner or specialist they want to see. The physicians are in private practice and most hospitals are independent but not-for-profit.

It was confusing. Two systems that I had heard being touted as the best did

> 'We could spend our entire gross domestic product on healthcare in useful ways. In fact we could probably spend the entire GDP on diagnostic tests alone – without ever treating a real disease.'
>
> John C. Goodman, *Priceless*[8]

not seem quite so good when I got a bit closer. Perhaps it was time to get a truly international assessment.

So, I am now in the OECD headquarters in Paris. The press officer takes to me to see a woman who, he says, has been much in demand to give presentations about healthcare systems. She has written an analysis which has caught many people's imagination. Along a corridor we come to a small room and I am introduced to a lively, charming woman called Isabelle Joumard.

I ask her to tell me about her research. She says that she analysed how effective healthcare systems are in relation to their costs. To put it another way, she looked at which healthcare systems produce the best results for the cash spent.

Isabelle Joumard at the OECD

I am sceptical. I have previous experience of how difficult it is to measure how well a healthcare system performs. How did she measure performance? As part of her answer, she mentions life expectancy. I exclaim that I am astonished she should take life expectancy as a measure! It is extremely misleading. Life expectancy depends far more on lifestyle – especially diet – than on the quality of the medical system. She smiles indulgently and replies

that her analysis included adjustment for lifestyle factors. It also excluded deaths by violence. She goes on to say she also used a measure of 'avoidable deaths' – deaths from conditions such as asthma from which young people should not normally die.

Amused by my scepticism, Joumard tells me that what persuaded her that these measures were meaningful was that they were 'highly correlated' with each other. The various measures she used produced similar results.

She suggests various papers I can read to get the full story. But it has been a long day and the thought of reading yet more OECD research papers fills me with dread. Yes, I will look at them, I assure her.[4] But in the meantime, could she tell me the answer, please?

She is reluctant to tell me the results of her extensive labours in a sentence. I cajole and encourage her, saying, 'This is turning into a long journey. Please give me a little guidance!'

Finally she relents. She offers me the result of her popular, learned study and her high correlations. What is the country with the most cost-effective healthcare system in the advanced world?

Australia.

Fine. I was not expecting that one. But Australia would be interesting. I was thinking of going there anyway.

I am now in lovely, spectacular Sydney. I am going to the Australian Club, which sounds charmingly old-fashioned. It turns out that the building I have been sent to does not look like a venerable gentlemen's club after all. I am going up in a lift in an office block. However, when I arrive at the top, the club has evidently held onto relics of its past, including a certain formal manner. I am greeted by John Graham, an immaculately polite, retired doctor of the old school.

He takes me to a table for two by the window which gives us a good view. I explain to him that I have been to the OECD headquarters in Paris where I was told that Australia has the most productive healthcare system in the world. What does he think?

'They must be looking at it through funny-coloured spectacles,' he remarks. Graham strongly feels that the quality of healthcare in Australia has deteriorated. Consultations are too rushed. The general practitioner does not have time – and is not trained – to get to the bottom of what a person is suffering from. He just follows a quick routine. He dishes out antibiotics, for example, which will be the right treatment for only one in ten of those he gives them to. For eight of the patients, antibiotics will be unnecessary and in one case he will have missed a different condition altogether such as jaundice.

Waiting times have become bad, Graham says. If you want a knee replacement, you can wait between eighteen months and two years. The bureaucracy has mushroomed, too. He is old enough to remember when healthcare in the state of New South Wales was administered by sixty-five bureaucrats. Now there are 15,000 of them. He has studied the proportion of people employed at the front line compared with managers, bureaucrats and so on. In his research, he bent over backwards to be fair, even including hospital gardeners as front-line staff since hospitals have gardens which need to be cared for and which are good for patients. Even after such a generous interpretation, he found that for every four people delivering healthcare, another three were not on the front line.

So there is a huge waste of money. But there is a kind of 'double whammy' of waste, too. First there is the cost of the administrators. Then there is the inordinate time which doctors and nurses must spend filling in the forms which the administrators create for them. Graham expresses all this in a tone of regret rather than anger, which only makes his remarks all the more persuasive.

After lunch, he takes me along a busy street to Sydney Hospital. It was founded in the nineteenth century and still has remnants of the old colonial architecture. In one part, substantial old stone arches run alongside a wide corridor open to the air at first-floor level. John says he can remember patients being placed in beds out in the open there. He reminisces about the days when the hospital was bigger and a centre of expertise where medical advances were made. Now politicians are trying to close it down. We go into various buildings. He retired only a year ago and all the staff know and obviously respect him. They call him by his first name and we are waved through wherever we go. He was probably working at the hospital before most of them were born.

In the emergency department, we talk to the senior nurse, who is exactly the sort of capable person you would want in that position. I ask her about waiting times for emergencies. She says that patients are put in one of five categories. Category One patients – the most serious – are seen straight away. Category Four patients have relatively minor injuries: for example someone might have turned an ankle but still be in some pain. He or she would be seen by a doctor within an hour. It all sounds pretty good. Then I mention to the nurse that Graham previously remarked that this emergency department is less busy than others. Ambulances are typically sent to a bigger hospital. She agrees. That is when she tells me about 'ramping'.

Sydney Hospital: patients' beds used to be put out onto the first floor terrace in the summer.

The nurse explains that sometimes, especially at bigger hospitals, they cannot accept all the emergency patients who arrive at busy times because there is insufficient capacity. So ambulances are told to wait on the ramp leading up to the entrance. Or else the patients are allowed into the hospital but continue to be attended by the ambulance paramedics so that officially they have not been admitted. This enables the hospitals to meet their target of seeing every patient within four hours of admission. Of course it is a tacit acknowledgement that they are probably not going to be seen within four hours of arriving.

The nurse says she has a friend who was in a serious condition and was kept on a trolley, waiting to be officially admitted, for two hours. Once admitted, she had to begin another wait to be seen by a doctor.

How often does this happen, I ask? 'At the big hospitals, every week. The usual times are Monday afternoons and Friday evenings.'

It sounds grim.

During my stay in Australia, I look into this some more. Jeremy Sammut, a healthcare analyst, tells me that over a third of emergency admissions to a public hospital have to wait more than eight hours for a bed.[5] That sounds positively frightening.

A few days later, I am having lunch with another doctor. We get onto the related subject of rationing of healthcare. Does rationing happen in Australia, I ask? He tells me I should talk to a specialist he knows. Without pausing, he makes a call on his mobile phone. He quickly tells the person on the other end of the line who I am and passes over the phone. I find myself talking to a specialist who does bone marrow transplants. This can be a life-saving operation for a certain kind of cancer. I ask if there is rationing in his field.

There certainly is, he says. 'We could do at least twice as many!'

So why doesn't he? Because the money made available by the government to pay for support staff and beds is restricted.

Does it matter? Does anyone suffer as a result? The specialist says that people who ought to have marrow transplants straight away have to wait. The doctors naturally try to prioritise urgent cases but there are some patients who have relapses because they have been waiting so long. They are often weakened so much by the relapses that they become unable to stand the strain of chemotherapy, which is part of the treatment. And since they cannot bear the chemotherapy, they die. The delay has caused their deaths. Medical rationing leads to deaths.

I ask whether he talks or writes articles about what is going on. He says it is against the terms of his employment. If it were revealed that he has said these things to me, he could be fired. He says no politician in Australia is telling the truth about healthcare rationing. No politician is willing to tell the truth and no doctor is allowed to.

This is depressing. Yet it seems there are some good aspects of healthcare in Australia. People can see a general practitioner quickly and easily. If their own doctor is not available it does not matter. They can see any general practitioner. Typically the government pays for most of the cost of a treatment but not all, so the patient has to contribute. I am told the doctors may do too many procedures because they get paid according to what they do, rather than how many patients they have. But seeing a general practitioner quickly is a good thing that does not happen everywhere.

Also the large minority of care in private hospitals seems to work well enough. There is a thriving market in private health insurance. Private hospitals and other medical care are encouraged by the government in clever ways. For example, the better-off have to pay an extra 1 to 1.5 per cent of their income to help pay for the government's health insurance scheme, Medicare. But if they opt out and take private insurance they do not have to pay this extra.

Private healthcare is big. One doctor tells me that 40 per cent of hospital care is provided privately. Mostly this consists of planned operations but the critical mass in private healthcare means there are even some private hospitals with emergency departments able to handle major incidents. A friend living in a Sydney suburb tells me that if members of his family have an emergency, they go straight to the local private hospital.

How does such a large private sector continue to exist after a number of decidedly left-leaning governments in recent decades, I wonder? A long-time resident tells me that the Labor Party has given up attacking private healthcare because private insurance is taken out by people fairly well down the income scale whose votes they need.

Overall, I am slightly disappointed. The numbers in Australia might look good from Paris but if OECD staff found themselves in an ambulance waiting on a ramp for a few hours before being admitted to hospital and then waiting some more, they would probably not be so impressed.

But there is one other advanced country that might be worth looking at. The OECD tends not to examine it because it is not a member of the organisation. It rarely appears in international comparisons of healthcare. This country is sometimes mentioned as having a good system and it happens to be on my way back to England.

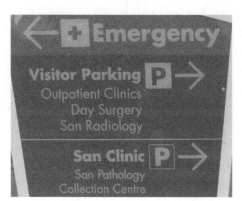

Sign to the emergency department of a private hospital in suburban Sydney.

My plane arrives in the early evening and across the wide bay are dozens of massive merchant ships and tankers. In the dying sunlight it is a wonderful sight and a reflection of how far the country has come. Singapore is now the second busiest port in the world after Shanghai.[6] Singapore was once a British colony. It was much poorer than Britain and its medical care was unsophisticated. But now babies born in Singapore are half as likely to die before their first birthday as those born in Britain. Life expectancy, for what it is worth, has surpassed that of the former mother country. It is eighty-two compared to eighty. I have heard no reports of 'ramping' or long waiting lists there. Do these good results mean the system costs a fortune?

On the contrary, whereas Britain spends 9.4 per cent of its national income on healthcare, Germany spends 11.3 per cent and America spends a staggering

17.9 per cent, Singapore spends a mere 4.7 per cent.[7] If Singapore had been included in the OECD comparison of cost-effectiveness, it would surely have come first. How does Singapore do it?

The most unusual aspect of the system is the way medical care is paid for. Money to pay the bills comes from a variety of sources. The system has been carefully assembled to try to reconcile competing aims.

One source of funds is the government. It provides a substantial subsidy to its own hospitals and clinics. This helps keep down the cost for those of modest means. It also provides further subsidies for the poor through some means-testing. Next there is a fund to help the poor who cannot manage any other way to pay for their healthcare. This is means-tested, too, to make sure that only the genuinely poor use it.

Then there is a government insurance scheme to protect against the cost of an exceptional, extremely expensive stay in hospital. Most people buy it because, again, it is subsidised.

Another source of payment is the patient's own pocket. The idea behind this is that people will not waste their own money as they might waste government money. In particular, most people except the poorest are expected to pay for their general practitioner and normal prescriptions with their own cash. Some element of 'co-payment' is fairly widespread in healthcare systems from Sweden to Australia. In systems where practically everything is covered by insurance, as in France and for many Americans, the cost of healthcare is very high.

This brings us to the last big source of cash, which takes place on a national scale only in Singapore: everybody is required to pay between 7 and 9.5 per cent of their income into a personal medical savings account called Medisave. Their employers pay slightly under half this amount. The money saved can only be spent on medical bills but the key point is that it remains the property of the individual. If at the age of fifty-five, the value of the Medisave account, combined with other savings accounts, is above a certain level, an individual can withdraw it. Moreover, when the individual dies, the saved money is distributed to whoever he or she has nominated without tax. The money in one's own personal Medisave account is used

> **'I was a student in Britain when the Labour government in 1947 implemented the National Health Service. Their belief that all people were equal and no one should be denied the best medical services was idealistic but impractical and led to ballooning costs. The British National Health Service was a failure. American-style medical insurance schemes are expensive, with high premiums because of wasteful and extravagant diagnostic tests paid for out of insurance. We had to find our own solution.'**
>
> Lee Kuan Yew, former Prime Minister of Singapore[9]

to pay for a great deal of one's healthcare. People can choose where they spend it. They have every reason not to waste it.

The ingenious aspect of the Singaporean system is the way it recognises the things that typically go wrong in healthcare systems around the world and finds ways to counter them. On the one hand, everyone is covered. On the other hand, there is competition, choice and the incentive not to waste money.

Even the government hospitals, which are semi-independent, compete with each other and with the private hospitals to attract patients. Patients can go to whichever hospital they prefer. The fact that hospitals get cash for treating patients may account for the fact that there do not appear to be long waiting lists. Almost everybody has the money available to pay for treatment because of the savings accounts. There are different levels of accommodation at different prices. The cheapest is in open wards in government hospitals which are 80 per cent subsidised by the government.

I am keen to see one of the hospitals and fortunately a visit to Khoo Teck Puat Hospital in the northern suburbs has been arranged for me. When I arrive, I find large modern buildings with gardens like those of a top-class hotel. I meet the manager, Liak Teng Lit, a veteran government official who grew up alongside the tough, determined creators of modern Singapore.

Khoo Teck Puat Hospital in Singapore. The lush garden is like that of a first-class hotel. The idea is that your heart-beat should slow down while you are there instead of speeding up as in most hospitals.

Liak takes me around the different wards. The lowest C-class open ward we see is full of people and has no air-conditioning. I would find it oppressively hot but perhaps local people are more acclimatised to the heat. The top A-class accommodation consists of private rooms which are quiet and cool. But I don't find them particularly welcoming.

These rooms have zero government subsidy. I mention that someone told me that the people in the A-class rooms get better treatment. 'That's rubbish,' Liak replies. He says that, in fact, one of his biggest problems is stopping the patients in the A wards being neglected. Doctors find it easier to do their rounds in the cheaper wards. They can move from one patient to another easily. Anyway, the doctors have no reason to prefer those in the A-class rooms. Most doctors are on a fixed salary.

There is one further, subtle advantage of the Singapore system. As a patient, you take responsibility for your own healthcare. You are not just told where to go by the government or an insurance company. You have your own resources and can make real choices. Yes, you have been compelled by the government to save. But you can use the money at any recognised hospital.

Are there any problems?

There is one thing which most advanced democracies would find shocking and unacceptable. Suppose a relative of yours – say your sister – has a serious medical condition that requires repeated stays in hospital and expensive drugs. Suppose, too, that the savings in her Medisave account have been exhausted. The government will come to you and your sister's other relatives, asking you to pay the bills from your own Medisave account. This is enforced family support. You might not even like your sister. You might not have seen her for thirty years. It does not matter. One person in Singapore tells me that this does not bring families together. It drives them apart. He also says that there are times when an elderly grandmother will not go for treatment because she does not want to drain the family finances. These are things that most democracies would not accept.

Another possible issue is that some people may not like the reluctance in the government hospitals to use the latest, most expensive equipment. And, in some countries, it would be reasonable to worry whether the vast sums locked up in Medisave accounts might one day be raided by a government in financial difficulty.

The Singapore system probably cannot be simply copied. In fact, I meet several people in Singapore who would like it to be changed in one way or another. The government, too, feels obliged to make little changes now and again to fine-tune it. Most people seem to want to increase the insurance element and reduce the amount of self-payment. But it must be admitted that the existing system appears to be the most cost-effective in the advanced world.

At this point, the reader might feel I should finish the world tour and come to a conclusion. But please come with me on one final journey. At least it is to somewhere warm where the people are friendly and the wine is excellent.

I am in Valencia, Spain. This is the region that includes resorts such as Alicante. But I am not at any resort. I am in an inland town called Alzira. Not familiar with it? That's not surprising. This is a nondescript sort of place that no tourist would dream of visiting. Yet a new kind of healthcare system began in this place. It has become known as the 'Alzira model' and it is studied and talked about far and wide. In fact, I first heard about it in Stockholm, of all places.

I am staying at a funny little hotel which is not exactly up to the highest international standards. My room is small and contains a fridge that is not plugged in. That does not matter since there is nothing in it anyway. In the morning, I am collected by a public relations officer who drives me the short distance to the hospital. The place seems normal enough – like hundreds of other hospitals. I am led to a meeting room where the manager and some senior staff are waiting for me.

The director general, Dr Manuel Marín Ferrer, is a short man with an air of relaxed authority. He speaks some English, but when he needs help, Dr Carlo Trescoli, a tall, urbane and friendly man, steps in.

They give me a presentation. The hospital has so many visitors from around the world that they are well prepared. Afterwards I ask questions and am taken on a tour. Then I interview a variety of people through the day to try to understand what is going on as well as I can.

I discover that the Alzira model was created in a roundabout way. No one planned it at the outset. In 1982, the Socialist Party in Valencia promised that Ribera – the health department in which Alzira is situated – would get a hospital. Years rolled by and no hospital was built. Hospitals cost money and there never seemed to be enough of it. While this was going on, it was becoming increasingly recognised in Spain that standards were low in many public hospitals. When I was in Madrid, before coming to Alzira, I asked someone how long you might have to wait to see a doctor in an emergency department. He told me it could be as long as seven days! I found it hard to believe. I had never heard of emergency waiting times being measured in days before.

So, in 1997, the national government passed a law decreeing that publicly financed healthcare did not have to be delivered by the government itself. The regional government in Valencia took advantage of this to find a way to build the long-awaited new hospital in Alzira. There was still no money but they had the idea of making a contract with a private company to design, build and – crucially – pay for a new hospital. In recompense for this, the company would run the hospital for ten years and then hand it back to the regional government. The private company would be paid a sum per year based on the number of people in the Ribera area and the amount would be no higher than the sum spent per capita elsewhere in the region.

For the regional government, the deal solved a political problem at no cost. In fact, the contract sounds so advantageous to the regional government and so tough on the private company that you might wonder why on earth the company would agree to it. How could the income over only ten years ever cover the heavy cost of building a hospital and produce a profit? I try to find the answers to this all day.

A cynic might think, 'Oh, they could make money by having long waiting lists and not treating people properly while taking the government's money.' But the contract was far too ingenious for that. Part of the deal was that if the people of Ribera voted with their feet and went to hospitals outside the department, the private company would have to pay the whole cost of their operations. The contract was deliberately unequal. If the situation was reversed and people from outside

Ribera came to the Alzira hospital, the company would only receive 80 per cent of the officially determined value of the procedures. So the Alzira hospital had to attract local patients in order to avoid heavy penalties. And if people came to them from elsewhere, the hospital had to find ways to treat them which were at least 20 per cent less expensive than what other hospitals managed.

How could the private hospital hope to survive in these circumstances, let alone make a profit? The savings in costs per procedure would have to be enormous. It turned out that the contract was indeed so tough that the company could not make it work. A compromise was made. The deal was eased a little and, surprisingly, in the course of making this compromise, the negotiators created the new element which made the Alzira model special: the regional government agreed that the company would take over primary care – care provided by general practitioners or local clinics – in Ribera as well as hospital care. This change had remarkable consequences.

But first, before we get to those, even after the original contract was made less tough, it was still very demanding. Throughout the day, I ask the people involved, 'How can you make a success of the contract when you have to pay for building and equipping the hospital and then you have to hand it back?'

Marín Ferrer tells me some ways in which his hospital saves money compared to public hospitals. 'We work the equipment from 8 a.m. to 8 p.m. instead of from 8 a.m. to 3 p.m.,' he says. The staggering thing about this remark is the way it reflects on the public hospitals. MRI scanners and advanced CT scanners are extremely expensive. Operating theatres are the most expensive part of a hospital. It seems the Spanish government-run hospitals allow this equipment to lie idle from three in the afternoon. Actually it is scandalous. For any enterprise, public or private,

Dr Marín Ferrer in a room overlooking operating theatres at the Ribera Hospital.

the cost of financing expensive equipment continues without pause, day and night. Equipment needs to be used as much as possible in order to carry the burden. As a private company, the Ribera Hospital has to pay attention to this or lose money.

There is a similar difference regarding the way the Ribera employs its staff. 'Public hospitals contract, say, sixty cardiac specialists who are paid their salary regardless of their activity,' says Marín Ferrer. But the Ribera Hospital adjusts the number of staff on hand to the level of activity. Staff also have their pay adjusted according to how well the hospital is meeting its targets. These targets include below-average inpatient mortality, keeping the surgical waiting list below ninety days and keeping average stays below five days. Everyone in the hospital is on the same side, striving to achieve these things.

Doctors at the Ribera work harder than in public hospitals and they get paid more. Their time is more productive. The beds are used more efficiently. The shorter-than-usual waiting time for surgery brings in more patients – from outside the area as well as from Ribera itself.

Now we get to why it matters that the contract was changed to include primary care: one of the big facts about healthcare which most people do not think much about is that hospital care is many times more expensive than primary care. When a patient is operated on in hospital and stays for five days or more, the cost is measured in thousands of pounds. But when a general practitioner sees a patient the cost is measured in tens. A healthcare system that can keep people out of hospital saves vast amounts of money.

So once the company had responsibility for primary as well as hospital care, what did it do? It provided lots of active, preventative care to keep people from needing to go to hospital. For example: in winter, people typically come to hospital suffering chronic bronchitis. When this happens at the Ribera, the hospital takes note of who they are and the following October, the primary care part of the

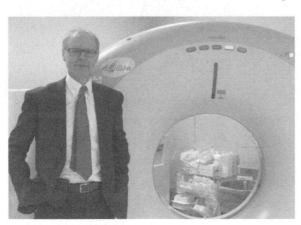

The author next to a CT scanner at the Ribera Hospital.

company contacts them and offers to visit, to see how they are. If they are having problems, they receive preventative treatment. In many cases, the monitoring and treatment keep them out of hospital as an urgent case in the winter. The benefits are two-fold: the healthcare system (paid for by taxpayers) saves money and the patient avoids a traumatic trip to the emergency department on a cold winter night.

People with known heart conditions are monitored, too. Many myocardial infarctions – heart attacks – can be avoided by monitoring the heart and offering early treatment. The Ribera now only has to admit half as many myocardial infarctions as before – an astonishing result.

The company similarly goes to great lengths to encourage people over sixty-five to have flu vaccinations each autumn As well as sending out letters, it does extra things like advertising on local radio. As a result, 95 per cent of over-65s have the injections in Ribera compared to the national average of 70 per cent.

In short, the company saves money through having pro-active primary care. It also has an incentive to keep the citizens of Ribera as healthy as possible. That, in brief, is why people from around the world make the pilgrimage to the modest little town of Alzira.[10] The introduction of this system has had the added benefit of encouraging the government hospitals in the region to improve their performance.[11]

So is the Alzira model the answer? Private companies in the service of the public good? It seems like an improvement on government provision wholly provided by government hospitals. And the idea of a government contracting out work to private companies has its echoes in some Swiss cantons, some Japanese regions and the British National Health Service.

Unfortunately there are some drawbacks. There is a danger of corruption – of government officials taking bribes to give contracts. This sort of thing has happened in parts of Italy when healthcare contracts have been awarded. Then there is the lack of choice. A Ribera resident has to go to a general practitioner employed by the hospital. Some of us would like to be able to choose a doctor who is not in the employ of the same company as all the others. There is also the danger that once a region has contracted out all of its care, it might reduce the funding and, when standards fall, put the blame on the private companies.

So which is the best system? Would you like to make a wholly logical decision based on objective evidence? Wouldn't we all! Unfortunately much of the 'objective evidence' clearly does not lead to an ideal solution. The statistics suggested Australia was particularly efficient, for example. But those waiting in an ambulance on a ramp outside a hospital would tell you that it is far from perfect.

> ## 'A healthy person is someone who has not been examined sufficiently well.'
>
> Tom Groot, VU University Amsterdam. The idea is well known among doctors that if you do enough diagnostic tests you can find something wrong with everybody. Therefore the potential cost of healthcare is virtually unlimited.

Again and again, I have looked at systems in different countries and found serious failings of one sort or another. Quite a few seem to have a strength which, unfortunately, is matched by a weakness. The Netherlands has a sophisticated method of paying hospitals but, for example, it does not seem very easy to get to see your local general practitioner.

What should we do then? Having admitted there is no wholly reliable way of reaching a conclusion, it might still be worth looking at which countries produce the best and worst outcomes for patients according to international measures. None of these measures is perfect or wholly reliable, of course, and many only cover a limited number of countries. But by looking at a mix, we might detect a pattern.

For example, which countries do best when treating cancer? The greatest variety of cancers is covered only in purely European research but, for a few common cancers, more of the world is covered.

How many people are alive five years after being diagnosed with breast cancer?[12]

The highest proportion of survivors:	The lowest proportion of survivors:
USA	Poland
Canada	Ireland
Australia	Czech Republic
Japan	UK
New Zealand	Denmark

The study does not include Switzerland. Neither this nor any of the following surveys include Singapore.

Which are the best and worst countries for colorectal cancer?[13]

Highest five-year survival rates:	Lowest five year survival rates:
South Korea	Poland
Japan	Czech Republic
Australia	Denmark
Iceland	UK
USA	Portugal
Germany	

Only advanced countries. There are six countries with the best survival rates because Germany and the USA in a sense drew. Germany had the better survival rate for women but the USA had the better survival rate for men. The study does not include Switzerland.

As another measure of healthcare systems, let's take the number of MRI scanners per capita. It is a rough and ready measure of the availability of advanced equipment.[14]

Most MRI scanners per capita:	Fewest MRI scanners per capita:
Japan	Hungary
USA	Poland
Italy	Australia
Greece	UK
South Korea	Portugal
Finland	Czech Republic

Only advanced countries.

One objection to the MRI figures could be that some countries prefer advanced CT scanners. So here are the figures for CT scanners as well.[15]

Most CT scanners per capita:	Fewest CT scanners per capita:
Japan	Hungary
Australia	UK
USA	Netherlands
South Korea	France
Greece	Belgium
Switzerland	Poland

Only advanced countries.

How quickly are patients treated? Unfortunately the figures are only available for a very limited number of countries. Still, it is an important measure and so seems worth including.[16]

Fewest patients waiting two months or longer to see a specialist:	Most patients waiting two months or longer:
USA	Canada
Germany	New Zealand
France	UK

The patients concerned are adults with chronic conditions. There were only eight countries in this survey. The others, in between, were the Netherlands and Australia.

Another litmus test is how many operations of various sorts are done. Let us take coronary angioplasty for example. The obvious difficulty with this one is that diets vary and so people who have more heart-friendly diets in the Mediterranean are less likely to need angioplasty. Fortunately no Mediterranean country is among the three best and worst anyway.[17]

Most coronary angioplasty operations per capita:	Fewest coronary angioplasty operations per capita:
Germany	Ireland
Belgium	Canada
USA	New Zealand

Similarly, the need for knee replacements is also affected by dietary factors. Arthritis is much rarer in Japan and perhaps Korea than in the West. But we can bear that in mind when looking at the results.[18]

Most hip replacements per capita:	Fewest hip replacements per capita:
Germany	South Korea
Switzerland	Poland
Belgium	Slovakia

Knee replacement is a less common operation and the countries concerned are slightly different.[19]

Most knee replacements per capita:	Fewest knee replacements per capita:
Germany	Ireland
USA	Hungary
Switzerland	Portugal

As this is a mixture of measures, we might also include the results of the OECD analysis of which countries obtain the best results for the money spent.[20]

Best health outcomes in relation to money spent:	Worst health outcomes in relation to money spent:
Switzerland	Ireland
Australia	Greece
South Korea	UK
Japan	Denmark

Doubtless other people would have chosen other measures but I did not choose these ones knowing what results they would produce.

On looking at them, I am astonished by how well the USA does. It is among the best countries in seven out of nine of these measures. Please note that these figures all relate to care before the implementation of Obamacare. One measure on which it most obviously does not excel is value for money. But even when cost is taken into account, it still is not among the worst – presumably because the results are so good.

One could doubtless find a string of measures according to which the USA would do

World healthcare piggy-backs on US innovation

USA	42%
UK	6%
France	4%
Canada	3%
Australia	1.5%

Share of pharmaceutical patents, selected countries.[21]

less well. Life expectancy, perhaps. But, as I mentioned before, simple life expectancy reflects diet and lifestyle more than the effectiveness of a medical system.

Should we conclude that the US system – currently undergoing huge changes – is a model for the rest of us? There are three reasons to hesitate. First, there is the extraordinary expense. The reasons for the amazing cost are a matter for a separate study all by itself. But whatever the reasons may be, the high price suggests something is not working well. Second, many people are not covered by insurance. They are not the poor because there is Medicaid. They are not the old because there is Medicare. They are the people not poor enough or old enough to have government-financed care and who have not bought insurance. Some argue that this is not

'Why do doctors and hospitals deliver so much unnecessary care? There are many reasons … Malpractice fears drive defensive medicine … But the most powerful reason doctors and hospitals overtreat is that most of them are paid for how much care they deliver, not how well they care for their patients. They get paid more for doing more.'

Shannon Brownlee, *Overtreated*[22]

as worrying as it first appears. You might even argue this drawback is worth it for the outstanding medical service received by the majority of Americans. But then we come up to the third problem: the existence of the uninsured appears politically unsustainable in a modern democracy. There are certain to be cases of people financially ruined by an illness in this system. Understandably these cases will cause outrage.

THERE IS NO DISPUTING THAT the US healthcare system is a dysfunctional muddle. It can be roughly divided into five segments.

First: corporate health insurance. This became a major part of American healthcare because of a historical accident. During the Second World War, wage controls were introduced but fringe benefits were not subject to them so employers used health insurance to attract workers.[24] Additionally, the contributions of employers to such schemes were made tax free.[25] Corporate health insurance generally provides excellent healthcare.

The second segment consists of people who are not employed by a company but who pay for health insurance. Their premiums are much more expensive because they are not part of a mixture of low-risk and high-risk patients. Also, the rates are pushed up because some individuals get insurance because they know they are going to use it a great deal while others do not buy it because they are young and healthy. Another thing that boosts the cost is that individual insurers get little or no tax relief.[26]

Since self-insurance is so expensive, millions of people do not take it out and they are not only the young and healthy. These people are the third segment: the uninsured. They can be ruined if they get an expensive illness.

The fourth segment consists of those at the poorest end of society. They are covered by Medicaid, a government programme. The fifth segment are the elderly, who are covered by Medicare, another

government programme. But these two programmes pay limited amounts for procedures and some doctors and hospitals refuse to treat them. One independent, non-profit hospital in America told me that it made a loss on Medicare patients and that the shortfall was made up by charging private patients more.

So the system is incoherent. It leaves a few to be ruined and many others to pay extraordinary amounts. Yet we have

A wondrous child-friendly waiting room in the paediatrics part of the Mayo Hospital in Rochester, Minnesota.

to acknowledge that in terms of medical performance, it appears to have better outcomes than any other.

The whole system has now been thrown into the air by the advent of Obamacare, formally known as the Affordable Care Act. This does not, as casual observers might imagine, introduce clarity and coherence. In theory, everyone will be obliged to have insurance and pay the same rate. But, in fact, people can opt out by paying a penalty. Those who opt out might include the young who are earning little and not expecting to get ill. So the cost of the insurance may rise because the average risk will rise. Meanwhile, some of the people who opt out of the programme will become seriously ill and be ruined.

Funding for Medicare is going to be reduced, which means that even more hospitals may find it uneconomic to treat Medicare patients. And as the government will effectively be establishing increased central control of medical care, there is a risk that greater bureaucratic burden will increase the cost of treatment. Something will have to give. One senior person at a hospital told me that thinking about it stopped her sleeping at night.

For a while at least, the excellence that has been built up over the decades will probably persist. But in the longer term, the system could reach some kind of crisis.

So if the USA is not the answer, is there anything else we can learn from the medical outcomes?

One noticeable aspect is that better healthcare is closely correlated with wealth. Look at the countries which appear most frequently in the tables above as being among the best: the USA (in 7 out of 9), Switzerland (4 out of 6), Japan (5 out of 8), (Germany 5 out of 9).

It is striking that these countries are among the wealthiest countries per capita in the world. Wealth leads to better healthcare. Indeed, it is possible to argue that if you want first-class healthcare, you should first get economic growth.

What else can we glean from the data? Let us look at the countries that come out worst in the tables: the UK (6 out of 9), Ireland (4 out of 8), and Denmark, Hungary and the Czech Republic (each 3 out of 8). The worst result of all is for Britain, which, exceptionally, is not one of the poorest countries. The distinguishing feature of British healthcare system is that it is mostly a government monopoly. In recent years there has been some contracting out by the government to the private sector. But there is generally no mechanism for people to access

Treatment for a small cut on the head: US$2,300

Oscar, aged twelve, attended an American summer camp and slept on the top level of a bunk bed. When he got out of bed one morning, he bumped his head against a sprinkler in the ceiling. It was a small cut but there was some bleeding. The camp rang his father and suggested the boy should see a doctor. So Oscar was taken to the nearest hospital. After a three-hour wait, a doctor dabbed on some anaesthetic liquid and 'glued' the skin tear in place.

The doctor's bill was $88.41.
The hospital's bill was $2,221.02.[23]

private healthcare directly unless they pay twice: once for government care through taxes and a second time privately. Because of this, most people only obtain government care. So the most monopolistic system also appears to be the least successful.

The Irish system is a close relative of the British one and also comes out badly. It has developed in different ways but the 1953 Health Act essentially meant the government paid most of the bills and supplied the overwhelming majority of the doctors. One difference is that there are some co-payments by patients. In both countries, private provision has gradually increased, partly because waiting lists for treatment have become national scandals at various times.[27]

After all the above, what should be the conclusion? What is the best system that a modern democracy might choose?

Clearly it should not be monopoly government provision. Yes, it might be an improvement for a government to contract out hospitals and even to follow the Alzira model. But this is not ideal either because of the lack of competition and real choice for the individual. At the other end of the spectrum, a system which leaves some people wholly uncovered for their healthcare costs seems unlikely to be acceptable in a modern democracy.

A system is needed where costs do not run out of control, as they have in many countries. Meanwhile hospitals, doctors and clinics need an incentive to come up with new drugs, devices and ways of treating people. It seems undesirable that those who want private care should have to pay for it twice, since this makes private care unaffordable for most people. It would be good for people to have free choice of hospitals and doctors. Everybody should be able to expect treatment.

If we agree on a list like that, what does it lead us to?

I suggest it might lead to a combination of the Singaporean and Swiss/Dutch models. The system could start with all of us having health savings accounts, as in Singapore: a personal account into which a percentage of our earnings is paid. We would use the money in this account for most healthcare bills such as seeing a general practitioner. This would

How many have to wait for their operation?[28]

Fewest:	Most:
Germany	Canada
Netherlands	Sweden
USA	Norway
Switzerland	UK
France	Australia

Proportion waiting four months or more for elective surgery, survey of eleven countries. The other one was New Zealand.

The contrast between the groups that did best and least well was dramatic. In none of the best-performing countries did more than 7 per cent wait more than four months. In all the relatively badly performing countries, at least 18 per cent were waiting for more than four months. I would not want to place too much reliance on the figures since some have varied dramatically over relatively few years and waiting times are notoriously prone to manipulation. However, I have included them because waiting times are very important and this is the best comparative information available. As always with medical performance, no comparative figures are perfect.

give us a reason not to waste money.[29] It would be vital to keep our health savings accounts out of the hands of the government by as powerful a constitutional lock as can be devised. And since much of the cost of healthcare will be paid out of our health accounts, our taxes could be reduced correspondingly.

What if the money in one's health savings account is not sufficient for a major medical bill? Then medical insurance would kick in. All of us would be obliged to take out medical insurance, as in the Netherlands and Switzerland. We would choose between companies which would compete to offer the best deals. The amounts we pay for the same cover would be the same as each other, regardless of age and prior conditions.

As for general practitioners, they would all be private and independent. Our relationship with doctors would go back to being personal and direct since we would pay them from our personal health savings account or in cash.

The advantage of this would go far beyond saving money by not having unnecessary treatments and tests. All sorts of suppliers would be inventive in creating medical services that are cheaper, faster, more convenient and better. In the USA, patients can order their own blood tests from competing diagnostic testing facilities.[30] It is far cheaper than going through a hospital and the results can be available online within forty-eight hours. Walmart, the large retail chain, offers hundreds of generic drugs at $10 for ninety days' coverage. Teladoc, a telephone doctor consultation service, provides advice from a qualified doctor at any time, day or night.

Hospitals could be both private and public. But perhaps they should be on a level playing field. The public ones should not be given subsidies or have losses guaranteed. It might be better to have few or no public hospitals so that all hospitals can compete on an equal basis. Existing public hospitals could be made into charitable trusts or sold to private companies. In the Netherlands, many hospitals are independent trusts.

When framing the best possible system, it is important to think, 'What could go wrong?' I can imagine a government fiddling with this system and undermining it. I would worry about excessive rules and regulations being imposed, increasing the costs. I would not be entirely happy that the health savings account and the insurance would be compulsory. But that compulsory element does seem necessary if we are to avoid

> **'The biggest change brought about by giving patients direct control over healthcare dollars is not on the demand side of the market. It's on the supply side.'**
>
> John C. Goodman, *Priceless*[31]

hard cases of people who are not covered causing outrage, leading to an aban-
donment of the whole system and replacement of it by something with even less
freedom. In any case, at present, in countries which do not have a system like this,
there is compulsory tax instead.

Some people have a strong aversion to private provision. To them, I would say
that the evidence against government monopoly provision is overwhelming. If you
want yourself and your loved ones to be seen reliably and quickly in an emergency
and you want a better chance of surviving a heart condition or cancer, a public
monopoly will not give you what you want.

The system suggested here would not be perfect. That's for sure. But my trip
around some of the healthcare systems of the world leads me to believe it would
be better and more economical than most.

4.

'Daisy, cross your fingers.'

The scandal of state education

IN 1977, MARC LE BRIS left teacher training school and went to work in the beautiful, rural region of Brittany in northwest France.[1] He had been taught at the school to scorn old-fashioned teaching methods. He believed that his predecessors were 'teachers of a previous era' and 'semi-incapable'.

He began work and found that he had a colleague who was the epitome of an old-fashioned teacher, dictating to his class in a high-pitched voice and getting children to read aloud – something Le Bris had been taught to regard as an absolute heresy. But he came to notice a curious thing: the students who came from the class of this teaching dinosaur did better than the others.

As time went by, he came to believe that what he had been taught at his teacher training school was quite wrong. Worse than that, the kind of teaching it promoted had been a disaster for education in France – a disaster that still has not been corrected. He also found that the new, inadequate methods had affected members of his own family.

A few years ago, Marc Le Bris's brother-in-law approached him. He and his wife were worried about their son, Martin. The boy was not doing as well as his older brother and his parents were coming to think that he was less able. They were even worried that he might be rather dim. Le Bris replied that Martin might be a bit of a rascal but he did not seem stupid – certainly not to the point of being unable to read.

The boy's parents explained that they spent one or two hours a day helping Martin with his school work, taking advantage of the way they had different shifts so that both

Marc Le Bris

could help him. But Martin's understanding was not getting better. It had reached the point where he did not like learning. There were sometimes screams and tears. Martin's teacher had talked about holding him back a year.

Le Bris looked at Martin's textbooks. He saw straight away that the school was using the 'whole word' method of teaching children to read, based on an educational theory which became fashionable in the latter part of the twentieth century. According to this theory, children should learn how to read by recognising words rather than letters. The teacher had even gone so far as to explain to the parents that they should not tell Martin the sounds of the letters. He should discover them for himself.

It was November. Le Bris suggested to the worried parents that they should try using the old-fashioned Boscher way of teaching, dating back to the 1950s, which emphasised letters. He gave them some simple instructions about how to do it. So the father started to teach his son to read in this way.

The following June, seven months later, Martin's teacher reported on how he was getting on. She said, 'We don't know what happened but suddenly, over Christmas, Martin made great progress!' Martin's mother, normally a quiet, reserved person, remarked pointedly that it was over Christmas that they had started teaching Martin the sounds of letters. The teacher blushed. She said that, in any event, what mattered was that the boy could now read. Quite so.

Marc Le Bris, his words suffused with anger and outrage, comments: 'In the end, it is the parents who teach the children to read. The teachers don't know how to.'[2] He feels guilty about the children he thinks he failed when he started teaching and was using methods that did not work. But at least he eventually perceived something was wrong and changed his method. But while he had the initiative and courage to change, the teaching colleges and the authorities did not. 'This has been going on for more than thirty years. More than 80 per cent of children are still subjected to dogmatic, stupid methods.'

State education for equal opportunity?

STATE EDUCATION OSTENSIBLY CREATES A level playing field for the children of the poor to compete with the children of the rich. But in many countries they reinforce the difference instead because the rich get their children into the best state schools and the poor are left with the rest. This phenomenon certainly takes place in Germany, France, Britain and the USA among others. In Germany, children from a privileged background are four times as likely to attend a

Gymnasium – the kind of school most likely to lead to university – as a child with similar grades from a working-class home.[3]

One way in which the rich get into the best state schools is by moving into the catchment area for those schools. This increases property values in the area, pricing out those who are poorer. In Britain, academic research has indicated that the best schools push house prices in a particular area 12 per cent higher than they would be if that area had the worst schools.[4] So there is a kind of auction for the advantage of the best government education. It is an auction which the rich tend to win, of course. As Professor Becky Francis has observed, 'equality of opportunity is being undermined by the greater purchasing power of some parents'.[5] It has even been found that one in twenty upper-middle-class parents go so far as to buy a second home in the catchment area of a specific school so that their children can attend it.[6]

What becomes of the children whose parents, unlike the parents of Martin, do not take it upon themselves to teach their children to read, Le Bris asks? They do not learn properly. But they are moved on to the next year anyway. Children are not held back for a year any more. Why? Because, he says, 'it would look bad in the statistics'. The title of the passionate book that Marc Le Bris wrote is *Et vos enfants ne sauront pas lire, ni compter !* – 'And Your Children Won't Know How to Read or Count!'

It might seem unlikely that more than one country would adopt and persist with a way of teaching that works so badly. But I have found that this has taken place in several countries at least.

We may have different ideas about the purpose of education. But most of us would agree that one thing that any schooling system should do is teach children who have been in its care for eleven or more years how to read and write. How well do the schools of the advanced world succeed in this fundamental task?

As part of my visit to the OECD in Paris, I am on my way to see Andreas Schleicher. He is the man who established the OECD's PISA studies of educational attainment around the world. All the OECD countries and a number of countries or cities which are not members of the OECD have taken part. Michael Gove,

'Next to the media in general and television in particular, our schools of education are the greatest contribution to the "dumbing down" of America. No one wants to know the actual results of these policies – whether they really help poor students. The ed school establishment is more concerned with politics – both academic and ideological – than with learning.'

Rita Kramer on US teacher training schools in *Ed School Follies*[7]

the former British Secretary of State for Education, has referred to Schleicher as 'the most influential person in education in the world'.

The press officer who arranged my visit takes me along a maze of smart, light corridors. Everything is modern with lots of straight lines and glass. We find an office on an upper storey with a large window looking over an internal courtyard.

Schleicher gets up and greets me with a firm handshake. He looks like everyone's idea of a dynamic, intelligent German in his prime. He reminds me of Martin Kaymer, a golfer whose final putt enabled the European team to win the Ryder Cup in 2012. I ask him: amid the great mass of information which he and his staff have collected – the latest PISA report consists of six substantial volumes – what is the conclusion about literacy? How well do the

Andreas Schleicher: 'If you have not learned to read by the age of fifteen, nobody will teach you.'

schools of the world teach children to read?

Schleicher is a precise man and asks what level of literacy am I seeking figures on. I specify 'functional literacy'. This is the literacy level that is good enough to be useful at work or in private life. A person is functionally literate, for example, if he or she can read a notice about donating blood and answer a fairly simple question about it. Answering the question does require a little intelligence but not much.

'Of the 200,000 adu[lts] [in Detroit] who a[re] functionally illitera[te] approximately ha[lf] have a high scho[ol] diploma or GE[D]

There are six reading levels defined in the PISA study. Schleicher tells me that those who manage to reach only level 1 are deemed to be functionally illiterate. He remarks that those who have not got further face a bleak outlook. If you have not learned to read by the age of fifteen, 'nobody

'How did I get through school when I couldn't read?'

Dexter Manley, professional American football player, giving evidence to Congress.[10]

will teach you'. So what is the percentage of children among OECD countries, who, after many years of schooling, cannot read properly?

Schleicher picks out one of the PISA volumes and finds the page with the percentages of children attaining the various levels of literacy in each country and the OECD averages. Adding together those below level 1 and at levels 1A and 1B, we work out that the level of functional illiteracy among the children of the advanced world is 18.8 per cent.[8]

I expected that the figure might be bad. But this is a truly appalling statistic. I remark that it is a terrible indictment of the educational systems of the advanced world. Schleicher does not disagree and observes, 'What is even more amazing is that they pass exams with this low level of literacy.'

Sample question from the PISA test

Blood donation notice from a French website:

Blood donation is essential.

There is no product that can fully substitute for human blood. Blood donation is therefore irreplaceable and essential to save lives.

In France, each year, 500,000 patients benefit from a blood transfusion.

The instruments for taking blood are sterile and single use (syringe, tubes, bags).

There is no risk in giving blood.

Blood donation

It is the best-known kind of donation, and takes 45 minutes to 1 hour.

The 450-ml bag is taken as well as some samples on which tests and checks will be done.

A man can give his blood five times a year, a woman three times.

Donors can be from 18 to 65 years old.

An 8-week interval is compulsory between each donation.

The test asks various questions about this notice. This is the question at level 2 – the level which indicates functional literacy:

An eighteen-year-old woman who has given her blood twice in the last twelve months wants to give blood again. According to 'Blood donation notice', on what condition will she be allowed to give blood again?

A correct answer is one that identifies that enough time must have elapsed since the previous donation. The answer will be marked as correct even if the time of eight weeks is not mentioned.[11]

We see many statistics about education in newspapers such as league tables of performance by schools and countries. But literacy figures rarely get any coverage. I suggest they are more important than any others. School systems that have not taught a large proportion of children to read have failed in their most basic task and damaged the futures of millions of people.

How many children are left functionally illiterate?

Shanghai	2.9%		Belgium	16.1%
Hong Kong	6.8%		Norway	16.2%
South Korea	7.6%		New Zealand	16.3%
Ireland	9.6%		UK	16.6%
Japan	9.8%		USA	16.6%
Singapore	9.9%		OECD average	18.0%
Poland	10.6%		Spain	18.3%
Canada	10.9%		Portugal	18.8%
Finland	11.3%		France	18.9%
Switzerland	13.7%		Italy	19.5%
Netherlands	14.0%		Austria	19.5%
Australia	14.2%		Greece	22.6%
Germany	14.5%		Sweden	22.7%
Denmark	14.6%			

Percentage of students below level 2 in reading, PISA study 2012, selected countries. The OECD figure Andreas Schleicher mentioned is slightly different because he was using the 2009 study.

Source: OECD[12]

Some countries do much better than others and we will come to the possible reasons why. But overall, it seems clear that the educational systems of most of the advanced world are failures, leaving an average of nearly one in five children functionally illiterate. It is an inescapable fact that all these systems are dominated by government schooling. Another question we will come to is whether private schooling would do better.

'The National Institute for Literacy estimates that 47% of adults in the City of Detroit are functionally illiterate.'[13]

Where did government schooling come from?

WE TEND TO TAKE THE dominance of government schooling for granted. But in each country, it is the result of different histories.

In France, the church dominated education until Louis XIV began to challenge it in 1666. The struggle for power between church and state continued right up to the nineteenth century with the state finally becoming dominant. In the middle of that century, the government minister responsible drew out his pocket watch and remarked, 'At this moment, all the students of the *lycées* [secondary schools] are explaining the same passage from Virgil.'[14]

In Germany, the Catholic Church also dominated education to begin with but the challenge of the Protestants in the Reformation temporarily created a vacuum in which private schools thrived. Then the Protestant ascendancy reached the point where the church used the power and tax-raising capacity of the state to enforce education of the sort it wanted. When the National Socialists came to power in the 1930s, they enforced teaching of Nazi views. Then, after the war, in East Germany, the communists enforced teaching of communist views. Three quarters of the teachers were fired for having signed their previous oath of allegiance to the Nazis.

In the USA, there was great diversity of schools in the early nineteenth century, which appears to have been quite successful. When Alexis de Tocqueville visited in 1831, he remarked that it was rare to find a New Englander who had not had the advantage of at least an elementary school education.[15] But from the 1830s on, politicians decided education should be made compulsory and this led to pressure to make it free – or rather paid for through taxation. Eventually all the states introduced compulsory education provided free at the schools they controlled. It was a similar story in England.

The sobering thing about the stories of France and Germany is the way education was seen by churches and governments of different sorts as a way of influencing the hearts and minds of children. But even nations which consider themselves liberal democracies are not free of the impulse to control the views and beliefs of the next generation.

I can imagine some people reading this and thinking, 'Yes, well, the statistics might not look great but there are plenty of schools doing a good job. Is there really a problem? Or is this a mere abstract thing without real consequences?' Let's see. What happens to people who cannot fully read and write?

Harriet Sergeant, a British journalist and author, wanted to understand why many white and Afro-Caribbean working-class boys were failing to go from school to normal jobs.[16] As part of her research, she went to West Norwood in south London to see if she could talk to the sort of youths who were dropping out of normal life. Accompanied by 'Swagger', a worker from a local community centre and former robber of security vans, she approached a small group of mostly black teenagers on the street. They were dressed in hoodies and low-slung baggy jeans, intimidating passers-by, glaring at shoppers, cadging cigarettes, shouting and laughing. She thought they looked as though they could turn violent at any moment. She assumed they had knives – perhaps even a gun. She had not thought about the fact that she was wearing an expensive watch.

The short, young leader of the group gave his name as Tuggy Tug. In her book, *Among The Hoods*, Harriet wrote that he was positively proud of his criminality. He showed her a red hoodie underneath his black one. He said he wore it in case he

Members of the gang befriended by Harriet Sargeant.

needed a quick change of identity. 'I want no one recognisin' me when I about my business,' he said.[17] He explained that he was looking for someone to mug and, as he spoke, he looked directly at Serge As I'd found when dealing with Robert Mugabe in Zimbabwe in 2000 in the escalating crisis there, having insight into what he was really doing and what he was really thinking and saying, greatly informed both my political response to, and my public handling of the crisis ant.

She asked why they were not at school. One of the group, calling himself Jiggers, was even smaller than Tuggy Tug and had scars on his little hands. He had a 'pinched, watchful expression'. He said he had problems with his English teacher. 'Why did them teachers keep askin' me questions? They knew I couldn't read but they kept on askin',' he said. Jiggers and Tuggy Tug, along with Bulldog and Sunshine, all admitted having trouble with 'them little words'. That is why none of them was in school.[18]

Swagger, Sergeant's escort, later described how he himself had been affected by illiteracy. 'I was embarrassed by my reading so I became the class clown,' he said. By the age of thirteen, he had become bored, frustrated and always in trouble. 'I didn't feel good about myself. I got no pride in myself. I was angry over every little thing. It did not take a lot to set me off.' No teacher seemed to notice or address the problem. 'So I think why not bunk school and go and do a bit of thieving?' he said.[20]

'50% of the chronical unemployed are n functionally literat

US Department of Educatic

That is how he became a criminal. Eventually he was caught robbing a security van and went to prison. 'We go from school to prison. I thought I would be dead by forty.'

Swagger's parents – first-generation immigrants from Jamaica working in good jobs – had hoped their only son would become a lawyer or doctor. But he said, shaking his head sadly, 'School shatters your dreams before you get anywhere.'

Swagger was unusual in facing up to what had happened to him. It is human nature to try to make the best of one's situation and see it in as positive light as possible.

Sergeant asked the gang members how they saw their future in the absence of education or jobs. 'Tuggy Tug answered for them all. That did not seem a problem. His heroes were rap stars and the older drug dealers in the area. "I know a man of twenty-one who owns five houses and he never went to school," he said.'[21]

The gang gave another explanation of why they had left school – one which, coming from young, illiterate criminals, is all the more remarkable. They complained of a lack of discipline:

Members of the gang complained about the lack of discipline at their school.

> 'You can sit on the desk with your shoes off, your socks hanging out, on the phone, doing your ting [drug dealing] and the teachers won't give a toss,' said Tuggy Tug.
>
> His friends all nodded, eager now to contribute. This was a subject that raised strong feelings… 'There's bare [lots of] people in your class just messin' around,' said one mixed-race boy called Sunshine. 'You don't feel like you're learnin' so what's the point of goin' to school?'[22]

These gang members felt that they were let down by their schools. And the failure of schools to teach them to read had, according to their own testimony, led them towards crime. In turning to crime, they were probably ruining their own lives as well as harming those who they mugged or robbed. Some of the gang have since gone – as Harriet Sergeant predicted at the time – to prison. Of course they are contributing nothing to the economy. They are costing money instead.

Their story suggests that a failed education and illiteracy, in particular, leads to crime. Is there evidence to support this idea? Here is some

'Sixty per cent of young black men who drop out of school land in prison by their thirties.'

Geoffrey Canada, 'Bringing Change to Scale'[23]

from the USA: only a minority of children are not taught to read proficiently, yet the overwhelming majority of those who get in trouble are from their ranks. Some 72 per cent of prison inmates have a low level of literacy and 40 per cent are at the lowest of five levels of literacy – almost twice the proportion in the general population.[24] These are remarkable statistics. It is as though literacy were a superb defence against criminal activity. As ever, correlation is not the same as causation. It is genuinely conceivable that some third factor contributes to children becoming both illiterate and criminal. Indeed we will consider later the role of parenting in this (Chapter 6).

Further support for the idea of illiteracy contributing to crime comes from the re-offending figures. Learning to read reduces the rate at which prisoners re-offend. The average effect is to reduce re-offending by 6 per cent and the best results can reach 14 per cent.[25] These and other similar statistics are so powerful and make so much sense that it seems overwhelmingly likely that illiteracy makes people more likely to be criminal in the modern world.

> '**What brings about the delinquency is not the academic failure *per se*, but sustained frustration which results from continued failure … When frustration can find no resolution into constructive or productive activity, one response, though not the only one, is aggressive, anti-social behaviour.**'
>
> Michael Brunner[26]

Why is illiteracy so powerfully connected to crime? It surely goes back to the comment of Tuggy Tug and his gang: if you can't read, you have trouble getting a job. It is exactly the same thing that officials in the Job Center in Madison, Wisconsin, said in Chapter 2. Most jobs require at least some ability to read. Even a driver needs to be able to read road signs. It is surprising how even some fairly low-wage jobs involve reading.

If a young man cannot get a job because he can't read, what is he to do? Live on welfare? Possibly. But the temptation to turn to crime is much greater than it would be if he could get a job. So we see two possible results of functional illiteracy: crime and unemployment. Both of them are damaging for those involved and the rest of society.

> '**The link between academic failure and delinquency, violence and crime is welded to reading failure**'
>
> United States Department of Justice

If we look at welfare recipients in the United States, an astonishing 90 per cent are high school drop-outs.[28] But it does not end there. Naturally those who cannot get work tend to be poor. That helps explain why among those who can read only at level 1, 43 per cent are relatively poor. Among those who read well – at level 5 – only 4 per cent are.[29]

There is another consequence. Poor education is also strongly correlated with unmarried parenting. Among young women aged sixteen to nineteen who are at the poverty level and below, those who cannot read well are six times more likely to have a child outside marriage than those who can.[31] Why should this be? There are probably quite a few reasons. I suggest one of them is that illiterate young women have difficulty getting a good job and so are more likely to be tempted to have a baby and to put up with living on benefits in public housing.

Overall, functional illiteracy is strongly connected to crime, unemployment, poverty and even unmarried parenting. It seems almost trivial to add that being unable to read also means never being able to appreciate history, novels or biography – in fact any of the world's literature.

It is not an exaggeration to say that the widespread failure of schooling is a tragedy for the individuals affected and for society.

What is going on in the world's schools that brings about such bad outcomes? What can be done to improve things? We have seen that centrally imposed teaching methods can damage literacy. But there must be more to it than that.

I am in San Francisco where I would like to visit a typical public school. Incidentally, I am using the phrase 'public school' here – and throughout the chapter – in the American sense to mean a government or state school.[32] I want to see a school with typical problems – not a basket case nor a model school. This is more difficult to achieve than it might seem. School boards like to show off their best schools, not their typical ones. In the couple of weeks before I arrived, I wrote emails to the school board asking to visit Balboa High School. It serves a relatively poor part of San Francisco. Its record is better than average but it's not at the top of the rankings. I did not get a definite 'yes' or 'no' in reply to my emails but now I have arrived in San Francisco, I have one more go at it. I ring the school directly and ask for the headmaster. To my surprise I get straight through and he says I can come round right away.

The main school building is big and around the

> **'Two-thirds of students who cannot read proficiently by the end of fourth grade will end up in jail or on welfare.'**[30]

...lked with eighteen-...r old Dorian Cain ...South Carolina, who ...s still struggling to ...d a single sentence ...a first-grade-level ...ok when I met him. ...hough his public ...ools had spent ...rly $100,000 on him ...r twelve years, he ...could not read."

Stossel, *Stupid in America*, ...elevision broadcast 2006

perimeter is a high fence. I enter a hallway with high ceilings and am directed to the reception office – a large, bustling, open-plan room with many people working at desks. The receptionist asks me to wait. While I am sitting there, I hear her take a call on a walkie-talkie. Immediately afterwards she makes a call herself. I hear her say something about 'getting an escort'. Soon after, she tells me I can go in and see the head. She shows me into an adjacent office where Mr Kerr – relaxed and genial – greets me.

I ask him straight away what that conversation concerning an 'escort' was all about. He explains that when a student wants to go to the toilet during a class, he or she has to have an escort to go there and come back. A teacher had phoned reception to request one. The receptionist had telephoned the security personnel to fix it up.

Why on earth is such a thing necessary, I ask? He tells me that when he became the head, the student body told him they did not like this system, which had been created by his predecessor. So Kerr agreed to abolish it and give the children the trust they wanted. But as a result, the toilets were defaced with graffiti and the floors were covered in urine so he decided to bring the system back.

The story gives some idea of what the school is up against. While we are on the subject of discipline, Kerr also tells me the children are not allowed to wear hats or the colours red or blue on their way to school. Why not? Because red and blue are the colours of two local gangs. If a child comes to school wearing red or blue, he or she may be approached by one of the gangs either to be invited to join or else harassed for wearing the 'wrong' colour.

Safety and discipline are obviously major issues. Another sign of this is that Kerr is proud that the fire alarm is triggered by the children only about once a year. He has been told that in another, even bigger, school in San Francisco, the fire alarm is set off once a week.

Despite this background, the school has improved its academic performance from below average to above average. I ask Kerr what he thinks are the key things that have helped achieve this. It is no surprise that 'making it safe' is the second thing he mentions. And the first?

'Putting in good teachers.'

I ask how he did this but he seems reluctant to say. Eventually, after we talk for a while and tour the school, he lets me have an idea of how it works. Eighty per cent of his teachers are 'exceptional', he says. But 20 per cent are not so good and he would really like to get rid of half of these and replace them with good teachers.

So why not do it, I ask?

'It takes years,' he replies. He says it is very difficult and time-consuming to make a teacher redundant in the public school system. And when finally you manage it, you are obliged to take a replacement from the 'consolidated list'. This is a list of teachers of the relevant subject who are available to be hired. There are doubtless some good teachers on the list, but a high proportion are teachers whom other schools have previously rejected. That is where fired teachers go: onto the consolidated list. So it is very possible that after finally removing a bad teacher, a head may be obliged to recruit another one.

Kerr, though, has worked out how to get around this problem – how to game the system. He proudly tells me that he requested an English literature teacher during one August – in the summer holidays. He was told, 'Oh, what a pity you didn't ask in April. We could have offered you plenty of teachers then.' But there were none available in August, which was exactly what Kerr hoped. And since none was available, he was allowed to recruit a teacher he knew and thought was good.

Kerr's techniques for recruiting better teachers do not always work but they usually do. That is clearly good for Balboa High and its pupils. Its rating has been rising towards a level at which it will be deemed 'exceptional'. But Kerr is a veteran head teacher. He remarks that novice heads get 'hazed'. They end up with the teachers that he and other experienced heads have finally managed to fire. The truth is, in this system, bad teachers do not go away. They get recycled. And of course the teachers know they are hard to fire – which seems unlikely to prompt a strong worth ethic.[33]

Bearing in mind that the school is rated as above average, I ask: what is the attendance rate? Kerr says it is 94 per cent. That does not sound very good and at one point, he says some children there feel that education is something 'done to them'. I can't help wondering whether the lack of motivation may be partly because there is no clearly identifiable public exam which would have a major effect on the students' careers.

Kerr is clearly appalled at the ignorance of some of the children at his own school. On his

'Dance of the lemons' – phrase used to describe the way that bad teachers fired by one school in America are hired by another.[34]

desk is a sign reading 'The buck stops here'. One of his students asked him what the sign was all about. He told the student that it was the sign that Harry Truman had on his desk.

'Who's Harry Truman?' the student asked.

How to get on as a teacher in the USA

IN THE EARLY 1990S, PETER Sacks left journalism to teach media studies at a community college – part of the public education system. He demanded effort and good behaviour from his students when he began. He gave marks he considered fair and the average grade he awarded was a C. But he received complaints from the students and demands such as 'I need an A in this course to graduate with honours!' As a result, he got poor evaluations from his students and this meant it was highly likely that he would lose his job.

He decided to lower his standards and become wholly indulgent and undemanding. His career as a teacher was at stake. He thought this was absurd but decided to make a kind of experiment out of changing his approach.

'I did almost anything possible to make them happy, all of the time, no matter how childish or rude their behaviour, no matter how poorly they performed in the course, no matter how little effort they gave … If they wanted to read the newspaper while I was addressing the class or if they wanted to get up and leave in the middle of a lecture, go for it.'

What was the result? His evaluations by the students became favourable and, in due course, he was granted tenure. In this *Through the Looking Glass* system, he was punished for maintaining high standards and rewarded for letting them go. He concluded: 'Nobody in the system had much of a stake in shoring up educational standards … just the opposite was the case.'

Peter Sacks wrote a book – *Generation X Goes to College* – about his experience.[35]

What about the standard of education generally in the US? Mr Kerr is gloomy about it. He says that in a survey, Americans aged thirty were asked from which country the USA had achieved independence. Forty per cent did not know.

The visit to Balboa and the story of ineffective teaching in France suggest a variety of possible reasons why so many schools around the world are doing badly. But what does the data say? Back at the OECD headquarters in Paris, part of the analysis they do consists of looking at characteristics of schools and seeing which are linked with good academic achievement. Discipline in the classroom is indeed correlated with better academic outcomes. Or to put in another way, bad discipline is associated with failure.

The best-performing countries tend to have so-called 'high stakes' public exams on which the academic futures of the children depend. To put it the other way round, the worst-performing systems tend to avoid high-stakes exams, preferring to announce that everyone is a winner. The best-performing countries also tend to benefit from one thing that is partly cultural: a belief that hard work enables almost any child to achieve success. This idea is particularly common in Asia. In

Japan, every child is obliged to learn to play an instrument – and does. There is, of course, a downside to emphasising hard work and high-stakes exams. In Japan and South Korea, some children work far harder than most Western parents would consider sensible or even humane. The expression 'examination hell' is part of normal language in Japan. At the other extreme is a Western view that children either have talent or they don't and that bothering to work hard is less important.

What other factors are there? Andreas Schleicher argues that teacher quality and status make a big difference. Some countries have teachers who are at the bottom end of educational achievement themselves. He also thinks it is useful if children who are doing badly are assigned the best and most effective teachers to bring them up to scratch. He emphasises the importance of motivation for everyone involved: the heads, the teachers, the children and their parents. And the PISA studies have found a correlation between the level of autonomy of schools and their achievement.

> 'On average a teacher in the bottom quintile of effectiveness covers only 50 per cent of the required curriculum in a school year, while a teacher in the top quintile covers 150 per cent.'
>
> Karl Weber, 'A Nation Still at Risk'[36]

In brief, the research suggests that the countries with the best outcomes have good classroom discipline, high-stakes exams, a belief in hard work and that every child can achieve, able teachers retained in the profession, independence for schools and a high level of motivation for everyone involved.

But since the systems of the world have generally done so badly, we can infer that it is commonplace for something like the opposite to occur: bad classroom discipline, avoidance of high-stakes exams, little belief in hard work or that every child can achieve, academically low-quality teachers in schools which have little independence and a lack of motivation among the people concerned.

'You stand at the front on the knife-edge of anarchy.'

'**A**LL TEACHERS HATE POOR DISCIPLINE** but the reality is it's very difficult to keep control in a rough school except by being friendly, getting the kids on your side. Being entertaining is the only way to do it. This is the opposite of what I thought initially (and to what you might think now). As a teacher you have no natural or assumed authority walking into a classroom. You have to earn it – hence the need for rapid cycling of activities – "fun and games" as the teachers call it. You stand at the front on the knife-edge of anarchy most of the time. When a class "loses it", it's distressing and uncontrollable. I saw it happen often in observation, with many good and experienced teachers. Swearing, constant disruption, laughter, throwing things, chairs pushed over, insulting the teacher, accusing them of racism. In some class groups, this was every single lesson.

'It was frustrating how prescriptive OFSTED [Office for Standards in Education] is about how to teach a subject. It felt like you were running through a formula. At the beginning you had to have a slide with the intended learning outcomes of the class. Lesson plans are required to be in sections of around five minutes. OFSTED likes teachers to change what they are doing often so there is a maximum of five minutes of a teacher talking and asking questions at the front. More than that seemed to be considered bad practice.

'There is a trend in schools to de-emphasise knowledge and promote skills. The idea is that knowledge we have now will be out of date so, instead, we should teach skills. This is a disaster for science. A little bit of teamwork, yes. But you need factual stuff!

'A big thing these days is AFL – Assessment for Learning. There is continual testing including at primary schools – closely defining what a child can do. Teachers seem to spend as much time on assessment as teaching.'

Mature science graduate who went through a teacher training course in England during which he observed many classes in different schools as well as teaching himself. The disorder and the damage done by teaching theories imposed from above are a penetrating window onto why British government schools do not do well. Similar problems exist in many government schools around the world.

What can be done to make things better? Setting about correcting these faults may well help. But before drawing conclusions let's look at another possible approach to the question.

Some people in the education business have looked at which individual countries get the best results with the idea of copying whatever system they have. So let's try that.

The top six places for functional literacy in the latest PISA study are taken by Shanghai, Hong Kong, Korea, Ireland, Japan and Singapore. Straight away, you can't help noticing something about them: five are east Asian.

This suggests that there might be something about Asia or Asians that leads to better academic performance. The most obvious thing

How many school days in a year?

USA	180
New Zealand	190
The Netherlands	200
South Korea	220
Japan	243

Source: Geoffrey Canada, 'Bringing Change to Scale'[37]

to anyone who has lived and worked there is the enormous emphasis on hard work and achievement. In Japan, it is seen as one of the prime duties of a mother to ensure that her child does well at school. And when Asians, notably those of Chinese origin, come to the West, they often bring a work ethic with them. They excel in American schools.

If hard work is the cause of the good Asian performance, that is interesting, of course, but it might be difficult to translate into government policy. One cannot just give instructions to 'be more motivated and work harder'. Something else is special about schooling in the Far East. Yes, there are government schools, to which the vast majority of children go. But it is normal for parents to supplement government teaching with private schooling and tutoring. In the jargon, this is called 'shadow education'.

In Japan, children often attend government-run schools for the first part of the day but then go on to privately run schools, called *juku*, afterwards. This is not just a luxury for super-rich parents. It is widespread. In year three at junior secondary schools, 65 per cent of children go to *juku*, 7 per cent have tutoring at home and 15 per cent take the cheaper option of correspondence courses.[38] The parents supplement government schooling partly because they want their children to get into the better upper secondary schools which are most likely to lead to better universities and jobs. But they may also believe that the government schools are not providing a good enough education.

Parents in South Korea, the number two country in the world for functional literacy, spend what has been called a 'staggering' amount on shadow education, equivalent to around 80 per cent of government expenditure.[39] Supplementary private schools there are called *hagwons*.

According to Andrew Coulson, an education analyst in the USA, 'most students [in Korea] sleep during some or all of their public school classes and then go to private *hagwons* after school until as late as two in the morning'.[41] Educationalist Michael B. Horn has reported from Korea that 'parents spend huge sums to send them [their children] to *hagwons* …, in which students do the "real" learning'.[42]

In Hong Kong, about 85 per cent of senior secondary students have some form of private supplementary schooling.[43] The proportion in mainland China does not appear to have been

'In a 2008 government survey, two-thirds of parents attributed the growing role of juku to shortcomings in public education. Their service is more personalised, and many encourage individual inquisitiveness when the public system treats everyone alike.'

The Economist[40]

established reliably but one estimate is that as many as 66 per cent of lower secondary school students receive extra private schooling.[44]

Governments and government-funded organisations around the world tend to dislike or resent supplementary schooling and demand that it should be regulated. But as the author of an Asian Development Bank report remarked, 'policy-makers may learn from the shadow. They should ask why it exists in the first place.'[45]

> 'Even though it's "free" at all levels, Greek households spend more for the education of their children (for private tutoring) than any other in the EU.'
>
> Aristides Hatzis, 'Greece as a Precautionary Tale of the Welfare State'[46]

The huge amount of supplementary private education in Asia should influence how we regard the PISA results. We cannot reasonably say 'We must learn from the success of Asian government schools' since we know the performance of Asian students has been affected by supplementary schooling.[47] In fact it would be more logical to say 'The lesson of the relative success of Asian education is that a boost from private education takes these places to the top of the tables'.

However, one of the top-performing countries is far away from Asia. It is very different. Finland has a history of being the best-performing country outside Asia in the series of PISA assessments. In the most recent study, it actually comes behind Ireland and Poland for functional literacy but it is the best outside Asia for science. Finland has no private schools. So what is it doing right?

I asked Andreas Schleicher, the creator of the PISA assessment, what he thought. He said Finland used to have a 'command and control' education system which stifled schools. But then, in the 1970s, the economy experienced a major crisis. GDP fell 18 per cent. As a result of this economic and financial crisis, school inspectors were abolished. Schools were consequently given more autonomy, akin to that in charter or 'free' schools. Suddenly Finnish schools came to be judged not by inspectors but by their success in exams.

The story supports the idea that autonomy and judgement of schools by results might be important. Another aspect of Finnish schooling highlighted in the OECD reports is the high status and qualifications of the teachers and their concentration on improving their performance. There is great emphasis on identifying and helping any child that falls behind, too. The schools are also small, which may or may not be significant.

> Switzerland an Canada do not hav national educatic ministries. Both g above-average resul on the PISA test

By chance, while puzzling over these things, I happened to meet a young Finnish researcher, who told me more about Finnish education from the inside. She told me there are elements of competition in the Finnish system. Her own school selected students by ability. When children get to the age of fifteen or sixteen, they face a fork in the road. Either they go to a vocational college or else they take a path that leads to university. It is a 'high stakes' moment.

I asked the researcher about discipline in the schools. It was as though I had asked about water in the sea. Yes, of course there was discipline. She took it for granted. She said that she herself was the biggest 'rebel' in her class. A keener, more dedicated 'rebel' would be hard to imagine.

She had a less than glowing view of the theme of equality that runs through Finnish education and which many admire so much. For her, it had drawbacks. This is part of an email she sent me:

> There is 'equality' even when people clearly have different interests and ambitions. For example until the age of 15–16 all students are divided into different classes based only on their surname or just randomly. Accordingly, students with a passion for a certain subject have to take the very same classes as those people who never do their homework and have zero interest in the subject.
>
> This is especially unfortunate in subjects such as maths and languages which require previous knowledge to learn something new. The brightest students felt discouraged from progressing and the most unmotivated people surely felt that sometimes the classes were too advanced.

She strongly felt that her schools had not stretched her and she had not had the chance to develop her full potential. She did not feel that Finland had pre-eminently good education and thought the universities were markedly inferior to British ones.

Several education policy specialists note how homogeneous Finland is. It has 3 per cent of immigrants compared to 9 per cent in Britain, 10 per cent in France, 12 per cent in Germany and 13 per cent in the US.[48] The academic performance of immigrants is often below average. Japan and Korea also have relatively few immigrants compared to other countries. So perhaps there is nothing wonderful about Finnish education at all. It could be a matter of high-stakes exams, good discipline deriving from the culture, low immigration or a mixture of these.

It turns out these are only a few of a host of reasons why academics feel there is reason to doubt whether the Finnish performance is quite as good a guide as the PISA study suggests.[49] There is not space to describe them all.

In view of this and the likely reasons for the success of east Asian students, it does not seem sensible simply to copy another country's system. We have, though, found some support for the ideas that discipline, private schooling and high-stakes exams can help. Is there some other way to find a system of education that could work better?

I am at the Summit Academy in San Lorenzo, California – a low building in a spacious suburban street. It's a calm, pleasant neighbourhood but the children at this school come from the poorer half of society. I meet the genial, bespectacled headmaster. After a short meeting in his office, I am taken from class to class. As I listen in to the lessons, frankly I am not convinced that the teaching methods are particularly good.

The headmaster has kindly arranged for me to talk to eight children. He has chosen a mixture of children – 'not just the easy ones'. Yes, there is Yasmin – bright eyed and enthusiastic – who sits opposite me and who, I guess, is probably something of an academic star. But there are others at the opposite end of the range.

I ask the headmaster if he would mind leaving us so the children can speak without worrying about his reaction to what they say. Generously, he agrees.

One of the eight is Michael. He looks Hispanic. He is in eighth grade, which would normally mean that he is about fourteen, but he was 'retained' in fifth grade. In other words he was held back and obliged to take that year again. So he must be about fifteen. I ask him what he thinks of Summit Academy. Is it good or bad?

'Not great but good,' he replies.

He was previously at a regular public school. I ask him how his life would be different if he was still there. He mutters one word: 'Juvie.'

I can't hear him very well but even if I could I wouldn't understand his reply anyway. The others explain. They say he means that if he had stayed at his previous school, he would now be in 'juvie' – juvenile hall or juvenile detention.

That's a big difference to make to someone's life. I ask how this school has managed to do this.

'We spend our whole life here!' he says with undisguised regret.

The hours are from 7.30 a.m. until 4 p.m. or 5 p.m. And then there is homework. I ask how he came to be at this school. Whose idea was it?

'My mom made me,' he complains.

Obviously he had not wanted to come. Why not? He says he wanted to go to Winton, a public school in the area.[50] Why didn't he want to come to Summit Academy?

'The uniform…' he mutters scornfully.

I suggest that he probably also has friends at Winton. He seems to agree.

Why did his mother make him come to this school? He says his sisters came here and his mother saw their grades improve. So she sent him here, too.

What does he expect his future to be? He says he thinks he will go to college but he does not sound sure about it. He says that when he finishes school he will become a missionary. After four years of missionary work, he wants to go to Brigham Young University, the Mormon university in Salt Lake City. And after that?

'A lawyer or athlete.'

It is hard to know how the rest of Michael's life will develop but, for the time being, in his own opinion, he is not in juvenile detention because of this school. A life that could have gone disastrously wrong from the start has not done so. If his life were the only one to be transformed by this school, its existence would be fully justified. But there are surely others, too.

But I am still not convinced I have got to the bottom of why this school has succeeded in changing Michael's life. I ask the others how things are different here. Mohammed, a burly black boy at the end of the row, went to a public school for only one year but he is eager to tell me the difference. At public school, he says, there were 'no lines, no uniforms'. Getting around from class to class was 'all your responsibility'. That sounds as if it could be a good thing but perhaps he was never told clearly where he was meant to go.

He says he was not supported in his public school as he is here. Here he can go to a teacher at any time. 'If you get a bad grade at the public school, you just get a bad grade. But here they follow up.' A much younger, slim black boy adds that in public schools, the teachers 'don't care. They don't pay attention so much to how you are doing.'

The themes they seem to keep coming back to are greater discipline and teachers who care.

Michael and Yasmin are on the left. Mohammed is at the far end.

It is tempting simply to conclude: 'Oh yes. That makes sense. Let's have more discipline in schools and teachers who care.' But it is not that easy. How do you get such things? If you have a command from government that 'discipline should be better' or 'teachers must care more' it is unlikely to have much impact. There is reason to believe that really good schools do not come by commands from above. So where can they come from?

Perhaps from a structure which improves the incentives and motivation of those involved. The school I am visiting – the Summit Academy in San Lorenzo – is a charter school, a member of the KIPP network of schools which mainly serves lower-income areas.[51] Charter schools are independent schools which receive money from the government according to how many students they have. There is no guarantee that the Summit Academy or any other charter school will attract students. A charter school has to have something which makes parents think it will be good for their child. The school and the teachers will only remain in place if parents think they are doing good work. This may provide a clue to where the motivation comes from.

Would education be better if there were more such schools with the autonomy and incentives of charter schools? Teachers' unions in America and Britain – where they are called free schools – campaign passionately against them. But in Sweden, where there is a far greater proportion of such schools, they are widely accepted. Local governments across the political spectrum go so far as to invite free schools into their area. Swedish socialists and even communists accept free schools. This suggests that they do not have to be a matter of left versus right tribal politics.

One man who is certainly on the left of the political spectrum is film maker Davis Guggenheim. In 2008, he directed a biographical film about Barack Obama for the Democratic National Convention. In September the previous year, Guggenheim was driving his children to school for the beginning of the new academic year. His familiar route took him past three public schools. His children weren't going to any of them. They were driving on to a private school. He was embarrassed about this: 'Years earlier my wife and I had researched our neighbourhood public school and discovered it wasn't up to snuff. So we did what other parents who can afford it did: we opened up our wallets and paid lots of money so that our kids could get a great education.'

'The Red Army'

Humorous phrase used to describe teachers in France.[52]

He felt guilty that he could pay to get his children into a good school but poor people could not. So he made a film about it. The film followed five children – all relatively poor – whose parents were trying to get them into charter schools instead of underperforming public schools. One was called Daisy. She was in the fifth grade and so aged ten or eleven. Daisy's dream was to be a doctor. But she was due to enter the local public school, from which six out of ten of the children did not even graduate. Her parents feared that she would have little chance of doing well enough to achieve her dream if she went to this school.

There was only one chance for Daisy to fulfil her dream. Down the street was a very successful charter school which had a good record. The difficulty was that it had 135 applicants for only ten places. The decision as to who would get in was random. It had to be by law. Entry was decided by a lottery.

Daisy and her father went to the lottery in person. Names were written on pieces of paper and then pulled out of a plastic box. Father and daughter sat there, serious and nervous. One name was read out after another. There were fewer and fewer chances left. Daisy's father felt that her future depended on the result.

He held his daughter's hand and said, 'Daisy, cross your fingers!'

More names were read out. There were only three places left, then two, then one, then none. She had not got in. The same happened to four out of the five children whose fortunes the documentary followed. The film is painful to watch. Hopes are dashed.

It seems awful that the futures of these children should have depended on lotteries. In one case,

Daisy's dream was to be a doctor.

the issue was decided literally by balls with numbers dancing in the air. The film evokes a sense of outrage. It brings home how desperately keen these parents, at least, were to get their children away from local public schools and into charter schools. These people had so few choices.

Some may be thinking, 'Well, possibly these particular charter schools may have been good, but what about charter schools generally? Are they better overall or were these just exceptions?' The academic papers on the subject get so complex that after a while looking at them one can begin to wish one was studying something simpler like nuclear physics. However, there is one study which was particularly well constructed and had a big sample size. It started at the point where the story of Daisy left off. After lotteries such as hers, obviously some children go to the charter schools and the rest go to regular public schools. This study followed both kinds of children in New York.[53] It was clever because we know for sure that the children in both cases had motivated parents keen enough to bother to try to get their children into better schools. So, in terms of the parents, we are comparing like with like.

We know quite a lot about the children in this study. They were poorer than average and more likely to be black or Hispanic. These were children who, on average, would do less well than those from richer neighbourhoods.

The study followed all the pupils in New York City who had been successful in lotteries and were enrolled in charter schools between 2001/02 and 2007/08. They were compared with others who had been unsuccessful in the lotteries and went on to normal public schools. The students in both groups did better than average for the areas where they lived, probably because they had motivated parents. But how did the ones that got into charter schools fare compared with those who lost out in the lottery – children like Daisy?

Those who went to charter schools gained an average of 3.6 points in maths test scores for each year that they attended compared to those who went to public schools. In English, the gain was 2.4 points per year. For a child who attended throughout – from the third to the eighth grade – the total gain in maths was 30 points. In English the gain was 23 points. This is a substantial difference in relation to a minimum score of 650 points to show proficiency and a relatively good score of 685.[54]

These students from Harlem – disproportionately poor and black – had caught up with 86 per cent of the typical difference between what they would normally achieve in public schools and the results in Scarsdale, an affluent New York suburb. In English, they had made up 66 per cent of the gap. To put it another way, charter schools gave the poor in New York City a far better chance of getting on even terms with the rich. It is an important achievement.

This is an impressive study, comparing like with like. But even in this case, academics are ingenious enough to find ways to cast doubt on the results. I would suggest, however, that the sample is so big and the results so dramatic that the quibbling begins to look like an unwillingness to accept what the evidence is telling us.

In the studies I have come across – of varying quality – there are predominantly two kinds of result both for Sweden and the USA. Some studies show a significant gain achieved by free/charter schools. Some do not. What is rare – in fact I do not know of any instance – is a study suggesting that free/charter schools damage educational achievement. The overall evidence is that free/charter schools do good. But in any case, they do no harm.

It is very possible, too, that their recorded performance will improve. When they started, both in Sweden and America, they were set up by all sorts of people – some with good ideas and some, no doubt, with bad ones. But a key aspect of free/charter schools is that no one is forced to go to them. So if a school performs badly, it is likely to lose customers and go out of business. Only successful schools are likely to grow.

It is also worth remembering that the PISA study found that good performance is correlated with autonomy. Free/charter schools are explicitly designed to have more autonomy.

How did Sweden come to have the highest proportion of free schools in the world?

Many people think of Sweden as the ultimate welfare state. They assume that everything is government controlled and run. But like most countries, it does not fit into the clichés about it when you get a little closer.

I am in a suburb of Stockholm going into a modern school. I walk through a large space like an open-plan office. But there are no children here because it is after school hours. At the far end is a smaller office where I meet Odd Eiken. Like many Swedes, he is a modest, uncontentious man. But appearances can be misleading. Eiken, when he was a government minister in 1993, introduced reforms which led to the creation of free schools in Sweden. His reforms have since led to one of the biggest changes in any nation's schooling for fifty years. Sweden now has the highest proportion of free schools in the world.

I ask him how Sweden, of all countries, came to introduce free schools. Several different things happened to make it possible, he says. Small village schools were being closed down by local governments. Parents in those villages wanted to find a way to keep their schools open. That had some influence. Another factor was that some people went to the European Court of Human Rights and argued that it was their human right to have choice in education and that this should include private education. The court did not exactly agree but it was sympathetic. This was influential since Sweden takes the concept of human rights seriously. A third factor was that, after years of left-wing governments, there was a change of view by the electorate and a more free-market government was elected.

Eiken also recalls an incident which clearly influenced him personally. When he was a child, his mother wanted him to change school. She was obliged to go to the local government as a supplicant, begging for a favour. She was told, 'No. This is the local school to which Odd has been allocated.' I guess, though he does not say so, that he felt embarrassed and angry that his mother had felt obliged to humble herself on his behalf. The experience made him see a totalitarian aspect to the education system as it was.

Odd Eiken's bill allowing free schools was passed. What happened then? At first, nothing much. It seemed a non-event, he says. Yes, some private schools turned themselves into free schools. Then, gradually, a few religious minorities and schools with particular education theories, like Steiner, established free schools. But this was on a modest scale.

Finally, companies began to get going. New ones were created by people who thought they could introduce better management or teaching methods. They began to create strings of schools, which enabled economies of scale. The company for which Eiken now works, Kunskapsskolan, created a pedagogical research and development department. He says his company now has thirty-three schools in Sweden and is still growing.[55] Companies have turned out to be the driving force behind the burgeoning number of free schools. Free schools currently account for 10 per cent of schooling in Sweden, Eiken says, and 25 per cent in Stockholm. He believes that, in time, a third of schools in Sweden will be free schools.

One welcome result has been open competition between different educational ideas. Previously, government schools had a somewhat uniform theory of teaching. Now, one company is consciously imitating private schools in Britain with students at desks facing the teacher and lots of team sports. Kunskapsskolan has particular ideas about school design. It believes in having no corridors in order to discourage bullying and to use space more efficiently. It develops educational resources centrally for use in all schools. Eiken is especially proud of a presentation on the French Revolution.

With this mushrooming of free schools, power lies with the parents to decide which kind of school will prosper. They are doing that simply by choosing which school to send their children to. The competition is intense.

I ask whether his company ever fires teachers.

'Oh yes!' he says. He says it is vital to be able to fire heads especially. Even a day with the wrong person in charge can damage a school. It seems it is easier to fire a teacher in Sweden than in America. So much for preconceptions.

What have been key elements in the growth of Swedish free schools?

1. Commercial companies have been allowed to establish them.

2. Local governments are not allowed to refuse planning permission for new schools except on very limited grounds. So former office buildings and warehouses have been converted into schools.

3. Odd Eiken argues that another key aspect has been that free schools get exactly the same cash per pupil as regular government schools and cannot charge parents at all. There are disadvantages to this but, in political terms, the advantage is that opponents cannot argue that free schools are unfair because they have extra funds.[56]

So is it all plain sailing for Swedish free schools? I suggest to Eiken that, over time, governments might impose more regulations and instructions, undermining the very innovation and independence which they offer. He replies that this is already happening. A second danger is that when free schools become a bigger part of the system, the government may cut back the money paid to them, leading to a slippage in standards or facilities.

But before concluding that charter schools are the best way to go, is it possible that there is something even better?

Which schools have the very best results according to the PISA study? The analysis in the 2009 edition divided all schools into three categories: public schools, government-dependent private schools and wholly private schools. Government-dependent private schools consistently did better than public schools. But wholly private schools did better still. On average, the reading performance of private schools was thirty-four points better than that of the public schools – a major difference.

The best-performing schools in the whole world, according to PISA, were the private schools of Shanghai. They had the best scores in all three subjects that PISA looks at. In maths, the Shanghai score was in a different league from the rest of the world – 646 compared to the next highest score of 579 for private schools in Korea.[57] The average score for OECD public schools was way down at 492.

What about those students who are less able? How good are private schools compared with government schools when it comes to teaching children how to read well? Government schools in Australia leave 19.2 per cent of their children functionally illiterate. But in the private schools, only 5.4 per cent remain so.

Black lives transformed by private schools

In 1997, a US charity offered subsidies to low-income children to go to a participating private school of their choice. There was a lottery to decide which children would receive the subsidies and which would not. Academics followed the fortunes of the children. This is how they fared:

Proportion going on to full-time colleges

Control group	26%
Those offered vouchers to attend private schools	32.5%

Proportion going on to selective four-year colleges, which tend to be more academic

Control group	3.0%
Those offered vouchers to attend private schools	6.9%

Source: Matthew M. Chingos and Paul E. Peterson, *The Effects of School Vouchers on College Enrollment*[58]

	Government schools	Private schools
Spain	3.5%	9.3%
Portugal	18.9%	7.1%
Australia	19.2%	5.4%
Ireland	23.4%	5.4%
OECD average	18.6%	5.1%
UK	19.2%	4.5%
USA	19.0%	3.1%
South Korea	7.1%	1.1%

Rates of functional illiteracy by school type in advanced countries where at least 5 per cent of children go to private schools. Japan omitted.[59] Source: OECD[60]

Of course it can be objected that, in many countries, children who go to private schools have wealthier, better-educated and more strongly motivated parents and that this is what boosts performance. This is true for many advanced countries. But it is not true for poorer countries like Indonesia and Tanzania where public education is rationed and it is the poor who buy private education more than the rich.

Andrew Coulson reviewed 150 different studies of the performance of public and private schools around the world.[61] Many adjust their results to take account of the social and economic position of the parents. In the overwhelming majority, private schools did better. Moreover in cases where the private schools were at their most independent and the government-run schools were most controlled, the difference was biggest.

More than 20 per cent of American public school teachers with school-age children enrol them in private schools – almost twice the 11 per cent rate for the general public.[62]

The World Bank produced a series of reports comparing private and government education in various developing countries between 1988 and 1994.[63] Often in these cases the parents of children at the private schools were poorer than the parents of those at government schools. In any case, the researchers 'controlled' for factors including differences in the wealth and educational background of the parents. The conclusion of the study of schools of Colombia and Tanzania, for example, was: 'Our results are robust. The estimated private advantage is large and empirically important.'[64]

These results tie up with some of the main themes of the PISA study. Private schools automatically have more of the autonomy which PISA suggests is important. They are accountable in the sense that if they perform badly, they lose customers and go out of business. Everyone involved, but particularly the head, is strongly incentivised to succeed. The head is likely to do whatever he or she can think of to ensure children are learning effectively. That will almost certainly involve maintaining discipline. Of course, the OECD does not endorse private schooling. That would offend the governments of its member-countries and would also go against – I would suggest – the organisation's unstated political outlook. But the research points, almost despite itself, to private education.

One further advantage of private education is that if a new teaching method works badly, private schools have a strong incentive to react quickly. This is in contrast to state schools, where a bad idea – such as the 'whole-word' method of teaching how to read – can last for decades before being abandoned.

It seems likely that the best results would come if countries moved all the way to thorough-going private schooling – not just charter or free schools. The poor could be given subsidised or free education through charitable schooling such as existed in abundance in late nineteenth-century in Britain and elsewhere. Unfortunately this is not practical politics in most countries.

If that is right, what should be done instead? Should we go for free/charter schools as the next-best option?

Perhaps. But the danger is that, over time, governments may impose more and more regulations and controls over charter schools so that they lose the autonomy that made them good.

The Netherlands introduced voucher schooling in 1917.[66] Government money was given to different kinds of independent schools as well as government schools according to the numbers of students. But in the following decades, rules were made about what schools should teach, how they should teach, how such schools could be created and so on. A system that once promised independence and competition saw it eaten away over ninety years. How does the Netherlands now score in the PISA tests? Better than average but it is not outstanding. This is consistent with the idea that some residual benefit remains from the reduced level of autonomy that remains.

> 'It would be fortunate if the best method of teaching were to be universally adopted. But who has it and on what authority? Let us therefore demand freedom of teaching.'
>
> Frédéric Bastiat[65]

Another problem with charter schools is that people are bound to object when money from their taxes is spent on schools which teach something they passionately disagree with. In Britain, some argue that no school that teaches creationism should receive public money, for example.

Because of these problems and others, some suggest that private schooling and parental choice can be promoted most successfully through tax credits or tax allowances.[67] In this system, parents pay private schools out of their own pockets and get tax relief for their payments, up to a specified limit.

But what about parents who cannot afford the fees even with tax relief? They can use money paid into scholarship schemes by companies and philanthropic individuals who obtain tax relief by paying into such schemes. In America, the growth of tax credit schemes has been dramatic. The number of children in them has risen from 36,000 in 2000 to over 301,000 in 2014.[68] One advantage is that it removes the objection 'I don't want my taxes to be used for teaching creationism'. It is always the parents' own money being used or that of willing donors.

In some countries, there would be scepticism that such schemes would reach the poor. That is why, in Florida for example, politicians have made a point of getting this kind of tax credit funding to the poor and disabled first.

But there is yet another possible approach, too. In Australia, government subsidies are paid to private schools. Some will be astonished by this and wonder how on earth it is politically possible. The answer is simple: the value of the subsidy is inversely related to the wealth of the parents. The poorer the children's parents, the bigger the subsidy. In this indirect way, poorer children are subsidised to get into private schools. The head of one of the leading private schools told me that over 15 per cent of Australian children go to private schools and nearly 24 per cent go to private but government-dependent schools, making a total of 39 per cent. This helps explain why the system has survived. Private and semi-independent schools and the parents of children in them are a serious political constituency. You don't easily get elected by attacking it.

The system also saves the government money. The head told me that each child at a public school costs the government A$13,600 but a child at a private school costs less than half that. Paradoxically, a majority of rich children do not go to private schools. Out of the 100 schools with the highest proportion of rich children, sixty-one were government schools. Perhaps competition from private schools makes the government schools try harder to attract students. Also, some Australian government schools are highly selective and obtain above-average academic results. So rich parents do all they can to get their children into them, obtaining a good education and saving money at the same time. This is a widespread phenomenon around the world: the rich often get the best state education for their children and the poor get the worst. But at least, in Australia, the poor have the possibility of going to private or semi-independent schools instead.

How does Australia do in the PISA tests? It comes seventh out of the major non-Asian countries in terms of functional literacy. On overall quality of schooling, it came sixth in the earlier 2009 PISA study. So it does pretty well. In fact, when I asked the head of one of the leading private schools in Australia how the subsidy to private schools had survived despite some left-inclined governments in recent decades, he said that one of the reasons is that private schools keep Australia at the upper end of the PISA rankings and the politicians know that.

It seems there is a surprising number of ways in which governments can encourage private or independent education:

1. Vouchers for free/charter schools.

2. Tax credits for parents, perhaps with tax credits for companies and philanthropic individuals to help the poor.

3. Outright subsidies to private schools with higher subsidies being given to schools with poorer parents.

Which is best? Each seems to have its advantage and disadvantages:

- *Charter schools/free schools/vouchers* – Sweden shows these can gradually expand but the Netherlands shows their independence can be eroded over the long term.

- *Tax credits* – Schools may retain more independence since parents and companies are spending their own money. But this system has not yet achieved a major presence in any country or state.

- *Direct subsidies to private schools* – they sustain a relatively large amount of private schooling in Australia but it may be difficult to introduce them where they do not already exist.

In each case, difficulties seem to arise. One of the biggest problems is that bringing about truly widespread private education – and the attendant benefits – seems to take so long. Is there a way in which fast, radical progress could be made? One way might be to introduce free/charter schools using the model of the privatisations that took place in many countries in the 1990s. Governments would simply privatise their schools.

In some countries, such as Britain, opinion polls show that most parents would like to send their children to a private school if they could afford it. So it is possible that a political party could attract support by promising that all parents who wanted to send their child to a private school would be able to do so.

'If you could afford it, would you send your child to an independent school?'

Yes	57%
No	25%
Don't know/no opinion	18%

Populus opinion poll (UK, 2012).

While 57 per cent of people would like to send their children to private schools, only 7 per cent do so. In most cases this seems likely to be because they cannot afford it.

Existing government schools could be offered by tender to cooperatives, churches, education companies, charitable trusts and associations of teachers and/or parents. Parents would then be able to apply to send their children to any school. The good would prosper and expand and the bad would go out of business. Where schools failed, the buildings could be offered for tender again. Successful companies and other organisations would soon increase the numbers of their schools under their management. Power would be in the hands of parents, not in the hands of governments.

The process could take place over five to ten years. This might be much quicker than any other method of spreading the benefit of private education. One should try to safeguard the system from creeping government control but frankly this would remain a danger.

Why hurry, some might ask? Why not just let slow growth of free/charter schools take place as in Sweden? Slow development would be better than none. But to accept slow development amounts to telling a child at a low-grade government school that will fail to teach him to read, 'Bad luck. You were born too early. If you had been born fifteen or thirty years later you might have gone to a good school.' It is not something that those who claim to care about children and their futures should be willing to accept.

This idea would represent a revolution in education and would attract opposition. But it is conceivable that a democracy might accept it since it would give choice and power to people.

> '**Public education in the United States is a government monopoly. Don't like your public school? Tough. The school is terrible? Tough.**'
>
> John Stossel, *Stupid in America*, ABC television broadcast 2006

I don't know whether something on this scale will ever be attempted. In the meantime, the evidence in this chapter suggests that the following policies could improve standards:

- More private schooling should be encouraged through free/charter schools or tax credits or subsidies to poorer students in private schools.

- Schools should have greater autonomy, combined with accountability through public exams.

> '**Much more valuable tha copying existing practices is th development of an education system that can be depende upon to constantly search o and deliver the best methoc over the long term**
>
> Andrew Coulson, *Market Educatio*

- School inspection bodies should be abolished and replaced with advisory bodies from which schools can obtain advice for a fee (as in Finland).

- Government legislation should safeguard the autonomy of free/charter and private schools.

- Private companies should be allowed to create charter schools as well as teachers or parents. Otherwise expansion is too slow.

- Local governments must not be allowed to obstruct the creation of charter schools through planning controls and other such techniques.

- Parents should have a choice of schools so that the schools have to compete to attract them.

- Bad schools should not be helped to survive by forcing parents to send their children to them.

- At fifteen, sixteen or seventeen, most children should get a job combined with vocational training. Only a minority should have purely academic higher education.

- Heads should be able to fire teachers without difficulty and hire better ones.

5.

'Do I have "stupid" tattooed on my forehead?'

Social housing – apple pie with poison in the filling

I AM SITTING IN A hired car in the accident and emergency parking area of the Hôpital Nord in Marseilles. It is cloudy and drizzling. The small car park is crowded and I am worried I might get in the way of anyone who arrives with an emergency. But this is where I have been told to come.

Soon, a man comes towards me and gets into the passenger seat. He has the air of someone used to dealing with all sorts of people, good and bad, without emotion. His clothes are informal but businesslike. He is a taxi driver but he is not going to drive me. He told me on the phone that it would be better not to make this journey in a taxi. It might get stoned. The gangs are suspicious of taxis because they might be used by undercover police.

I have asked him to show me a mixture of different public housing estates in Marseilles. The local newspapers are packed with reports about five murders that have taken place in the past two weeks, mostly in or near public housing. In one case, a car was torched with a man inside. He had been shot in the head. The killings have generally been part of turf wars between drug-dealing gangs. Extra police have been sent to Marseilles by the tough-talking minister of the interior, Manuel Valls (who later becomes Prime Minister).[1]

My guide, Yves, is a friend of the brother of someone I know. He says we will start with an estate where there was an attempted murder last night. He tells me the victim is in hospital 'in a bad way'.

The road winds up a hillside in the outer part of Marseilles where tourists never go. To one side, some blocks of flats about twelve storeys high stand like tombstones, surrounded by rough land. Few people are to be seen. It is bleak. We climb further and turn up a side road into a public housing estate. We have arrived at the edge of a group of three or four wide blocks of flats grouped together. I pull into a parking space.

'Shall we get out?' I say. 'I would like to walk a bit.'

Yves looks reluctant and I am not sure whether he will get out too. I open my door anyway. He emerges a little later. I lock the door and start walking up the hillside on the left-hand side of the estate. I look at the block of flats on my right. Yves seems to be following slowly, lagging behind.

'There are plenty of cars parked here,' I remark. 'It looks like some of the people here are not in poverty.'

He mishears me and replies, 'Yes, the people are in poverty.'

I start trying to explain what I meant but nervously he interrupts: 'Keep your voice down. They will be listening.'

The Solidarité social housing estate in Marseilles.

I ask him to walk faster so that we look as if we are going somewhere. But still he hangs behind. He is agitated. I climb further up and then turn round to look down on Marseilles beneath us. It is grey and grim. The bustling centre seems far away.

Eventually, I give way to Yves's unspoken urging that we should get back to the car. We walk back and get in. He relaxes and as we start off, he says, 'You see the man at the bus stop in the black hoodie? He is the *chouf*.'

I glance out and see a man hunched over with his hands in his pockets, his face barely visible under his hood. 'What is a *chouf*?'

'He is the look-out for the gang that controls the estate. A *chouf* is there all the time. He tells the gang when anyone comes.'

'When who comes?'

'The police or someone who wants to buy drugs.'

As we drive on down the slip road, I exclaim, 'But this estate… it was designed by an idiot! There is only one entrance! The gang only has to watch this one road and they can protect themselves against the police. It is like a medieval castle. That would have a single entrance, too. The estate is designed to be a castle for a gang!'

I ask Yves the name of the estate.

'Solidarité.'

Solidarity! How ironic! French politicians and trade unionists frequently appeal to the ideal of 'solidarity'. It is a central part of French political thought and tradition. The estate we have just visited is subsidised housing for the poor, intended to bring this ideal of solidarity into reality. Instead, it is an isolated, threatening place controlled by a criminal gang: the very opposite of solidarity.

Where next?

We drive for quite a while and I have no idea where we are but he tells me the next estate is called Font Vert. Eventually I see a sign for it as we turn left at a T-junction and soon after we are right inside. We drive along a narrow road with a big block of flats immediately on our left. The ground-floor flats are slightly raised above ground level but nearly all are tightly shuttered. Even on the first floor, plenty of the flats have their shutters closed too. Only at the higher levels are they not being used. I remark on this to Yves.

He says matter-of-factly, 'They are like prisoners.'

We see a woman and child and I wonder aloud what it is like for them to live in this environment. Are they scared? Do they get abused? Yves says that sometimes a gang stores its drugs in the flat of a single mother. The woman might get some cash in payment but in any case she dare not refuse. I guess the gang stores drugs at her flat so that if the dealers' own flats are raided by the police, no drugs will be found. If the woman's flat is raided, she won't risk her life by saying who left them with her.

'A den of thugs.'

'Very large housing estate with ten blocks, several drug dealers associated with the Flemish and the Irish, all armed.'

'It looked a bit like a concentration camp' – from a veteran of the A.F.N.

Comments about Font Vert on Wikimapia, April 2013. 'A.F.N.' is probably a reference to an organisation involved in the conflict at the end of France's colonial time in north Africa.[2]

Yves says that a gang can suddenly burst into someone's flat and start using it to deal drugs or guns. I recall a recent newspaper article saying that Kalashnikov rifles change hands in Marseilles for between €1,000 and €1,500.

The block of flats we are driving alongside is long. Finally we get to the end of it and where the narrow road turns left – on the far side of the corner – is a torched car. It is just a charred skeleton. I am startled to see it quietly sitting there as if this were normal. I remark on it. Yves replies that there are places where there are dozens like that. Cars are burned for fun.

We leave by the only exit. There is one way in and out. We have not stopped for a second. We certainly have not got out of the car.

A torched bus in Marseilles in 2006. A 27 year-old woman was badly burned on two-thirds of her body.

We drive on to another estate: Les Busserines. Yves tells me we must stop in the street outside. He does not want us to go into this one at all. He points to the nearest ground-floor flat. The windows are shuttered and all possible entrances – all the windows and the front door – are protected with heavy-duty metal bars. It is like a fortress.

We drive on to another estate: Marine Bleue. It is, appropriately, painted blue in parts. It sits on a hill and many of its flats must have fine views. Again, it has one entrance and exit. We drive straight through without stopping.

Finally we reach La Castellane or, as Yves pronounces it in his Marseilles accent, 'La Castellang'. It is the most famous estate in Marseilles because Zinédine Zidane was brought up there. Zidane, the son of Algerian immigrants, was arguably the best footballer of his generation and a French hero. He won the World Cup with France in 1998. He was named World Player of the Year three times. He also famously head-butted another player when playing in the 2006 World Cup final. He was sent off and the head butt possibly cost France the match. Zidane said his opponent had repeatedly insulted his mother and his sister.

Intriguingly, Zidane feels a strong loyalty to the estate where he grew up. He once said, 'I am still proud to be who I am: first a Kabyle [an ethnic group in Algeria] from La Castellane.' La Castellane is mentioned before his identity as a Frenchman.

The estate is a huge group of buildings rising up on a hill – a phalanx of tall blocks. The road going up past it is wide and busy. We stop on the far side and look across. Yves tells me that there is, again, one entrance and one exit. He will not go into the estate. He says that if a gang blocked the road, we would be trapped. Once again, he points out the *chouf* standing at the bus stop very close to us. As usual, he is wearing a hoodie.

He tells me a *chouf* is paid €150 for a shift from 8 a.m. to 1 p.m. 'It is much more profitable than going to school and getting a job. They are better off than being a manager. They have Rolex watches, Boss, Prada…'

Yves sounds as though he shares their values, according to which these brand names are powerful symbols of success.

I ask if he agrees to pick people up from the estates.

'Rarely', he replies.

Has he had a bad experience?

'Not myself. But I have friends whose cars have been stolen or burned.'

I drive us back to our original meeting place at Hôpital Nord. I pay Yves for his time and he gets out. Then I drive to the centre of town.

It is drizzling and overcast. I walk to the Old Port – the tourist part of Marseilles with many restaurants surrounding the harbour. They are all full so I walk away from the port and eventually find an Indian restaurant where I can have lunch. I write up my notes as I wait for my order to come. Only as I am writing there do I realise that during our tour of five housing estates and after all the talk in the newspapers of a tough security clampdown, I did not see a single police officer.

Of course, not all the social housing in France is as grim as the estates I saw in Marseilles. Only half an hour away, in Aix-en-Provence, I walked through some reasonably pleasant ones without much trepidation. And some social housing in France is positively luxurious, as we will see.

But the variations in quality should not distract us from the fact that social housing – in France and around the world – has been riddled with problems. This is rarely discussed or admitted. The problems include gangs on frightening estates but go far beyond that, too. Housing is of key importance yet barely noticed or debated. Many people think of social housing as an obviously good thing like apple pie. But it has poison in the filling. And the core problem is this:

The amount of social housing varies dramatically

0–5%	Australia, Greece, Italy, Norway, Portugal, South Korea, Switzerland, USA
6–10%	Belgium, Canada, Germany, Ireland, New Zealand
11–20%	Finland, France, Poland, Spain, Sweden, United Kingdom
More than 20%	Austria, Denmark, Netherlands

Source: OECD.[3]
More detailed figures for Europe in endnote.[4]

1. Social housing often contributes to unemployment

For decades, less well-off people in Britain have received housing benefit – money to help pay their rent. This sounds considerate and reasonable. But if these people have been unemployed and have then taken a job, 65 per cent of what they have earned has disappeared in reduced housing benefit. In addition, they have lost other benefits such as tax credits and council tax benefits. As the left-leaning Joseph Rowntree Foundation put it in 2013, 'they can face an effective taper rate of 96 per cent and be left with four pence from every additional pound of gross earnings'.[5] Someone earning £7 an hour would have to work for fourteen hours to be £4 better off. Of course nobody would work for fourteen hours to earn £4. It has been an extraordinary discouragement to extra work.

Then there is the discouragement to working at all. In 2006, the Institute of Fiscal Studies calculated that 3.6 million people who were working would lose less than 30 per cent of their net income if they lived on welfare benefits instead. Out of those, 1.9 million would be less than 20 per cent worse off on benefits.

23%

Proportion of social tenancies in Britain held by someone in full-time work[6]

In the circumstances, it is remarkable that so many of them were working at all. But what these figures could not show was how many people had decided it was not worth working for such a small financial gain. As the research by Kathryn Edin showed (see Chapter 1), a very large proportion of such people will have other, undeclared income. This problem has gradually got worse. The rise in rents between 1979 and 2006, for example, resulted in higher levels of housing benefit and therefore increased the disincentive to work. As a result, housing benefit in Britain has been a major contributor to high unemployment.

Something similar, though less extreme, has taken place in the USA. Rent in public housing (equivalent to social housing) depends on individual circumstances but usually is 30 per cent of income after various adjustments. If someone takes a job, the rent automatically goes up. He or she also has to pay social security payments of 7.5 per cent and may lose entitlement to Medicaid and food stamps. There will be income tax, too. Again, social housing has reduced the incentive to work and added to unemployment.

1.9 million Briti workers would g more than 80 per ce of their net income staying at home welfare benefit

Source: 'Financial Work Incentiv Britain: Comparisons over Time between Family Types', Institute of F Studies (2

'Like many other benefits, and in combination with them, housing benefit creates an unemployment trap.'

Rebecca Tunstall, *New Statesman*[8]

Some people might be tempted to think, 'Well, this one is easy! Just lower the rate at which the rent subsidy is reduced. If someone gets a job, reduce the rent subsidy by only, say, 20 per cent. Then people will keep more of their income from working and still have plenty of incentive to work. Problem solved!'

Unfortunately it is not that easy. If the subsidy reduction is made more gradual, large

numbers of extra people will become entitled to it and so they too will have a
reduced incentive to work. The cost of the whole system will jump, too, at least in
the short term.[10] This is a difficult knot to unravel. That is why it has been put to
one side for so long.

Does this problem apply to all countries with social
housing? No. At least, not as severely as in Britain.[11]

How do other countries avoid the problem? In some,
housing benefits – or rents, as the case may be – are not
adjusted according to income. It's as simple as that. It might
sound extremely tough. It means that those who lose their
jobs and are hard up must continue to pay full rents and,
if they can't afford them, they can lose their homes. What
countries would be so hard? What countries would treat
their people in way that seems so un-welfare-state-like?

One of them is Sweden. If you lose your job in Sweden
you are entitled to generous unemployment benefit as a
result of the insurance contributions you have paid while
working. You will be able to continue paying your rent. But
when the insurance money runs out, you will have to use
your savings. If the point is reached where you can no longer afford the rent, you
are likely to lose your home and have to move to something much more modest.

Social housing is different in Sweden. You do not get it on the basis of need. You
get it only if you reach the top of a waiting list and can afford the rent.[13] So people
in social housing in Sweden are in utterly different circumstances from those in
Britain or America. The Swedish model is not unique. According to the OECD,
the Netherlands, Denmark and Luxembourg also have 'broad-based' allocation of

social housing, which means it is aimed at a
wide spread of people, not just the poor.[14] These
countries probably avoid some of the worst
unintended consequences of social housing.
The crucial point is that, in so far as rents or
housing benefits are not adjusted for income,
they do not discourage work.

One might ask, 'What, then, is the purpose of social housing in these countries? If it
provides housing to a broad mix of the population, why should some minority part of
the "broad mix" be in government-subsidised

> '**Modelling showed
> that reducing the taper
> [of housing benefit]
> from 65 per cent to 36
> per cent reduced the
> number of people facing
> very high marginal tax
> rates … however, the
> number facing fairly
> high rates grew.'**
>
> Joseph Rowntree Foundation[9]

Social housing and unemployment

People with no qualifications *not* in social housing who are workless	43 per cent
People with no qualifications in social housing who are workless	70 per cent
Lone parents *not* in social housing who are workless	35 per cent
Lone parents in social housing who are workless	64 per cent

Source: Economic and Social Research Council[12]

housing while the rest is not? If it confers an advantage on those in social housing, is that not unfair on the others? If it confers no advantage, what is the purpose?'

Frankly it is hard to see one.

There are further problems caused by social housing.

2. Social housing can contribute to the incidence of lone parenting

Why does Sweden have a lower incidence of lone parenting than Britain or America? Sweden, after all, is well known for a culture in which the independence of women is celebrated. It is meant to be a land of free living and loving. In Britain, a two-parent family is still held up as the ideal and America is still quite a Christian country. There is probably no simple answer to this question but the following story points to one possible factor.

The Pruitt-Igoe Myth was a television documentary which argued that the well-known failure of the Pruitt-Igoe project – 'project' is the American term for a social housing estate – did not mean that all public housing was a bad idea. But in the course of this documentary in favour of social housing, former residents of Pruitt-Igoe, in St Louis, Missouri, were filmed speaking about fathers who left their families so that the mother and children could qualify for public housing.[15] They also spoke of children denying to officials that their father was living with them. It is a grotesque thought that fathers would leave their families or that children would deny the presence of a father, but the situation can arise because the cost and allocation of social housing in America, as in Britain, is adjusted according to the needs of the tenants.

When housing is allocated on the basis of need, preference tends to be given to single, unemployed parents because they have dependent children. If the rent – or housing benefit – is adjusted according to means and need, then a lone unemployed mother will be granted a lower net housing cost than a couple where one of the two is working. In this way, social housing can make lone parenting a less unattractive option than it would otherwise be. It can penalise couples.

I have not seen an academic study attempting to measure the impact of social housing allocation on lone parenting. But the proportion of lone parents in social housing is certainly much higher than in the general population in America and in other countries with similar systems. In Britain, nearly half of all lone parents live in social housing whereas only a tenth of couples do.[16] The logic of the incentives in these countries is that social housing has the potential to increase the incidence of lone parenting. But not in Sweden, or at least, to a far lower extent.[17]

It seems possible, at least, that the difference in the way that social housing is allocated and charged might help explain why Britain and America have more lone parenting than Sweden. Britain and America are, in fact, respectively the European and world capitals of single parenting (see Chapter 6).

3. Crime and fear

I saw during my journey around Marseilles how crime can establish itself in social housing. Cabrini Green, in Chicago, is another example of this. It once housed more than 15,000 people. It was described in *USA Today* as 'a virtual war zone, the kind of place where little boys were gunned down on their way to school and little girls were sexually assaulted and left for dead in stairwells'.

But projects do not have to be gigantic to become crime centres. Dunbar Village in West Palm Beach, Florida, consists of only 226 units. In 2007, a teenager knocked on the door of a young single mother and told her that her car had a flat tyre. Nine more teenagers suddenly barged into her flat, brandishing guns and demanding money. They proceeded to rape and anally rape her multiple times. They beat up her twelve-year-old son in the room next door.[18] The details of the story are horrific and do not need to be described here because what really brings home the nature of the estate at that time are the comments made by other residents in the wake of these horrible crimes.

Citoya Greenwood, who lived there with her four-year-old daughter, said, 'I try to be in my house no later than seven, and I don't come out. I don't even answer my door anymore.' On the Fourth of July, Independence Day, 'we didn't know if we was hearing gunshots or fireworks,' she told a reporter. Patriciea Matlock said, 'So a lady was raped. Big deal. There's too much other crime happening here.'[19]

'So a lady was raped. Big deal.'

The two teenagers who were charged with committing the crimes were said to be 'mostly fatherless, bouncing between homes'. The mother of one of them said that she herself was raped twice, at the ages of seven and twelve.

In the year leading up to the multiple rapes of the single mother, police were called 717 times – almost twice a day – to Dunbar Village. Whenever overhead lighting was put in, it was immediately destroyed by gunfire. City officials were considering putting in bullet-proof lighting. 'Isn't that quite a commentary on what the situation is there?' remarked Molly Douglas, the city commissioner. 'I just bow my head sometimes and think we just couldn't possibly have enough officers to take care of all of this.'[20]

This degree of lawlessness is hard to imagine for those of us living well away from such places. Back in Marseilles, they would understand. A magistrate there remarked, 'We have some gang members who refuse to leave prison because they fear being shot as they go out.' Interior Minister Manuel Valls referred to 'about forty' housing estates in Marseilles as 'sensitive' – a euphemistic expression used in France to mean 'dangerous'.[21] 'It is a war between the law of the state and barbarity,' he said. The Marseilles criminal trade in cannabis is concentrated in the public housing estates. A ton of cannabis was seized by police in less than three months at the beginning of 2013 along with twenty rifles, including ten Kalashnikovs.

> **'Public housing has a long record of looking attractive at the time of the ribbon cutting and then going quickly downhill.'**
>
> Howard Husock[24]

Such anecdotal evidence is supported by the statistics: the risk of burglary in social housing in Britain is more than twice as high as in owner-occupied housing – 4.2 per cent compared to 1.7 per cent, according to official figures.[22] But even this is almost certainly a major understatement. Much of the crime is simply not recorded.

A reporter for the left-leaning *Observer* newspaper went to Clyde Court estate in Leeds and asked a woman whether she had tried to have an anti-social behaviour order (ASBO) – a court injunction against bad behaviour – put on the local gangs who were making her life a nightmare.[23]

'Do I have "stupid" tattooed on my forehead?' she replied. 'The only way to make an ASBO stick is to give evidence in court and if you do that, your life won't be worth living.'

> **'In the areas origina built as flatted coun estates …18 per ce feel unsafe alone ev at home or outsi in daylig**
>
> Professor John Hills, referring to estates in Eng

Why have so many social housing estates got higher crime levels than elsewhere? It may be partly due to the first two problems of social housing: high levels of unemployment and single parenting. Both tend to lead to higher levels of crime (see Chapter 7). Then there are the common areas which nobody owns that are typical in such estates. No one has a strong incentive to protect these areas and keep them in good condition. The burnt-out car I saw in Font Vert was just left lying there. If it had been on property that someone owned, it would surely have been removed as quickly as possible. Social housing is, of course, owned by someone – often the local government. But local governments tend not to deal with such problems with the urgency of private owners.

Pretty well everyone now thinks that building massive public housing blocks was a mistake which has contributed to the crime problem. And having only one through road – as in the estates I visited in Marseilles – seems like a terrible blunder. It is hard to know what weight should be given to the different possible causes of crime in social housing. But it is certain that crime is much higher than elsewhere and many residents live in fear as a result.

4. Waste

A significant portion of social housing deteriorates to the point where it has to be destroyed. In other words, it turns out to be a total waste of time and money.

We have already referred to the failure of the Pruitt-Igoe project in St Louis. It was designed by a highly prestigious architect, Minoru Yamaseki, to house 85,000 families. It was built in 1954–6 but deteriorated to the point where it was 25 per cent vacant. It was demolished after just twenty years. The big Cabrini Green project in Chicago – also referred to earlier – was built in stages between 1942 and 1962. It was 'closed' in 2010.

So many estates have deteriorated badly that it has become US government policy to fund the destruction of some estates and replace them with new ones. The programme is called, without irony, 'Hope VI'. Prior to 1995, the units that were demolished had to be replaced one-for-one with new units. But there was not enough money to build the replacements so this rule 'effectively prevented demolition even of very deteriorated developments'.[26] Eventually the rules were relaxed with the result that 200,000 public housing units were torn down between 1995 and 2008. The total number of public housing units dropped from 1.33 million to 1.16 million.

In Britain, a website called Wikia has a list of sixty-four council housing estates that have been demolished.[27] The source is not official and is probably incomplete but I cite it because I am unaware of any full, authoritative list. A typical one on the Wikia list is Lee Bank, in Birmingham. This was built in the 1960s and officially opened by Queen Elizabeth. Most of it was demolished in stages between

2000 and 2007. One building on the estate, Charlecote Tower, was destroyed in a controlled explosion in 2000.

In France, construction of the Cité des 4,000 near Paris – so named because the vast estate was intended to have 4,000 units – began in 1956.[28] It took more than ten years to build and began to go wrong in the familiar ways involving crime and physical deterioration. After a child was shot dead there in 1983, President Mitterrand visited it.[29] Problems continued and, after the death by gunfire of an eleven-year-old, Nicolas Sarkozy, then a tough-talking minister of the interior and later President, also visited.

But visits by presidents and ministers did not arrest its decline. The Debussy block was demolished in 1986, the Renoir in 2000, the Ravel and Présov blocks in 2004, the Balzac in 2010 and the 'little' Debussy in 2012. There is a poignant contrast between the way these blocks were named after French cultural icons of art, literature and music and the grim reality of crime and violence that took place in them.

In Béziers, the Capendeguy estate was blown up spectacularly on 27 January 2007. The event has been uploaded a number of times onto YouTube so you can see for yourself the scale of the destruction.[30] It was built thirty-five years previously, in 1972.[31]

The waste that has taken place in social housing has been on a massive scale. I have only mentioned a few examples. As far as I know, nobody has written a full account of all the destruction.

People were taxed to pay for these massive projects. But, instead of providing decent accommodation for the poor, as intended, they made life miserable and dangerous for the residents and ultimately had to be destroyed. In some cases, deterioration began within five years of construction.

Demolition of the Carpendeguy estate in 2007.

5. Allocation of social housing can lead to corruption

In February 2005, it emerged that the French Minister of Finance, Hervé Gaymard, his wife and eight children were living in a prime location not far from the Champs-Elysées at the expense of taxpayers.[32] He protested that he came from a humble background. He said he was 'the son of a shoemaker ... I do not have money'. He claimed that he needed the flat. But then it was revealed that he already owned a flat in Paris, albeit one that was not as big. It was rented out, bringing him money while he had free, luxurious accommodation that had not been declared. He had done nothing illegal but he had to resign. It then emerged that the Budget Minister, too, enjoyed an apartment paid for by the government and similarly owned a flat in Paris that was rented out.

This sort of thing has been a recurring theme in France. Previously, President Chirac's government was involved in scandals, some involving 'the abuse of state-paid apartments'.[33] And before that, President Mitterrand's administration was also accused of corruption. As a BBC reporter put it after the Gaymard affair, 'the disastrous impression has been reinforced of a self-serving caste of leaders who follow their own moral codes, cut off from the concerns of mere citizens'.[34]

IN PARIS, I MEET A specialist in housing, Nicolas Lecaussin, director of development at the Institute of Economic and Fiscal Research, at a café not far from the Arc de Triomphe. He suggests that I might find it interesting to see the office of the national government agency responsible for social housing. I don't have to walk far. After our meeting, I walk around the Arc de Triomphe and find Rue Lord Byron, a stone's throw from the Champs-Elysées. It is a narrow street that bends as it goes downhill. The buildings are elegant – probably constructed in the nineteenth century.

One is particularly wide and reaches up six or seven storeys. It has a highly polished brass plaque outside with the words 'Union nationale des fédérations d'organismes d'H.L.M'. These are the offices of HLM, which stands for *habitations à loyer modéré* ('housing at moderate rent'). Another brass plaque identifies five other organisations, four of which also have HLM in their names.

The role of HLM is to provide housing for the poor. Much of this housing is in suburbs in drab blocks. But the officials responsible for them are located in one of the smartest, most expensive parts of Paris and, indeed, the world. The entrance has a decorated metal canopy like a luxury hotel. I step back to look at the building and notice an old sign in the stonework: 'Hotel Lord Byron'. So the offices were indeed formerly a smart hotel. This does not count as corruption on a narrow definition. But I personally find it sickening.

The corrupt allocation of housing does not happen only at a high level. In November 2012, a regional newspaper reported that 'several dozen families have been victims of a huge swindle'. They had paid between €1,000 and €1,500 in cash bribes to obtain social housing in Montpellier. The families had then discovered that some of the flats in question were already occupied. They had been duped. They were victims of a crime but, of course, they were also breaking the law themselves by paying bribes. The total number of people who were tricked will never be known because, as the local newspaper commented, 'in admitting it, they confess, de facto, their complicity in corruption'. The fact that 'dozens' were involved gives us a hint of how commonplace this is.

Also, in the comments made about this story online, no one expressed scepticism about it. On the contrary, everyone concurred that bribery in social housing allocation was widespread. One commented, 'I know … people who have obtained social housing – a maisonette with a garden – they lived as a couple with nearly €4,000 [per month, presumably] income but with well-placed relations [named individual], the town council and the municipal police, they became entitled to it in less than a month and they are still there. They pay €350 [per month] rent, they have social housing and they go to Cuba each year, never failing to have a week's skiing at Serre Chevalier, and have two Touaregs [a large, luxurious 4x4] parked outside.'

The same person claimed to know three other similar cases, all of them among his or her acquaintances and all involving 'pulling strings'. Another wrote, 'There are hundreds and hundreds who have got their homes by pulling strings'.

I found general acceptance in France that allocation of public housing is often corrupt. No one is surprised if the friends and/or mistress of a mayor are allocated particularly desirable apartments. The idea that subsidised social housing is there to help the less well off certainly exists in France but is abused. It has even been claimed that more affluent families rent public housing than rent private housing.[35]

Does this kind of thing happen only in France?

I am now in a taxi in Manhattan being driven to Harlem. The driver is a middle-aged, Hispanic man of ample proportions. He says he has lived in Harlem and the North West Side for forty-seven years. He remarks that I won't be able to get a taxi from Harlem back to my hotel. Cabs looking for fares don't go there. I ask what the apartments are like in the Ulysses Grant project, which I am intending to visit. He says that they are good. In fact you could wait a long time to get in there. It

Part of the Ulysses Grant 'project' in Harlem.

would certainly be three or four years and could even be nine or ten … unless, that is, you pay someone 'under the table'.

I had not expected to hear of people paying bribes to get into Harlem. He explains that Harlem used to be 'bad' – meaning violent and dangerous – in the 1980s but now it is better. It is far from being smart but it is nevertheless in Manhattan and not too far from better areas.

'How much would someone need to pay to jump the waiting list?' I ask.

'Oh… $6,000, $7,000', he replies.

Later on during my stay in Manhattan, I ask another taxi driver if he has heard of this sort of thing. He is black, in his forties, and tells me he lives in Newark, New Jersey, 8 miles west of Manhattan.

'Oh yes!' he says. It turns out that he knows plenty about it and can explain the economics of it. A flat in the Ulysses Grant project might cost $800–$1,000 a month. But it is in a relatively desirable area. A flat across the road from the project and rented privately would cost $1,600 a month – up to twice as much. So you can save $7,000 or more a year by getting into Ulysses Grant. I ask him what you would have to bribe someone to jump the waiting list. Would it be the $6,000–$7,000 mentioned by the other taxi driver? He thinks that is too much. He suggests a month's pay – perhaps about $3,000.

He adds that one person has been arrested for paying money like this 'because it is against the law'. You don't say! It is also not exactly what the creators of social housing had in mind.

Of course, the word of two anonymous taxi drivers is not exactly proof perfect. But I have no reason to disbelieve them. It is also worth mentioning that this kind of crime is hard to detect and prove. Both parties to the crime want to keep it secret, as we saw in France. Both have broken the law. But proof does emerge occasionally, as it did in the case mentioned by the taxi driver and again in another country thousands of miles away.

Douglas Norris, a senior client services officer in the housing department of New South Wales, Australia was a white, middle-aged man, balding from the front of his head. He had a moustache and a tiny beard under his lower lip. The department had 40,000 people on its waiting list.[36] With so many in the queue, priority was given to those 'in urgent need' or aged over eighty. In 2003, Norris was approached by Bruce Murray, a tenant on the estate for which he had responsibility. Murray wanted to move from his bedsit to a one-bedroom flat.

Norris replied that it could take years to get to the front

Douglas Norris.

of the queue. He then allegedly added words to the effect that 'you scratch my back and I'll scratch yours'. He asked for a payment of A$500 and promised that, in return, Murray could have a one-bedroom flat in only two weeks. That is how Norris's little bribery business began.

The Independent Commission against Corruption subsequently identified seven individuals who had jumped the queue by paying him.[37] The details of the story show how difficult it is to get hard evidence of corruption of this sort. Obviously neither the person who gives the bribe nor the one who receives it will report it to the police and the payment is likely to be in cash. Norris would have got away with it indefinitely but for an informer. Even with an informer, though, it took an expensive police operation to obtain adequate evidence. So it is impossible to know how widespread this kind of corruption is. But we can be fairly confident it happens in France, the USA and Australia at least.

6. Some social housing subsidises the rich

Frank Dobson is a bluff, cheerful member of the British Parliament. He draws a salary of £67,060 – more than twice average full-time earnings – plus expenses and he is automatically a member of the favourable pension scheme provided to MPs.[38] He has had a fairly successful political career, being Secretary of State for Health from 1997 to 1999. At that time he had a salary of over £72,000 – more than three times average earnings at the time – and enjoyed the perks of office such as a chauffeur-driven car.

Where would you expect such a well-paid, successful man to live? He actually lives in social housing – a three-bedroom flat in a smart mansion block in central London at a subsidised rent.[39] We know it is subsidised because he has said that he could not afford to rent privately. 'Market rents in our area are phenomenal,' he said.

Dobson is getting a subsidy from taxpayers. People who earn less than him are helping to pay his housing costs. Is this what 'social housing' is for?

Bob Crow, leader of a trade union, reportedly had pay and perks worth £140,000 in 2012 – six times average income.[40] He was living in social housing in London at an 'estimated' rent of £150 a week – a small fraction of the open market rent.[41] The subsidy to him from poorer people was even more grotesque.

Are these isolated examples? No. In October 2011, there were 15,000 people in Britain living in social housing despite having earnings of more than £80,000.

Similar stories can be told in France and elsewhere. Where the rent for social housing is not subsidised, it is

> **'15,000 tenants in social housing … have household incomes of more than £80,000'**
>
> Daily Mail, 7 February 2012[42]

no scandal that the rich should live there. But where ordinary taxpayers are subsidising the rich, social housing has become an insult to its original purpose.

7. Social housing can reduce mobility

Most tenants of social or public housing have obtained their homes only after years of waiting. So they are reluctant to give up the accommodation and the subsidy that is part and parcel of it. They are discouraged from moving to where they might be able to get a job or, perhaps, a better job. They may be discouraged from moving to be near an elderly parent who needs their help.

In New York City, the average tenancy in public housing is twenty years.[44] The turnover of tenancies in London social housing is a mere 3.5 per cent a year.[45] These are measures of how social housing can reduce the ability of people to move where it might suit them, damaging their personal freedom, their well-being and the economy generally.

> **'Almost a fifth of council households – some 720,000 – earn more than the national average wage'**
>
> *Daily Mail*, 7 February 2012[43]

8. Waiting lists

In San Francisco, I did a little tour of some of the housing estates. Some blocks were boring but otherwise not too bad. One was in a prime area – a development called North Beach Place at the end of the picturesque cable car line that approaches Fisherman's Wharf. These blocks were in good condition, although it may have helped that they were relatively new.

I looked at the San Francisco public housing website to learn more about public housing in the city. The latest developments and refurbishments looked attractive. One could easily get the impression that here, at least, public housing is working out.

Still browsing the website, I came to a page with details of the percentage of housing reserved for people in various low-income bands. Below that was a question: 'How long is the Public Housing waitlist?'

> **'Waiting lists for social housing are increasing ... In England, for instance, housing waiting lists increased ... to over 1.8 million households in 2011 (an increase of 76 per cent since 2000). In France, 1.2 million applicants are registered on waiting lists for social housing and 630,000 in Italy.'**
>
> Alice Pittini, 'Housing Affordability in the EU'[46]

The answer was: 'The Waiting List is currently CLOSED.'

> **'Most agencies have long waiting lists for public housing and some no longer accept new applications because of the size of the backlog.'**
>
> Center on Budget and Policy Priorities, USA[47]

Long waiting lists are normal for public housing around the world. Even if social housing were otherwise a successful idea, the problem would remain that many people have to wait many years to get it. And in some cases, such as San Francisco, you cannot even get on the waiting list. It is worth considering why the waiting lists are so long or even closed. Here is one reason:

9. Cost

When social housing in Britain was given a major push following the Second World War, it was thought that it could be an economical way of building homes. The financial credibility of the government would enable public housing to be built cheaply. The government could borrow at a lower interest rate than individuals. And after the cost of construction, further costs would be zero because rent would cover the maintenance bills. Indeed, that is more or less how it turned out ... for a while.[48]

Then three rising costs spoiled the picture. First, many estates became riddled with crime and degraded so the cost of maintaining them rose. Next, people refused to live in these blocks so no rent came in at all. Finally for several decades there was high inflation and it was politically difficult to raise the rents in line with rising prices. Rents were increased to some extent but housing benefit was used to help those who were short of money.

This was a financial time bomb. More and more people were discouraged from work because if they took a job, they lost their housing benefit. So numbers on housing benefit soared and the cost rocketed from £400 million in 1980/81 to £12.6 billion in 2003/4.[49] Social housing that was meant to be self-financing after the initial building cost became a financial disaster. Similar events took place elsewhere in Europe, and in Australia, New Zealand and the USA.

The Public Housing Capital Fund in America, which handles money for building and renewing public housing, spent $2.5 billion in 2010 and the Operating Fund spent nearly twice as much.[50] But these sums were a fraction of the cost of housing vouchers: just under $18

San Francisco social housing.

billion. The total federal budget appears to have amounted to $45 billion.[51] But considerable state expenditure must be added to that to arrive at the real annual cost.

There is also an overhang of capital spending that needs to be carried out but has not been done yet. The Center on Budget and Policy Priorities – a left-of-centre organisation in favour of public housing – has calculated that the cost of paying for 'unmet needs' in public housing for capital repairs and improvements would be $22 billion.[52] But it adds that some developments may require more substantial work: 'If, for example, 100,000 units were replaced rather than renovated, estimated capital needs would rise from $22 billion to $32 billion.' It is a big sum considering that public housing is relatively small in the USA compared to other countries. What is the total cost of public housing in France? I am told that even those who specialise in the subject find the financing impossibly obscure and cannot estimate the total cost. Quite possibly, no one knows. But the sum is likely to be enormous.

•   •   •

I have listed a daunting number of problems that tend to arise with social housing. Have any countries managed to avoid them?

It looks as though the best – or perhaps least bad – outcomes have been in countries such as Sweden where public housing has continued to be for everyone and has not been used as a means-tested method of helping the poor although even Sweden has suffered from problems 6, 7 and 8 on the list above. But now the European Union appears to be pressing Sweden and others to give up this model and switch towards the means-tested approach which has been such a spectacular failure in Britain and the USA. At a meeting in November 2012, an EU representative faced complaints and criticism from the Netherlands, France, Austria and Sweden for demanding that public housing should only be for those of low income.[53]

In any case, the manifold problems of social housing have led to a significant decline in this aspect of most welfare states. In Britain, the proportion of people living in social housing fell from 31 per cent in 1979 to 17 per cent in 2012.[54] In America, the number of public housing units fell 10 per cent in the twelve years from 1995.[55] In Australia, between 2004 and 2010, the proportion of social housing also declined even though the quantity remained more or less constant, because the total amount of housing of all kinds continued its long-term, rapid increase.[56] Germany saw a dramatic fall in social renting as a proportion of all rented property, from 26 per cent to 11 per cent between 1987 and 2001.[57]

Many tactics have been used to try to save public housing. But there is reason to doubt that any is satisfactory (see box).

Things that have been tried to improve housing for the poor

a) **Rent control**. This was introduced in Britain as a temporary wartime measure in 1915. It continued until 1980–89 when it was progressively ended.[58] To prevent landlords evading it by evicting tenants, tenants were given long-term security of tenure. The result of this was that owning property to rent became a terrible investment. Properties ceased to be properly maintained and the supply of privately rented accommodation available to the poor declined. It was a disastrous policy.

Dwelling stock of privately rented homes in the UK during the period of rent controls (thousands).

Source: Office for National Statistics[59]

b) **Low-rise social housing in mixed areas instead of massive blocks**. This kind of housing may well be less prone to crime and degradation. However if the housing is in a good area and pleasant and the rent is subsidised, there is bound to be a waiting list, most people will not get it and it is unfair; if, alternatively, tenants are given money to pay a market rent, they will probably face particularly big unemployment traps because the rent will be high; or, if there is neither a rent subsidy nor a tenant subsidy, the units might as well be a private development.

c) **Cheap financing to help poor people buy their own homes**. This may be of some benefit provided that the supply of new housing is flexible and can respond to the stimulated demand. Otherwise the measure just causes higher prices. There is also a danger with policies of this sort: in 1999, US banks were encouraged by the government banks 'to extend home mortgages to individuals whose credit is generally not good enough to qualify for conventional loans'.[60] This became known as 'sub-prime' lending. Many people who could not afford to buy did so anyway. They subsequently lost their homes. This contributed to the financial crisis that began in 2008.

d) **Housing associations**. These semi-independent organisations which manage social housing are meant to be more flexible and local than city governments with the result that the management is better. Even if that is true, they do not remove the essential problems with public housing such as unemployment traps and unfairness.

e) **Insistence on providing some 'affordable housing' as a condition of allowing private housing development**. This practice causes new housing to be less profitable and therefore less attractive to developers. It therefore results in fewer apartments being built than would otherwise be the case. In some cases, entire projects cease to be commercially attractive and nothing is built at all. As the market in housing is fungible – total supply affects all prices – the net effect is likely to be to make housing on average more expensive than it would otherwise be.

f) **Shared or partial ownership**. This enables people to have a stake in ownership. It effectively increases the ability to buy. But, if the supply of housing cannot be increased in response to higher demand, it will only result in higher prices.

g) **Compulsory savings accounts which can be used for home purchase**. This has been adopted in Singapore. No unemployment trap is created and there is no unfairness between people in similar positions. As a result of the scheme, there is mass ownership of property in Singapore. It has one of the highest home-ownership rates in the world: 90.5 per cent.[61] Relatively poor people own their own homes, which provides them with a major asset. But there are two concerns: that it might only work well in a society as well organised as Singapore; and that the domination of the system by government reduces personal liberty.

Holland Close, Singapore: government-built flats which are owned by the inhabitants.

Leo Siew Tiew, a taxi driver in Singapore, bought his four-room flat with two bathrooms for S$96,000 in 2,000. The building was created by the Housing and Development Board and was subsidised. He was able to use money from his compulsory savings. He is delighted that his flat is now worth S$400,000.

h) **Giving priority in public housing to those who get work combined with personal counselling for those who have problems getting work**. These two ideas have been combined in what could be called 'the Atlanta experiment'. Renee Glover took over the Atlanta Housing Authority in 1994 and created a revolution in US public housing with these policies.[62] They reversed the unemployment trap problem because they provided tenants with an incentive to get work instead of the opposite. They also removed bad tenants. The results were remarkable: the employment rate of household heads increased from 18.5 per cent in 1994 to 62 per cent in 2010. An underclass was turned into a working class.

The idea of giving housing predominantly to those in work rather than those 'in need' echoes that used in much of eastern Europe under communist rule. In Poland, for example, those who got work often received accommodation which was tied to their jobs.[63] As for giving personal advice in people's own homes, this is like the approach of Octavia Hill in nineteenth-century Britain. Her estates were financed privately and tenants were actively counselled.

The concerns with attempting to replicate the Atlanta experiment are: that it might take a particular place and special people to get it up and running; potential damage to the communities to which troublesome tenants are moved; high cost; and obtaining democratic support for such 'tough love'.

j) **Taxing empty property to increase the amount of property available for occupation**. This is likely to make property ownership less desirable and thus, in time, reduce the amount of housing created and exacerbate any shortage. It would be better to counteract any reasons that owners might have to leave property empty, contrary to normal commercial incentives. Such reasons are likely to be government regulations or taxes.

k) **Price controls on new property**. China has tried to control housing prices by diktat.[64] Predictably some building projects have been cancelled. This will certainly lead to less housing than there otherwise would have been and this, in due course, is likely to lead to higher prices – the very opposite of what is wanted. In 2012 Caixin Online, a Chinese newspaper, reported: 'Price controls have been blamed for suspensions or cancellations of large numbers of new housing projects, which means new housing supplies are sure to fall over the next few years and push prices higher.'[65]

Whatever ingenious schemes are devised, some problems do not or even cannot go away. In the end, there are only three approaches to social housing and all of them lead to a dead end:

1. If the *rents* are subsidised, there are sure to be waiting lists and it will be unfair to those who are excluded. The excluded people will also be paying through their taxes for the subsidies enjoyed by others, adding to the injustice.

> ### 'The rent is too damn high!'
>
> Name of a minority party in the 2010 election for New York governor, subsequently used as the title of a book by Matthew Yglesias.[66]

2. If the *people* are subsidised by being means- or needs-tested to determine how much help they should have with the cost of their rent, the financial incentive to work will be reduced, leading to higher unemployment. This will reduce the long-term ability of the poor to get out of poverty.

3. If you do not subsidise either the *rents* or the *people*, there is no purpose to public housing.

On this analysis, there is no good option. Social housing simply does not make sense. Is there any way out of this three-way trap? Perhaps. It is not called 'social housing' but it addresses the problem that social housing was meant to deal with.

The fundamental thing that most of us want is that the poor should be able to get reasonable housing. People on different political sides can probably agree about that at least.

Let's step back and look at what has actually happened in many advanced countries. The fact is that the opposite has occurred. It has become increasingly difficult for the poor to get housing. Things have got worse, not better. They have got worse during the past century, during which social housing has been a prominent part of welfare state policy.

On the face of it, this is odd. Advanced countries across the world have seen substantial increases in the incomes of the less well off. The relatively poor can afford many things more easily than before. Food as a proportion of the average budget in the UK has fallen from over a third in 1947 to only 11.6 per cent in 2013.[67] In America, the cost of food, which took up 42.5 per cent of average expenditure in 1901, fell to 13.2 per cent just over a century later.[68] For the poor, the drop was even more significant.[69] Annual holidays of only a week were normal in the 1950s. Now the relatively poor are granted – and can afford – holidays

of four weeks or more. The proportion of people aged 16–54 in households owning mobile phones in Britain reached 99 per cent in 2012.[70] The one big, jarring
exception to the poor getting richer is housing. The cost for the average household has jumped from a mere 8.8 per cent of expenditure to over a quarter since
1947.[71] Once again the impact of this on the poor will have been even greater.
That is why the subsidies paid to people for their housing have had to increase,
adding to the discouragement to work. It is the increased cost of housing that is
at the root of the problem.

Housing has leapt over food as a major cost for average families

Percentage weightings of food and housing in the British Retail Price Index. The weightings reflect the amount that
is estimated to be spent on each category. The weighting of food has fallen partly because people are wealthier
and partly because food has become cheaper in real terms.

Source: Office of National Statistics[72]

Why has the cost risen? To look into this, let's compare Germany and Britain.
They are surprisingly similar. Since 1970, both have experienced similar population
growth.[73] They have had comparable economic growth – albeit at different times.
And their population densities are not very different either.[74]

There is one big difference. In Britain, the cost of housing has soared. In Germany it has not. In Britain, the average price rose 232 per cent in real terms between 1975 and 2014.[76] Over the same period, the cost of German housing actually fell 8 per cent.

How many people per square km?

Singapore	7,405	Switzerland	198
Hong Kong	6,787	France	119
Malta	1,299	Spain	93
Netherlands	495	Ireland	66
Japan	351	USA	34
UK	259	New Zealand	17
Germany	235	Canada	4
Italy	206	Australia	3

Source: World Bank[75]

Index of real house prices in Germany and the UK rebased to 100 in 1975.

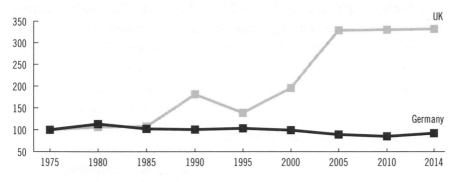

Source: Federal Reserve Bank of Dallas[77]

The rise in house prices in Britain has meant that the cost of housing has become a bigger multiple of average salaries. The figure has been volatile but, as the years have gone by, the lowest ratios in the cycle have been higher and so have the highest. In 1981, a Briton on an average salary had to pay 3.5 times his or her salary to buy an average home. That figure rose to a peak of 5.0 times in the late 1990s.[78] At the peak of the following boom in 2007, the ratio reached nearly 6.5.

Among those who rent unfurnished accommodation privately, rent in Britain amounts to just over 30 per cent of their income.[79] This is the average. According to the Office of National Statistics, the proportion spent by the poor on housing is more than twice as much as the proportion spent by the richest.[80] Housing has gone from being a significant cost for the poor to a dominant one. Or, to put it another way, the rising cost of housing has made the poor poorer.

While the ratio of house prices to salaries was rising in Britain, it was falling in Germany.[81] In 2013, the cost of housing – measured per square metre of an apartment – took up a significantly smaller part of a German's net income than in 1991.[82] Another way of measuring this is to look at the cost of 100 square metres (1,080 square feet) of a 'typical upscale housing unit' and compare it with average per-capita GDP. In Britain, 100 square metres cost 80 times average per-capita GDP in 2014, one of the highest ratios in the world.[83] In Germany, it was only 9.6 times.

Just as the poor have disproportionately suffered from rising prices in Britain, so they have disproportionately benefited from stable prices in Germany. Of all the contrasts in this book, this must count as one of the most important for anyone interested in the living standards of the less well off. What accounts for the contrast in house prices in Britain

'In the 2012 Mercer Cost of Living Survey, no German city ranked among the fifty most expensive expat destinations worldwide.'[84]

and Germany? The answer is simple enough to be understood by an eleven-year-old. It is a matter of supply and demand. In Britain, the supply of housing has increased very slowly despite substantially increased demand. Therefore prices have risen. In Germany, supply has increased faster and has met the increased demand.

In 2010, for every 100,000 people in Britain, 15 hectares (37 acres) of land were developed for new housing. In Germany, new development amounted to 50 hectares (123 acres) – more than three times as much.[85] Over the longer term, the rate of building new dwellings per capita in Germany has ranged from 10 to 110 per cent a year more than in Britain, according to the European Union.[86] New homes in Britain are also less spacious than in Germany – an average of 76 square metres (820 square feet) compared to 109 square metres (1,170 square feet).[87] Furthermore, the average size of a British family home has been shrinking. It fell by 2 square metres (22 square feet) between 2003 and 2013.[88]

Housing in the USA has become less affordable

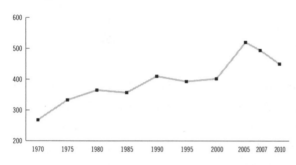

Ratio of the price of new single-family homes to median household income.[89]

Why is it that supply of new housing in Germany has responded to demand much better than in Britain? Some people like to suggest rapacious builders in Britain hoard land to push up prices and increase their profits. But there is nothing to prevent new entrants in the house-building business starting up and taking advantage of these supposedly artificial high prices. In any case, it seems unlikely that British builders are any more rapacious than German ones.

A more credible explanation is that it is more difficult to obtain permission to build new homes in Britain. Land with permission to build has therefore become extremely valuable. In 2011, in Oxford, for example, it cost £4 million per hectare while agricultural land was worth a mere £16,000 per hectare. Land with permission to build is so rare that it is worth 249 times more than land without permission. Even in far less prosperous areas of Britain, such as Liverpool, land with permission to build is worth over 100 times the value of nearby agricultural land.[91] Barratt, a house-building company, says that, as a rough national guide, land with permission to build is worth fifty times land without permission.[92]

> 'What's needed is bold action to deliver new homes and lots of them ... Millions of young people and families are priced out of a home of their own.'
>
> Anne Baxendale, Shelter[90]

The cost of land with permission to build in England has soared. The average figure tripled in only sixteen years, between 1994 and 2010, going from £731,168 to £2,371,549 per hectare.[93] These figures are not just for hotspots like London but the whole of England.[94] The cost has rocketed simply because it is so difficult to obtain the permission.

Housing has been a major part of how welfare states have gone wrong. The poor have been hurt above all. And what has been at the root of this problem? The planning system! It is like a detective story at the end of which you find the villain of the piece is a bureaucrat in a local office who never meant any harm to anyone. The bureaucrat, though, is of course only the instrument of policies which most people – including most politicians – have not thought about very much.

Plenty of countries have their own versions of the British planning problem. The list of countries with price rises of over 90 per cent

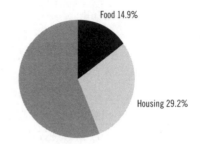

The poor spend twice as much on housing as on food in the USA

Food 14.9%

Housing 29.2%

Percentage of expenditure by Americans with incomes between US$15,000 and US$19,000.[95]

between 1980 and 2008 includes Australia, New Zealand, Norway and the Netherlands. Meanwhile other countries which have, like Germany, allowed new housing to meet demand include Switzerland and Japan.

Not all countries have priced people out of housing

Countries where prices have gone up less than 20 per cent (or fallen), 1980–2008:	Countries where prices have gone up by 90 per cent or more, 1980–2008:
Germany	Australia
Japan	Belgium
Portugal	Finland
South Korea	Ireland
Switzerland	Netherlands
	New Zealand
	Norway
	Spain
	United Kingdom

Changes in real house prices between 1980 (or earliest year available) and 2008.

Source: OECD[96]

The relationship between planning controls and house prices has been studied by many academics. Over and over again, they have found the same thing. Even if you look at apparently crowded places with physical restrictions on development such as Hong Kong and Manhattan, restrictive planning controls have increased prices. Kristian Niemietz, after studying a sheaf of studies from around the world concluded, 'There is overwhelming empirical evidence that planning restrictions have a substantial impact on housing costs.'[97] The USA provides a useful natural experiment since planning control there is largely managed by the individual states and even individual cities. Again, it has been shown that high prices are a response to restrictive planning. In Houston, Texas, where there are minimal controls, housing is truly affordable and more people have accordingly been moving there. Even with a rising population – and therefore increasing demand for housing – Houston has remained affordable. The median home price in recent times has been only 2.3 times median family incomes (2009 figure).[98] This compares with a ratio of 7.1 times in the San Francisco/Oakland area where there are substantial restrictions on development. In 2006, eleven out of twelve states which had price-to-income ratios above 4.0 had some form of restrictive planning.[99] At the other end of the scale, twenty-four out of the twenty-five states where housing was affordable – a ratio below 3.0 – did not have restrictive planning.

Further evidence comes from the timing of events. Housing became unaffordable in California ten years after restrictive planning legislation.[100] In Oregon it was six years after. In King County, Washington, which includes Seattle, it was four years after a boundary was drawn to prevent urban development.

'Everyone agrees not to give permission for land to be built on. But who pays the price? French people who have seen the price of land that that they would like to buy fly out of reach.'

Nicolas Sarkozy, former French President.

Between 1997 and 2010, the price of housing in France jumped 143 per cent while wages rose only 33 per cent.[101] So property became less affordable. Why? Construction costs rose only 44 per cent during this time so that was not the problem. The culprit was the cost of land with planning permission.[102] It rose at least 300 per cent.[103]

Some countries have tried to restrain rising house prices in various ways. They have tried taxing houses or restricting the amount of money lent to house buyers. Such things do not help in the long term. High prices are telling us that there is unsatisfied demand. The only full answer to unsatisfied demand is increased supply – more housing.

Which leads to a final question: how do countries which allow more building manage it? Germany and Switzerland must have their fair share of people who do not want new buildings to spoil their views or invade their countryside. The answer is that building in these countries is by no means uncontrolled. But two circumstances apply. First, planning control is local and, second, taxes are received locally. So local governments have a strong incentive to allow development because taxes imposed on people who are attracted to live locally form a significant part of their income. At the same time, the new housing is more likely to be in sympathy with what local people will accept because it is decided by local politicians who want to be re-elected.

The conclusion seems unusually clear. We would all like to see the poor in decent housing. Many attempts to achieve this have focused on social housing but these efforts have often gone wrong – in some cases, horribly wrong, leading to high rates of unemployment and ghettos of crime. In some countries, housing has become less affordable for the poor – the very opposite of what pretty well everyone wants. The only way to turn this around is to make more land available for building by changing the planning system to incentivise local councils to permit it. Such a policy would benefit, above all, the poor.

6.

'In our liberal society, there is a group of staunchly conservative people: children.'

Inconvenient truths about parenting

I AM IN LONDON, GOING to a talk at the Daiwa Anglo-Japanese Foundation. It has elegant offices in a white stucco terrace facing Regent's Park. On arrival, I am greeted in a polite, deliberate, civilised way. That's how they do things.

The speaker this evening is a young academic from Oxford called Ekaterina Hertog who has done some unusual research. She has made a study of Japanese unmarried parents. Ekaterina says it is well known that there is something unusual about Japanese parenting. The number of children born out of wedlock is tiny compared to most of the rest of the world. In most advanced countries, the proportion of births to unmarried women has risen enormously. In Britain and the USA the figure is up to 43 per cent. But in Japan, the number has barely passed 2 per cent. She set out to discover why.

Some people might respond, 'Oh well, Japan is probably socially conservative. That's the reason.' But that kind of generalisation does not seem to hold water. Ekaterina says that the divorce rate in Japan has risen substantially, just as it has in other countries. The way

Only a tiny proportion of children are born out of wedlock in Japan.

Japan has been notably different from other countries has been in its tiny number of unmarried mothers.

For her research, Ekaterina personally interviewed sixty-eight unmarried mothers in Japan. As if this were not enough, she also interviewed twelve divorced, single mothers. One thing soon became very clear. Most of the unmarried mothers felt terrible about having had children out of wedlock. Half of them remained extremely keen to marry the biological fathers of their children. Ekaterina was astonished by how much they wanted to marry 'even the seemingly least attractive ones'.

Take Yoshiko. She was clearly a capable woman – a full-time nurse, earning more than the man she was living with, who was only working part-time. She told this man she was pregnant and, perhaps, she hoped that he would at least offer to get a full-time job to help pay the bills. But no. He said he was willing to get married but only on the following conditions: 'I like my life as it is. You work, care for the child and do all the housework. I won't help.'

In the West, such an attitude would cause outrage but Yoshiko was so keen to marry the father of her child that she agreed. In the end, the man did not marry her after all. He decided against it when he discovered that Yoshiko had epilepsy.

You may think that Yoshiko would want nothing further to do with this dreadful character. She was doing well in her job and managing to look after her new-born child. Her boss encouraged her to improve her qualifications by doing a PhD. She was not in desperate need of the man. Yet, even then, Yoshiko told Ekaterina she would marry the man if she could.

Why? And why, as Japanese mothers are so determined to marry the fathers, do they feel it is not so bad to be divorced?

In her talk, Ekaterina discusses the various possible explanations put forward by senior academics. But I suspect no one has talked to more unwed mothers in Japan than she has. She has reached a clear idea of what is motivating these women.

'To bring a child into existence without a fair prospect of being able, not only to provide food for its body, but instruction and training for its mind is a moral crime, both against the unfortunate offspring and against society.'

John Stuart Mill[1]

She says there is a widespread belief in Japan that the best framework for a child to develop successfully is with the two biological parents. The mother is seen as the one with primary responsibility for making sure the child works hard and develops successfully. Meanwhile the father's job is to provide a role model, especially to boys. He can maintain discipline so that while the child is indulged by the mother, he or she is kept in order by the father. If the child has problems, like doing badly at school or being naughty, it is believed he or she can be put right by the concentrated efforts of the mother. Presumably this is made easier if the father is out earning the money.

Digging deeper, Ekaterina quizzed the women about whether they would marry a man who was not the father of the child. She found that they were cautious. They believed another man is not as good for the child as the biological father. One remarked, 'These days there is a lot of child abuse, isn't there? Towards others' children. Because this happens often, I am afraid.' Ekaterina reports: 'Marrying anyone apart from the child's biological father was often perceived as putting one's own happiness ahead of that of the child.'

So it all amounts to a certain understanding of what is best for a child and a certain belief that the mother has to do her best for her children. But why then are Japanese women willing to divorce if they think that married, biological parents are so important? Ekaterina suggests that Japanese women believe that by getting married in the first place, they demonstrate that at least they have tried to give their children the best possible chance in life. There is less blame if they have made the attempt. We should also remember that the Japanese divorce rate, while much higher than it used to be, remains lower than in many Western countries. This is despite the fact that many marriages are between couples who, in Western countries, would not have married in the first place. Overall the proportion of children brought up by lone parents is significantly lower than elsewhere.

> # 'The worst abuse against a child is the absence of a parent.'
>
> Title of a paper by Ekaterina Hertog describing the attitude in Japan.[2]

Japan provides one belief system with regard to parenting. Now let's look at another at the opposite end of the scale. The difference is one of the most dramatic in welfare. In Japan, one in fifty children is born out of wedlock. In Sweden, well over half of children are born that way.

I am now in Stockholm and I have been asking those I interview whether people in Sweden are concerned that unmarried parenting might be bad for the children. The question is usually met with a look of puzzlement. It is as though such an idea had never been put to

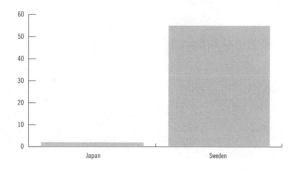

One of the biggest contrasts in the modern world

Births outside marriage, 2010.

Source: OECD[3]

them before. It is outside the normal range of discussion. I also ask whether there has been any research on the subject that has been published in Sweden. Again a look of surprise and uncertainty. It seems the subject is just not on the agenda.

How can that be? The issue is certainly discussed in other Western countries such as Britain and America. A possible answer finally emerges in conversation with an academic, Andreas Bergh.[4] He makes a remark which would be astonishing in many countries. He says divorce is 'viewed positively' in Sweden. Why is that, I ask? Because it shows women are able to live independently of men, he replies.

I follow up his comment in conversation with other Swedes, trying to establish how they think about the subject. Gradually I come to believe that the independence and equality of women is viewed as being of such pre-eminent importance in Swedish society that if it conflicts with other ideas or aims, it is likely to win. In fact, the point may have been reached where anything that might interfere with the independence of women is regarded as automatically unconscionable.

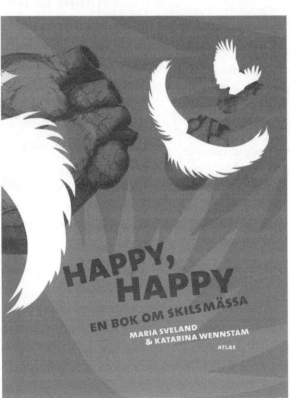

That is why, I suspect, there is no appetite in Swedish society to consider the possibility that lone parenting might be damaging for the children. It might interfere with the freedom of women. Similarly, it is widely assumed in Sweden that day care from an early age does children no harm. I suggest that is because day care enables women to go to work and be independent. In Sweden, parental leave ends when a child is one year old and people there believe that day care from that age is fine. Many people would applaud this.

Incidentally, some people assume that all the Nordic countries are pretty much the same and share similar attitudes. But Finland has a different system and different views, it seems. Financial support

Happy, Happy, published in Sweden in 2011, celebrated divorce as a positive, liberating experience. The flying objects are hearts.

for parents there continues until the child is three years old. Many Finns believe day care before that age can damage a child. It is hard to know whether the rules reflect the different beliefs of people in Sweden and Finland or whether the rules created the beliefs. Perhaps there has been some mixture of rules and beliefs influencing each other. Juho Härkönen, a Finnish sociologist who works in Sweden, suspects that the rules have influenced the beliefs. Human beings have a tendency to believe that behaviour that is endorsed by their government and is widespread must be all right. They also, of course, resist any suggestion that they are doing anything wrong themselves.

Now let's go to a place where things are different again – to Rome. I have arrived at a part of the university not far from the city centre and the famous tourist sites. I go into an old courtyard and find a throng of students and a lively sense of chaos. There are student posters all over the place and a slight sense that the students have taken over. I ask directions and walk up a floor or two to where I find a little office. Amid the bustle, Professor Pugliese suddenly comes in. He is an old-fashioned sort of professor, striding around making confident assertions. This turns out to be the shortest interview in all my research since he has to be elsewhere very soon and is going to hand me over to one of his colleagues. In fact, we talk as he is standing in the doorway, obviously in a hurry to go. It is frustrating but the thing about such professors is that, however assertive and content with themselves they might be, they sometimes make interesting remarks.

I ask him about single parents in Italy and he declares, 'In Italy, single mothers are wealthy!' I am puzzled but he storms on, saying that the upper class in Rome has a lower marriage rate than the rest because being a single mother is a luxury which only the rich can afford. With that, he sweeps out.

After he has gone, I pursue the subject with his colleague and, later, with others. He has pithily highlighted the key thing about lone parenting in Italy. There is very little support for it from the state. That's why only the rich can afford it.

> **'In Italy, single mothers are wealthy!'**
>
> Professor Pugliese

But why is there so little state help for lone parents?

Everyone I speak to takes up the same theme: it is all about the family. The family is the first port of call in the Italian way of thinking about social policy. In principle, it comes before any resort to state welfare. There are important exceptions: pensions, healthcare and education. Otherwise, the Italian belief system is focused on the family as the main source of welfare. The family should provide accommodation for those without homes. It should provide care for the elderly. And if a daughter has a baby but no husband, she may well stay with her parents. The family is an attitude of mind, an ideal and an obligation.

So what happens, I ask, to a young mother who has no man to provide for her and who also, for some reason, cannot get help from her family?

I discover that it depends where she lives. The issue is handled by each region according to its own ideas. But, in some regions, women in this situation may be granted accommodation in *case-famiglia* – 'family houses'. These are small groups of flats run by charities or individuals and subsidised by the local government. There is a parental figure present. A typical *casa-famiglia* might consist of three flats joined together with one kitchen and washing machine between them. A single mother would be lucky to get her own private flat.

Does the mother get a free place at a kindergarten for her child? Perhaps. In some regions, a single mother might get some preference but it varies and there is no guarantee. Italy has the lowest provision of day care facilities in Europe. It all comes back to the family. The family is expected to look after young children.

The father of the baby, in such cases, is pursued for support and, in theory, must pay substantial amounts. But, of course, the father is not always successfully tracked down and made to pay.

Overall, the picture for a single mother without support from a man or her family is much less attractive than it would be in many other countries. If the mother is entitled to substantive benefits at all, it will only be for up to nine months. Then she must work. It is not an attractive option. That is why only the rich can afford it.

You may not be surprised to hear that the rate of lone parenting in Italy is relatively low. Is this due to the culture – the ideal of the family – or is it because the laws make lone parenting unattractive? The two things seem to influence each other and – in combination – they are powerful.

We have now seen three countries with different ideas and also different kinds of state welfare for lone parents. There always seems to be an interplay between the cultures and the welfare systems. This is only a snapshot, of course. All these countries have seen significant changes and they continue to change. Many Italians are concerned that their country is becoming more like Scandinavia. The family is ceasing to be such a cornerstone. A word has been coined to describe what they regard as worrying: defamilisation. The rate of unwed parenting has risen from 4.3 per cent in 1980 to over one in five in 2007.[5] The proportion of children living in single-parent households has increased to one in ten. This is one of the lowest rates of single parenting in the advanced world but it is still quite a shock for Italy.

'It is regarded as a tragedy if a child leaves home at eighteen.' 'Horrible!'

Two people in Madrid emphasising to the author how important families are in Spain.

In some places, though, there is no concern about the trend. The European Union is positively encouraging things that are part and parcel of it. The EU has a target for increasing the availability of day care outside the home.[6] When people talk of day care, they always mean care that is done by people outside the family. The OECD, too, is content that families are losing their grip and that state care is taking their place. These international organisations have taken the view that the Swedish model is best. Their top priority for social policy is similar to Sweden's: enabling independent working women. They are not concerned that there may be any consequent damage to children and implicitly they do not believe that people should stay married for the sake of the children. The only thing that worries the OECD is that single parents tend to be relatively poor. The OECD's preferred solution to this problem seems to be simply to give them more money.

So the trend around the world is overwhelmingly in favour of 'defamilisation'. The proportion of births outside marriage across the advanced world has jumped to a new level. It has happened in a single generation. In 1980, one in nine children was born outside marriage. By 2007, the proportion had soared to one in three. No doubt since 2007 it has continued its rise. The proportion in England and Wales reached 44.3 per cent in 2007 and five years later had moved on to 47.5 per cent.[7]

The worldwide boom in births outside marriage

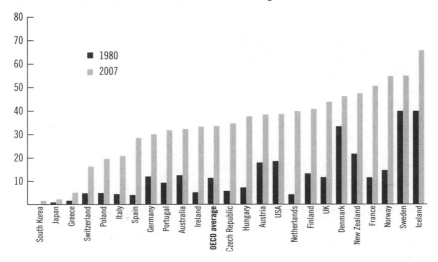

Percentage of children born outside marriage in 1980 and 2007.

Source: OECD, *Doing Better for Families*[8]

By 2007, 15 per cent of children in the advanced world were being brought up by lone parents, 11 per cent by cohabiting couples and 72 per cent by married couples. Since then the proportion with lone parents has increased and in future years it will inevitably continue to do so as the much higher proportions of children now being born to unmarried parents grow up. True, some of the single parents will marry the fathers or mothers of their children. Some, too, are cohabiting at the time of the birth. But even allowing for this and other such factors, it is sure that the proportion brought up by a lone parent will rise. So also will the proportion brought up in households where one of the adults is not the natural parent.

The trend across the world is emphatic. You might even think it is a force of nature and irresistible, whether for good or ill. But is it?

We should, perhaps, note that the numbers in different countries are still very different from each other. In Iceland, two out of three births are outside wedlock. In South Korea, only one in sixty-six is. The extreme variation suggests that being in the modern world does not necessarily mean that mass lone parenting is inevitable. Perhaps there is not a force of nature and we are at a time in human history in which things could turn out in a variety of ways.

One of the biggest contrasts in the modern world

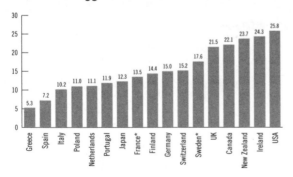

Percentage of children living with one parent (2007). This is a selection of the countries covered by the OECD statistics.

*France and Sweden have the highest rates of children raised by cohabiting couples – 21.0 per cent and 30.5 per cent respectively – and it is possible that, since cohabiting couples tend to break up more readily than married couples, the lone-parenting figures in these countries will increase.
Source: OECD, *Doing Better for Families*.

Ironically Sweden, of all countries, shows that trends in this area can be arrested or even reversed. Births to unmarried women rose quickly between 1980 and 2002.[9] But since then the proportion has plateaued and even fallen back a little. Meanwhile the marriage rate has rallied – from four per thousand adults at the turn of the century to five in 2011, slightly above the European Union average.[10]

The stories from Japan, Sweden and Italy show that there are all sorts of different ideas around about parenting. Who is right about the crucial issues of lone parenting, divorce and the care of infants?

For a start, does lone parenting tend to damage children or not?

There are hundreds of studies on this but let us first pick out one which is unusual because it looks at how happy children are. Often you hear parents say that what they really want for their children, above all else, is for them to be happy.

The research was done by Gundi Knies and her purpose was to look at whether being poor makes children less happy.[11] She drew on figures from a major long-term study of British families with a sample of 4,900 children. These children aged ten and over were asked to assess their level of happiness.

One can imagine that some people associated with the study might have been expecting it to show that being relatively poor makes children unhappy. But that was not the result. Knies found no connection: 'Household income is not associated with child life satisfaction in any of the models we estimated.' Only when the circumstances were so bad that the child suffered 'material deprivation' was happiness affected by income per se.

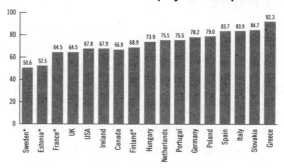

How many children are still brought up by married parents?

Percentage of children living with their married parents. Some of these children are very young and their parents will divorce. So the percentage of children who spend their whole childhoods with their married parents is sure to be lower. These OECD figures fail to distinguish between married couples who are both the natural parents and step-families. So these figures include step-families.

*These countries have among the highest proportion of children living with cohabiting parents: Sweden 30.5 per cent, Estonia 23.9 per cent, France 21.0 per cent and Finland 15.8 per cent.

Source: OECD, *Doing Better for Families.* Selected countries. No figures shown for some countries such as Japan and Australia.

Knies found a completely different factor had a much bigger impact on the happiness of children. The figures showed that it made a really big difference what kind of family the child came from. Those children with two married parents were significantly happier than those from lone-parent families. As Gundi Knies put it, 'the family living context appears to impact hugely on child life satisfaction, living with both biological parents being associated with the greatest happiness.'[12]

One of the unusual advantages of this study is that it differentiates between biological parents and step-families. The result is striking. The study indicates that the children in step-families are significantly less happy than those with their biological parents. More remarkably still, children in step-families are also significantly less happy than those with a single parent.

There is more lone parenting in the USA, Britain, Ireland and Canada than there is in Sweden, Denmark or Finland.[13]

In parenthesis, it is worth mentioning that another finding of this study was that the happiness of these children was quite strongly correlated with whether or not other children at their school 'misbehaved'. The more misbehaviour, the bigger the damage to their happiness. It seems possible that bad or undisciplined schools may help contribute to making children unhappy as well as causing them to do less well academically.

Since there are so many studies of parenting, it would be easy for an author – including me – to pick ones which suit his purpose. So it is important to go to an overall assessment of what the research about lone parenting tells us. A 'meta-analysis' – or 'study of studies' – pools together, with suitable adjustments, the results of many other studies. Paul Amato, Professor of Family Sociology and Demography at Pennsylvania State University, has done several meta-analyses of this subject. What is his assessment?

> Compared with children who grow up in stable, two-parent families, children born outside marriage reach adulthood with less education, earn less income, have lower occupational status, are more likely to be idle (that is, not employed and not in school), are more likely to have a non-marital birth (among daughters), have more troubled marriages, experience higher rates of divorce, and report more symptoms of depression.[14]

It is a devastating summary. The clear answer is that children are better off with their two married, natural parents.

The next issue on which people have different beliefs is the similar but distinct one of divorce. What about those who start off married and then get divorced? How do they fare? Amato says that there are fewer studies of this and there is 'some variation' across the results although generally the outcomes are comparable. For example, one study with a big sample compared how many children dropped out of high school in the USA. The proportion of children of continuously married parents was 13 per cent. The figure jumped to 37 per cent for children of unwed parents and fell only slightly to 31 per cent for children of divorced parents. The rate for children of the divorced was better than that for the never-married but not by very much.

One of the most influential pieces of research into the effect of divorce on children was the California Children of Divorce Project in the 1970s. Academics carefully followed sixty families where the parents were getting divorced. One of the special things about this study was that the researchers spoke to the children several times over. This sometimes got them closer to what a child was really feeling. Robert, for example, was not visited frequently by his father. At the first interview, he told researchers smilingly, 'I have a grand time on his visits' and added, even though he had not been asked, 'I see him enough.' But, in his third interview, Robert admitted that he missed his father intensely. He longed to see his father every day and was profoundly hurt that his father did not come more often.[16]

Children have a strong sense of loyalty to their parents. They want to respect and love them. The study found that 'children lied bravely to protect them [their parents] and to camouflage their own hurt feelings'. This is surely one of the reasons that many parents who divorce often do not understand how painful it is for the children. The children don't tell them. Many divorcing parents believe – or like to believe – that it would be better for the children, as well as themselves, if they divorced. But that is not how most children see it. The study found that fewer than one in ten children was relieved by their parents' decision to divorce even when there was actual physical violence between parents.[17] The report commented, 'Whatever its shortcomings, the family is perceived by the child at this time as having provided the support and protection he needs. The divorce signifies the collapse of that structure and he feels alone and very frightened.'

> 'I suffered when my father left my mother. Now the state is trying to organise the separation of mothers and fathers and I don't want children to go through the same thing I went through.'
>
> Frigide Barjot, author of *J'éduque mes parents* (which can be loosely translated as 'Educating My Parents').[15]

> matter how well-intentioned ents are, no matter how lised they feel they are being, r divorce or separation ays makes children unhappy. ays. Parents separating is just a storm but a hurricane howls through family life … cking children's security.'
>
> pe Leach, *Family Breakdown*[18]

A further issue on which people around the world differ is cohabitation. In some countries, notably Sweden and France, it has become widespread. Supporters of this trend say there is no need for a piece of paper called 'marriage'. In any case, young children are hardly aware of whether their parents are married or not. They have their parents together and that is the main thing for them. Unfortunately cohabiting couples are far more likely to break up. One study in the USA found that a quarter of cohabiting parents broke up within just a year of their child's birth. A separate study of first births found that after five years, 31 per cent of cohabiting couples had split up – almost twice the proportion of married couples (16 per cent).[19]

'There is one group who are bucking the trend. In our liberal society, there is a group of staunchly conservative people who feel that divorces should not be granted except for very weighty reasons. They are children.'

Asta Leppä in *Helsingin Sanomat*, a Finnish newspaper.[20]

It is actually rare for children to be brought up continuously by cohabiting couples. One study found that less than half of one per cent of adolescents aged sixteen to eighteen had spent their entire childhoods with two continuously cohabiting, biological parents. Some have married, of course. But the majority break up, leaving the child with a single parent. In Britain, Harry Benson of the Marriage Foundation estimates that nearly two-thirds (65 per cent) of cohabiting couples who have children are likely to break up by the time a child reaches fifteen.[21]

What about lone parents who find a new partner? Amato says the studies show that when a single parent re-marries, children have similar problems to children of single parents. He adds, chillingly, 'step-children are overrepresented in official reports of child abuse'. Of course, the vast majority of step-parents do not abuse their step-children. But a child is at greater risk. The fears of the Japanese single mother quoted by Ekaterina Hertog have some basis in fact.

Children from broken homes are also far more likely to become juvenile delinquents. A review of the evidence in 1998 concluded that the risk of delinquency was double for children from broken homes and that this association was remarkably consistent over time and in different places.[22] A British study of boys in Newcastle found that 53 per cent of those who had experienced divorce or separation in the first five years of their lives were convicted of a crime by the age of thirty compared with only 28 per cent of the others.[23] In a long-term study of working-class boys in London, 29 per cent who came from 'disrupted' families were convicted of juvenile crimes compared to 18 per cent of children from 'intact' but otherwise similar families.[24]

One might hope that this was just a matter of adolescents going through a bad phase after which they would recover. But the same study found that just over a third of boys from the disrupted families had criminal records as adults compared to 22 per cent from intact families.

This study also looked into whether the child's prospects are improved if a lone mother establishes a relationship with another man. The reverse was the case. The most damaging thing for a child appears to be a series of changes in who looks after him or her. The more changes, the worse.

There is a lot still to be done in disentangling exactly which circumstances tend to do the most or least damage. But it is overwhelmingly clear that children whose homes break up are dramatically more likely to turn to crime. It follows that in countries where there is a high incidence of broken families there will be a higher level of crime than there otherwise would have been. The figures suggest that children from broken families are at least 50 per cent more likely to commit crimes. So if a country's rate of broken parenting rises from, say 5 per cent to 50 per cent, it is conceivable that the crime rate will rise by 20 to 25 per cent above what it would otherwise have been. And since crime is the ultimate anti-social behaviour, it is likely that other kinds of anti-social behaviour will also be significantly more common than they would otherwise have been.

> **'24 per cent of prisoners have been in care at some point during their childhood.'**
>
> UK Ministry of Justice[25]

Some suggest that the bad effects of single parenting and broken families are not mainly due to single parenting itself but rather because single parents are often poor. But many of the studies already cited separate out the impact of being poor from the effect of family breakdown. The one for boys in London, for example, found that broken parenting was correlated with a much higher likelihood of crime even after controlling for the parent being relatively poor and other possible confounding factors. But to what extent does it make sense to separate out the impact of the parent being poor anyway? Other things being equal, being a single parent brings with it the likelihood of being poorer than someone with a partner or spouse. One income amounts to less than two. Yes, the father may pay money to the mother. But the statistics show that a woman is far more likely to be relatively poor if she is a single parent.

> **'...you finish high [sch]ool, get a job, and [get] married before [hav]ing children, you [hav]e a 98 per cent [ch]ance of not being in [pov]erty.'**
>
> [Mayo]r Bloomberg

A lone mother may also have greater expenses such as paying for more childcare. Furthermore it is more expensive for the father and mother to have two separate homes than a single one. Being relatively poor is part and parcel of single parenting, divorce and separation. As Mayor Bloomberg asserted in an advertisement displayed in New York, 'if you finish high school, get a job, and get married before having children, you have a 98 per cent chance of not being in poverty'.

Our main concern in all this is the children. The damage to them is of pre-eminent importance. But bundles of academic studies provide evidence that single and broken parenting do not make the adults happy either. An influential review of them concluded, 'Science tends to confirm Grandma's wisdom. On the whole, man was not meant to live alone and neither was woman. Marriage makes people happier.'[26] Or to put it more grimly, lone mothers are far more likely to get depressed. One Canadian study with a large sample found that single mothers were about twice as likely to have suffered a period of major depression in the previous year as married mothers. The figures were 15.4 per cent for single mothers compared to 6.8 per cent for married ones.[27]

Single mothers are less healthy, too. Another Canadian study found that mothers who had experienced a heart attack or stroke were 3.3 times more likely to be lone mothers than 'partnered'.[28] Married women also live longer: a large-scale long-term study found that among women aged forty-eight, 90 per cent lived to at least sixty-five whereas only 60 per cent of the divorced and never-married did.[29]

Which older people get depressed?

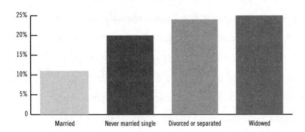

Percentage of people aged fifty-two and older reporting four or more depressive symptoms.[30]

As for the fathers – who are usually the ones without custody – they are also less happy. The same study found that their longevity was similarly affected. Long-term studies have shown that men's psychological well-being is improved by marriage.[31]

Why does marriage make adults happier? One American sociologist, Dr Linda Waite, found that marriage encourages more healthy behaviour.[32] Partners monitor each other's health. Married people are less likely to drink excessively or take illegal drugs. Not surprisingly, men and women who live without adult company are more lonely. Some socialise more in order to compensate, but they return to a home which contains no other adult who cares about them.

Overall, there seems to be a pretty clear answer on all the related issues of lone parenting and divorce. Marriage tends to produce better results for all concerned.

But what is the truth about the other major area where different countries have contrasting views: day care for infants?

Looking at this subject is a bit like walking onto the battlefield of Waterloo or Gettysburg. The ground is littered with the dead and wounded. Jay Belsky's story reflects just a part of this.

Jay Belsky was an able student of child development and worked under Urie Bronfenbrenner, one of the most eminent academics of the time, on a review of the effects of day care on children.[34] Most people regarded the resulting paper as giving day care the green light. It argued that there was little scientific evidence that day care did harm. The paper was very well received.[35]

Over the next eight years, Belsky was repeatedly asked to write and talk about the subject and he reported the same message. Then he wrote a review about the effect of the quality of childcare. He found that if caregivers were attentive, stimulating and affectionate, a child's development could be enhanced. This kind of high-quality care occurred when caregivers were reasonably well trained and the number of children per caregiver was fairly low. This research was applauded and it contributed towards him receiving an award for 'Distinguished Early Contribution in Developmental Psychology' from the American Psychological Association.[36]

> '**Over time, the accumulation of a shared history may become, in itself, a source of meaning, self-definition, and well-being.**'
>
> One of the findings of an academic study of marriage.[33]

A few years after that, in 1986, he was preparing another talk about childcare. He says, 'As I worked my way through the newly emerging evidence, I realised I could no longer tell the same story I had been telling.'[37] So he talked at the conference and wrote in the journal about 'a slow steady trickle of disconcerting evidence' linking day care in a child's first year with things such as 'insecure infant–parent attachment' and increased levels of aggression and disobedience at three to eight years of age. He concluded that childcare in the first year of life should be regarded as a 'risk factor'. A 'risk factor' is not the same as a disaster and may be nullified by other factors. He delivered his talk to an annual convention of paediatricians and published it in a relatively obscure newsletter.

To his astonishment, his article created a 'firestorm'. Articles appeared in the *New York Times*, the *Washington Post*, the *Wall Street Journal* and *Time* magazine. He was accused of being against day care, opposed to women working outside the home and of being 'more or less a misogynist'. 'It was rather amazing how quickly supporters and admirers turned me into the devil incarnate almost overnight,' he wrote later. He came to realise that he had 'run smack into the wall of political correctness before the term was even coined'. He had violated 'the 11th commandment of the field of child development: "Thou shalt not speak ill of day care."'[38]

Belsky later found and reported evidence of actual harm. He was pilloried for doing so. It was as if no one actually cared about what was true. It seemed to him as though the orthodox view was more important to some people than the well-being of children.

The extraordinary outcome of the outrage and controversy was that the American government commissioned a major long-term study costing millions of dollars to get to the bottom of the issue. Belsky, as a leader in his field, was commissioned to work on this but so were his critics. People with opposing views had to work in harness.

They fought over the shape of the great study and the interpretation of the findings. Belsky's account of it sounds like a harrowing marriage counselling session full of angry recriminations. It was called by some 'the study from Hell'. However, at the end of it all, the National Institute of Child Health Study of Early Child Care was produced – one of the biggest such studies ever to have taken place.

What was its conclusion?

There was not just one, unfortunately. There were hundreds, some of which appear, at first sight, to contradict each other. But the green light on day care definitely turned to amber. The research showed that caution was called for. Damage to children was identified. On the other hand, it was not a clear case of 'all day care before the age of three is bad'. According to the report, many things influence how a child turns out and day care is only one of them. It can have a damaging effect but this may be so small as to be insignificant depending on the amount of day care and other circumstances.

Contrary to the earlier emphasis on the quality of day care, the key factor arising from the research seemed to be the quantity.[39] Extensive childcare emerged as a 'significant predictor' of 'problem behaviours' in kindergartens. The greater the quantity of childcare, the more likely the child was to demand lots of attention, get jealous easily, boast, argue a lot, be disruptive and get into fights. Childcare by a relative came out significantly better than childcare in a centre.

Negative behaviour persisted right up to the oldest age assessed by the study: fifteen years. The children had 'significantly' fewer social skills and poorer work habits. One of the most striking results was that when children had a lot of day care, the 'sensitivity' of the mother to the child was lower. There was more 'flatness of emotional engagement with the child', lower sensitivity to the distress of the child and less stimulation of the child's 'cognitive development'. The children correspondingly had 'less positive engagement' with the mother.[40] In other words, there is a risk that a large quantity of day care can damage the quality of the interaction between mother and child. Childcare was only one factor, though. The study also found it was a risk factor if the parents were relatively poor or unmarried.[41]

The paper concluded that 'the negative effects [of day care] found in these studies are not large' but 'even low or moderate risks are significantly multiplied by their widespread prevalence'.[42]

There has been plenty of other research since, of course. A major study by Stanford University and the University of California, Berkeley in 2005 gathered data from more than 14,000 infants in kindergarten, their parents and their teachers, measuring social behaviour and skills, like aggression and bullying, sharing, cooperation and engagement in classroom tasks. It found: 'Attendance in pre-school centers, even for short periods of time each week, hinders the rate at which young children develop social skills.'[43] It also found that the negative impact on social behaviour was particularly strong 'for black children and children from the poorest families'. But the effect was not limited to any one race or class. Middle-class, white children who attended pre-school suffered lower social skill levels than similar children who remained at home in the care of a parent. Meanwhile, another study found that children in day care have higher levels of cortisol – a hormone induced by stress – than children being cared for by their mothers.[44]

What about the age from which a child has day care? It is clear from the various studies that the first year is critical and day care then is not appropriate. Beyond that, the evidence is not so easy or clear. The National Institute study suggests that the total amount of care matters, not so much when it is given. Another study – specifically of boys in their second year – found that those with 'moderate' or 'high' other risk factors were 'significantly' more likely to have problems with 'interactions and behaviours' if they had more than twenty hours a week of non-maternal care.[45] It seems there is no definite age at which an 'all clear' sounds.

The quality of care matters. Unfortunately there are reasons to be concerned that, in many countries, this is deteriorating.

In Sweden, the number of infants cared for per adult has increased dramatically. Jonas Himmelstrand, who studies childcare issues, says that an experienced pre-school teacher he talked to remembers that in 1980, there was

> 'The most recent studies convincingly suggest that neither a pro-day care nor an anti-day care stance is tenable because the effects of day care on children depend on the caring institution and its personnel and on the age, family experiences and characteristics of individual children being cared for.
>
> Naturally parents who are seeking more and more day care for younger and younger infants are looking for economic improvement in their own lives, but not many would do so if they believed that they earned money at their children's expense.
>
> It is clearly and certainly best for babies to have something close to full-time mother care for six months at least – conveniently linked with breast-feeding – and family care for a further year and better two. Using financial or career penalties to blackmail women into leaving infants who are scarcely settled into life outside wombs that are still bleeding is no less than barbarous.'
>
> Penelope Leach, *Children First*[46]

a ratio of two and a half young children per adult. But today, the ratio can reach as high as 5.7 children per adult (seventeen children to three adults).[47] In Britain, the government has announced that the number of infants that may be looked after by a child minder will be increased from four to six. This obviously reduces the time available for each infant. In several countries, it seems that the initial quality that may have been possible with small numbers of children per adult has become financially more problematic as the numbers have grown.

Himmelstrand has argued that Swedish people, in their extensive use of day care, are not genuinely 'following their hearts'. The same thought has been expressed by Penelope Leach, the British child development specialist, who wrote: 'People are expected to feel strongly about their children, but not to act upon those feelings.'[48] Many mothers feel awful when they first leave their infants at day care. They may quell their emotions because they know that what they are doing is normal. They may assume that as everyone else is doing it, it must be all right.

It seems possible, to put it no higher, that the feeling that some mothers experience in this situation is an instinct that has evolved because the child truly does want and need her at this time. Humans are, of course, different from monkeys but it might be worth mentioning one of the most famous experiments in all psychology since it is highly relevant.

A baby monkey pathetically clings with its hind legs to its cloth 'mother' while drinking from its milk 'mother'.

Harry Harlow sought to establish what an infant monkey really wants. If previous psychologists like Freud were right, what they wanted from their mothers was milk. To find out, Harlow put baby monkeys into cages with two available surrogate 'mothers'. One was made of cloth and the other was made of metal but provided milk. Which would the babies choose? The outcome was clear and poignant. The infant monkeys spent nearly all their time with their cloth mother, 'clinging to, climbing on and pushing themselves into the soft folds'.[49] But, of course, they need milk and one of the photographs from the experiment shows a little monkey hanging on to the cloth mother with its hind legs and reaching across to take milk from the metal mother. The monkeys were so attached to their surrogate mothers that they did not want to leave them even for milk.

In another experiment, young monkeys were put with their cloth mothers in a room full of toys. After a while, they would eventually climb down from their 'mother' to explore but would often return to touch her and re-connect. If the cloth mother was removed from the room, all play would stop and 'frantic screaming ensued'.[50] In essence, this is a sad story of an infant being deprived of its sense of security.

Human infants can also scream when removed from their mothers at an early age. Or else they may go quiet.[51] John Bowlby observed that when children are separated from their attachment figures for a long time, as in a hospital stay, they quickly descend into passivity and despair. When children know they have a secure attachment figure available, they go out and explore confidently. He argued that when children are denied a stable and enduring attachment relationship – raised, for example, by a succession of foster parents – they are likely to be damaged for life.[52]

> 'The priority for any formulation of childcare policy should be: will this be good for the child's well-being? Sadly this question is very rarely asked. The growing child is simply viewed as an impediment to work.'
>
> Jill Kirby[53]

Where does all that leave us?

The picture is not clear and different people will react differently to the evidence. Personally it leaves me with considerable concern about children being packed off to a large quantity of childcare sessions before the age of one. I am also somewhat concerned about it for children under two. I feel there is reason to be cautious about it even up to the age of three. Penelope Leach summarised it this way:

> Of course nobody can say, 'At such and such an age your child needs you to be around this many hours a day and any fewer will be disastrous for him or her,' but it would be fair to say, 'The more you are around, the better, and the younger the child, the more it matters.'[54]

After reading the research on the subject, I confess I look back at how my own children were raised and wish we had given them more parental care for longer.

Some may be thinking, 'This discussion of day care and parenting is all very well but what has it got to do with welfare states?'

The relevance is this: welfare states may be influencing the incidence of both lone parenting and day care. In this way, they may be affecting the happiness and well-being of millions of children and their parents.

Do welfare states affect the rates of lone parenting and day care?

Let's take lone parenting first. There is plenty of anecdotal evidence of this. But what is needed is a proper academic survey comparing benefits in different countries and analysing whether these benefits have changed the rate of single parenting.

Fortunately one person has done such a study: Libertad Gonzales at the University of Barcelona. Because her work on this is so significant, I have come to Barcelona mainly for the purpose of talking to her about it.

Libertad Gonzalez: welfare benefits can increase the rate of lone parenting.

It is a lovely sunny morning when I reach the part of the university where she works. The buildings are unusual – like military barracks around a rectangular parade ground. I go in and find a series of long corridors with doors into rooms at regular intervals as if they were monks' cells. These are the offices of the academics.

I find Libertad's door and, after saying hello, she suggests we go outside for a coffee. We find an unpretentious little coffee bar nearby and I quiz her about her findings. In her studies, she concluded that a difference of €1,000 per year received by lone mothers results in a difference of two percentage points in the rate of lone parenting in that country. So, in a given country, an extra 1,000 of benefits would result in the rate of lone parenting being, say, 7 per cent instead of 5 per cent. Her conclusion, despite the caveats which academics tend to add, is pretty clear. Welfare benefit levels do influence the amount of lone parenting.

But I want to check out how her calculations were arrived at. I ask her if her figures were based on the people most likely to be affected by benefits – the relatively poor. No, she says. They were based on the overall female population. So her figures – while powerful enough as they stand – understate the effect on the less well off.

Next I ask her if she included the value of subsidised or free housing given to lone parents in certain countries. No, she says, she did not. Again, this means the power of benefits to influence lone parenting is likely to be understated since free or subsidised housing can be very valuable.

The poor are influenced towards single parenting by welfare benefits more than the rich

Social class A: 2%

Social class E: 23%

Rates of teenage pregnancy by social class of the woman's father in Britain.[55] Teenage pregnancy here acts as a broad brush proxy for single parenting.

'ACCORDING TO THE AUSTRALIAN INSTITUTE of Health and Welfare, "a relatively high proportion of substantiations [of reported child abuse and neglect] involved children living in lone mother families". The Australian Institute of Family Studies estimates that child abuse in such households is "about two and half times higher than would be expected given the number of children living in such families".

'This problem was created by the Whitlam government when it introduced the single mothers' pension in 1973. This made it possible for women who did not work and did not have bread-winning husbands to raise children at taxpayers' expense. What has ensued is the rise of a dysfunctional underclass of welfare-dependent single mothers with a complex range of personal and social problems, including substance abuse, domestic violence, and an inability to properly parent children ...

'But we are reluctant to admit this because telling the truth about "diverse" family structures is not politically correct. We are culturally deaf, as it were, to the fact that all "families" are patently not equal when it comes to securing the welfare of children.'

Dr Jeremy Sammut, research fellow at the Centre for Independent Studies, Sydney.[56]

As we saw in the previous chapter, the countries with the highest rates of lone parenting respectively in the world and in Europe are the United States and Britain. These are countries where the allocation of housing is based primarily on need so single mothers are favoured. There may be no stated priority for single mothers but there is a de facto priority.[57] Single mothers account for 57 per cent of working-age households in public housing in the USA. Only 8 per cent of all public housing households are married couples.[58]

So the evidence from Libertad Gonzales's work is that the benefits offered to single parents increase the rate of single parenting. Her findings are likely to understate the reality because she did not focus on the poor – those most likely to be affected – and did not include the impact of subsidised housing, which may well have as much or more impact than cash benefits. True, there are some less focused studies which have come to more mixed conclusions. But most, like Libertad's, do not look particularly at those on low incomes or the impact of subsidised housing. The country-by-country analysis overwhelmingly suggests that, yes, welfare states can increase the rate of lone parenting. Italy, for example, has barely any benefits for lone mothers and has a low incidence of lone

'Shoes under the bed'

Government officials in Britain and the USA from time to time visit the homes of single parents receiving welfare benefits to check that a boyfriend is not living there. They look for such things as men's shoes under the bed and toilets with the seat left up.[59] If they find a boyfriend or husband is living with the woman, her benefits will be reduced or withdrawn.

parenting. Britain has a history of special benefits for lone mothers and a much higher rate of lone parenting.

As for whether government policies affect the amount of day care, that hardly needs discussion. The incidence of day care for infants is far higher in those countries where the state subsidises it than in those where it does not. In Sweden, where it is highly subsidised, 92 per cent of children aged between one and three are in day care – an extraordinary figure and far higher than in most other countries.

> '**I have discussed the German principle of generational solidarity at a number of seminars and conferences in Britain and Australia, and on every occasion, somebody ventures the opinion that it is "unfair" to expect grandparents to pick up the tab if the parents fail in their responsibilities to their children. But if it is unreasonable to expect grandparents to contribute to the upkeep of their grandchildren, how much more unreasonable is it to expect complete strangers to do so through their taxes?'**
>
> Peter Saunders[60]

To sum up: some welfare states are, by their policies, encouraging single and broken parenting. It is pretty clear that these things tend to damage children. Other welfare states are encouraging day care, which is probably of declining quality and may also harm children depending on the quality and circumstances. Overall, to put it bluntly, welfare states are causing unhappiness for millions of children. These children are consequently doing less well at school. A higher proportion of them are becoming criminals, which ruins their own lives and damages the lives of others. And among adults, too, there is greater unhappiness and loneliness.

Sweden is a wonderful country but frankly it is in denial about these things. That is not to argue that the position in Japan is ideal either. There the position of women is at the opposite extreme and surely unduly limits their ability to enjoy and enhance their lives. But the ideas there about the importance of parental care are closer to the mark than Sweden's. Of the three countries we looked at to begin with, Italy's way of parenting and caring for children seems closest to the best, without necessarily being ideal.

The key thing that more of us would probably like to aim for is some way to combine a sense of duty to the children we bring into the world with reasonable respect for the interests of adults. But this isn't easy. On one hand, we want women to be able to pursue careers as they may wish and be independent. But on

> '**We know the statistics: t children who grow up withou father are five times more likely live in poverty and commit cri nine times more likely to drop of school and twenty times m likely to end up in pris**
>
> Barack Obama, 2

the other hand, children appear to benefit from care from their mothers in their early years. Also we might want to avoid encouraging single parenting by not offering taxpayers' money to subsidise it. But, in the short term, that means that more single mothers will go out to work and be unable to care for their infants as much as would be ideal.

These problems are not easy to resolve. It is certainly desirable that marriage should re-establish itself as the overwhelmingly normal way to bring up children but even here caution is required. It may not be necessary or respectful of human liberty to create subsidies for marriage. It is probably only necessary to remove as much as possible of the discrimination that exists in some countries against marriage in favour of single parenting. The financial and emotional advantages of marriage and the benefit to the children are clear. They have led people to marriage in the past and should be able to do so again. Marriage should not need government help – only the removal of policies which have undermined it.

> 'Family members helping each other only represents a "huge saving to the government" if you think the government should be paying and providing for everything.'
>
> Peter Saunders[62]

This is a difficult area but, bearing in mind the experiences of different countries and the research, here are the policies I would suggest:

- Single mothers should be given no priority over married couples in the allocation of social housing.

- Single and married parents should be given a personal tax allowance in respect of each child. This is better than a cash grant because it automatically encourages at least one parent to work.

- Social insurance (earned through contributions) should provide women – whether with a partner or not – with an income for the first three months after a child's birth.

- If a mother has no partner or husband and has not worked to gain insurance, she should be expected to pay for her own accommodation or else live with her parents. In cases of emergency need, she should be able to seek assistance from charities, subsidised by government, running hostels as in Wisconsin.

- Any state subsidies for day care should be matched by allowances for home care, including by family members, otherwise the state is incentivising parents to have their children looked after by non-family members.

- Government subsidies for day care should not be extensive because they might unintentionally encourage lone parenting.

- If a single mother works, some of the cost of day care should come from her income so the natural incentive to prefer child care by family members is not removed. This would also reduce the cost to taxpayers.

Some of these policies are normal in various countries. In other countries, they might be highly controversial. But in the end, most people believe the interests of children should have priority. The evidence is that they benefit from having their two natural parents married and with them. They want the loving care of their mother for a large part of their baby and infant years. Children, as Asta Leppä has said, are 'staunchly conservative people'.

'People used to be grateful and eager. Now the attitude is: "I want this. You get it for me."'

The effect of welfare states on behaviour

I T'S 1953 AND THE BIGGEST British sporting event of the year is the Cup Final match between Bolton and Blackpool. Both sides have some of the country's best footballers playing for them: Nat Lofthouse, for Bolton, is one of the greatest centre forwards Britain has ever produced. Stanley Matthews, for Blackpool, is a brilliant right-winger who plays for England too.

Bolton starts sensationally. Lofthouse scores within ninety seconds and Bolton builds on this beginning. With three-quarters of the match gone, Bolton leads 3–1.[1]

Then Stanley Matthews gets through on the right wing and sends a cross to Stan Mortensen, who scores. The Blackpool team keeps feeding the ball to Matthews because of his ability to dribble past other players. But Bolton is still ahead 3–2 with only two minutes left. Blackpool then gets an equaliser from a free kick. Finally, in injury time, with only seconds remaining, Matthews again gets through on the right wing and his pass leads to another goal. So Blackpool wins 4–3 at the

Nat Lofthouse: gracious in defeat.

last moment. It's a sensational game. But for Lofthouse, this must be a moment of great disappointment. How does he react?

If he were a typical modern English player, he would bury his head in his hands, absorbed in his own misery. But this is 1953. Behaviour is different. Lofthouse and his fellow Bolton player Malcolm Barrass stand and applaud Matthews, the very man who has robbed them of victory.[2]

Let's go back a little further. It's 1936 and Adolf Hitler is the Führer and Reichskanzler of Germany. The Olympic Games are being held in Berlin and Hitler wants them to demonstrate the superiority of the Aryan race. But Jesse Owens, a black athlete from the USA, is stealing the show, winning gold in the 100 metres, 200 metres and the 100 metres relay. He is also entered for the long jump. In the qualifying heats, Owens does a foul in his first attempt and comes up short in his second. He is only allowed three goes. If he fails in his last attempt, he will not be in the final.[3] Luz Long, his greatest rival and a German, goes up to him. He suggests Owens should change his marks for the run up. Owens takes his advice and successfully qualifies. He then goes on to win gold, pushing Long into second place.

What does Long do after being defeated, knowing that he himself helped bring this about? He hurries over to Owens to be the first to congratulate him. Owens and Long run round the stadium together in a joint lap of honour.[4]

Such sporting behaviour sometimes still occurs today. But it is surely rarer. Behind it lies a certain idea of how people should behave. Sir Donald Bradman, considered by many to be the greatest batsman who ever lived, described a part of it:

> When considering the stature of an athlete or for that matter any person, I set great store in certain qualities which I believe to be essential in addition to skill. They are that the person conducts his or her life with dignity, with integrity, courage, and perhaps most of all, with modesty. These virtues are totally compatible with pride, ambition, and competitiveness.[5]

But gradually a change has taken place. In cricket, it was certainly under way by the mid-1960s. That was when 'sledging' made its first appearance in Australia. 'Sledging' is the practice of insulting an opposing player to try to put him off his game. A typical tactic is to suggest that the batsman is useless. Another is to make a joke implying that the sledger has had sex with the batsman's wife.[6]

This was a distinct change. Sunil Gavaskar, another of the game's greats, said that in his early years in the game, there was some good-humoured banter in key matches.

But what was banter in days gone by – and which was enjoyed by everyone, including the recipient of it – today has degenerated to downright personal abuse.[7]…

I played more than one test match for my country [in fact he played 125] with and against bowlers who took hundreds of wickets and there was hardly a word uttered in anger on the field. Yes, towards the end of my career I did get referred to a couple of times by a part of the female anatomy and, more than anger, it saddened me to hear that.

Some players, such as Shane Warne, one of Australia's most talented spinners, have been proud of their insults. According to Warne, Merv Hughes, another bowler, claimed that a quarter of his wickets were due to sledging.[8] The idea that winning is of prime importance has been taking precedence over the idea that one should behave decently and honourably.

What about honesty in sport? Gary Sobers, another cricketing legend, used to tell the umpire if a ball he caught had bounced on the ground beforehand, with the result that an opponent who might have been declared 'out' was not. He cared more about being honest than winning. But the idea that one should be honest has faded. Gavaskar commented, 'Thanks to the win-at-all-costs theory, appeals are made even though the fielders know that the batsman is not out. There is the other side, of course, where a batsman knows he is out but stays put.'

It is striking that those at the forefront of sledging and dishonesty have been from Anglo-Saxon countries: Australia, New Zealand and Britain. Prominent players best known for opposing it have been from India and the West Indies. Viv Richards from the West Indies, another all-time great, was infuriated by such behaviour. When Hughes repeatedly stared him down after bowling in a match in the Caribbean, Richards finally snapped: 'This is my island, my culture. Don't you be staring at me. In my culture we just bowl.'[9] It is as if the Third World was trying to give the First World a lesson in manners.

Stories of cheating and insulting opponents have spread to many sports. Often the media does not condemn it. That shows how far the change in culture has penetrated. It has even reached the point where television commentators congratulate players on their cheating. According to one American correspondent, 'complimenting players who trick a referee occurs in every televised NBA [National Basketball Association] game I have ever seen'. Naturally such attitudes are imitated by children. In middle schools, 'basketball players train on how to move their body to make it look like they have drawn a foul'. Or as one journalist put it, 'parents … encourage their prepubescent children in Little League to imitate Derek Jeter and Dewayne Wise and fake getting hit by a pitch'.[10]

Some people may feel that the sporting gestures of previous generations were silly and misguided. They may think that sledging and cheating are fine and sensible – just part of the modern game. They make excuses: 'everyone does it and you would be a fool not to' or 'the reason for the change is just the extra money now' and so on.

Stepping back a bit, it is worth recognising that, at all times and places, people tend to accept what is normal. We are all swept up in the culture of our time. Many people resist the idea that their culture has deteriorated compared to an earlier generation even if the evidence is clear. That is understandable. But I would ask the reader to imagine that we are flying over time and space, trying to observe objectively. As we fly high above, we look down on different countries and cultures in past centuries. Look at how dramatically morals and attitudes have changed.

There are extraordinary contrasts. We see soldiers in the First World War on both sides showing astonishing courage and willingness to face death. We marvel at how that they believed they were fighting in a great and glorious cause. The idea of honour keeps cropping up at various times but in different forms. We see aristocrats in the seventeenth century prepared to fight a duel to the death if their 'honour' is impugned. During the reign of Henry IV of France perhaps 10,000 gentlemen died for their 'honour'. The Chevalier d'Andrieux killed seventy men in duels before his thirtieth birthday.[11] Here the concept of honour seems to have a lot to do with asserting one's status, dignity and courage.

This idea of honour has something in common with that of Japan in the nineteenth century and before. Samurai committed suicide – 'seppuku' – if they felt they had been – or would be – dishonoured. Again, it seems largely a matter of personal dignity achieved through courage. The Japanese concept of honour persisted into the Second World War. Allied troops in Burma watched in astonishment as a platoon of Japanese soldiers marched in good order into the river to commit suicide to avoid the 'dishonour' of capture.[12] The ideas of 'giving face' and 'loss of face' have been a continuing part of life in East Asia to varying degrees. This concept of personal dignity has included the idea that losing one's temper is undignified.

A somewhat different concept of honour appears in *Othello*, first performed between 1601 and 1604. It includes such things as doing one's duty, being faithful to one's spouse, courage and honesty. One of the characters, Cassio, says, 'Reputation, reputation, reputation! Oh, I have lost my reputation! I have lost the immortal part of myself, and what remains is bestial.'

Two centuries later, 'honour' of another kind appears in *Pride and Prejudice*, published in 1813. One of the characters, Lydia Bennet, has an affair with George Wickham. Jane Austen takes it for granted that Lydia's whole life will be ruined as a result. In fact, the whole family's prospects will be destroyed. Obviously that is a big contrast with many countries now.

Then there are some completely different systems of belief. If we go across to America in 1917, we find many Quakers refusing to serve in the First World War because they were opposed to all forms of violence. Several other religions have had embedded in them a duty of people to contribute money or goods to the religious order concerned and/or to the poor. In Britain, people had to contribute a tenth of their grain to the church. Among modern Mormons, the practice of giving a tenth of one's income remains strong today. In Islam, the prophet Mohammed initiated the *zakat*: money that had to be given by adherents to the poor. In these religions, there seem to be two ideas combined: that one should give money as an act of piety – to honour God – and also as an act of kindness. One thing that has influenced believers to be virtuous has been a promise of paradise accompanied by a threat of hell, otherwise.

If we fly back further to the second century AD, we find the Roman aristocracy widely adopting an approach to life which we now call 'stoicism'. At an outpost of the Roman Empire, we find the Emperor himself, Marcus Aurelius, writing down some of this philosophy: 'So what is left worth living for? This alone: justice in thought, goodness in action, speech that

It was taken for granted that Lydia Bennet's affair would ruin her life.

cannot deceive, and a disposition glad of whatever comes, welcoming it as necessary, as familiar, as flowing from the same source and fountain as yourself.'[13] It amounts to an ideal of personal behaviour.

Let's swoop forward now to England in 1549. The Book of Common Prayer has just been published. The writing of it was guided by Thomas Cranmer, who had been made Archbishop of Canterbury by Henry VIII. It includes a powerful concept of mankind's sinfulness and, implicitly, an insistence that we humans should strive to do better. It includes these words: 'We have left undone those things which we ought to have done and we have done those things which we ought not to have done, and there is no health in us.'[14] It is hard to imagine a more unequivocal assertion of mankind's sinfulness.

Moving further ahead to 1973, we see the first showing of a L'Oréal advertisement with the tag-line 'Because I'm worth it'.[15] We have gone from a Christian belief in original sin to an assertion of 'original virtue' or worth.

The purpose of this journey has been to suggest that cultures, values and even national characters can and do change. The Italians today bear little relation to Marcus Aurelius. Not many Frenchmen are now keen to fight duels to the death.

I want to suggest that in modern times – and in the course of only one or two generations – attitudes and behaviour and so on have also changed or begun to change in some countries. The stories from football, athletics, cricket and basketball at the beginning of the chapter illustrate part of the change that has taken place in some Anglo-Saxon countries from one set of attitudes to another. These are only anecdotes, of course. It is very difficult to prove such changes with objective statistics.

Let's look at another part of modern life. It is not that long ago, in 1946, that the American film *It's a Wonderful Life* had its premiere. The film celebrates a man who behaves kindly and decently. He sacrifices any chance of being famous or rich in order to do what is decent. Another film, *High Noon*, a classic western starring Gary Cooper, was first shown six years later. It praises a man for his courage in standing alone and facing likely death in a good cause.

It's A Wonderful Life celebrates a man who behaves decently and kindly.

Now let's fly forward to 2011. We find another American film in which very different behaviour is treated as normal and acceptable. *Bridesmaids* is a comedy in which much of the behaviour is mean and selfish. 'Gross-outs' proliferate, including vomiting, farting and defecating.[16] The *Inbetweeners Movie* is another comedy released the same year. A British film this time, it is about a group of teenagers who go on holiday in Greece to get drunk and have sex.[17] There is an almost complete absence of kindness shown by any of the characters. Instead there are insults and humiliations. Both these films were popular. People who enjoyed them may think that it is ridiculous to take them seriously. They were comedies, not moral lectures. But all films, plays and novels reflect something of the culture from which they spring and probably help spread that culture. The comedies of sixty or seventy years before, such as *Bringing Up Baby* with Cary Grant and Katharine Hepburn, had no such meanness or vulgarity.

I am suggesting that changes in sport and films reflect how to some degree our cultures, attitudes and beliefs have changed over the past generation or two. If that is right, why has it happened?

There are plenty of possibilities: the development of feminism and women's rights, which, in turn, might perhaps have been encouraged by the reduction in the importance of the physical strength of men as agricultural work and military prowess have become less significant; the vast increase in wealth across the world; the advances of science and the possibly related decline of religion; improved medical techniques and hygiene, which, along with greater wealth, have increased life expectancy; improved contraception, reducing the degree to which women need be concerned about becoming pregnant as a result of sex. There are many candidates.

But one other factor that may have changed behaviour in modern societies could be the development of welfare states. How could this work? In a variety of ways.

1. Welfare states → unemployment → crime?

I have argued (Chapter 2) that more people are unemployed because of welfare states. A number of studies indicate that unemployment causes alienation from the rest of society. Younger unemployed males, in particularly, can feel resentment and anger. Their resentment may make them feel rebellious and believe that selfishly grabbing what they want is justifiable.

It is true that only a minority of people are unemployed at any one time. But a much bigger – and growing – part of the population has at one time or another been through this depressing and disaffecting experience. Unemployment rates are higher among the young and young men are known to be more likely to behave anti-socially than any other category of men or women.

The ultimate in alienated behaviour is crime. Do the unemployed commit more crime? The bare figures are startling. In a study of British prisoners, two-thirds had been unemployed before their imprisonment.[18] This is a strong correlation but it is not immediately clear which thing causes the other. Does being a criminal cause unemployment or the other way round or both? Previously convicted criminals certainly find it harder to get jobs because of their convictions. But does unemployment cause crime?

One indication of what is going

The unemployed are more likely to commit crimes

Percentage unemployed in the general population and percentage unemployed before imprisonment in Britain.

Source: Social Exclusion Unit report[19]

on is what criminals themselves say. In one study, over half of prisoners said unemployment was a contributing factor leading to their crimes.

A study in France provides more rigorous evidence. It looked at changes in unemployment in different areas to see whether rising unemployment led to a consequent increase in crime. It found that 'increases in youth unemployment induce increases in crime' and that 'this effect is causal for burglaries, thefts and drug offences'.[20] The use of the word 'causal' in academic literature is notable because particularly good evidence is needed before the word is used. Normally a study only says that one thing is 'correlated' with another. Meanwhile another study of 402 districts in Germany found that youth unemployment 'plays a prominent role in explaining property crime, namely housing burglary'.[21] It is true that a causal relationship between unemployment and crime is not supported by all the different kinds of study but the evidence that does support the idea is extremely strong.[22]

One unexpected finding of the research is that the unemployed seem more likely to be the victims of crime too – at least of violent crime. One study – albeit on a small scale and only of male-on-male homicide – found that 70 per cent of murder and manslaughter victims were unemployed.[24]

Unemployment does indeed appear to lead to higher levels of crime. So welfare states which cause high unemployment are responsible for a higher level of crime

Torching cars has become a New Year's Eve tradition in France. On New Year's Eve 2013, it was considered good news that 'only' 1,0[...] cars had been burned.[23]

than there would otherwise be. Moreover crime is the tip of an iceberg of anti-social or uncivil behaviour.[25]

2. Lone parents and broken families → crime and uncivil behaviour

I have also argued that some welfare states have caused more lone parenting and broken families (see Chapter 6). I suggested that this has tended to damage the children in many ways and has made them more likely to turn to crime. Some of the statistics on this are dramatic.

A study of US prisoners found that 43 per cent had lived in a single-parent household for most of the time they were growing up and a further 14 per cent had lived in households with neither parent.[26] So a majority of prisoners had not spent most of their young years with both their parents. At the time – 1991 – this was a big contrast with the average population in the USA. A national long-term study of youths subsequently found: 'Family background matters. Adolescents raised in families where both parents are present are much less likely to engage in crime.'[27]

In Britain, one study found that more than a quarter of prison inmates (27 per cent) had been taken into care as a child – a stunningly high statistic considering what a small percentage overall is taken into care.[28] And, again, family circumstances have been crucial because most times a child is taken into care, he or she is not living with both natural parents.[29]

There are some studies in which the significance of lone parenting or broken homes appears as a relatively minor factor. However, such studies break down possible factors into multiple categories such as 'poor parenting', 'lack of parental controls', 'lack of parental closeness' and suchlike. This can be misleading by minimising the fact that these difficulties are more common among lone parents.[30]

Some criminologists argue that the key thing explaining different levels of crime around the world and through history is the influence of others who lead people towards crime. That idea is entirely consistent with the theory that an intact family with both natural parents provides a strong influence against crime.[31]

Lone parenting is, of course, only one factor. It would be remarkable if its effect could be detected in national crime figures. But just in case, I have looked at whether there is any correlation at all. I have had to use dates that are not ideal. The effect of unwed parenting should probably take at least twelve to fourteen years to show through fully in crime levels and suitable figures with a gap of that length are not to hand. Despite these obstacles there is indeed a correlation between national rates of lone parenting and rates of assault. The R squared figure – indicating the strength of the correlation – is only 0.235, which is relatively low. But it is remarkable that there is any correlation at all.

Is there a link between lone parenting and crime?[32]

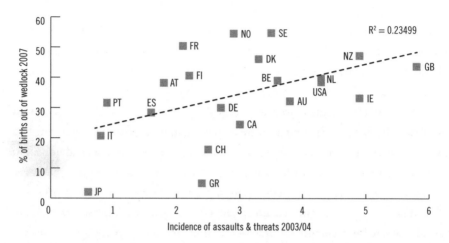

Overall, to the extent that welfare states increase lone or broken parenting, they cause crime to be higher than it otherwise would be. Again, it is likely that crime is an indicator of other anti-social behaviour. One might add that, to the extent that welfare states encourage and implicitly approve of lone parenting, they undermine the sense that parents previously had that they should stay together for the sake of the children. In other words, some welfare states discourage a sense of duty to children.

3. Poor-quality state education → crime and uncivil behaviour

An astonishingly high proportion of children – 18 per cent – have been left functionally illiterate by their schools, as we saw in Chapter 4. I argued there that the remarkably common failure of government schools to teach children to read properly tends to lead to crime. I should add that some criminologists hotly contest the idea that literacy is linked to crime. They suggest, for example, that criminals tend to be young males of a certain social background and that others from a similar background may be no more literate than the ones who end up in prison.[33] This kind of debate is difficult since so many factors are at work simultaneously. An Irish study persuasively summed up its conclusions like this: 'There is no suggestion that the relationship is a simple causal one ... However there is a considerable body of evidence showing that poor literacy skills restrict a range of life choices (particularly employment), and thus become a pre-disposing factor in criminal activities.'[34]

If we were in a society where it was easy to get and keep work despite being illiterate, there would be no reason for poor literacy to cause crime. That was the situation in the early nineteenth century and before. Now, though, literacy is necessary for most kinds of work. And nowadays, functionally illiterate children are legally required to stay at school even though they cannot follow what is being taught. Is it not inevitable that they become frustrated and irritated?

Tuggy Tug and his gang turned to crime and gang life as a way of getting the self-esteem that all of us seek.[35] Education and employment had been closed off to them mainly because a government school failed them. They had, as the Irish report put it, 'a restricted range of "life choices"'. In fact, Tuggy Tug was affected by all three factors mentioned so far: lone parenting, unemployment and a failed education. If you put these three together, the combination is social dynamite. Welfare states have increased the incidence of all of them.

There is a further way in which government schooling may have affected attitudes and behaviour. In many countries it has come to be seen as dogmatic or wrong to teach children values. The idea is that children should discover them on their own. In the USA, this idea gained popularity in the so-called 'values clarification' movement. As Jonathan Haidt has written: 'Values clarification ... urged teachers to refrain from imposing values on anyone. Although the goal of inclusiveness was laudable, it had unintended side effects. It cut children off from the soil of tradition, history, and religion that nourished older conceptions of virtue.'[36]

The decision not to teach values has not

Basic training for the twentieth-century English gentleman

If you can keep your head when all about you

Are losing theirs and blaming it on you,

If you can trust yourself when all men doubt you,

But make allowance for their doubting too;

If you can wait and not be tired by waiting,

Or being lied about, don't deal in lies,

Or being hated, don't give way to hating,

And yet don't look too good, nor talk too wise:

The first verse of 'If' by Rudyard Kipling.[37] After all the 'ifs', he concludes: 'Yours is the Earth and everything that's in it, And — which is more — you'll be a Man, my son!' The poem is in praise of uncomplaining courage, modesty, decency, self-reliance and self-control.

happened everywhere, of course. When I visited the Gan Eng Seng primary school in Singapore, there were signs hanging from the dining room ceiling with words in big letters such as 'STRIVING', 'RESILIENCE' and 'AMBITIOUS' along with encouraging sentences such as 'Happiness springs from doing good and helping others'. There are also schools which still promote religions. In British private schools there is some remnant of the values that were traditionally taught there in the past, some of which are captured in the Rudyard Kipling poem 'If' (see box). It is fair to say, too, that some values are taught in schools now in place of the ones that have been dropped. They include racial and religious tolerance.

Some people object to religious schools. Others may not agree with the values promoted by the Singapore school. Yet others may not approve of the values of personal behaviour that remain in British private schools. None of us is going to agree with all the values that have ever been taught in either government or independent schools. But it is Orwellian to have the state impose a uniform idea of values or beliefs on all schools. The only way to have variety and freedom in schools is for parents to have the power to choose which schools they want for their children. It seems possible, at least, that, given such a choice, parents would like schools that did esteem personal behaviour such as politeness, consideration for others, perseverance and suchlike.

4. Government interventions in housing → crime and uncivil behaviour

Government housing also appears to have had a damaging effect on behaviour. This operates in several ways.

First, government-built estates in many countries have become centres of crime and fear (see Chapter 5). In estates such as the ones I saw in Marseilles, one can see in action the theory of some criminologists that a major cause of crime is criminals influencing others to become criminal. In some estates, there is simply no choice but to join a gang.

Second, government housing in some welfare states contributes to unemployment (Chapter 5), which, in turn, encourages crime. Third, government planning controls have made housing far more expensive in some countries than it would otherwise be. This makes it more difficult for poorer people to buy reasonable housing, which may contribute to crime. The British Ministry of Justice analysed where prisoners live before going to prison. It found that only 15 per cent of the men and 7 per cent of the women were owner-occupiers. So only a very small proportion of owner-occupiers commit crimes compared to the rest of the population. This does not prove the case but it does suggest the possibility that home ownership discourages crime.

It is conceivable that the fact of owning a home gives a person a different psychological framework – a sense of having a stake in society and a certain self-respect. The country with the highest rate of home ownership – Singapore – is also one with very low levels of crime although, of course, there are other factors involved.

When young people convicted of crimes were interviewed for one study, more than a third said lack of accommodation was the factor

'I pass through Lyons. What can I see? Not the historic buildings. Not the tourist hot-spots or the Michelin-starred restaurants. I see big blocks of social housing. I see hundreds of walls covered in graffiti. Are the two connected?'
Notes made on the train to Aix-en-Provence.

most likely to lead them to re-offend.[38] And people who have served short prison sentences are two to three times more likely to re-offend if they do not have access to suitable housing.[39]

Housing matters. Housing that the poor can afford matters because we want the poor to have good lives, because it can affect unemployment rates and because it may reduce crime. Unfortunately government planning controls have made housing unnecessarily expensive in many countries.

5. Means-tested benefits, high taxes and social security → dishonesty

Some welfare states have encouraged fraud on a massive scale. Kathryn Edin and Laura Lein found that all but one of 379 poor single mothers had a source of income in addition to their welfare benefits (Chapter 1). Most had incomes of a sort that should have been but were not reported to the

Shashi Bacheta and Jeffrey Cole claimed £40,000 in benefits while sailing around the world on a luxury yacht".

welfare benefit officials. Two out of five were working but not reporting their income to the tax authorities. To put it bluntly, they were committing fraud. They knew it, too. That is why Edin found she only got to the truth after welfare recipients were interviewed several times over and convinced that they were not going to be reported.

If such fraud is widespread among recipients of other kinds of means-tested welfare benefits, this amounts to millions of people across the USA and in other countries. These are people who are simply trying to get by but the circumstances they are in have led them to lying and cheating, week by week, month by month and even year by year.

There is cheating and lying among taxpayers, too. Those who have salaries from big companies or the government have little opportunity. But the self-employed and small businesses have plenty. They have a strong incentive because the costs of many welfare states have led to high tax and social security rates. I am not aware of research like Edin's on tax evasion, but anyone who has ever paid or received cash for work is aware that it is widespread. Fraud teams report that they detect it relatively easily. Proving it and mounting a prosecution is the time-consuming part.[40] In the USA, academics have estimated that 18 to 19 per cent of income that should be reported isn't.[41] They also found that the rate of evasion has risen dramatically since the end of the Second World War. The rate of evasion is linked to the federal income tax rate and the amount of unemployment.

A reflection of this avoidance is the boom in black economies (see Chapter 8). Many payments for services are being made in cash, evading both sales and value-added taxes and also income taxes. Again, this represents further millions of people who are, to be blunt, lying and cheating.

The first President…

'I can't tell a lie, Pa; you know I can't tell a lie. I did cut it with my hatchet.'

Reputed answer of George Washington, aged six, when asked if he knew who had killed his father's favourite cherry tree. The story may be exaggerated but for generations it was used to extol the virtue of honesty.[42]

A recent President…

'I want to say one thing to the American people. I want you to listen to me. I'm going to say this again. I did not have sexual relations with that woman, Miss Lewinsky. I never told anybody to lie, not a single time – never. These allegations are false. And I need to go back to work for the American people.'

Bill Clinton, January 1998

DNA taken from his semen later proved that President Clinton misled 'the American people'. The change in American culture is reflected in the way President Clinton lied and even more in the way he was not wholly disgraced. Moves were made to impeach him but he continued in office and was treated with considerable respect in following years.

It seems likely that the more people lie, the less they feel ashamed of it. They come to feel, 'Well, everybody else does it. Why should I be the one person who tells the truth?'

6. State subsidies for lone parenting and care for the elderly → the rise of entitlement and the death of duty

I am in Lower Hutt, a sunny little town in New Zealand. I have come to interview Erin McMenamin, the manager of Supergrans – a charity which advises people who are having difficulty coping. Erin is a doughty character – the sort who says what she thinks but has a big heart, too. I ask: what problems do the people she helps have? She tells me that some have simply never learned how to do things.

She tells me about mothers who can buy flour and vegetables at the store but have no idea what to do with them when they get home. They have never learned to cook. Others have no idea about budgeting or living economically by going to food banks and so on. A large proportion of her clients seem to be lone mothers. Some have just escaped from – or need to escape from – a violent partner. She tells me that often 'their own mums are young. They have no role models and no support. There is multi-generational ignorance.'

> many as one fourth of drivers the state [California] are using abled placards fraudulently.'
>
> Los Angeles[43]

I ask about the influence of welfare benefits and she is typically frank. She says some people like the lifestyle of not working. When a Supergrans counsellor advises lone mothers against having another baby, some reply, 'If I don't have another baby, I'm going to have to go back to work!'

Erin has run Supergrans for a long time so I ask how things have changed. She says violence and drugs have increased. 'The ability to accept where they are has decreased. People used to be grateful and eager. Now the attitude is: "I want this. You get it for me."'

So does she feel less sympathetic than before? She says she is 'totally' less sympathetic than when she started but then the positive side of her nature revives and she

Erin McMenamin: 'people used to be grateful'.

adds, 'but the better ones outweigh the bad ones – and the bad ones can be turned around.'

Erin has seen a sense of entitlement develop that was not there before. It is difficult to prove this has happened or that welfare states have caused it. But it is telling that someone who has been on the front line of welfare for so long has no doubt about it. Many welfare benefits are, indeed, legal entitlements. When people have these entitlements, it is understandable that they should come to think in terms of demanding them.

> **Neither we nor our customers are here to be verbally or physically abused.**
>
> **Anti-social behaviour will not be tolerated. We will refuse to serve anyone who behaves in an unacceptable way.**

Typical sign in public buildings in England. This one is in Hammersmith Town Hall.

The psychology of this is different from earlier times when help might be requested from other family members or a friendly society or charity. Then people probably felt a sense of duty to try to get back to being self-reliant again as soon as possible. But when people receive government money to which they are entitled, no sense of obligation is likely to be felt. There is no awareness that it comes from other people, some of whom are not rich. The government is perceived as a kind of bottomless pit.

Another testimony comes from Dr Richard Dumont 12,000 miles away in Montpelier:

> I have seen a decline of politeness and an increase in incivility over the past two decades. When I started, there was what one could call respect for the white gown. Now everything has changed. Doctors, like nurses, too, regularly find themselves being verbally attacked for practically nothing.
>
> A classic scenario: someone describes to us minor symptoms and we ask them to make their own way to the hospital. But they have not got what they wanted so they explode. The aggression ranges from saying, 'I am going to come and smash your face in' to 'arseholes', 'buggers' or worse. Verbal violence has become routine.
>
> I think these people think of the emergency services as a right and that the moment we do not agree to their demands, they think they can do anything.

Across the channel, in Britain, it is now not uncommon to see signs in public buildings such as hospitals and post offices saying that verbal or physical aggression against the staff will result in prosecution.

A sense of entitlement has increased in many countries accompanied by a willingness to complain. Meanwhile, at the other end of the spectrum of attitudes, the sense of duty has declined. In previous generations, it was common for a couple – even one whose marriage had turned out disappointingly – to stay together 'for the sake of the children'. This was thought of as a duty to the children, who should not be expected to pay for the mistakes of their parents. The idea of such a duty has dwindled. The welfare state has played some role in this.

People used to feel a duty to care for their parents. But welfare states have undermined that sense of duty by assuming responsibility for aged people. As a result, more and more aged people live alone or in institutions where they tend to be unhappier than they would be with – or close to – their adult children.

The very use of the word 'duty' has declined. Professor Patricia Greenfield used Google's word count tool, Ngram Viewer, to examine a million books published in the USA between 1800 and 2000 and 350,000 books published in Britain. The use of the word 'duty' declined by two-thirds over that time.

It is likely that many reading these words will feel, 'Yes, and a good thing, too! What a relief to be liberated from the shackles of such an antiquated burden!' But the other side of a 'duty' is a person who benefits. Yes, a duty to visit

'He every now and then, with evident increase of pain, made a greater effort with his vocal powers, and pronounced distinctly these last words: "Thank God, I have done my duty"; and this great sentiment he continued to repeat as long as he was able to give it utterance.'

From the account by Dr William Beatty, the ship's surgeon, of the last hours of Admiral Lord Nelson, who was mortally wounded during the Battle of Trafalgar in 1805 (picture below).[44] Nelson's words reflect the importance he gave to the concept of duty.

an aged mother might be a burden for the visitor. But for the mother there is the pleasure and comfort of seeing a beloved child.

In France, Pierre Garello, an academic, remarked to me, 'France is a very centralised country but the people are very individualist.' By 'individualist' the French often mean something akin to 'self-centred' or even 'selfish'. It may be no coincidence that France is both 'centralised' and 'individualist'. It makes perfect sense that if a centralised government is taking all the decisions about how society is run, the only thing left for the individual to be worried about is his or her own personal interest. Direct, person-to-person kindness is crowded out. The idea of being a civil individual – looking out for others and society generally – is made pointless.

Another possible effect of welfare states may be to lower expectations of one's own behaviour and resourcefulness. People may have become so used to the state providing and deciding things that their confidence in their own ability to fend for themselves or assist others has been reduced.

The idea that one's self-esteem should be based on an idea of oneself as an honourable person who does his or her duty – a concept expressed by people as far apart in cultures as Emperor Marcus Aurelius and Rudyard Kipling – has been under attack. From my own experience in Britain, I know that concepts such as sinfulness, wrong, duty, decency and honour all existed during my childhood in the 1950s and 1960s. They rarely figure in discussion today. People now expect little of themselves in terms of self-denial and duty. They feel that they have a 'right' to do what pleases them. They do not

Death of the concept of duty

Frequency with which the word 'duty' has appeared in English fiction.

Source: Google Ngram Viewer

feel shame at their own behaviour. 'Shame' is another word that has fallen into disuse.

Does this really matter? Perhaps it just seemed a better world to live in when people wanted to do the right thing – to do the best for their country rather than the best for their political career; to do the right thing by their wives or husbands rather than leave them because a new lover was more exciting; when there was more reason to trust one's fellow human beings.

•   •   •

I have suggested six ways in which welfare states have tended to change – and usually damage – attitudes and behaviour, the real stuff of a civilisation. The routes have been through unemployment; lone-parenting; illiteracy; housing; means-tested benefits combined with high taxes; and the undermining of personal responsibility. In some cases the evidence is clear. In others, it is hard to prove but the logic is there for those willing to follow it. All in all, the effect of some welfare states, at least, on the spirit, culture and behaviour of people has been damaging.

Before leaving the subject, let me respond to an objection to this line of argument which is perfectly reasonable. If welfare states give so much encouragement to crime and incivility, as I have suggested, why have the crime figures been falling?

Overall levels of crime have indeed been falling around the world. Some of the reported drops are astonishing. In New York City, car thefts have fallen 93 per cent.[46] There used to be 500 or so robberies of banks, building societies and post offices a year in Britain in the 1990s. In 2012, there were a mere sixty-nine.[47] The old fashioned bank robber is going out of business. The world appears to be becoming a more law-abiding place and governments in several countries have boasted about how their policing policies have made their countries safer. They are sometimes irritated when the public, in surveys, say they are still afraid of crime.

Why should crime suddenly be falling? Are people genuinely more respectful of the law? Are they behaving better? Or is something else going on?

The fall in crime has thrown up a great range of explanations. Each has its group of intelligent academic supporters (see box).

'Watching the ever-increasing costs of the welfare state in Britain and Sweden, we decided to avoid this debilitating system. We noted by the 1970s that when governments undertook primary responsibility for the basic duties of the head of a family, the drive in people weakened. Welfare undermined self-reliance. People did not have to work for their families' well-being. The hand-out became a way of life. The downward spiral was relentless as motivation and productivity went down. People lost the drive to achieve because they paid too much in taxes. They became dependent on the state for their basic needs.'

Lee Kuan Yew, Prime Minister of Singapore 1959–90[45]

Why has reported crime gone down? Some of the possible explanations.

- **THE RISE OF PRIVATE SECURITY:** the number of security guards in Europe increased 90 per cent in ten years. They now outnumber police officers. Cars are fitted with electronic security devices which make them more difficult to steal. The proportion of British households with a burglar alarm rose by half to 29 per cent between 1995 and 2011. Bullet-proof partitions have been introduced in banks. Video recorders have been installed in shops and many other places.

- New technology has improved policing: it is now impossible to walk down many city streets without being monitored by a video camera. DNA testing means it is easier to prove someone was at the scene of a major crime. 'Predictive' policing has had some success – sending police officers to where trouble is likely.

- Ageing populations: young men are the most likely people to commit crimes and as a proportion of the population they have been going down.

- Reduced lead in petrol: the idea might sound absurd but the evidence is surprisingly good.[48]

- Increased imprisonment: increased imprisonment rates per crime committed have been followed by lower crime levels in some countries and vice versa.[49] However, this idea is fiercely contested.

- Increased confidence in the rule of law. A long-term trend over centuries has resulted in people relying more on the state to enforce justice rather than trying to enforce it themselves.

- Increased wealth is correlated to lower crime levels and may have played a part.

- Reduction in the number of valuable, easily stolen things: thieves used to steal DVD players but now that they only cost £25, they are not worth the trouble and danger. More people have bank accounts and credit cards so they keep less cash in the home or in their pockets.

Let's take one of the more common explanations for the fall in crime: improved defences against crime through technology and increased private security. If this is the true cause, it is possible that the underlying tendency towards crime or willingness to commit it has not fallen at all. It might even have risen.

The biggest falls have been in 'property crimes'. These are the sorts of crime most likely to be affected by new technology. Cars are now much more difficult to steal than before. Car thefts have consequently fallen dramatically but clearly that does not necessarily reflect any improvement in honesty.

The use of video surveillance – CCTV cameras – has soared. It seems that the first town to use a video camera may have been Olean, New York in 1968.[50] From that small beginning, the use of them has exploded. In the United Kingdom in 2011, it was estimated that there were 1.85 million cameras in use and that the average person on a typical day would be seen by seventy cameras.[51]

Similarly there has been a rapid growth in the number of private security personnel – mostly security guards. In Canada in 2006, there were more private security personnel than police officers – three for every two, in fact.[52] In the European Union, it has been calculated that the number of security guards jumped by two-thirds in only eight years, between 1999 and 2007. The number rose from 600,000 to 'well over' one million.[53]

What about crimes against people?

The most reliable evidence comes from 'victimisation' surveys, where people are asked about crimes they have experienced recently, such as over the past year. The only truly international survey suggests a mixed picture. In some countries, including the USA and Germany, the number of assaults went down between 1989 and 2003/4. In others, including England and the Netherlands, they went up. We should note that any increases are in the face of the spread of security cameras and the vast increase in private security guards. More recent international survey figures, for 2010, only allow long-range comparisons for seven advanced countries but assaults actually increased in six of them: Denmark, Germany, the Netherlands, Sweden, Switzerland and the United Kingdom. The only exception was Canada.

Assaults appear to be increasing in some countries

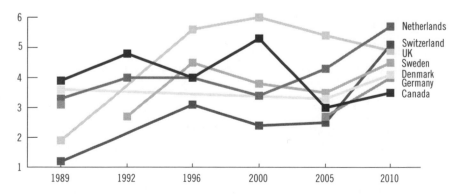

Percentage of people saying they were assaulted or 'threatened in a way that really frightened' them in the previous year.

Source: International Crime Victims Survey[54]

The United States has a long run of crime statistics which suggests that the incidence of all forms of crime, including violence against other people, has gone down.[55] These figures suggest a peak between 1980 and 1990 and a substantial fall since. However, the latest levels of reported robbery and aggravated assault are still dramatically above the levels in 1960 when the statistics begin. The rate of aggravated assault is more than two and half times higher than it was in 1960.

Violent crime has fallen but is still much higher than in the early 1960s and before

Year	Robberies	Aggravated Assaults
1960	60.1	86.1
1961	58.3	85.7
1962	59.7	88.6
1963	61.8	92.4
1964	68.2	106.2
1965	71.7	111.3
1966	80.8	120.3
1967	102.8	130.2
1968	131.8	143.8
1969	148.4	154.5
1970	172.1	164.8
1971	188.0	178.8
1972	180.7	188.8
1973	183.1	200.5
1974	209.3	215.8
1975	220.8	231.1
1976	199.3	233.2
1977	190.7	247.0
1978	195.8	262.1
1979	218.4	286.0
1980	251.1	298.5
1981	258.4	289.3
1982	238.8	289.0
1983	216.7	279.4
1984	205.7	290.6
1985	209.3	304.0
1986	226.0	347.4

1987	213.7	352.9
1988	222.1	372.2
1989	234.3	385.6
1990	256.3	422.9
1991	272.7	433.4
1992	263.7	441.9
1993	256.0	440.5
1994	237.8	427.6
1995	220.9	418.3
1996	201.9	391.0
1997	186.2	382.1
1998	165.5	361.4
1999	150.1	334.3
2000	145.0	324.0
2001	148.5	318.6
2002	146.1	309.5
2003	142.5	295.4
2004	136.7	288.6
2005	140.8	290.8
2006	150.0	292.0
2007	148.3	287.2
2008	145.9	277.5
2009	133.1	264.7
2010	119.3	252.8
2011	113.7	241.1

Robberies and aggravated assault per 100,000 people in the USA.

Source: Uniform Crime Reporting Statistics.[56]

Despite substantial falls in overall crime in many countries, the reduction only takes us back to where we were three or four decades ago. Compared to the 1950s or 1930s, most advanced countries remain dramatically more crime ridden.

Looking over the evidence, I would suggest that a rough summary of the history of crime might go like this: over the centuries, crime appears to have fallen. But the second half of the twentieth century saw a remarkable rally. The timing varied somewhat from one place to another. Afterwards, there was a fall in property crime but crime against people did not fall much or even at all in a number of countries.[57]

I would suggest that the role of welfare states in this may have been to contribute to the major rally in the second half of the twentieth century. And subsequently, it may have caused crime now – especially crime against the person – to be higher than it otherwise would be. We might also note that among the many ideas that attempt to explain falling overall crime, one is absent. I have nowhere seen it suggested that the fall in crime is because people have become more decent and honest.

But all this is without counting a category of crime that is not recorded even in victim surveys. People do not report crimes they are committing themselves. There has surely been a vast expansion of fraud in claiming welfare benefits and declaring taxable income.

Have all welfare states had a similar impact on attitudes and behaviour? No. Not all welfare states are the same. Not all encourage lone parenting to the same extent. Not all have created crime ghettoes in social housing. The incentive to lie about income is much less strong in countries where tax and social insurance payments are lower.

It follows that the impact of welfare states on levels of crime, anti-social behaviour and attitudes has varied considerably. Britain has unfortunately made most of the mistakes that can be made. In the first half of the twentieth century, it was a country whose people – rich and poor – were internationally admired for their behaviour. Sadly those days are gone.[58] Other countries have suffered similar effects but Britain acts as a warning of just how much a nation can be changed by a welfare state.

We should also acknowledge that the people whose behaviour and happiness have been most affected by welfare states are the ones who have been most in contact with them and most dependent on them: the less well off. This helps explain an increased division between the poor and the rest – a 'coming apart' as Charles Murray has called it.[59] Only less well-off women receive welfare benefits or subsidised housing as a result of divorce or separation. Accordingly, the breakdown of marriage has been most widespread among the less well off. Only those poor enough to claim means-tested benefits have had an incentive to lie or been discouraged to work. Only those with a low ability to earn have been tempted by benefits to be unemployed instead. To be in a position where one has an overwhelming temptation to avoid regular work, to lie about income or wealth and to do informal, unrecognised work instead is a miserable condition for a society to put any of its members in.

The advantage of the continental systems, where most benefit payments are insurance payments, is that there is less incentive to lie about one's means. However, the drawback is that social insurance contributions can be so big that people are again prone to working in the black market to avoid paying them. It is true that the better off also have an incentive to lie, to evade income tax. But most of them are employed by companies or governments and have little scope to do so.

All of us, though, are affected by the changes of behaviour and attitudes in our society. We are influenced by people we meet. If we come across rudeness and cheating, we are more likely to do the same. Where divorce and lone parenting are commonplace, people think it is normal and therefore there is nothing wrong or regrettable about it. None of us is immune to the influence. The more cheating there is in sport, the more everyone accepts it. Once a critical mass of people accept the idea that winning is more important than behaving decently, it is difficult for anyone to stand out against that view.

Most of us would agree that these changes in behaviour and attitudes are undesirable. We would rather live in a society where there is less crime and anti-social behaviour, where everyone – not only those in particular parts of town – feels safe walking in the street at night, where cars are not torched and gangs do not terrorise a neighbourhood and where everyday politeness and consideration are normal. We would prefer a society where people can trust each other and where they give and receive help from each other as family or friends. Welfare states have shown a tendency to undermine this kind of society. In this way they have diminished our civilisation.

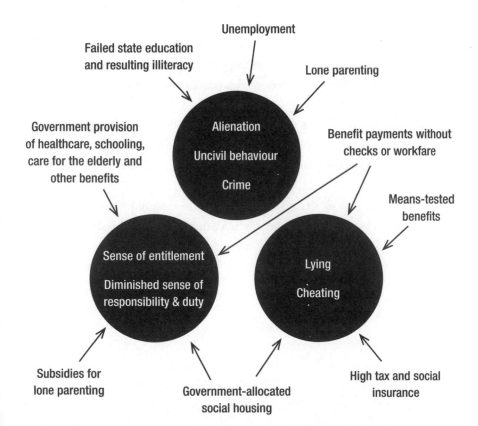

It may seem a Herculean task to try to reverse such tendencies. It may seem pointless even to suggest ways to improve things. Yet there are things that can be done.
One can at least try simply to remove, as much as possible, the elements of welfare
states that have caused the problem. Here are some possibilities:

1. Means-tested benefits should have the smallest possible role since they create a temptation to lie.

2. Levels of taxation should be as low as possible for the same reason.

3. Social insurance should go into personal savings plans rather than general government income. That way people have less reason to lie about their income.

4. Welfare benefits should be kept down to a level where it is always worthwhile
   for the low-paid to work.

5. Any special housing or cash benefits for lone parents that are not also available
   to couples be minimised so that the natural disincentives to lone parenting
   are not too much reduced.

6. Lone parents should be expected to go to their families for accommodation
   and support before any question of government support.

7. Diverse, independent schools should be the norm to improve literacy and
   enable the teaching of a variety of values rather than a uniform dogma or
   absence of values imposed by government.

It is no good pretending that measures such as these would have an immediate
impact. Cultures take years and decades to change. This would only be a start.

8.

Not to be read by anyone under the age of forty

Pensions and their unexpected consequences

I AM IN WARSAW HURRIEDLY walking along Świętokrzyska Street to get to a meeting. I can see in the middle of the square nearby the extraordinary monster-building given by the Soviet Union to 'the people of Poland' but not received with universal pleasure. It is in communist-gothic style with curious details reminiscent of gargoyles.

After a while, I reach some dignified streets from the nineteenth century and then Krakowskie Przedmieście, a wide main road. On the other side is the presidential palace. I am going to meet a government official but, to be embarrassingly honest about it, as I rush from one appointment to another, I sometimes have not had time to investigate exactly who I am going to see. I know this person is someone working for the government on social security but I am not entirely sure what she does.

The presidential palace is grand: a wide, elegant, white building of classical design. I tell the guard at the gate who I am going to see and am directed to a particular entrance. I cross a parade ground and go to the door indicated. I am straight away confronted by security procedures like those at an airport but on a smaller scale.

The Palace of Culture and Science donated by the Soviet Union to 'the people of Poland'.

That done, I am told to wait in a small area with a few chairs. Soon, a woman comes down and invites me to follow her back up some stairs. The decor is in a traditional style. She leads me along a corridor and into a large, high-ceilinged room. But this turns out to be just an ante-room. We continue on to the far side, to an impressively solid wooden door. She knocks and we go in. She introduces me to 'the minister'.

I feel a fool for not having realised I would be meeting someone so senior. The minister is Irena Wóycicka, a woman with severe black hair and bright intelligence.[1] She stands to greet me then goes to sit on an Empire chair behind a massive wooden desk. Friendly and efficient, she quickly assesses my lack of knowledge of the subject and briskly proceeds to tell me a little horror story.

It started long ago, before the Second World War. The Polish copied the kind of social insurance pioneered in Germany by Bismarck. Contributory schemes were created covering pensions and other elements of social security for various trades or professions.

During the war, Poland was invaded by both Germany and the Soviet Union. By the end of it all, the Soviets had installed a communist government. This government unified all the different social security schemes under its control. The scheme became, as the minister remarks, 'very huge'.

An innocent from Britain or America might assume that this 'very huge' system involved large amounts of assistance to the poor and unemployed. But no. Unemployment wasn't the big cost. 'Employment was mandatory,' the minister crisply explains. So what became 'very huge'?

As the post-war baby boom generation grew up, despite the 'mandatory employment', there was a lack of jobs for people to do. The government thought that the way to deal with this problem was to get older people to stop working and let younger ones take their jobs. They encouraged older workers to retire early by offering attractive terms. Wóycicka adds, rather defensively, that this sort of tactic was adopted in a number of countries around the world, which is perfectly true. There was a widespread idea that older workers should not keep jobs from young people setting out in life. But Poland seems to have taken the idea further than most. The result was that the cost of pensions was inflated by early retirement on notably generous terms. So pensions became a major component of government spending.

Then things got worse. The communists were ejected from power in 1989. It was an extraordinary time. The new Minister of Finance, Leszek Balcerowicz, was a radical who loathed communism and appreciated capitalism as only someone who has lived under communism knows how. He masterminded what became known as 'shock therapy' – a sudden break with fixed prices and top-down economic control.

Wóycicka remarks that this time of national upheaval would not have been a good moment to change the social security system. In fact, benefits were indexed to maintain their real value. But one result of the big changes in the Polish economy was an increase in unemployment and fear of unemployment. Unemployment benefits were small. So people migrated to where the benefits were bigger: disability pensions and retirement pensions. The cost of both ballooned.

Wóycicka remarks drily: 'Poland and the Netherlands were the two champions of disability' – meaning they both had burgeoning numbers of people claiming disability benefits. Naturally, a variety of counter-measures was adopted: there was 'bigger control of doctors'; benefits ceased to be indefinite and people were checked out every three years. Poland also became a 'pensions champion'.

The government was determined not to get into unsustainable debt so there was only one way to pay for this: dramatically increased contributions. Total social insurance contributions jumped from 23 per cent of wages to 45 per cent! The burden on employees was extreme. Naturally some reforms were made to try to reduce the problem. In 1999, the rules were changed so that, in the future, pensions would be based on contributions instead

Leszek Balcerowicz masterminded 'shock therapy' in Poland.

of salaries. Also some pension contributions began to be invested in real assets – a 'funded' system. But the latter was expensive since, if contributions went into actual investments, they were not available to pay the pensions of people already retired. More recently, the amount going into funded pensions has been reduced.

Now it has been proposed that the retirement age should be raised by three months every year. Another proposal is that the women's retirement age should be raised in line with that of men. But raising retirement ages causes a lot of opposition. Eighty per cent of the population is against it, Wóycicka says. Nevertheless, as a result of all the measures that have been and are being taken, the cost of Polish pensions is forecast to fall in relation to the size of the economy.

Well, that's good news, certainly. But I leave the minister and the presidential palace with the impression of a massive problem being grappled with.

Exactly how big is it? In 2005, the cost of paying government pensions in Poland amounted to 11.4 per cent of all economic activity – a staggeringly high proportion.[2] But if that still does not sound like much, let us put it another way. Pensions amounted to more than a quarter of all Polish government spending in 2007 – more than twice as much as in Britain, America or the Netherlands.

Leaving the presidential palace, I walk along Krakowskie Przedmieście, bustling with cars and trams, heading in the direction of the historic centre. I pass War-saw University, cross a big intersection and eventually reach a quieter street, Nowy Swiat, lined with traditional shops. At last, I reach my destination: Blikle. This is a charming Polish version of the coffee houses of Vienna but smarter than most of them with white tablecloths and uniformed staff. This is where two women, Aleksandra Wiktorow and Zofia Czepulis-Rutkowska, have told me to meet them.

They arrive and settle on to a cosy banquette while I sit opposite them. They are friendly and cheerful. Aleksandra is a comfortable, smiling woman who used to have a senior government job. Zofia, who speaks better English, clearly has had government experience too. In the course of our convivial meeting, I ask if they can explain more about the Polish pension horror story.

In the battle to contain the exploding cost, they tell me, pensions stopped being linked to wages. They were linked to prices instead – which normally rise more slowly. But at one time, even this was damaging because wages fell. Another ploy was to stop indexing some of the extra money being paid to spe-cially privileged groups such as miners, teachers, construction workers... the list seemed long.

Talking of privileges, they say, do I know about the retirement age for police-men? No. In 1995, they were given the right to retire at the age of thirty-five. Not to be outdone, the military soon obtained the right to retire at thirty-five, too.

'This must have been a great victory for the trade unions,' I say.

'Oh no! It was not the trade unions.'

Aleksandra and Zofia explain that the extraordinarily low retirement ages were negotiated by high-ranking police and military officers. A new government was in power which wanted support from the police and army. It also wanted votes. The support and votes of police officers, soldiers and generals were effectively bought by committing other people's money for years to come.

At this point, some readers may be thinking, 'This does sound shoddy but is it really so bad? Does anyone suffer as a result?' Let's look at the consequences of the generous early pensions granted in the past and the exceptionally generous pen-sions of certain government employees.

Money has to be found to pay for these pensions and it comes from social insur-ance. Let's look at someone who pays for them. Take someone employed at a cost to his employer of £11,800 a year. That is after including his employer's social insur-ance. After that is removed, the pay of the employee comes down to £10,000 a year, which is a little above the national average.[3] From this, the employee's social insur-ance contributions must be taken, bringing his income down to £8,250. Then there is taxation, which further reduces the take-home pay to £6,750. There is clearly a big drop from the £11,800 cost to the employer down to the £6,750 in the worker's pocket. It is a major wedge (see Chapter 2).

Imagine the frustration in, say, a small town where the boss of a carpentry workshop employs a teenager he has known all his young life. The worker would obviously like more cash in his pocket and the boss is tired of paying a fortune to what probably looks like the bottomless pit of social insurance. Would it not be tempting for him to say, 'Well, Dominik, how about if I pay you half the money officially and put the rest directly in your pocket? That way we both gain.' If you think that might be the case, you will not be surprised that the World Bank estimates that the black economy in Poland amounts to 26 per cent of all economic activity.[4]

Of course, not everyone has the opportunity to work for cash on the side. A major company can't do this. But major companies are affected, too. A Polish business's rival in Hong Kong, say, can pay lower wages yet still have better-paid employees. Therefore it is able to offer products at better prices than the Polish business, and so it grows, benefiting the Hong Kong economy and all who live there. Such growth passes Poland by.

The Polish situation is unfair too. Money earned by the worker is going to someone else's pension. The current worker will certainly not get anything like a reasonable return on his pension contributions. He could even make a loss. Why? Because the pensionable age is bound to be pushed up. The amounts paid in pensions will have to be subtly reduced compared to national income. Only in such ways will the vast burden of pensions be managed, especially given the fact that people in Poland, as everywhere, are living longer. It all amounts to a kind of theft perpetrated by those who are now pensioners against current workers.

To put it bluntly, the post-war generation voted for itself big and early pensions, sometimes with outrageous privileges, and thus guaranteed that the current generation of workers would be saddled with national debt and pensions with low returns. How should this be seen? Irresponsible? Selfish? As an example of how democracy can be the enemy of justice? Doubtless when the generous pensions were created they were depicted as wonderful, perhaps even rather heroic. They turned out to be plain greedy.

As I leave the charm of the Blikle café and my two genial companions, the burden of Polish pensions seems worse still. I have the impression, though, that the Polish pensions disaster is an extreme case – the unfortunate result of particular circumstances.

Later I look at the figures for other countries. I discover that Poland is not unique. It is not even the worst case. The cost of pensions amounts to over a tenth of national output in Poland. In Greece it amounts to 11.9 per cent. But Greece is not the worst case either. Pensions amount to an eighth of output in France. But the worst case of all is Italy. The cost is a staggering 14.1 per cent of GDP. In Italy, pensions absorb 29.4 per cent of all government spending, crowding out many other things.

National pension burdens compared

Government spending on pensions as percentage of gross domestic product in selected countries for 2007. Source: OECD[5]

The charts above and below show plenty of major countries with big pension burdens but they also show countries with much smaller ones.

Public pensions as proportion of government spending

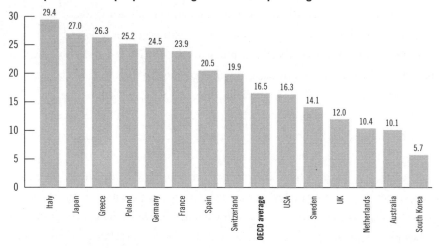

Public pensions as a proportion of government spending, selected countries. Source: OECD[6]

I can imagine some people still thinking, 'Well, yes, I can see that pension spending has ended up higher than intended in plenty of countries. Clearly some economies are needed. But it is all manageable, isn't it? I'm still not convinced that much harm has been done.' What are the real consequences?

1. Current workers are going to get a poor return on their pension contributions

Poland is an example of a common problem. Europe will simply be unable to pay the pensions it has promised. Pension obligations in nineteen of the European Union member countries are about five times their official gross debt, according to a study commissioned by the European Central Bank.[7]

Europe has the highest proportion of people aged over sixty in the world and the proportion is going to rise dramatically – from 22 per cent of the population in 2009 to 35 per cent by 2050.[9] The situation is 'totally unsustainable', according to Jacob Kirkegaard at the Peterson Institute in Washington.[10] And like any genuinely unsustainable situation, it will not be sustained. The money will not be paid. People currently working will not receive the incomes in retirement that they are theoretically expecting. Younger people will get less or will be paid from a later age or both.

When government pensions were first created in Germany under Bismarck, life expectancy was barely forty years and you had to wait until you were seventy to get a small pension. Since then, German life expectancy has almost doubled but the pensionable age has been reduced to sixty-five and the value has been increased.[8] A policy that was cautious became irresponsible, presumably because politicians sought votes without caring about the consequences.

Governments are continually 'surprised' by the degree to which life expectancy rises. To be surprised once or twice might be forgivable but the surprise is perennial.

The OECD, referring to its member countries generally, says, 'Many pension reforms will result in large cuts in benefit levels at a given retirement age and might risk a resurgence in old-age poverty,'[12] and again, 'Half of OECD countries are already increasing pension ages or will do so.' It amounts to a betrayal of promises given to people by governments. But that is not the end of it: 'However, most of these hard-won increases [in pension ages] will be outpaced by increases in life-expectancy.' In other words, even the cutbacks announced or expected will not be enough.

According to Richard Jackson, a specialist in the field, stabilising government spending on pension payments as

he pension reforms of)01 radically changed the erman pension system, ducing the generous placement rate from proximately 70 per cent final salary to a predicted per cent by 2030.'

an De Deken, assistant professor, partment of Sociology, University of sterdam[11] a share of GDP would necessitate cutting benefits 'in almost every developed coun-try' by between 30 and 60 per cent.[13] Yet 'workers remain highly dependent on public pensions and entirely unprepared for large benefit reductions'. He wrote these words in 2000. Pensions in many countries have been cut back since then so it is worth looking at his more recent views. According to his most recent estimates, the cost of maintaining the current generosity of pension schemes would add an extra 7 per cent to government budgets by 2030.[14]

'The median ages of Western Europe and Japan, which were thirty-four and thirty-three respectively as recently as 1980, will soar to forty-seven and fifty-two by 2030, assuming no increase in fertility.'

Richard Jackson[15]

In a desperate attempt to fulfil promises made, younger workers of today and the next generation will be required to pay more money. It does not matter whether the bill is paid through social insurance or tax, it amounts to the same thing: an even bigger subsidy of one generation by the next and with even more damaging results.

In Japan, the government has calculated that the early post-war generation will do perfectly well out of the pen-sion system but those born later will fare worse and those born recently will do worst of all.

> Estimation result shows that the net benefit rate is 1.0 per cent for the genera-tion born in 1950, minus 5.3 per cent for the generation born in 1970 and minus 13.0 per cent for the generation born in 2010. Thus, the younger generation suf-fers the larger net burden and intergenerational inequality should not be ignored.[16]

It is a kind of rolling rip-off by one generation of the next. In many countries – as in Poland – the post-war baby-boom generation voted itself generous pensions. It allowed itself to believe that it was perfectly fine for each generation to fund the pensions of the one before. Politicians and voters conveniently ignored the obvi-ous fact that life expectancy was rising. They kept the retirement age unchanged. They ignored the fact that the ratio between numbers of retired people and num-bers of active workers would be utterly transformed.

In France, as recently as 2012, President François Hollande carried through a pre-election promise, making things even worse – reducing the age at which people can receive pensions from sixty-two to sixty. He reversed, at least in part, the modest reform of his predecessor, Nicolas Sarkozy. This demonstrates how difficult it is in a democracy to push through sensible reform. Perhaps the people who happily voted for Hollande and for more money for their own pen-sions liked to imagine that this was a gain for all French

'[By 2030], in Italy, Spain a Japan, more than half of adults will be older than t official retirement ag

Richard Jacks

people without consequences. Not according to the OECD: 'If a pension system is financially unsustainable, the scale of changes needed in the medium or long term will be more sudden and painful.'

Despite the Canute-like gesture of President Hollande, the underlying reality is that in France, as elsewhere, future pensions are being cut back. *Marianne*, a French magazine, put it like this:

> Over the years, a succession of reforms of pensions have succeeded each other: the age at which pensions will start has been increased or the conditions have deteriorated and each time it is promised, sworn, that it will be 'the last of the last'. In particular, the key variable, that of the rate of replacement, that is to say the amount of the pension as a percentage of salary, has not ceased to fall.[18]

And there will be more in that long line of 'last' reforms in France. There were 4.2 people of working age for every French pensioner in 2011. This ratio will collapse to 1.9 by 2050 according to *The Economist*.[19] The figures are even worse for Germany.

In France, the pension age will now rise to sixty-seven from 2023. Germany is heading towards the same age. It will happen everywhere and to a greater extent than so far announced.

Many advanced countries around the world now have a choice of evils: either break the promises made to those who have made contributions in the past or tax and penalise the next generation to an extraordinary degree. In fact, most countries are doing a mixture.[20] Some must also squeeze spending on every other budget such as education, defence, foreign aid and so on. It is difficult to cut the healthcare budget because ageing populations also necessitate more spending there, too.

The problem tends to be discussed by the European Union and the OECD as if it were some unfortunate event that has arisen without any human agency. That is not true. The failure to pay pensions as promised and the penalising by one generation of the next are the unfortunate creations of the welfare states of the world.

Any young person now entering the workforce has good reason to feel angry at the generation retiring now. The figures below for the USA give an idea of just how big the inter-generational theft is. The contrast between the gains received by the

> 'The retirement age for Greek jobs classified as "arduous" is as early as fifty-five for men and fifty for women. As this is also the moment when the state begins to shovel out generous pensions, more than 600 Greek professions somehow managed to get themselves classified as "arduous": hairdressers, radio announcers, waiters, musicians, and on and on and on.'
>
> Michael Lewis, *Vanity Fair*, October 2010[21]

post-war generation and the losses of the current generation amounts to over $170,000 per person. The contrasts in Poland, France and Italy are probably even greater.

Early generations have ripped off later ones

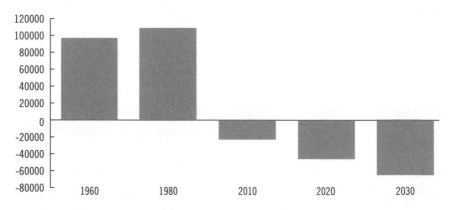

Difference between social security (pension) benefits received and social security taxes paid by a single man on the average wage in the USA after various adjustments to make the figures comparable. The years shown are when he reaches sixty-five. Source: Urban Institute[22]

'Increases in retirement ages are underway or planned in twenty-eight of the thirty-four OECD countries. These increases, however, are expected to keep pace with improved life expectancy only in six countries for men and in ten countries for women'

OECD[23]

This new generation will have to pay through the nose to finance the pensions of the old while they themselves get miserable or negative returns on their own contributions. Young people will not demonstrate in the streets or refuse to pay only because of a natural desire to respect their parents coupled with ignorance of what has happened. But the post-war generation – my own generation and before – should be ashamed.

2. Big contributions to fund state pensions have encouraged black markets

I suggested that the high level of tax and social insurance in Poland is, at least, part of the reason why Poland has such a big black market. Could that be true elsewhere, too?

The biggest pension burdens are carried by Italy, France, Greece, Germany, Poland, Japan, Spain and Sweden (see chart on p. 194

Big pension burde
→ high tax and
social insurance
contributions
→ black econom

'National pension burdens compared'). So how big are the black markets in these eight countries?

Three of them – Italy, Greece and Poland – are at the top of the league when it comes to 'shadow economies'. Two others have above-average black economies. Two are a little below average. Only Japan is notable in having a relatively big pension burden but a small black economy. Japan, though, spends less on other welfare state benefits such as incapacity benefits. So this is consistent with the idea that the wedge between the cost to a business of employing someone and the money actually received is a significant influence.[24]

Who has got the biggest (and smallest) black economy?

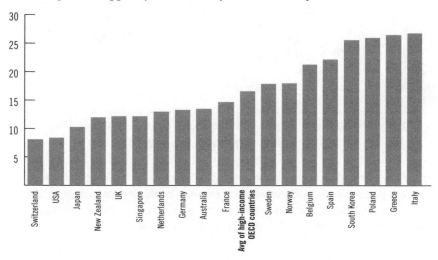

Shadow economies as a percentage of total economic output, selected countries. Source: Friedrich Schneider, Andreas Buehn and Claudio E. Montenegro, 'Shadow Economies All over the World'[25]

Sweden and Norway are often regarded as countries which are civilised and law-abiding. But they are also countries with large social contributions and taxation. Sweden has made moves to bring its pension burden under control but has anyway found plenty of other things to spend money on. And yes, they do indeed have black economies of above-average size.

What about the countries which have relatively small pension burdens: Korea, Australia, the Netherlands, the UK, America and Switzerland? Strikingly, five of the six also have smaller-than-average black economies. Korea is the exception. One of the possible explanations for this is that Korea has a dramatically higher proportion of self-employed workers than other countries. They have more opportunity to do transactions which do not appear in the books.[26]

Does any connection between large pension burdens and large black economies show up if we look at the national figures? A scattergraph does indeed suggest a modest correlation.

Big government pensions appear to encourage black economies[27]

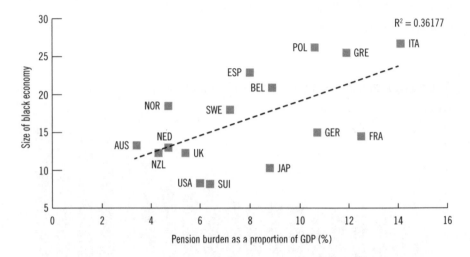

Size of shadow economies as percentage of GDP plotted against public expenditure on old age and survivor benefits as a proportion of GDP. Big government pension schemes create a large tax and social insurance 'wedge' which encourages black economies. Please note that the outlier of Korea has been omitted. If it were included the R squared figure would fall from 0.36 to 0.123. Sources: OECD and World Bank.

Of course pension costs all by themselves do not wholly account for the size of black economies. Governments impose heavy taxes and social insurance contributions for other reasons, too. So it is remarkable that pensions are influential enough to show any correlation at all.

Among those who study black economies, however, the influence of social contributions and taxes will come as no great surprise. According to a World Bank study of black economies,

> in almost all studies it has been ascertained that the overall tax and social security contribution burden are among the main causes for the existence of the shadow economy ... The bigger the difference between the total cost of labor in the official economy and the after-tax earnings, the greater the incentive to avoid this difference.

And for good measure, 'reducing the tax burden is the best policy measure to reduce the shadow economy, followed by a lessening of fiscal and business regulation'.[28]

Do we need to ask what is wrong with black economies? We might as well. There is a Panglossian tendency about which tends to think 'whatever exists is fine'. But black economies are inherently unfair. Two people work. One pays a large part of his or her income to the state while the other does not.

Secondly, they encourage dishonesty. Those involved are knowingly and deliberately lying. Once lying becomes normal in one context, the practice is easily transferred to others. Eventually that leads to a reduction in mutual trust.

Thirdly, a black economy makes the problem of funding an overlarge pension system even more difficult!

3. Big state pensions can contribute to unemployment

The big wedge caused by government pension schemes also contributes to unemployment (see Chapter 2).

As an experiment, I have tried to see if the boost that big pension burdens give to the wedge – and thus to unemployment – shows through in unemployment levels.

Big government pension schemes tend to create unemployment[29]

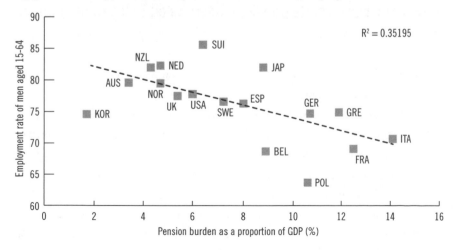

Please note that no country has been excluded from this scattergraph as an outlier. Source: OED statistics.

There does indeed appear to be a modest correlation. Again, no one would claim pension burdens are the sole or overwhelming cause of unemployment. But a connection makes sense and the scattergraph provides evidence to support the idea.

And there is a likely follow-on consequence: when there is unemployment, there is more emigration of working-age people to other countries. Migration from Spain to Germany reached 30,000 in 2012, a 45 per cent increase on the previous year. Immigration from Italy was even higher at 42,000, up 40 per cent.[30] These elevated figures were partly a response to problems that might be temporary. But some migration patterns were established prior to the 2008 crisis. The number of French people living in other countries has built up over time. It is estimated that 300,000 French people live in London and another 200,000 in Belgium.[31] This is clearly not because France is a poor country. It is because those who cannot get jobs in their own countries or where their net pay is severely reduced by tax and social insurance naturally seek employment elsewhere.

We see a kind of domino effect: dysfunctional, overstretched state pension systems causing high taxes and social contributions, which increase unemployment and then prompt emigration. The emigration is primarily of working men and women. When they move, of course, they no longer pay pension contributions in their own countries. By leaving, they help make the pension crisis back home even worse.

Big pension burden → high tax and social insurance contributions → unemployment

4. In many cases, state pensions have failed to make old people better off

The ultimate irony is that often the 'generous' state pensions have not made people better off in their old age. Millions of people have been given the impression by their governments that a good pension will be paid to them. This has been true in France, Britain, Italy, Germany and Spain at least. But the amount that many people in these countries are receiving now is less than they were led to expect. But because most people believed their governments, they saved less than they otherwise would have done. So many people in advanced countries have disturbingly small savings. They are poorer in old age.

More than half of American workers have less than $25,000 in savings.[33] In Britain, the average savings of people retiring between the ages of fifty and sixty-four was £91,900 in 2010, which, if used to buy an annuity, would mean an annual income of £4,000 or less – a pittance.[34] And as this is an average figure, obviously a large proportion of these people – probably a majority – had less.

What has made this even worse in some countries is that some less well-off people of working age have been on welfare benefits which are means-tested and only paid to those who have little or no saving. This has created a perverse incentive not to save. These people have thus become dependent in old age on a state pension that is totally inadequate.

State pensions were created partly to ensure that people would not be poor in old age. But instead, in some cases, they have turned out to be a trick which has led people to save too little and see out their lives in severely reduced circumstances.

Countries where the old are disproportionately more likely to be poor than the general population include many with large government pension payments such as Greece, Japan, Spain and Italy.[36] Poland is the exception. In Poland, the old are less likely to be so poor but this is unlikely to last.

countries where people know that the state will not provide for them, saving is a major part of the way of life. In Hong Kong, for example overall national gross savings were 34 per cent of GDP in the 1990s before there were any mandatory or government pension schemes. At the same time, the gross savings rates in Germany, France and Italy were in the region of only 20–22.5 per cent.[32]

5. Public employee pensions are a scandal and a ticking time bomb

Related to government pension schemes for the general population are the schemes for government employees. They are related but different. Bill Lockyer, the state treasurer of California, asserted in 2011 that public employees were not getting particularly generous pensions.[37] Lockyer said the average was $2,500 a month, equivalent to $30,000 a year. It would be a lot of money for many people around the world but in America it did not seem extravagant.

Daniel Borenstein, a columnist for the *Contra Costa Times*, was surprised by the figure and decided to take a closer look. He found it was misleading. The 'average' cited by the treasurer included public employees who had worked for as little as five years. If, instead, you took only those public service workers getting their full benefits,

'Even average wage earners with a full career can no longer accumulate sufficient entitlements to be assured of a retirement income above the social assistance level, and hence might still have to depend upon means-tested benefits during their old age. As a consequence, an increasing number of wage earners no longer has an interest in saving to supplement their public pension.'

Johan De Deken, on German pensions.[35]

the average state employee retiring in 2009 was receiving nearly $67,000 a year, a really generous package.

He then discovered that those working for local government in California were receiving even more. In his own county, Contra Costa, the average pension for new retirees was $85,500. Moreover, two-thirds of these pensioners were members of the California government pension system and through this were also entitled to social security benefits worth a further $19,000 on average, making a total of over $100,000.

Meanwhile, over on the other side of the country, a local newspaper in Newark, New Jersey did a similar investigation when it was similarly claimed that government employees had modest pensions. The *Star-Ledger* found that the average for those who had done twenty-five years' service was $40,000.[38] Teachers got a better deal, receiving $46,486, and police officers and firefighters did outstandingly well with average pensions of $73,571. These figures

President Sarkozy and the problem of French pension reform.

can be compared with median pre-tax earnings in the USA of about $45,500 at that time.[39]

The cost of growing obligations for pension payments of public sector employees in the USA and elsewhere is a time bomb. It gets little attention partly because public sector employees have every reason not to publicise it. But the damage will become more obvious in due course and, in some cases, it already has.

In Detroit, generous public sector pensions helped provoke a major financial crisis. An emergency manager was appointed and said the cashflow problem made the city 'insolvent'. A lawyer specialising in bankruptcy commented that the lack of funding for the pension fund and healthcare benefits for the retired 'could be the tipping point where the city ends up having to file bankruptcy if there's no concessions made'. In New York City, the annual pension contributions jumped from 6 per cent of the city's annual spending in 2002 to 18 per cent ten years later. The proportion is still rising. In California, the city of Stockton, with a population of just under 300,000, filed for bankruptcy. What was its biggest debt? An obligation to the California Public Employees Retirement System.[40]

Two economists, Robert Novy-Marx and Josh Rauh, tried to work out the combined effect of all the shortfalls in unfunded state employee pension schemes in the USA. They calculated that to fund them properly would require the average US taxpayer to contribute an extra $1,365 a year.

In America, we can see that the situation is bad. But America is relatively transparent in its public affairs. We can't be sure just how substantial are the obligations lurking beneath the surface elsewhere around the world. Even the OECD, with all its resources, remarks, 'The disclosure of these promises [to public sector workers] is all too often less than transparent which may be hiding potentially huge fiscal liabilities that are being passed on to future generations of workers.'[41] It is rare for the OECD to use such stark language.

Many countries do not publish estimates of these liabilities but the OECD has tried to work out the figures for a small selection. On the basis of this report, the troubles of the USA are not the worst. There are much bigger unfunded liabilities in France, Finland, Britain and Germany.

'Potentially huge fiscal liabilities … are being passed on to future generations of workers.'

OECD[42]

The public sector pension time bomb

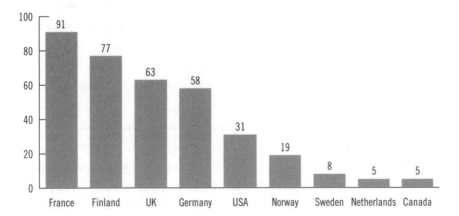

Net unfunded liabilities of the examined public sector pension plans on a fair value basis, per cent of GDP in 2008.

Source: OECD[43]

These liabilities are not included in publicly acknowledged national debts. If one adds them to national debts, the figures are truly alarming. In France, the pension debt added to other debts amounted to 152 per cent of GDP in 2008. In Britain it came to 138 per cent. These figures are daunting – the more so because since 2008, the national debts of most countries have significantly increased. Estimates were not done for Spain, Italy and Poland and one might fear that their hidden pension debts are as bad or worse.

6. The cost of big unfunded government pensions can lead to demands to allow more immigration

A website called Left Foot Forward in Britain carries the headline: 'How best to support an ageing population? More immigration.'[44] The author cites the well-established concerns that there will be fewer working-age people in future to support more retired people. Then he refers to a comment from the Office for Budget Responsibility: 'Higher net migration, close to levels that we have seen in recent years, would put downward pressure on borrowing and public sector net debt, as immigrants are more likely to be of working age than the population in general.' The conclusion of the article is that 'allowing more people of working age into the country would ... take some of the strain off the welfare state.'

It would indeed, at the margin. But the reprieve would be temporary and minor unless the structure of the pension system were changed.[45] It is a strange way to decide upon mass immigration, though, isn't it? Create an unsustainable pension system and then try to keep it going a little longer by encouraging mass immigration? Even if it worked, it would be an admission of national incompetence.

•   •   •

These six problems with government unfunded pension schemes are daunting. Those now entering them are sure to get a poor or even a negative return. The burden of government pensions has contributed to the creation of huge black economies and widespread unemployment. In many cases, they have deceived people, causing them to save too little and be poor in old age. Public employees have often been granted advantageous terms at the expense of everyone else. The unfunded cost hangs over the finances of many nations – an inheritance of debt for the next generation.

Some of us may be tempted to say, 'OK, then. Let's get rid of state pensions altogether. They have obviously failed. Government involvement in saving for old age has done more harm than good.'

That may well be true. But it seems unlikely that democracies will be willing to give up all government involvement in pensions. In which case, we need to find a better way of running them. What could that be? Are there any countries that have had more success with pensions? If so, how have they managed it?

One measure of success is whether older people are poor compared to the general population. It is far from being a perfect measure (see the note accompanying the bar chart below), but it is somewhere to start. On this basis, it appears that the Netherlands has done relatively well. Its older people are less poor compared to the general population than in other countries.[46]

Where pensioners are relatively poor

Percentage of over-65s with income less than 50 per cent of median household incomes. Source: OECD.[47] These figures should be treated with caution since accurate income figures are difficult to capture and subject to the honesty or otherwise of tax returns and benefit claims. Also a country might provide generous pensions that are not sustainable. Meanwhile, someone deemed to be 'relatively poor' in Switzerland may well be richer than someone with an average income in Greece.

So what is the Dutch system? First, there is a basic pension paid to everyone who has lived or worked in the country. People become entitled to it at a rate of 2 per cent of the full pension for each year they have lived or worked there. The full value amounts to 29 per cent of average earnings so it is basic – not luxurious.

The second element consists of thousands of funded occupational pension schemes. They appear to be compulsory for most people. Some schemes are run by pension funds and the rest by individual companies.[48] In either case, the value is transferable when someone changes job. The pensions are mostly based on the individual's average earnings during his or her working life. The pension funds have real investments – in bonds, shares and bank accounts.

It must be admitted that the system has had a few setbacks. Payments were reduced by 1.9 per cent on average after the weakness in the financial markets in 2008.[49] Some cutbacks have been as high as 15 per cent.[50] Rising life expectancy has also led to increases in the age at which the pensions are payable. But the Dutch system has two big pluses: the government has not built up a huge unfunded liability and the level of payments is high compared to other systems. Payments from Dutch private pensions amount to 5.2 per cent of GDP – one of the highest levels in the world. The Dutch system certainly seems better than average.

The fact that it is 'funded' – that is, it has real investments behind it – seems to be a key reason for its success. But if we are going to consider a funded system, there are two other models worth looking at.

I am in Singapore and a think tank there has succeeded in arranging for me to meet Thurman Shanmugaratnam, the deputy Prime Minister and Minister of Finance. A taxi deposits me at the side of a busy street in the centre of town. I look up

Thurman Shanmugaratnam: 'compulsion is not what makes Singapore different'.

and see a modern tower of offices looming over me – the Ministry of Finance. I go in and pass through security before going up in a fast lift to the floor where Shanmugaratnam works. There I am ushered into a large and, frankly, rather grim internal meeting room. It has chairs but no windows. Suddenly the minister marches in followed by a small entourage. He is a tall, slim, balding man of Indian heritage with dark areas under his eyes. He radiates active intelligence. He is a prime example of how clever people in Singapore are sometimes fast-tracked to the top. The interview turns into one of the most demanding I have ever done. He deals with issues so quickly and definitively that I have to hurry to think of further questions to ask.

We cover a wide range of subjects but before long we come to the Singapore pension system. All Singaporeans are obliged to contribute to personal accounts with what is known as the Central Provident Fund. Their money is invested in bonds, shares and even gold. They can choose fund managers and individual shares within certain rules. But it is compulsory for everybody to pay into the scheme.

Some people in other countries might be unhappy about the compulsory element, I suggest to Shanmugaratnam.

He deals with the objection briskly. The element of compulsion is not what makes Singapore system different, he declares. Many other countries compulsorily take money from workers to pay for their welfare. What is different about Singapore is that it is transparent, it is funded and it retains the element of self-reliance. In many Western countries, governments have been short-termist. Large and often unquantified liabilities have been built up for the future.

Frankly, all this is hard to deny. I suggest, though, that it is normal for governments to think short-term. It is a response to democratic pressure for immediate results. He does not accept that it is inevitable. If a government goes ahead and puts the argument that something makes sense for the long term, the opposition has to deal with that argument, he says. As ever with the Singapore government, the attitude is bold and clear.

The Central Provident Fund accords with what people believe in, says the minister: doing well through work rather than welfare; the family; building prosperity and contributing to the community. He points out, perhaps with a little pleasure at the irony, that the fund – the focal point of the Singapore system – developed from arrangements created by Britain when it was the ruling colonial power.[51] He is too polite to add that Singapore has kept and successfully developed this system whereas the 'mother country' has taken another direction with inferior results.

How does the Central Provident Fund work? Workers and their employers pay a lot of money into the scheme to build up a personal fund which the individual can use to pay for housing and healthcare as well as pensions. Up to the age of thirty-five, the employee must pay in 16 per cent of earnings and the employer a further 20 per cent. On the face of it, this appears like another damaging wedge – a big gap between the cost of employing someone and the amount the person actually receives. But this is different because all the money paid in continues to belong to the individual. So he or she need not feel the payments are disappearing. Each individual can see, year by year, how money is building up in the personal account or, to be more precise, accounts.

'It is fairer and sounder to have each generation pay for itself and each person save for his own pension fund.'

Lee Kuan Yew, former Prime Minister of Singapore[52]

Part of the contributions goes into the individual's pension fund – known as the Special Account.[53] This part starts at 6 per cent of income, rises to a high of 9.5 per cent between the ages of fifty and fifty-five, then falls suddenly to 2 per cent and declines further thereafter.[54]

Below is a young woman's statement of her account with the Central Provident Fund. You can see she has been employed for less than two years but already she has savings of almost S$15,000 (about £7,000). The Medisave Account shown on the statement is for healthcare and the Ordinary Account is normally used to buy housing, although any excess can also be used for other purposes including investment and education.

Cash in the Special and Medisave accounts attracts an interest rate of at least 5 per cent at present when total savings in the fund are $60,000 or less.[55] This is a good rate since inflation is very low in Singapore. But savers can choose to make other investments once they have saved a basic minimum in this deposit account.[56] Though the rules are complex, one can gain exposure to share markets through approved unit trusts run by well-known international companies such as Allianz, Franklin, Fidelity, Templeton, Aberdeen, Schroders and Legg Mason.[57] In one account, they can also put up to 10 per cent of their money in gold funds.

CPF STATEMENT OF ACCOUNT

STATEMENT PERIOD JAN TO DEC 2011	NAME HUI :		ACCOUNT NO.

TRANSACTION DATE	CODE	FOR MTH/ YR OF	REF	ORDINARY ACCOUNT (OA) $	SPECIAL ACCOUNT (SA) $	MEDISAVE ACCOUNT (MA) $
01 JAN	BAL			2,122.54	568.35	707.42
18 JAN	CON	DEC2010	A	598.06	129.94	182.00
17 FEB	CON	JAN2011	A	598.06	129.94	182.00
19 FEB	DPS			-36.00		
15 MAR	CON	FEB2011	A	598.06	129.94	182.00
19 APR	CON	MAR2011	A	598.11	142.97	181.92
18 MAY	CON	APR2011	A	598.11	142.97	181.92
16 JUN	CON	MAY2011	A	598.11	142.97	181.92
15 JUL	CON	JUN2011	A	598.11	142.97	181.92
17 AUG	CON	JUL2011	A	598.11	142.97	181.92
19 SEP	CON	AUG2011	A	598.11	142.97	181.92
17 OCT	CON	SEP2011	A	598.12	155.93	181.95
16 NOV	CON	OCT2011	A	598.12	155.93	181.95
16 DEC	CON	NOV2011	A	598.12	155.93	181.95
31 DEC	INT			134.55	120.07	85.40
31 DEC	BAL			9,398.29	2,403.85	2,976.19

REF A : NATIONAL UNIVERSITY OF SPORE

Miss Hui (aged about twenty-four) saves for her pension

The rules are complex but one can detect a few themes. One is that people should save in order to provide for themselves. A second is that particularly attractive terms are offered to those who have less money. Third, the government does not want people to blow all the money at retirement and then have nothing to live on.

Unfortunately, we do not have readily to hand comparative statistics to show how well or badly the elderly in Singapore do compared to elsewhere because Singapore is not a member of the OECD. But it appears difficult to reach old age in Singapore without having built up savings. It seems probable, at least, that the elderly are relatively well catered for. It seems even more likely that the current and new generation of workers will do a lot better with their savings than those in the vast majority of Western countries. Exactly as the first Prime Minister of Singapore, Lee Kuan Yew, intended, the old generation is not being unfair to the new.

But there is a third model for funded pensions, too. Back in 1974, Chile had a traditional, unfunded pension scheme. It suffered from the typical problems of such schemes taken to an extreme. Contributions needed to be enormous to pay existing pensioners. They amounted to more than half a worker's salary. This gave rise to exactly the sort of problems already described and on a big scale: mass evasion, a large black economy and very high unemployment.[58]

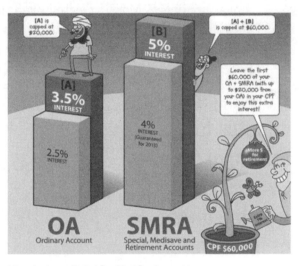

Interest rates on Central Provident Fund accounts.

Something had to be done. A new system of personal retirement accounts was created. As in Singapore, contributors could choose how to allocate their pension funds. They were similarly able to see the value of their individual plans grow. But there were two key differences: the scheme was not compulsory and people did not have to save via a government agency. They could go direct to a fund manager.

It is true that once this scheme was in place, a large minority of the population remained outside it and low-paid people became entitled to very modest pensions.[59] However, it is worth remembering that at the beginning of this process, Chile was an extremely poor country with a pension system already in meltdown, unlike the others we have considered. Moreover since this system has existed, Chile has grown enormously in prosperity. The pension scheme is obviously not the only reason but it may well have contributed.

In 2008, the system was reformed again and the basic state pension element was increased. But the investment part was retained and in 2012, a study by actuaries Melbourne Mercer with the Australian Centre for Financial Studies ranked the Chilean pension system above those of some advanced countries including the USA, Japan, France and Germany.

Several countries have moved in the same direction. Denmark in the 1980s started increasing the proportion of privately managed, funded pensions. Funded occupational pensions were made all but universal in the 1990s. Since then, personal funded pensions have also been encouraged. In Sweden, reform began in 1994 which also led to the development of pensions backed by investments. It is only a minor part of the system but at least some pension income is now backed by real investments. Moreover individuals can choose the fund managers who will look after the money. The Polish also moved towards funded personal pension funds, although this element has subsequently been reduced.

> ‘The major impetus for reform of the Swedish system was the threat of financial disaster.’[60]
>
> OECD report, ‘The Swedish Pension Reform Model: Framework and Issues’

One of the advantages of personal pensions with actual investments is that people seem happier to declare their incomes and pay their contributions. They understand that the money remains theirs and is not disappearing perhaps never to return,

In Chile, the size of the black economy admittedly is bigger than that of the average advanced country. It is estimated to be 19.5 per cent, compared with a 16.6 per cent average for advanced countries. But Chile has a smaller black economy than Belgium, Spain and Italy and, compared to the rest of South America, it is outstanding. It has the smallest black economy of any country on the continent. The black economy of Brazil is twice the size. Singapore, meanwhile, has a black economy of 13.0 per cent – below average for advanced countries and probably significantly smaller than that of nearby countries in south-east Asia.

After all these stories and experiences, what conclusions should we draw?

First and above all, we should conclude that typical state pensions have been among the most disastrous parts of many modern welfare states. One of the key reasons for the multiple problems they have created is that they have been unfunded. Funded pensions have performed better in countries as diverse as the Netherlands, Singapore and Chile.[61]

What might be the best way to reform?

I would suggest that the majority of pension payments should come from funded pension accounts under the control of each individual. It might work something like this:

What can go wrong with personal funded pensions?

The stock market might fall. Over the length of a working life, stock market returns including dividends have been positive in most countries.[62] However, it is worth guarding against the risk that savers of modest means might find they suddenly lose a significant part of their savings just before they retire. One possible answer is to provide better-than-normal cash returns on the first tranche of savings. Only when savings have gone beyond this minimum would people be free to invest in normal investments such as cash deposits, bonds, managed funds, property, gold or shares.

Fees and other transaction costs can be high. An important part of the design of the system should be to make sure that contributors can avoid high charges unless they deliberately decide that a high cost fund is what they want.

Individual liberty is constrained by compulsory contributions. True, but this is no worse than existing systems in which money is taken in social insurance and all personal control and ownership is lost.

Governments can raid them. True again, but the risk can be reduced if the whole population has a stake in the system and there are constitutional safeguards.

- Everyone should have considerable freedom to choose his or her investments.

- The pension funds should be compulsory for everyone in employment. (In some countries, voluntary schemes have had poor take-up. If everyone is involved, this provides greater political protection from raids on the investments by governments.)

- Even with universal involvement, the integrity of schemes should be heavily protected by law. Experience in Britain, Australia and Poland has shown that governments find it hard to resist the large pots of money in funded pensions.

- A truly basic pension might also be paid to everyone who has been resident in a country for a long period. This makes means-tested benefits less significant and means-tested benefits discourage work, honesty and self-reliance. The Netherlands has this and New Zealand has started a version of it, too.[63]

- The retirement age should rise automatically with life expectancy.

- All public servants should take part in the same pension scheme as everyone else. Any extra benefits that may be justified for a particular public service job should be transparent and paid outside the pension system. Members of parliament and ministers, above all, should have no special treatment. In addition to the question of fairness, special pensions might cause them to care less about the success of the system used by the general public. Special terms for public servants should be seen for what they are: a form of corruption.

How can a country with an 'unfunded' pension scheme make the transition?

The method recommended by most specialists is to let the older generation continue with existing pensions while the next generation starts the new system. Those in the middle would have a mixture. It must be admitted that there is a problem of affordability: the new generation must pay, to some extent, both for their own and for their parents' pensions. But this difficulty can be reduced by significantly increasing the retirement age and failing to index pensions to match growth in the economy.

This is not politically easy. But old government pay-as-you-go unfunded pension schemes have been a failure. Funded personal pensions would mean elderly people would be better off for generations to come.

9.

'While her dear father lived, any change of condition must be impossible for her. She would never quit him.'

Who cares for the elderly?

EMMA WOODHOUSE LIVES WITH HER elderly father and cares for him. He is a nervous man, but she comforts and reassures him. They have a family friend, George Knightley, whom Emma has known since she was a child. The two of them enjoy bantering with each other. They have had a few serious disagreements, too, but finally they have come to realise that they love each other.

Knightley proposes to Emma. She wants to marry him but she says 'no'. She cannot go to live with Knightley because she believes she has a duty to her father to stay with him as long as he lives. 'While her dear father lived, any change of condition must be impossible for her. She would never quit him.'

Knightley does not complain or try to change her mind. He recognises and accepts her wish to fulfil this duty. Fortunately they find a way to resolve the problem: Knightley suggests that he could come to live with Emma at her father's home for as long as he is alive. That way they can marry and Emma can continue caring for her father.

This is the climax of *Emma*, written by Jane Austen

Emma Woodhouse with her elderly father.

and published in 1815. Most people who read it probably do not particularly notice that it is accepted as normal and right that Emma feels she has a duty to her father and that even her suitor accepts that this duty exists.

In another of the most famous nineteenth-century novels, *Great Expectations* by Charles Dickens, published in 1861, Clara Barley – much further down in the social scale – is pursued by Herbert Pocket. She, too, takes it as normal and right that she should continue to live with and care for her father. He is extremely eccentric and difficult. He 'roars' and bangs on the floor. But still she stays with him. She 'holds dutifully to her father as long as he lasts', says Dickens. Only after he dies does she consent to marry Herbert.

This is not only a matter of women looking after their parents either. In the same novel, John Wemmick, a bill collector, also takes care of his father. Dickens describes the father as 'a very old man in a flannel coat; clean, cheerful, comfortable and well cared for, but intensely deaf'. Wemmick fires a cannon every day and the father takes pleasure in being able to hear it.

Children used to live with or near their elderly parents and take care of them around the world. Of course it did not take place in every case. But it was usual. In Sweden, a detailed study of family life in the nineteenth century revealed that 'at least half of the population [over 65] had a child living close to them in every age group'.[1] At the age of eighty-five, an elderly person had a fifty-fifty chance of living in close proximity with one or more adult children. Care of elderly parents by their children in Sweden was so orthodox then that it was legally enforceable up until 1956.

Until recently there was also legal and institutional pressure for children in Germany to take responsibility for the care of their parents.[2] In Belgium there is still a remnant of it – a legal obligation for children to pay for the care of their parents if the parents run out of money. But generally since the nineteenth century, an extraordinary change has taken place. While, in some countries, the idea that children should take responsibility for their parents remains, in others it has almost completely disappeared.

The typical crunch moment is

Does Granny live with her children when her husband dies?

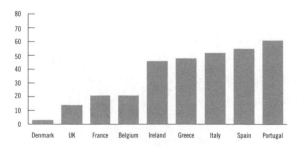

Percentage of women aged sixty-five and over without a partner living with their children.[3]

when an elderly woman is widowed. Will she live alone or with one of her children? In Portugal, Spain and Italy over half of women over sixty-five who are without a partner live with their children. In Denmark, only 3 per cent do. The incidence of older women living with their children is twenty times higher in Portugal than Denmark. The contrast is extreme.

A second set of statistics covers all women over sixty-five including those whose partners are still alive. It has the advantage of covering a few extra countries and it shows that, in some countries, adult children are living with both their parents. In these multi-generational households, the elderly are not necessarily frail.

How many women over sixty-five live with their children?

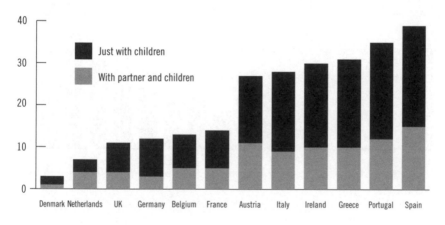

Percentage living with just their children (dark bar) and living with their partner and children together (light bar). Figures prior to 2000.

Source: Institute for Social and Economic Research[4]

In this chart we see that the Netherlands and Italy are similarly poles apart. Only a fraction of Dutch women over sixty-five live with their children – 7 per cent. In Italy, four times as many do – 28 per cent.

Why are there such big contrasts in the way people treat the elderly?

It is tempting to say, 'Oh well, the Mediterranean countries have a strong tradition of extended families' or, 'The Catholic countries are the ones which look after their elderly.' But these generalisations are not to be relied on. Most countries – perhaps all – previously had a tradition of children caring for their parents. Japan is a country where it is common for children to live with and care for their elderly parents. More than 61 per cent of Japanese women aged over eighty live with one of their children.[5] Japan is obviously neither Catholic nor Mediterranean. Moreover if it were just a matter of Mediterranean culture, why would almost as many women over sixty-five live with their children in Austria as in Italy?

Take another measure of family life: in Austria, 7.5 per cent of children – not adult children – live in multi-generational households. That is twenty-five times more than in Sweden. Of course, neither of these countries is Mediterranean.

Children living in multi-generational households

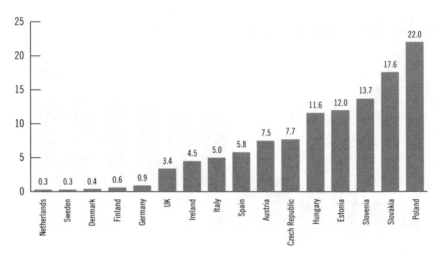

Source: OECD, *Doing Better for Families*[6]

It could be that a culture – along with political ideas – influences the shape of the welfare state, which in turn affects how people treat their elderly – reinforcing or undermining past practice.

If it is not simply a matter of Catholicism or being on the Mediterranean, what other factors could be at work? Let's go back to the contrast between the Netherlands and Italy.

In the Netherlands, people pay social insurance through their working lifetimes and part of the premium pays for long-term care in a home if it is needed. This is part of the system and people are consequently encouraged to believe it is normal for the elderly to go into a home rather than be cared for by the family. Indeed it goes against the grain to pay for something and then not use it. That is surely one of the reasons why the proportion in care homes in the Netherlands is five times that in Italy, and this reduces the proportion who are cared for by family members.

How many are in residential care?

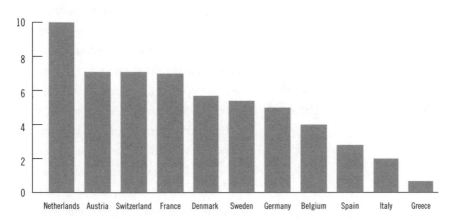

Percentage of people aged sixty-five and over in residential care homes.[7] The difference between the Mediterranean countries and the Netherlands is dramatic. But Germany and Belgium also have much lower rates, probably due to current or previous laws requiring adult children to take responsibility.

The provision of care for the elderly outside the family has similarly been much greater in Denmark than in Portugal.[8] Denmark was once described as 'the envy of the world' in its government-provided care for the elderly.[9] That could help account for why older women are more than eleven times more likely to live with their children in Portugal than in Denmark. In contrast, Japan has kept its provision of institutional care for the elderly comparatively modest. So the continued high level of family care there could well be a response to this history of relatively low government provision.[10]

The idea that the financial arrangements organised by governments affect family care is supported by some academic studies. Gary Engelhardt and Nadia Greenhalgh-Stanley studied the effect of changes in Medicare payments for healthcare in the home that took place at different times in different places between 1997 and 2000. They concluded that 'elderly housing and living arrangements are quite responsive to social insurance benefits'.[11]

The overall effect of the changes was to make

Ten per cent of residents of England and Wales provide unpaid care for someone with an illness or disability.[12]

government provision for the elderly more modest.[13] It seems likely that this is why the proportion of elderly living in 'multi-generational' families in the United States ended a long-running decline and rallied a little, from 17 per cent in 1990 to 20 per cent in 2008.[14]

If it is true that government policies are framing, however unintentionally, how families live, perhaps governments should be thinking in terms of whether their influence is for good or ill. Do they really wish to diminish the importance of both the immediate and the extended family?

The decline in the proportion of elderly living with their children appears to have ended in the USA
1900: 57%
1980: 17%
1990: 17%
2008: 20%

Percentage of Americans aged sixty-five and over living in a multi-generational family.[15] According to Pew Research, one of the possible explanations is 'cuts to Medicare enacted in 1997'.

Are government-run care and the crowding out of the family's role the best thing for the elderly? Governments, especially in Europe, along with the European Union and the OECD, often take it for granted that they are.[16] They support taxing everyone and then giving the money only to those who have government-provided care. But are they right? Is it truly in the interests of the elderly?

How would the elderly *like* to be cared for? The question rarely seems to be asked.

But, unusually, it was posed in a Japanese government survey. People were asked where they would like to receive long-term care if they came to need it. One in five wanted to go to a care home, nursing home or hospital. The vast majority wanted to receive long-term care at home, either independently of their family (46 per cent) or with the help of their family (28 per cent).[17] It seems that some parents would love to live with or near to their children. But others genuinely do not want to and would rather be independent as long as possible. Some may prefer to put up with a bit of loneliness because they feel they should not be a burden for their children in the prime of their lives.

I wonder what readers of this book would reply if asked where they would like to be living aged, say, eighty-five. Alone? In an institution? With family? Very close to family?[18] Of course there is a wide spectrum of circumstances. What is best in one case would not work in another. Some

'Asked where th
would like to spe
their last da
Americans alm
always say at hor
surrounded by peo
they love ... In real
though, ... more th
30 per cent die i
nursing home ... a
over half end up i
hospit

The Econor

people aged ninety are still married, hale and hearty. Others twenty years younger are highly dependent.

There are four basic living arrangements: living with a partner; living with family; being in an institution; and living alone. Let's look at how things go for people in various circumstances.

The Pew Research Center interviewed people aged sixty-five and older about whether they felt lonely. Among those who lived with others, 8 per cent said they were lonely. Among those who lived alone, the proportion was more than three times bigger (28 per cent).

Are older people happy living alone?

EXPERIENCE LONELINESS

Living alone	28%
Living with others	8%

OFTEN FEEL SAD OR DEPRESSED

Living alone	28%
Living with others	15%

Source: Pew Research Center[20]

The Johanniter aid organisation in Germany supplies elderly people with buttons attached to wrist or neck bands. Subscribers, who generally live alone, can press the button in an emergency to summon help. Every day, the organisation receives nearly 3,000 emergency calls from their 110,000 customers. In more than half these cases, no one has fallen down or become ill. People have pressed the button just to have someone to talk to.[25]

It may seem like a statement of the obvious but – just in case there is any doubt – lonely people are not happy.[21] As John Cacioppo and William Patrick put it, 'social isolation is on a par with high blood pressure, obesity, lack of exercise, or smoking as a risk factor for illness and early death'.[22] And again, 'individuals with the highest baseline scores for loneliness were also the ones most likely to be admitted to a nursing home over a four-year period'.[23]

People who live alone are more likely to suffer a decline in both their health and their mental abilities than those who live with others. So it is no surprise that those living alone are twice as likely to enter a nursing home as others. This is according to a study of studies – a 'meta-analysis'.[24] It is a massive difference.

n Hamburg, social orkers came across n old woman who adn't spoken with nyone for two ears other than the upermarket checkout oman.'

egel Online International[27]

Some people may think, 'Well, living in a retirement home will mean an elderly person is not lonely. So that would be the best thing.' But it is not contact with just anybody that mitigates a feeling of loneliness. It is not even the amount of time spent with other people. It is the nature of relationship: 'the individual's ratings of the meaningfulness, or the meaninglessness, of their encounters with other people.'[26] When it comes to quality of this sort, the natural intimacy of being with family members and old friends is likely to be best.

Those who are married are the least lonely and the least likely to go into a nursing home.[28] Living with children is not as good as being married but the results are much better than living alone. In a study of over 8,000 people over ten years, nearly one in five of those living alone went to a nursing home.[29] Of those who remained married, fewer than half as many did. Those who lived throughout with one of their children were in between. The chances of going to a nursing home were reduced by a third. These are powerful indicators of the importance of family life to happiness and well-being.[30]

How many went to a nursing home?

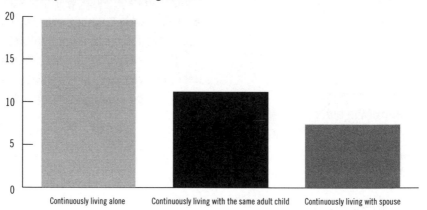

Percentage of people aged seventy and over admitted into a nursing home during a ten-year study.[31]

What are the results like for those admitted to a nursing home or a residential home? One study in England and Wales compared elderly people in residential care with those at home – both those living alone and those living with family.[32] The researchers used the Geriatric Mental State exam to gauge levels of depression. They found 9.3 per cent of those living at home were depressed but the figure soared to 27.1 per cent for those living in residential care – nearly three times as many. The study concluded that 'depression was highly prevalent' in residential homes.

Will granny *really* be happy in the care home?

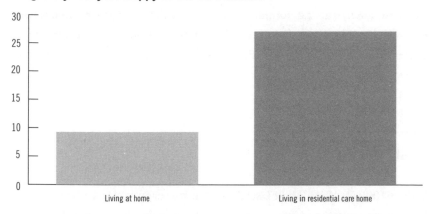

Rates of depression among those living at home and those living in residential care homes. Based on a study in England and Wales.[33]

The researchers investigated various symptoms of depression. They even asked people if they wished they were dead. A remarkably high proportion of people living at home – 12 per cent – said that they did. We should remember that it is likely that many of them were living alone. Among the elderly who had moved to care homes, however, the proportion wishing they were dead jumped to 21 per cent – more than one in five.

How many of the elderly 'wish they were dead'?

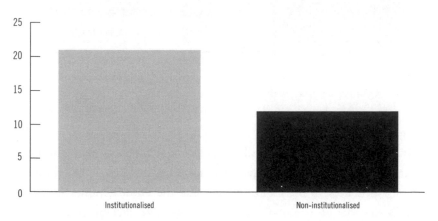

Proportion of elderly who say they wish there were dead who live at home and who live in a residential care home.[34]

That study was of people in residential care. One would expect depression levels to be worse still in nursing homes. One study was done of residents in a nursing home in Berlin.[35] It found that over a third suffered from minor depression and a further fifth endured major depression so that, in total, 56 per cent of residents were depressed.

Would you like to live here?

I **AM VISITING AN ANGLICAN RETIREMENT** village in the suburbs of Sydney. The village is on a big site with its own attractive roads lined with trees. It is like being in a separate world.

There are three kinds of accommodation. Those in relatively good health live independently in well-landscaped, attractively designed flats. They can buy in services such as laundry and help with cleaning. They can eat in their flats or go into one of the dining rooms to have meals. They can also take part in organised activities.

For those less able to cope, there are large residential homes. People in these blocks have their own rooms with plenty of their own possessions. They share living rooms and can take part in

organised activities. It looks well run. But with plenty of old people gathered together – seeming quiet and perhaps depressed – these homes frankly are not places where I would go, given a choice.

Finally, those residents who are seriously disabled or bed ridden go to the on-site nursing home. I was not taken to that building but was told that life expectancy there is significantly shorter than in the residential homes.

Academics reading this may well be thinking to themselves, 'Hang on! The causation could be the other way around. It could be that depressed people are more likely to go to care homes, not that care homes make them depressed.'

This is indeed a theoretical possibility and it would be excellent if someone could unpick the truth with a really long-term study that saw people through a variety of experiences. In the meantime, we must use a little common sense. Yes, it is surely true that people who are depressed are more likely to go to a care or nursing home. Depression and loneliness tend to lead to health problems. But the figures for depression in institutions are on such a major scale that it seems likely that the main thing is that being in residential care – let alone in a nursing home

– causes depression. We know from many other studies that social interaction is important and contact with loved ones particularly significant. We also know that people like to have some control of their own environments – where they go and when they get up in the morning. Many of us have personal knowledge of people who were cheerful and full of life but who, without any other change in their lives, went to institutions and became depressed. Some of us, sadly, have known people who, soon after admission, died.

On the basis of this and other evidence, it seems that there is a kind of progression from the best circumstance for well-being for the elderly to the worst:

1. Living with a spouse.

2. Living with an adult child.

3. Living alone – this tends to be more lonely but the feeling can be mitigated by plenty of social activity.

4. Living in a care home – significantly more depression.

5. Living in a nursing home – a majority of people are likely to be depressed.

Some people might think, 'Well, Granny might not be particularly happy in a care or nursing home, but at least she will be well looked after by professionals.' Is that right? Among those who are elderly but not in institutions, between 5 and 10 per cent suffer from malnutrition. But, in some studies, up to 60 per cent of those in institutions have been found to be malnourished.[36] The study in Berlin mentioned above revealed 22.8 per cent malnourished and a further 57.9 per cent 'at nutritional risk'.[37] It is a shock that malnourishment is so common in places which exist for the very purpose of looking after the elderly.

In mitigation, one should mention that depressed elderly people tend to be malnourished and reluctant to eat. However, there is some evidence that, even in hospitals, there can be inadequate efforts to help elderly people with their meals. The Care Quality Commission found that 38 per cent of inpatients in England said they did not get enough help with eating or only 'sometimes' did.[38]

> **'I just want to hold the hand of one of my children or grandchildren each day!'**
>
> Elderly woman in a care home, talking to the author

The chairman, Dame Jo Williams, commented, 'Time and again we found cases where ... people were left without call bells, ignored for hours on end, or not given assistance to do the basics of life, to eat, drink or go to the toilet.'[40] In a poll of 1,000 nurses in Britain, almost 30 per cent said they would not trust the hospital they worked in to take note of malnutrition if one of their own relatives was a patient.[41] Malnutrition, of course, leads to further problems such as lower resistance to disease and a greater likelihood of injury through falling.

Ten per cent of NHS hospitals ... failed to meet standards on treating patients with dignity and respect. Only 2 per cent of private hospitals had the same failings.'

Daily Mail, citing Care Quality Commission report. The report explained that common themes in the hospitals which did not treat people with respect were 'lack of privacy, call bells being out of reach, and staff speaking to patients in a condescending way'.[39]

In one study in America, it was found that 92.5 per cent of nursing home residents did not drink enough.[43] Some elderly people need to be reminded and encouraged to drink many times in order to get them to take enough.[44] When staff do not have the time, this does not happen.

One indicator of how good nursing homes are at looking after their patients is how frequently they fail to manage medical problems which should be within their capabilities. Congestive heart failure, asthma and diabetes are examples. An alarmingly high proportion of admissions to hospital from nursing homes are of this sort, indicating that residents have not been well cared for. In one study in Los Angeles, 45 per cent of hospitalisations should not have been necessary.[45] In a study in the state of Georgia, the figure reached 67 per cent.

Another indicator of poor-quality care is the incidence of pressure ulcers. The variation is dramatic – anywhere between 2.2 per cent and 23.9 per cent in American nursing homes, according to an assessment by the Institute for Healthcare Improvement.[46] The vast majority of pressure ulcers can be prevented with the right equipment and care. In one nursing home, the incidence of heel ulcers – one of the most common kinds – was reduced by 95 per cent simply by the use of heel protectors.[47] This sort of thing can be prevented relatively easily but – clearly – often isn't.

'There was a tiny lady of ninety-thr[ee] no longer ill but too frail to return hor[ne] At first she was very jolly and t[old] me in her fluting, refined voice ab[out] her father, who managed a fam[ous] biscuit company, and about courting the Wrens. Over three weeks I sa[w a] change; her voice became faint, she [sat] with her head hanging down, breakf[ast] untouched. No one helped her to e[at]. No one thought to investigate h[er] and why she had suddenly become [so] weak. "God help me," she whispe[red] as I held her ha[nd]

Jane Kelly describing one of her experiences [as a] visitor at a British National Health Service hosp[ital]

There is reason to fear that drugs may be used excessively in nursing homes, too. A US government report revealed that 14 per cent of residents of nursing homes receive so-called 'atypical anti-psychotic drugs'. An astonishing 88 per cent were used for reasons that were 'off label' – meaning reasons other than those for which they are intended.[48] 'Off-label' use can be for sound medical reasons but this should be the exception, not the rule. Such drugs are sometimes used as a so-called 'chemical cosh' to make it easier to look after agitated patients. Unfortunately their use can lead to life-threatening nervous system problems, diabetes, low blood pressure and dizziness. The government report found that 22 per cent of the time these drugs were not administered in accordance with the official standards with regard to unnecessary use.[49]

A British study found that more than a quarter of elderly people with dementia were being given anti-psychotics (of all types) and that in most cases they were being given them as sedatives.[50] These are drugs that are meant to be given for short periods and as a last resort. Their use is meant to be reviewed regularly but this was often not done. They can make dementia worse.

Be Nice To Your Kids They'll Choose Your Nursing Home

Humorous fridge magnet.

I should emphasise that of course there are care homes that are run conscientiously and well. But there are also cases where care is worse than inadequate. It is callous or even cruel. In some cases, people have become suspicious and have set up hidden cameras, discovering some very unpleasant things.[52] A notorious case took place at Winterbourne View, a care home in England. A BBC reporter secretly filmed carers pinning patients down, slapping them, dousing them in water and taunting them. An official report stated that there was 'considerable' physical violence against patients and some required hospital treatment as a result.[53]

The difficulty with this and other such reports is that it is hard to know how common such treatment is. Naturally while inspectors or relatives are visiting, such behaviour stops. It

'...ch day, hundreds of ...usands of nursing home ...dents are given anti-...chotic drugs, even though ... ...se drugs are inappropriate ...d life-threatening for the vast ...ority of residents to whom ...y are given.'

...delman, senior policy attorney for the Center for ...are Advocacy, in his statement to the Senate Special ...ittee on Aging[51]

has been found that the elderly are reluctant to report it because they 'don't want to make a fuss' or they fear they might be treated even worse in revenge. The same difficulty of measurement goes for bad treatment by carers who visit the elderly in their homes to help them get out of bed, wash them and prepare a meal.

NEWS ITEM, WEDNESDAY 13 FEBRUARY 2013: 'A quarter of care provided for the elderly in their own homes is "unsatisfactory" according to the Care Quality Commission.' BBC Radio 5 live has an interview with Valerie, an elderly woman who receives care at her home. The interviewer, Rachel Burden, asks Valerie what she thinks of the care she gets.

Valerie says it used to be bad. She remembers a day when the carer was late for the first visit – to hoist her out of bed. The carer said she was sorry but her car had broken down, and added that she would not be coming for the second visit at all – to toilet Valerie and give her lunch – because she would have to collect her car.

'Who will come instead?' asked Valerie.

'No one,' the carer replied.

Rachel Burden asks how things have got better since that day. Valerie says that, about four and half years ago, she was allowed to move to a different system. Instead of the caring agency being chosen by her local government, she was allowed to use money allocated to her to choose the care agency herself. She says she has now got a much better service from an agency called Nightingale. She has the same carer every day except when that carer has a day off. When that happens, she is told who will be coming instead.

Valerie says she likes having the same person coming to help her. Some agencies think it is bad for carers to become friendly with the elderly people they look after, but elderly people appreciate it, Valerie says. They do not like just anybody coming into their homes.

In England, local councils are responsible for home visits by carers. An inquiry conducted by a trade union, Unison, found that 73 per cent of councils commission visits that last only fifteen minutes.[54] The union's spokesman, Heather Wakefield, said,

> Imagine trying to provide personal care to an incontinent 94-year-old with dementia, clearing up any mess they have made, feeding them and giving them medicines, all in just fifteen minutes. There is no time left to have a conversation, let alone provide some compassionate care before rushing out. No wonder home carers tell us they are depressed about the standard of care they are forced to provide.

In theory, those in greatest need such as the woman described would be allocated a longer slot of thirty or forty-five minutes. But councils are short of money and the large proportion of them which sometimes provide very short visits suggests that many people may be getting peremptory, inadequate care.

Cost is an important and growing problem, causing a decline in the quality of the care that governments provide. In the USA, the Congressional Budget Office projects that public and private spending on long-term care for the elderly will more than double from 1.3 per cent of GDP in 2010 to 3.0 per cent in 2050.[55] Frankly they would be lucky to get away with such a modest increase given the ageing population. In Japan, the cost of government expenditure alone – following the introduction of a new long-term care insurance system in 2000 – doubled in only six years to reach 1.2 per cent of GDP.[56] Denmark starts from a higher base. Its government expenditure already stands at over 2 per cent of GDP,[57] so as the population ages a rise in cost of such proportions or anything like them would be hard to manage.

When governments first started offering care for the elderly, of course, life expectancy was much lower, and it is the number of the most elderly which is set to rise fastest. In Britain, the population aged over eighty is set to soar from three million to eight million between 2008 and 2050.[58] The ratio of younger working people to older people is collapsing, with the same implications for elderly care as for pensions. The figures for Japan are forbidding. In 2000, there were 3.9 working-age people for every person over sixty-five. By 2050, there will only be 1.3.[59] Younger people have got to pay for the pensions of older people and also care for them. There is one bit of good news, however: the elderly are generally healthy for longer than in previous generations.

But the rising cost pressure means that, around the world, savings in the cost of caring for the elderly have been made in every way you can think of. Staffing levels have been reduced, resulting in less personal attention. Waiting lists have been allowed to rise. Priority has been given only to those in the worst condition, so people who, in truth, cannot cope well have been left to fend for themselves. In Australia, the elderly who are deemed to be 'low priority' can wait months before even being assessed.[60] In a number of countries, homes for the elderly have increasingly been contracted out to private companies to reduce the cost per person. Governments have encouraged the elderly to stay at home with offers of 'in-home' support, which is vastly cheaper than institutional care. And when that has not saved enough money, there has sometimes been a reduction of the amount of such support and it has been provided only to those in the worst circumstances.

The responses vary from country to country. But everywhere, cost is a major problem and governments accordingly want more elderly people to stay at home. Some politicians claim they have come to realise that people are happier at home. In reality, all have been influenced by the soaring cost.

In the Netherlands, where nursing and care homes dominate, they admit – openly or otherwise – that the cost is getting too much. I talked to Esther Mot, a Dutch economist, who expressed some jealousy that the cost of the German system to the government was not expanding as fast as in the Netherlands.[61] Why is that, I asked? Because in Germany, people are expected to pay more of the cost out of their own pockets. she said.

Vic is a taxi driver in Sydney. He is a Sikh and says that part of his heritage is a belief that children have a duty to look after their parents in old age. The money he earns in Australia will help enable him to fulfil his duty to his parents.[62]

All of the above – the cutbacks to government care due to cost and the greater happiness of the elderly in or near their families – seems to lead to one conclusion: that adult children should more frequently take care of their elderly parents. I am not suggesting that this is the best thing in all cases. Far from it. In this particular area of welfare – more than any other – it is dangerous to prescribe any universal rule. But in view of what we know about how sad and lonely elderly people can become in institutions and bearing in mind the worryingly poor care they can receive in care homes, in nursing homes and when a carer visits only once a day, it could, perhaps, be regarded as a moral duty of children to be ready and willing to live with and help care for their parents. This applies above all to the elderly who are widowed or otherwise living alone.

Many people in the West may not like this suggestion. They might regard it as an interference in their freedom to live their own lives. They have become accustomed to the idea that social insurance has been paid so the state should provide. But this approach has simply not proved to be humane – to be kind to the elderly.

Jane Kelly, who has been a hospital visitor and seen old people ignored by their families, wrote:

> Over the past six decades, we in the developed north took a rather patronising view of people in southern Europe who seemed to cherish family above any civic sense, or those in the developing world relentlessly having babies to care for them in their old age. But our own experiment in cradle to grave care seems to have failed so maybe they were right all along.[63]

Jane visited Peter, a 75-year-old disabled man. He had nowhere to go so the council allocated him a tiny room with a flickering strip light. It didn't even have a kettle. Jane followed him to this miserable place.[64] To her surprise, Peter mentioned he had a sister in the same city. Jane phoned her.

'What has it to do with me?' the sister said angrily. 'The state should look after him.' She added, 'You'd better get your finger out!' as if it were Jane's responsibility to get the state to look after him better.

Jane asked Peter's sister if she might at least bring her brother a kettle.

She replied, 'Will I get recompensed for it?'

We might, each of us, remember that one day we ourselves will probably be old. In the US, 70 per cent of those who reach the age of sixty-five can expect to need long-term care during their lives.[65] Do we ourselves want to be institutionalised or isolated?

In Sweden, a pensioner died in his home in Tumba, a town south-west of Stockholm.[66] His bills continued to be paid by direct debit. His pension was paid by bank transfers directly into his account. The man had relatives but they were not in regular contact so no one realised that he was dead. Eventually his body was discovered in 2011 because broadband was being installed in the building so people finally entered his home. The food in the refrigerator was found to date back to the beginning of 2008. His body had been lying there for three years with nobody knowing or caring.

In a similar case in Stockholm, a man was found two years after he had died because some plumbing work needed to be done.[67] One of the people interviewed afterwards remarked, 'One wonders how many dead, lonely people are lying across the city.'

In Japan, the phenomenon of 'lonely deaths' has its own special word: *kodokushi*.[68] Inevitably it is happening increasingly because more people live alone. The number of people over sixty-five living alone in Japan jumped from 880,000 in 1980 to 3.86 million in 2005.[69]

In Germany, Klaus Pawletko, director of Friends of the Elderly in Berlin, has seen a lot of poverty during his career. But he says, 'old people actually find being alone much worse than their financial difficulties'. He adds, 'hardly anyone in Germany talks about that'.[70]

While greater family care for the elderly may be desirable, it must be admitted that there can be problems. An Indian woman tells me that a married woman in her

> 'The research found that the closer elderly people live to their children, the less lonely they feel. Older people who see their children once a month or less are twice as likely to feel lonely as those who see their children very regularly.'
>
> Women's Royal Voluntary Service paper, reported in *The Times*.[71]

country is expected to look after the elderly parents of her husband. It is one thing to look after one's own elderly parents but to look after someone else's, even one's husband's, is bound to be less attractive.

In Japan, where a tradition of women looking after the older generation has continued albeit less widely than before, there have been surveys indicating a significant proportion of family carers admit to feelings of hatred for those they care for.[72]

***

AT THE UNITED COMMUNITY CENTRE in Milwaukee, Wisconsin, some of the elderly are resident but others are collected from their homes by bus each day. This helps enable families stay together because the adult children can go out to work, happy in the knowledge that their mother or father is being looked after during the day. Most of the elderly are Hispanic so, to make them feel at home, the central lounge is designed like a Latin American plaza. There is a balcony and birds in cages. The centre offers activities, exercise and social life. Ricardo Diaz, the executive director, says his centre has good facilities for bathing people, which is appreciated because often adult children are embarrassed to help their parents wash. The elderly can also see young children who attend the charter school which is part of the centre. They are not in a ghetto entirely reserved for old people.

A wife may be in the prime of her life and wanting to develop a career. She may not want to care for elderly parents, whether they are her husband's or her own. Perhaps this is why the issue is taboo. To advocate caring for elderly parents comes up against some people's idea of feminism – that women should be able to have careers as uninterrupted as those of men. Even in Spain and Italy, women are increasingly taking full-time jobs. Of course men can be expected to care for their parents, too. But in practice it happens less often.

We should, perhaps, think that it is important for a person – whether a woman or a man – to put a higher priority on caring for an elderly, widowed parent than on a career, at least for a while. In most cases, it should be possible to provide help for an elderly person without sacrificing a whole career. There are all sorts of solutions that can be found. Care can be shared by different family members. Outside help can be brought in.

In Italy, many people try combine family care for their elderly with freedom for the wife by hiring *badanti* – women from poorer countries who are paid to live with elderly people and look after them. They may well live with the extended family in fact. *Badanti* generally come from nearby countries such as Romania, Moldavia, Ukraine or Bulgaria but some come from South America.[73] In Rome, I was told that there are 1.2 million *badanti* out of 1.5 million carers in Italy but some estimates are lower.[74] Something similar happens on a smaller scale in Britain. Many live-in carers come from Zimbabwe and other parts of Africa. The difference in Britain is that they usually live with the elderly person and no one else.

The right course of action depends on individual circumstances. Some elderly may genuinely not want – let alone need – help from their children. Others may be bed-bound and affected by dementia or incontinence or both. They may need turning regularly to avoid bed sores. Some may require medication three times a day and be barely able to speak. Looking after someone in that condition is extremely stressful. To expect a family to do that unaided, at home, would be asking an enormous amount. But the majority of elderly people are in a far better condition and it is quite possible for them in live with or near their children without being a great burden.

The point that repeatedly emerges when looking at the issue is that there is no universal, best answer. Despite this, it is possible to suggest one clear theme to how governments should approach it: they should do nothing that discourages families from looking after their own. In practical terms, that means equality of treatment between families who look after their elderly and those who do not. At present, many countries effectively favour those who leave strangers to look after their parents. This discourages something that makes elderly people happier and healthier.

I **AM IN MADRID AND DOLORES** Navarro Ruiz, minister for social and family affairs in the city, is telling me about the help provided for the elderly in Spain. One service is provided specifically in Madrid. Members of her department make regular telephone calls to elderly people on their list who are living at home to check that they are all right. This gives the elderly some reassurance and human contact. It is extremely popular and appreciated.

No discrimination against families which look after their own.

Another unusual aspect of care there is that Spanish regional governments are required to pay money to families who look after disabled parents. Therefore there is no discrimination against families looking after their own compared to putting them into institutions. This is in high contrast to most countries, such as France, where money is only paid if the care is given by someone outside the family. Spain's lack of discrimination may be laudable but it increases the cost – in the short term, at least. The Netherlands tried something similar and was shocked by the rocketing expense. It cut the programme back to a fraction of what was originally intended.

There are also positive steps that could be taken. One tactic would be to create compulsory savings accounts which could be used to fund care for the elderly as well as general medical care. A key feature would be that the money could be used to fund care by the family as well as by institutions. To maximise innovation and reduce costs, these savings accounts should not be supplied by governments but by friendly societies, mutual societies, trade unions, professional associations and for-profit companies. If the funds turned out not to be needed, the money would become part of the person's estate and could be bequeathed like any other asset. Of course, in some cases, the savings would run out. So to cover at least basic care in these circumstances, governments could also require compulsory care insurance. Only when all this provision was exhausted would the state step in. Again, assistance should go to those cared for by their families as much as for those in care homes or alone.

The central idea of removing obstacles to family care should influence other government policies, too. If an elderly person wants to live with an adult child, there may not be enough room. Both may need to sell their homes to buy a bigger one together. But this kind of flexibility is discouraged in many countries by high stamp duty on homes. Accordingly it is desirable to minimise or abolish stamp duty. It is similarly important that housing should be plentiful and not too expensive because this helps enable family care. In a British survey, half those who said they would not take in an elderly parent needing 24-hour care said lack of space was a reason.[75] Housing is a key issue when it comes to care for the elderly as in other areas of welfare.

One advantage of the scheme described above is that it would be less likely to run out of money, as state schemes have – causing services to be cut and the elderly to be left in dire circumstances. Furthermore, it would mean that care is not given on the basis of means-testing, which can create a perverse incentive not to save. In a means-tested system, people know that if they spend all their money, the state – or, rather, taxpayers – will pick up the bill. Some means-tested care should be available but only as a last resort and perhaps provided by charities with government support.

The drawback of compulsory savings and insurance accounts, of course, is the element of compulsion. But without compulsion, there will be many who make no provision and then have to be provided for, through compulsory taxation, by those who have. Effectively one form of compulsion – saving – would replace another – tax. And the requirement to save, unlike tax, would provide some freedom, dignity and choice if we need help. The saved money could also be used flexibly to provide what is really needed in individual circumstances.

'The government and the church both stress the importance of family life but neither dare speak out about the fact that it has completely broken down at both ends of life and is probably no better in the middle. I think that I can stand back to look at this because I am gay and I have always lived alone and look on this as a sort of outsider. Now approaching 70 with both my parents dead, I look back on their life and see one that was supportive of their own parents and of me. I would like to thank God (but as an atheist I cannot) that they did not farm me out to carers at any age. I did let them down by moving away for work, so I did not help them as much as they deserved.

'I have just been talking a friend who is thinking of moving closer to her two sons but is afraid to be too close. I assured her that this would be impossible. Sometimes it seems we have forgotten what it is to be human.'

Online comment signed 'Alan Thorpe' in response to an article in *The Times*[76]

Such a system would not be perfect. No system of care for the elderly will ever be so. But it would result in millions of elderly people enjoying a happier old age.

10.

'All animals are equal, but some animals are more equal than others.'[1]

The public sector

T HE PUBLIC SECTOR PROVIDES LARGE parts of the services provided by welfare states around the world. It supplies education nearly everywhere, healthcare in varying degrees and pensions usually.

The public sector is often depicted as worthy and admirable. Here is David Cameron, speaking in 2006, before he became Prime Minister:

> Public service – the concept of working for the good of the community – is a high ideal. We see it in our doctors and nurses, our police officers and our soldiers. But we also see it in many, many areas of our civil service and local government.[2]

Journalists, too, tend to treat the public sector with respect. In this case, Eduardo Porter in the *New York Times* argued that it is better than the private sector:

> Our track record suggests that handing over responsibility for social goals to private enterprise is providing us with social goods of lower quality, distributed more inequitably and at a higher cost than if government delivered or paid for them directly.[3]

'Trust me. I'm a civil servant.'

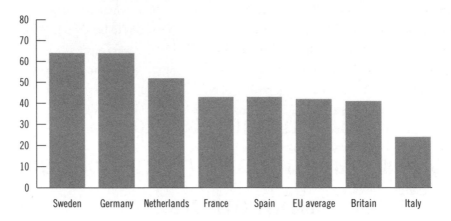

Proportion of people saying that their public administration functions well. Source: Censis using Eurobarometer data (2010)[4]

Some people praise the public sector and add in condemnation of private enterprise as an alternative provider. They say that it is wrong for companies to make profits out of educating children, or caring for the sick. Often public servants are thought of as decent people doing their best for others while receiving low incomes. Is that fair?

We're in a room full of teachers in New York City.[5] Some are reading books. Others are doing crossword puzzles. A few are playing chess. Yet others are debating with each other. One is painting a watercolour. Another is planning a holiday. They are spending the whole day in this room. They are not teaching any classes at all.

Every day they come to this room at the same time as other teachers go to schools. They leave at the same time, too. They are paid the same. They have the same holiday entitlements, too. The only difference is that they are not teaching.

There are plenty of rooms like this in New York City – enough to contain more than 700 teachers. The cost to taxpayers of paying for these non-teaching teachers is between £35 million and £65 million a year.[6] But why aren't they teaching?

Some of them are considered by their former schools as incompetent or lazy. Some have been accused of improper conduct such as sexual harassment of students. Others have been accused of crimes. For these or other reasons they are not allowed to teach.

The rooms in which the teachers sit all day are officially described as 'temporary reassignment centers'. Colloquially they are called 'rubber rooms' because staying in them can make you go crazy and a 'rubber room' is slang for a padded cell.

Of course it is understandable that some teachers should be suspended while accusations are resolved. But why are there so many? Because these teachers are in limbo for a long time. Typically their cases take two to five years to be resolved. Why does it take so long? The explanation is that there are many layers of state laws and agreements with unions which severely restrict the ability of schools to fire teachers.

This is how the 'rubber rooms' were in 2009. Since then, the ones in New York City have been closed. After their existence became a public scandal, the mayor and the union made a deal: cases would be dealt with more quickly but the teachers could stay at home. Yet even after this deal, the cases were still not dealt with very much faster. The problem did not go away. It was only made less visible – swept under the carpet.

Is the New York City experience a one-off?

No. Firing teachers is difficult in many American states.[7] In Illinois, one in 2,500 is removed. For comparison, the figure for doctors is one in fifty-seven and for attorneys one in ninety-seven. Teachers are close to being unsackable. In New York State, disciplinary hearings for teachers last eight times longer than the average US criminal case. The total cost to taxpayers of the teachers who are waiting for these hearings is $65 million a year.[8]

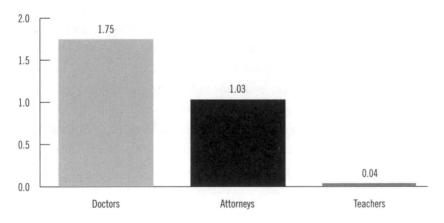

Percentage in each profession losing their credentials in Illinois. Source: *Waiting for 'Superman'*[9]

Since it is so difficult and expensive to fire teachers, schools are reluctant even to try. If a school finally manages to get rid of a bad teacher, he or she joins a pile of teachers who must be hired when other schools need new teachers. Bad teachers don't get fired. They get recycled. And if a school has to fire a teacher, it has to fire the most recent recruit regardless of merit.

Michelle Apperson won the title of Teacher of the Year in the Sacramento City

Unified School District. Soon after she was made redundant along with 400 others when the number of teachers was cut due to shortage of money.[10] Why did they pick the Teacher of the Year? Because she had less seniority than other teachers.

Stephen Wright, a tenured teacher at Downers Grove School District in Illinois, was warned by the district against 'improper touching' of female students.[11] He had also asked his classes for synonyms for oral sex and asked students why semen tastes salty. For these and 'other confirmed improprieties' the district eventually fired him. The cost to the school district was $134,799 in legal fees. Within a year, Wright was back teaching in another school.

According to a local newspaper, 'none of the tenured teachers fired in the last decade have had subsequent action taken to revoke or suspend their teaching certificate [in Illinois]'.[12]

Some may think, 'Does it matter much if some good teachers are fired and some not-so-good ones have jobs for life?'

Eric Hanushek and Steve Rivkin examined the difference made by teacher quality. They concluded that if students had good teachers instead of average ones for four or five years in a row, the effect was as big as the difference in attainment between students entitled to free or reduced-price lunches and those who are not. That, of course, is the holy grail of education: to give decent opportunities to the poor. Hanushek and Rivkin also found that if the bottom 5–10 per cent of teachers were replaced with average ones, the USA would move from being below average in international comparisons to being one of the best.

Let's put it more bluntly and emotionally: the difficulty in firing low-quality teachers damages the education of American children. Above all, it affects the children of the poor – those who cannot afford to move to a prosperous neighbourhood to get their children into a better school with better teachers.

How has it happened that teachers are so difficult to fire, damaging the futures of millions of children? Because teacher trade unions have used their power to make it this way. The rules are designed for the benefit of union members, not children. This is not public service as praised by David Cameron – a form of philanthropy. It is selfishness.

A. J. Duffy, president of the most power[ful] union in California – the United Teachers Los Angeles – revelled in adopting a gangs[ter] style of dress. He wore two-tone shoes a[nd] suits with wide lapels. Behind his desk wa[s a] picture of Marlon Brando playing a Mafia b[oss] in *The Godfather*.[14] Duffy led a boycott of the *L[os] Angeles Times*, which dared publish a serie[s of] articles in which test scores were used to ass[ess] the effectiveness of teacher[s]

Some may think, 'But this is not a public sector problem. This is a union problem.' Yet the two things are connected.

How have unions achieved so much power in education? Only because education is virtually a government monopoly in the USA. The American teacher unions provide a case study of how the public sector can combine with unionisation to cause harm to the public.[16] In America, first the public sector established monopoly of supply in education. Next, because of this monopoly, teacher unions were, in due course, able to become powerful. This took place through the 1960s and 1970s.[17] Third, they used their numbers and money from subscriptions to

> '**Getting bad teachers out of the classroom is essential if kids are to be educated effectively. Yet the formal rules prevent it.**'
>
> Terry Moe, *Special Interest: Teachers Unions and America's Public Schools.*[13]

obtain political power. Between 1989 and 2010, the two big teacher unions – the National Education Association and the American Federation of Teachers – together made bigger political contributions than unions representing any other trade or profession. They gave twice as much as the Teamsters Union, for example. A full 95 per cent of these donations went to the Democratic Party.[18] Fourth, they used their power to promote their interests, getting for themselves better pay and conditions and making it difficult for teachers to be fired. This raised the cost of education and damaged the interests of children.

The contrast with the private sector is this: in private enterprise, companies that produce services at a higher price and lower quality do not survive. If unions force a company to pay higher wages and reduce the quality of what is offered, the company goes bust. Consequently the union loses the power it established. But in the public sector, no matter how badly a government monopoly fails, it continues in place. Therefore unions can be as demanding as they like. This is how unions have come to be much more powerful in the public sector than the private. It is why the issues of union power and the public sector are connected.

> nfortunately, considerable power
> the National Union of Teachers
> pecially – seems to have ended up
> the hands of Leninists ... The ultra
> t has survived in the trade union
> ovement despite its disappearance
> m mainstream politics ... Some
> ions have become a sort of Jurassic
> rk, in which otherwise extinct
> ologies can live again.'
>
> O'Brien[595]

Some people will be thinking that the case of American teachers is an extreme one. That may be true. Children's lives are damaged. That causes anger. But the story demonstrates that it is wrong to assume that the public sector is always and inherently philanthropic. Many individual American teachers are philanthropic. But collectively they are not.[20]

I would ask those who have a gut reaction in favour of the public sector to bear with me. Of course there are decent, hard-working people within it. But it is only right, if we truly want the best results for the public, such as the best education for children, to look at ways in which the public sector has let the philanthropic ideal down. It is quite a list.

1. The public sector has a tendency to give itself special privileges

Let us take public sector pensions. All across the USA, police officers receive special pensions. In most states, firefighters do too. There is a considerable range of occupations in the public sector which get such special pensions. In about half the states, wildlife/conservation officers receive special consideration. Park or forest rangers get special pension terms in a similar proportion of states. In seven states, a 'motor vehicle inspector' gets favoured treatment and, in three states, so does a 'dispatcher'.[21]

The proportion of public employees who receive special treatment is rising. The idea of what is 'arduous' in public service keeps on expanding. In Florida, the number of categories of workers entitled to special pension terms was increased on five occasions between 1993 and 2011. The numbers of workers entitled to them rose 53 per cent.[22] In California, in 2000, the number of employees eligible for enhanced or early retirement jumped 30 per cent and the number eligible only for regular retirement plans fell.[23]

JACQUES ATTALI WAS AN ADVISER to François Mitterrand, the French President, from 1981 to 1991. After the communist regimes of eastern Europe began to fall in 1989, Attali was made head of a new bank set up by Western governments although his background was not in banking. The European Bank for Reconstruction and Development was meant to offer financing to help eastern European countries re-build themselves. Before long, it became a scandal. The *Financial Times* reported that it had spent £55 million on the refurbishment of its offices – the second set of offices it had occupied.[24] Of that money, £750,000 had been spent on replacing one kind of marble with another. The bank's expenditure on itself was more than its entire lending during 1991 and 1992, its first two years of operation. As a result of this and other revelations of extraordinary self-indulgence, Attali eventually resigned. But there was no punishment or fine. He was allowed to keep the salary he had been paid of £250,000 a year, tax free. He had travelled by private jet at the expense of the bank.

Attali was later involved in another scandal known as Angolagate. Yet, despite these two scandals in his curriculum vitae, in 2007, President Sarkozy made him president of a commission to study obstacles to economic growth. Senior public servants sometimes seem to keep getting public sector appointments almost regardless of their behaviour.

There are many jobs in the private sector which could be considered equally arduous. Builders have demanding physical jobs but get no special pensions. Private investigators experience stress, like police investigators, but get no privileged pensions. Those working with the mentally ill on behalf of charities receive no privileges and often very low pay. The public sector seems quick to regard its employees as 'special' – more special and deserving than other people.

In many cases, the public sector regards all its employees as special. All civil servants in Britain – teachers, local council administrators, cleaners and so on – are entitled to pensions of a defined value related to salary, which is inflation indexed. Such favourable terms are practically unknown to the rest of the workforce. In Ontario, Canada, nearly all public sector workers have pensions based on their salaries but only just over half of employees in the private sector do.[26] In many other countries public sector workers again have better pension schemes than everyone else. Who funds these better schemes? The rest of the public, of course. It all amounts to a transfer of wealth from the general public to public sector.

French public sector workers retire younger

Average age of retirement in France.

Source: *Le Figaro Économie.*[25]

In addition to this, workers in the public sector are less likely to face compulsory redundancy. We saw that US teachers are almost unfireable. A study in Ontario found that public sector workers are less than a fifth as likely as workers in the private sector to be fired.[27]

Some will be thinking, 'Yes, but the security of public sector jobs and the gener-osity of their pensions merely compensate them for being less well paid.' It is true that average pay in the public sector in many countries is below that in the private sector. But the public sector often includes a higher proportion of low-paid jobs such as cleaning and clerical work. The Fraser Institute did a study comparing pay for people of similar qualifications and ages doing similar work in Ontario. The conclusion was that those in the public sector are paid 14 per cent more.[28] In the United States, another study found that public sector workers in similar jobs were paid between 3 and 19 per cent more than those in the private sector.[29]

Policy Exchange, a British think tank, looked at public sector pay and concluded, 'When controlling for the differences like age, experience and qualifications, the hourly pay premium for a public sector worker was 8.8 per cent as of December 2010.'[30] In Greece, the wages of workers in the government-run railways averaged €65,000 in 2012. A former Minister of Finance exclaimed, 'There isn't a single pri-vate company in Greece with that kind of average pay.'[31] It may well be that public sector workers were once paid less than those in the private sector. But that is cer-tainly not the case any more.

Government employees have more days off sick

Average days off sick in 2010 in Britain. The median annual cost of days off sick in the public sector was 46 per cent higher than in the private sector (£1,040 compared to £710). The cost for taxpayers of the extra sick days was £5 billion.

Source: Confederation of British Industry[32]

All this might be justifiable if the public sector employees were working longer hours than those in the private sector. The US Bureau of Labour Statistics has detailed figures derived from timesheets of all the hours that someone actually works. The survey therefore captures such things as length of holidays and work done at home. Using these figures, Jason Richwine made adjustments so that similar jobs and qualifications could be compared. He found that the average employee of the US federal government works 2.2 hours a week less than his or her equivalent in the private sector – a difference of slightly more than 5 per cent. Over a full year – incorporating time taken out of work for sickness as well as holidays and hours per day – a federal employee works the equivalent of three weeks a year less than other people. It's a difference of just over 6 per cent.

Richwine found that state and local government employees were working even fewer hours than the federal government workers above. It is true that teachers work fewer hours than others because of school holidays, but Richwine excluded teachers from his calculations.

It would not be fair to say that public sector workers enjoy special privileges always and everywhere. But in many cases and many places, public sector workers get better pension terms, have higher pay, work less, have more days off sick and are less likely to lose their jobs. The people who pay for this consists of everybody else. The public sector often takes advantage of the rest of the population.

> **'I asked myself exactly where I had landed … an absurd universe in which the people who do the least declare that they are overwhelmed and where one works for thirty-five hours not in a week but in a month.'**
>
> Aurélie Boullet, writing under the pen-name Zoé Shepard, on her experience as a high-flying young civil servant. She had passed tough exams to get her job but once she was in post, she was scandalised by how little she and her colleagues were expected to work.[33] She was also angered by the substantial salaries and benefits given to the bureaucrats while front-line public servants, such as nurses, teachers, social workers and the police, were starved of cash.[34]

2. The public sector tends to be inefficient, wasteful and over-manned, resulting in higher costs

Britain led a global wave of privatisations of nationalised industries between 1980 and 2000. One of these was of British Gas Corporation. It had 91,500 employees and, before privatisation, some people claimed it was overmanned and inefficient.[35] Was it?

Well, four years after privatisation, it had 12,000 fewer employees. Within another four years, it had shed a further 12,000 employees. There seems to have been no suggestion that customer service deteriorated. If anything, the opposite took place.

So, in retrospect it seems that, as a public sector operation, it had 24,000 more employees than were needed to run the business – an excess of 26 per cent. It was inefficient and heavily overmanned. The public, through charges and taxes, had to pick up the bill.

Fewer staff are needed in the private sector

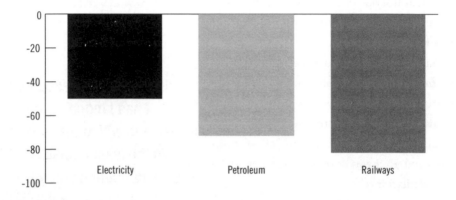

Reductions in net employment in Argentinian public sector businesses after privatisation. Overmanning in the public sectors of developing countries can be on an astonishing scale. In a study of privatisations around the world, researchers remarked, 'A number of highly protected and deeply politicised enterprises have seen huge declines in net employment.'

Source: World Bank.[36]

The electricity-generating companies in Britain employed 26,700 people when they were nationalised industries.[37] After three years in the private sector, the number of employees had been reduced to 10,400 – a fall of 61 per cent. It appears that the business had been extravagantly overstaffed.

Teachers in Poland are only required to teach for eighteen hours a week. In some cases, they teach more than eighteen hours but, if so, they get an overtime rate. Teachers are well known for having second jobs particularly as insurance salesmen.

When gas and electricity were nationalised industries, strikes took place occasionally, causing disruption and inconvenience to the public and businesses. When they were in the public sector, the unions were strong and could threaten to turn the lights off or keep the country in the cold. Once the state monopolies were broken up, the power of the unions to make such threats diminished. The number of strikes has dwindled to practically zero.

In some countries, it goes beyond excessive staff employed to do the business of the organisation. In the USA, Britain and Spain, for example, public sector unions are so strong that the taxpayer is obliged to finance full-time union employees, too. They are not helping provide the service in question at all. But they are certainly adding to the costs.[38]

There are two kinds of privatisation. One kind creates a market of competing companies. The other is just contracting out work to private companies. One drawback of the contracting-out kind is that a contract might be awarded to a company or official who has paid a bribe. When in Italy, I was told that there had been scandals of this sort in the south of the country involving healthcare contracts. One involved prostitutes being hired in an attempt to make sure that the contract was given to a particular company.

'Los liberados'

Nickname for union officials in Spanish companies and in government who receive a salary but work full time for the union.[39]

But let's ask why governments contract out work at all. They know they will be criticised by the public sector trade unions. One often finds that governments do not explain why they are contracting out but the answer is simple. Governments contract out almost always because their budgets are under pressure and they find it is the only way they can afford to do what they want to do. They keep quiet about this – the real reason – to avoid inflaming any conflict with the public sector unions. Saving money was the reason why the regional government in Valencia contracted out the construction and operation of a hospital in Alzira (see Chapter 3). Valencia got a cheaper hospital service and better results.

Saving money is also the main reason why the operation of many prisons in the USA and elsewhere has been contracted out. Has money actually been saved? Adrian Moore looked at fourteen studies of the subject.[40] Two found that the contractors cost about the same as the public sector. The other twelve found savings of between 5 and 28 per cent. Did privatisation damage the way these prisons were run? Not according to six studies comparing their quality. In fact, one way in which costs have been reduced is through minimising the number of violent incidents. That has been achieved in some cases by improving conditions such as by providing prisoners with more opportunities for work, education and recreation.

Sometimes private sector administration is simply less bureaucratic. One warden in a privately run prison explained that when he needed some minor piece of office equipment, he did not have to go through some long and complex state purchasing process. He just went out and bought it.[41] In Britain, a time-study was done of the work done by a social worker on a single case. It was found that only

14 per cent of the time was actually spent in the family home and even that was mostly used for collecting information to fulfil reporting requirements.[42]

Social worker or paper worker?

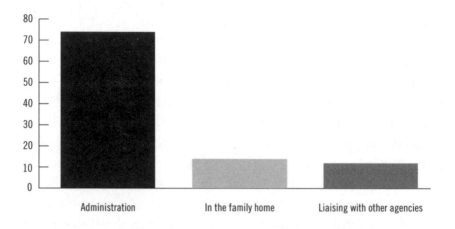

The proportion of time spent by a local government social worker dealing with a single case in Swindon.

Source: The Life Programme[43]

Waste and inefficiency can arise in various ways. In October 2002, *The Economist* carried an article about massive improvements which Tony Blair, the Prime Minister, was promising in the National Health Service: 'Tony Blair talks ecstatically about a new consumer focus – from hospital appointments booked online at times convenient to patients to electronic medical records that can be accessed wherever the patient is.'[44] This was going to be a step change in efficiency. Patients were going to be able to go to their computers and fix appointments. They would be able to see their records online. Doctors anywhere in the country would be able to look up patient records in an instant.

But even at that early stage, *The Economist* sounded a warning note.

> [Tony Blair] is depending on IT to deliver the goods. Yet large government IT projects have a habit of going spectacularly wrong. The government thinks it has learned the lessons of past IT disasters. The new Office of Government Commerce has created something it calls the Gateway process, a sensible enough system of appraisal and review, which it believes will cut down the number of 'rogue' projects. But it is far from clear that the government

understands why IT projects in the public sector are particularly susceptible to failure.[45]

In accordance with *The Economist*'s fears, the project stumbled from one failure
to another. Contractors withdrew despite incurring losses of hundreds of millions
of pounds. Doctors made criticisms. Costs mounted. I had supper with someone
in the information technology business in 2006 who told me that the new NHS
computer system was never going to work and this was common knowledge in
the industry. Still it ploughed on. More money was spent. Finally in 2011, a House
of Commons committee made a damning report. A month later, the government
belatedly brought the project to an end. Some elements of it have survived and
have been of use. But the majority of the cost – some £12 billion – was wasted.

What was the problem?

The Economist, in its 2002 article, had commented: 'Big projects are difficult to manage whether public or private. But the most intractable problems
arise from attitudes that are distinctively public-sector.' It suggested that, in the
private sector, companies focus on lower costs and improved competitiveness.

'But politicians (*vide* Mr Blair), desperate
to find quick fixes and unencumbered with
any understanding of what technology can
and can't do, often expect miracles.' Moreover, '"Change management" is never easy,
but in the public sector it is especially hard
because there is too little competitive pressure
pushing it, and there are too many powerful
unions holding it back.'[46]

Long after the failure of the NHS computer project, a computer magazine obtained
records released under the Freedom of Information Act. Its report did not receive much
attention but it was revealing. The records
showed that Blair had pressed the NHS to
hurry up the project so that the expected benefits could be seen quicker – by 2005, when a
general election was due.[47] This helped con-
tribute to the failure of the project. *The Economist*'s assertion that politically
motivated interference was one reason why public sector projects go wrong
was vindicated.

> 'Senior people issue
> airy instructions –
> usually in response to a
> [newspaper] column –
> but, not understanding
> management, they do
> not know how to follow
> through and ensure
> things are done.'
>
> Dominic Cummings, former UK government
> special adviser.[48]

No one, as far as is known, was sacked as a result of the huge waste of money. Certainly neither the head of the NHS nor the Prime Minister was removed. There were few apparent consequences for anyone in the public sector. This points to another reason why the public sector can be wasteful and inefficient: the lack of accountability and clear responsibility that often exists. In the public sector, 'the buck doesn't stop here'.

In sum, there seems to be a rogues' gallery of reasons for public sector inefficiency and extra cost: more bureaucracy; lack of focus on costs; lack of competitive pressure; powerful unions; politically motivated interference and lack of accountability.

3. The higher costs of public service lead to higher taxes and public debt

In France, where public servants are particularly numerous, a magazine expressed widespread exasperation with public services there. Its front cover carried a photo of an empty counter, complete with 'Position Closed' sign, where an official should have been attending to members of the public. The headline was: 'PUBLIC SERVANTS, the pets of power: While the deficit soars out of control, they are twice as numerous as in Germany ... but where are they hiding?'[49]

It was a cry of frustration at an excess of public servants who, despite their numbers, provide poor service. Everybody has to pay for the self-indulgences and waste. The people who pay include the poor. The poor pay sales or value added tax. In many countries they pay income tax, too. It is wrong that the poor should be taxed to finance the waste and early pensions of the public sector.

4. The public sector tends to create excessive regulations

Blake Hurst was brought up on a farm in America.[50] At the age of fourteen, he was put in charge of feeding two steers and planting and harvesting 40 acres (16 hectares) of corn. He kept the books for the whole operation. After four years, he had saved enough to pay for his college education.

That was a generation ago. Now, he would not be allowed to do any of this work except the book-keeping. It is against the regulations.

Blake buys fertiliser from a small-scale supplier. The supplier tells him he has been fined about a third of his annual profit. Why? Because he failed to complete his 'Risk Management Plan' correctly despite hiring a consultant to do it for him. The form concerned is so big that it is held in a binder 3 inches thick. The supplier must pay the large fine and re-file his plan online. The instructions on how to complete the form are 110 pages long.

All the forms, fines and regulations infuriate Blake and his supplier. But why were they created? Was there a reason?

Let's take the rules that make it difficult for young teenagers to do work in American farms. Yes, there was a reason. They were created to protect children. Hilda Solis, Secretary of Labor, was one of the people in favour of such rules. She was concerned for the well-being of children. She did not want them to be 'robbed of their childhood'.[51] She, with the cooperation of others, passed laws and created the regulations. She believed what she was doing was good.

It must be intoxicating to feel that with the stroke of a pen one can improve the world. That is probably an important reason why public servants create so many regulations. In France, there are regulations to ensure that two wheelchairs can pass each other on the pavement. Any branch or street sign that gets in the way must be removed.[52] Wheelchair access is required – not just recommended – in more and more places such as hotels, historic houses, hospices and care homes. France has a law protecting the coastline from overdevelopment. One can readily imagine and sympathise with the desire to preserve something natural and beautiful. A law was passed to enforce it. The intention is quite obviously to do good.

Such regulations sometimes come out of a scandal. In Britain, there were concerns that the police were not always maintaining proper standards in their investigations. So they were required to fill in forms showing that interviews had been conducted properly. Politicians were seen to be acting to make the world a better place.

And so the rule books grow. In France, the tax code, the labour regulations and the planning laws all more than doubled in size between 2002 and 2012.

Regulation inflation

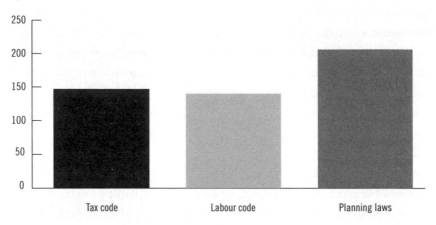

Increase in pages of government regulation in France in the ten years to 2012.

Source: *Le Point*[53]

Finance ministers doubtless used the tax code to encourage desirable things like investment. The labour code was extended to give further protection to employees. The planning laws were changed to ensure that nothing unpleasant should blot the landscape and that new homes should be more energy-efficient.

The French government has the distinction that it counts up the number of its regulations – something that only a centralised country like France can do. It has found that its citizens enjoy the benefit of 400,000 rules.[54] At the current rate of growth, it cannot be long before the count reaches a million. Even then, no doubt, there will be more injustices, depredations and nuisances to counter. More regulations and forms will have to be created to combat them.

In most cases, regulations are created to make the world a better place. In other cases, they are created by politicians to please the public. How could things that come from such intentions do any harm?

'The head of a small company [in France] counted up. Last year he had to reply to thirty-seven questionnaires containing 7,047 questions.'[55]

Take the regulations insisting that children should not be used for work on farms. Yes, children are protected from exploitation. They can have childhoods free of remunerative work. But might children not gain satisfaction and life skills from being entrusted with work at a young age? They could earn money and ease the budget of their family if it is poor. They might save, as Blake Hurst did, to finance a college education. Without such work, some children might not be able to afford a college education. Such are the possible unintended consequences which regulators may not always take into account. Perhaps the regulators might also have done the parents the honour of letting them take the decision.

What about the regulations on fertiliser supplies and the voluminous, complicated 'Risk Management Plan'? One consequence is that suppliers have to spend money on consultants or spend their own time filling in the forms. So the financial return on their investment in the business will be lower. This means they are less likely to have money to expand and invest. The money they must spend on a form-filling consultant might have been spent on new plant or on research and development. The extra cost of fulfilling the regulatory requirements is likely to add to the price of fertiliser and thus the price of food.

> 'If I employed someone I would have to completely change my tax and VAT status. It would be complicated and I would need to employ an accountant.'
>
> A self-employed gardener in Aix-en-Provence. She could grow her business by employing an assistant but does not do so because of the extra burden of the regulations this would entail.

Wheelchair access is required for new student accommodation in France. So rooms are made 20 per cent bigger, which means the cost is higher and, since there is no extra money, fewer students are able to get student accommodation.[56] Meanwhile, the law protecting the coastline has affected the little town of Plouvien in Brittany.[57] A very short section of the town boundary runs along the inland end of an estuary, miles away from the sea. As a result, almost no building is allowed in Plouvien. This has prevented the construction of a factory which would have provided employment.

In Britain, planning regulations for building in Britain mean that the cost of obtaining permission to build a house has come to cost as much as the bricks used in its construction.[58] Housing is therefore more expensive than it otherwise would be and fewer people can afford homes. The police, meanwhile, have been required to fill in forms answering 1,099 questions when conducting major crime investigations.[59] According to a report on this, 'we have armies of people filling in spreadsheets trying to prove their force meets this or that standard. There is one-third of policing that we could cut out.' To put it another way, the excessive regulations mean that fewer policemen are available to fight crime.

The unintended consequences of regulations are a kind of undiscovered continent. There are 2.4 times as many companies in France with forty-nine employees as there are with fifty.[60] Why? Because once a company has fifty employees, it is required to introduce profit-sharing, to set up three employee worker councils, and to submit plans to the worker councils if ever it wishes to fire anybody. Therefore small companies are discouraged from growing into middle-size ones, which means lower economic growth than might otherwise have taken place.

> 'Residents who live near a proposed relief road at Manchester Airport were recently left scratching their heads to be asked in a consultation: "Is your gender identity the same as the gender you were assigned with at birth?"'
>
> Daily Mail[61]

Contracts with government for support of hospices in Britain can run to hundreds of pages.[62] Dealing with them and making sure all the terms are fulfilled is expensive. Therefore hospices cannot afford to take in as many people as they otherwise would or else they must save money by giving their elderly customers less care. More subtly, a mentality may be encouraged whereby staff in hospices may come to think of themselves as following a set of rules rather than doing things from an impulse of loving care. As Michael Howard, chairman of Help the Hospices, put it: 'hospices began as a response by local people to a lack of dignity and compassion for dying people … We must not allow hospice care, as a humanitarian response to a deeply human issue, to be eroded by inappropriate regulation and red tape.'[63]

Regulations affecting companies can be so extensive that only big companies can afford them and survive. That means fewer small companies, less innovation and less competition. In Manhattan, the number of small finance or insurance companies fell 23 per cent between 1998 and 2010.[65]

The above may seem to some people like a collection of unfortunate events of no great significance. Are regulations so widespread that they make a substantial impact? What is the big picture?

> 'Paper tax
>
> Phrase coined by a French think tank describe the burden of form-filling

The World Bank examined whether varying levels of state control of the economy and regulation could help explain different rates of economic growth. The answer was 'yes' – or, to put it in the bank's more academic way:

> Diverging patterns of reform contribute to explain the puzzling disparities in growth outcomes over the past decade … Our empirical results seem to suggest sizeable benefits from further progress in reforming the regulatory environment and in reducing the role of the state in business activities.[66]

Among the findings, the World Bank concluded that employment protection reduced investment.

John Dawson and John Seater, two economists in North Carolina, have looked at the leading studies of the impact of regulation on growth. They comment, 'Almost all these studies conclude that regulation has deleterious effects on economic activity.' They themselves studied the effect of regulations in the USA and concluded that extra regulation created since 1949 has reduced economic growth by 2 per cent a year.[68] This is an astonishingly large amount. The cumulative effect over time is huge. John Dawson and John Seater estimate that the economy in 2005 was only 28 per cent of what it would have been if the amount of regulation in the USA had remained at 1949 levels. To put it another way: the USA would

> ## 'WHAT INTUITION TEMPTS US TO BELIEVE:
> Someone needs to plan, and central planners know best.
> ## WHAT REALITY TAUGHT ME:
> No one knows enough to plan a society.'
>
> John Stossel, *No They Can't*[67]

have been more than three times richer without post-1949 regulation. They comment that this result – which at first seems so remarkable – is in accord with other studies using different methods.

The World Bank has made an index of 'ease of doing business' – a combination of measures such as the number of days it takes to set up a new enterprise.[69] It is, in part at least, an indication of the burden of regulations. The top-ranked countries for 'ease of doing business' are:

1. Singapore
2. Hong Kong
3. New Zealand
4. USA
5. Denmark
6. Norway
7. United Kingdom
8. South Korea
9. Georgia
10. Australia

The countries where it is easy to do business have become prosperous or have been growing fast. Some will be surprised to see Georgia, a relatively poor, formerly communist country, on the list. But after it adopted a policy of low regulation, it had one of the fastest growth rates among such countries. It suffered through war with Russia in 2008 but the average growth rate prior to that – from 2004 to 2007 – was 10 per cent.[70]

Countries rated badly for 'ease of doing business' tend to have lower per capita incomes. Most tellingly, they have lower incomes than other countries in the same region. Indonesia and the Philippines, for example, have less 'ease of doing business' and their people are poorer than those in Singapore and Malaysia.

A tale of two territories

AFTER THE SECOND WORLD WAR, Hong Kong was a territory with practically nothing. Many people were living in shanty towns. It had a small public sector and few regulations. It had no restrictions or taxes on imports at all.

Meanwhile France was endowed with centuries of civilisation and development. It had a large, centralised government headed by some of the best-educated people in the world – an elite. It created laws and regulations to protect its important industries: farming, car-manufacturing and so on. Under France's leadership, the European Union developed its Common Agricultural Policy to protect farmers from international competition.

How did the two places progress in the following decades?

By 2012, France's GDP per capita was $36,785 according to the World Bank and it ranked twenty-seventh in the world. Hong Kong had GDP per capita of $51,170 and ranked eleventh.[71] The land of free trade, small public sector and zero protectionism had overtaken historic France.[72]

GDP per capita in international dollars reflecting actual purchasing power

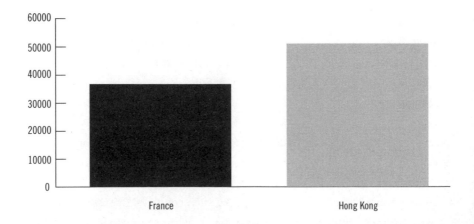

Source: World Bank, 2012 figures.

So regulations can do major damage to national economic performance as well as causing other unintended consequences. What should we do about them? Should we abolish them all? Surely not. Some regulations are bound to be beneficial even when all their unintended consequences are included in the equation. But they should probably be minimised. There should be a prejudice against them. Possible unintended consequences should be considered as carefully as benefits. In fact, they should be considered more carefully since they tend to be subtle or indirect whereas the benefits are obvious.

We should probably also guard against the first reaction of politicians, the media and others when something goes wrong. The first reaction tends to be to create a new rule, but sometimes that is not the best answer. The story about the governors of California and Texas illustrates this (see box). Or let's suppose a policeman abuses someone he arrests. People might demand that in future forms are filled in to provide evidence that prisoners have been well treated. Instead of this, we should perhaps simply demand that the policeman concerned is charged and fired. We are surely all aware that filling in a form does not genuinely prove that a suspect has been well treated anyway.

What does a governor do when he meets a coyote?

'THE GOVERNOR OF CALIFORNIA IS jogging with his dog along a nature trail. A coyote jumps out. He attacks the governor's dog and then he bites the governor. The governor starts to intervene but reflects upon the movie *Bambi* and then he realises he should stop because the coyote is only doing what it does naturally. So, instead, he calls Animal Control. Animal Control captures the coyote and bills the state $200 for testing it for diseases and $500 for re-locating it. He then calls the veterinarian, who collects the dog and bills the state $200 for testing it for diseases. The governor then goes to the hospital. He spends $3,500 getting checked for diseases from the coyote and getting his bite wound bandaged. Of course, being California, the running trail gets shut down for six months while the Fish and Game Department conducts a $100,000 survey to make sure the area is now free of dangerous animals. The governor then spends $50,000 of state funds implementing a 'Coyote Awareness' program. The legislature then spends $2 million to study how to better treat rabies and, in fact, how to permanently eradicate the disease from the world at large. Of course, the government security agent is fired for not stopping the attack and the state spends $150,000 to train a new protective agent for the governor with special training regarding the nature of coyotes. And then PETA [an animal rights group] contests the re-location and files a $5 million suit against the state.

'The governor of Texas is jogging with his dog along a nature trail. A coyote jumps out and tries to attack him and his dog. The governor shoots the coyote with a state-issued pistol and just keeps on jogging. The governor spent 50 cents on a .38 calibre cartridge and buzzards ate the dead coyote.

'And that, my friends, is why California is broke and Texas is rich.'

Richard Fisher, president of the Federal Reserve Bank of Dallas, describing what a business friend in Los Angeles told him was the difference between California and Texas.[73]

5. A powerful public sector enables abuses of power

Lisbeth Salander, a young woman, behaves very abnormally and a court decides she must have a legal guardian. Her first guardian is kindly but he dies and he is replaced by Nils Bjurman. Bjurman sexually molests Lisbeth and demands she give him oral sex. She resists.

Nils Burman abuses his state-given power.

He says, 'If you are nice to me, I'll be nice to you. If you make trouble, I can put you away in an institution for the rest of your life.'

So she submits and does what he wants.

This is a scene from the best-selling Swedish novel *The Girl with the Dragon Tattoo*, by Stieg Larsson. It is an illustration of how public sector officials have the potential to abuse their power. This power is particularly great because the public sector is frequently a monopoly. The individual cannot switch to a competitor.

Coca-Cola is a powerful and rich company. But if you don't like it for any reason, you can buy Pepsi, fruit juice or water. If you want social housing, however, there is probably only one place you can go. We have seen (in Chapter 5) how an Australian civil servant abused the power that his government position gave him and how, in France, such abuse appears widespread.

In the United States, the Internal Revenue Service (IRS) discriminated against organisations that were on the right of American politics.[74] When such organisations applied for an advantageous tax status, they were more likely than left-wing organisations to be subject to delays. President Obama called the scandal 'inexcusable' and remarked, 'I will not tolerate this kind of behaviour in any agency, but especially in the IRS, given all the power that it has and the reach that it has into all of our lives.'[75] That is exactly the point. This scandal was disturbing because of the 'power … and the reach' of the agency. There are many other government agencies that have similar power, including social workers, courts, social housing officials, customs officials, regulators of industries, doctors in government hospitals and so on.

The scandalous behaviour of the IRS in the USA and the housing official in Australia became public because these two countries are relatively open and people there aspire to behave decently. In some countries, they would not become public at all. These things are difficult to prove even in countries like the USA and Australia. But the fact that they may be exposed probably makes public servants more likely to behave as they should. In less open societies there is surely much more abuse of public sector power.

When eastern Europe was under communist rule, if you wanted something from a public servant, you routinely had to give a bribe. Public servants had power in many situations. As one study of bribery noted, 'the allocation of economic resources depended primarily on administrative decisions by public officials. Bribes, payoffs and kickbacks were therefore a way of influencing these decisions.'[77] A habit or way of life was established, unfortunately, and became part of the culture. As recently as 2010, it was estimated that

> **'The mystery is over. After a month of waiting, it turns out that an 84-year-old woman in Florida has won the $590 million Powerball lottery. As for how much tax she's going to have to pay, the IRS said it's too early to tell because they don't know whether she's a Republican or Democrat.'**
>
> Jay Leno, American talk show host, joking about the IRS political favouritism scandal.[76]

bribe-giving is more than eight times more common in the former communist countries than in the rest of Europe.[78]

Another abuse of power takes place when public servants cover up their own incompetence. In 2010, there were many warnings about dreadful failings at Morecambe Bay NHS Trust.[79] The Care Quality Commission conducted an inspection over two days and gave the trust a clean bill of health. This finding was completely wrong. It is now believed that, between 2001 and 2012, up to sixteen babies and two mothers died owing to poor care at a maternity unit that was part of the trust. Another nine infants were born with permanent brain damage.

'Power tends to corrupt and absolute power corrupts absolutely.'

Lord Acton writing to Bishop Mandell Creighton, 1887

When this emerged, the commission conducted an internal review of what had happened in the original inspection. It was highly critical of the way the inspection was done. But at a meeting where the chief executive was present, an order was given to delete the review so it would never be seen by the public. Only due to the bravery of a whistleblower has the truth about this cover-up become known.

6. Intimidation of the public sector's own employees

This is one of the less obvious ways in which the public service sometimes does not live up to any philanthropic ideal. In England, a terrible scandal took place in Mid Staffordshire National Health Service Trust between 2005 and 2009. The neglect of patients by staff at Stafford Hospital was so dreadful that between 400 and 1,200 patients died unnecessarily through thirst, starvation, wrong or non-administration of drugs and so on (see also Chapter 11).[80] The official inquiry tried to establish why the appalling treatment was not discovered earlier, before so many lives were lost. It found that 'an explanation of staff's reluctance to come forward with concerns was that they were scared'. Furthermore, 'staff lived in an atmosphere of fear … promoted by the managerial styles of some senior managers'.[81]

The government had set targets for hospitals to attain. So the managers could damage their careers if they failed to meet these targets. This led to bullying and lies. Of course, bullying takes place in the private sector, too. But the public sector does not make a bright, cheery contrast, as some imagine. The fact that it is often a monopoly employer makes its bullying all the more frightening. An employee who is fired by a near-monopoly provider like the NHS does not just lose a job. He or she loses a career.

7. The public sector often provides poor service

We have referred to quality of service in passing before. But it is a subject by itself.

Hospitals in Valencia, Spain, until very recent times rarely provided an epidural anaesthetic to women giving birth (see Chapter 3). They told women it was not good or even possible for them to have them. The situation changed when the contract for running a hospital was given to a private company. This hospital offered epidurals. So women started coming from across the region to give birth at this hospital. Then, and only then, did the public sector hospitals start to provide this service too. This is a classic case both of poor service by the public sector organisations and the excuses used to justify it.

Sometimes people do not realise how poor the service is that they are getting from a public sector monopoly. In Argentina, prior to the privatisation of the water supply, in many areas a lot of people did not understand how many deaths were being caused by low-quality water. It is estimated that after privatisation the improvement in purity saved the lives of about 500 infants and young children a year.[82] The greatest effect was in the poorest areas.[83]

In Britain, in 1987, it was normal – it simply seemed part of the way of the world – that a quarter of public telephones were out of order.[84] After privatisation the proportion was reduced to 4 per cent. Similarly it was not uncommon up until 1987 to wait weeks to have a telephone line connected to a house or flat. Officially the proportion of requests met within eight days was 59 per cent. After privatisation, the proportion rose to 97 per cent.[85]

There are many such examples. The public sector often offers an inferior service, sometimes even resulting in loss of life as in Argentina. The public is typically unaware of the poor service because there is no competition and therefore no way of making a comparison.

Those who say they reject the idea that public sector service tends to be inferior sometimes reveal a different view by their actions. Civil service employees in Spain are allowed to choose private or public healthcare.[86] More than four out of five choose private care.

Another revealing phenomenon is that failure by a public sector institution has to be on a major scale to be considered interesting enough to warrant news coverage. A private sector institution that makes even one mistake attracts enormous attention. Why? Surely because poor service is considered unsurprising in the public sector.[87]

•　　•　　•

After this list of seven charges against the behaviour and performance of the public sector, let me again emphasise the difference between criticising a system and the people in it. There are plenty of public sector employees who work hard and go beyond the call of duty. They are all the more admirable for doing their best when they are in circumstances that make providing a good service difficult. But overall, the public sector services tend to be wasteful, inefficient and expensive. They give themselves special privileges, cause taxes to be higher than they need to be and provide inferior quality of service. This can damage the education of children and the delivery of healthcare. It can make the poor poorer and seriously damage economic growth. In view of all this, it makes sense to hand over as many as possible of the public sector's operations to the private sector.

The private sector is sometimes regarded as greedy, ruthless, uncivilised and unkind. It can exhibit any of these characteristics – like the public sector. But the advantage of the private sector is that competition creates an incentive to provide good service. If a company fails to provide a good service or product, it is likely to lose business to a rival which does. Companies want to keep a good reputation for the same reason. Supermarkets offer fresh milk and helpful assistants because, if they do not, they will lose out to other supermarkets which do. Historians of human behaviour have even argued that commerce has been a factor in the development of civil behaviour. In the feudal system, aristocrats had less reason to be polite and helpful than a shopkeeper. A shopkeeper has a reason to be polite and friendly to everyone: he wishes to keep his customers.

'When governments contract with the private sector, efficiency and innovation do not come about because private firms have some magic pixie dust, unobtainable by the public sector, to sprinkle about. It is competition that creates efficiency and innovation, because competition punishes inefficiency and inertia.'

Adrian T. Moore, 'Private Prisons: Quality Corrections at a Lower Cost'[88]

The private sector service is not better regardless of its setting. A private sector monopoly is no better than a public sector one. It is competition that provides the spur. That is one reason why contracting out is the inferior form of privatisation. Yes, it can save money. Yes, there is or should be competition between suppliers to get the contract. But the public sector is usually the monopoly lead contractor. In the disastrous NHS computer project, the public sector contracted out to private companies. It was an incompetent monopoly contractor.

There is also the danger in contracting out that private companies may bribe public sector employees. Another problem is that the public sector may be so desperate to save money that it reduces funding to the point that the contractor can only make the work financially viable by providing an inferior service. Then the private sector takes the blame. There have been signs of this happening with Swedish free schools. For these reasons and more, wherever possible, the public sector should avoid contracting out. What is the alternative?

The best outcomes emerge when there is continuing competition between different companies and perhaps other organisations such as charities, mutual societies, trade unions, churches and trusts. For example, schools can be run by competing organisations. Pension schemes can be compulsory, but the consumer can be given a choice between competing fund managers. Private or charitable hospitals can compete. Funding for their work can be provided by competing private insurance or savings schemes.

> '**No force ... except the force of competition has ever done anything to keep producers in order.**'
>
> Sir Ernest Benn[89]

The principle can be and has been applied in many areas. Competition between providers already exists in healthcare in the Netherlands, Switzerland, Germany and Singapore. It exists in schooling in Sweden and, to a smaller degree, in the USA and the UK. Pensions in Chile, Hong Kong, Australia and elsewhere incorporate competition between fund managers.[90]

There are still dangers even here, however. As mentioned, governments can create regulations which increase the costs of providers and create barriers to competition, making it expensive for new companies to enter the field. This has already started in welfare in Sweden.[91] Too many regulations can stifle innovation. Another danger is that governments can put a brake on funding so that the standard of service provided by all competitors deteriorates.

There is no sure defence against such things although in some cases it might help to put some kind of guarantee in the constitution. Otherwise the best defence can be public opinion, in which case the more people who are dependent on the system the better. If everybody is using, say, compulsory private health insurance, a government might hesitate before cutting the funding back.

There is always great scope for human beings to run things badly. There is no foolproof plan. But the record shows that we have a better chance of good service at a reasonable price when private sector competition replaces public sector monopolies. And nowhere is this more important than in schools and healthcare, where the education of children and lives are at stake.

How to use the private sector

DO

Facilitate competition rather than contracting out if possible.

Allow for-profit companies, trusts, churches, trade unions, trade associations, mutual societies and friendly societies to join in the competition.

Give all or most of the population a stake in the continuing existence of competition. Let people be the customers, not government.

Allow public sector entities to compete with the private sector only on a level playing field.

Create constitutional guarantees of the independence and funding of services paid for by government but provided by the private sector – especially schools.

DON'T

Overregulate, stifling the variety and competition that drives innovation, ambition, high standards and choice.

Create regulations which inhibit competition by creating barriers to entry.

II.

'It's like putting all bus drivers through astronauts' training.'

The training and qualifications bonanza

IT IS EARLY EVENING IN Rome. I have had a long day of interviews and, now, at last, I am meeting Kishore Jayabalan of the Acton Institute to have supper. I have run out of energy and am happy simply to enjoy his company and that of his friends. It is a warm evening and we go to a little open-air restaurant where we are joined by others. It is a friendly, relaxed occasion – the very image of Italian conviviality. The welfare states of Italy and the world can take a rest. My notepad is closed and my glass is full.

The last person to arrive is a young man called Adriano. We chat and I ask what work he does. He replies that he is a student. He is completing his studies this year. I am astonished. He does not look young enough to be a student. I ask how old he is.

'Twenty-nine,' he replies.

'Twenty-nine!' I exclaim. 'How can you still be a student at twenty-nine?'

'Actually I am finishing my studies earlier than most. Many of my friends won't finish until they are thirty.'

'Thirty!' I know it's rude of me to show my surprise but Adriano isn't offended. If anything, he is bemused. For him, it is normal.

The conversation moves on to other things, but the idea of students continuing until they are twenty-nine or thirty must be sticking in my mind because, as we walk away from the restaurant, I fall into conversation with another of Kishore's friends and ask if he could tell me more about it. He says that it can take five years to get a first degree. Then one gets a master's degree and finally a doctorate. There is no hurry.

But why do people want to spend these years getting higher and higher academic qualifications when, in most cases, they are not going to be academics?

'To get a job,' he replies. It emerges that people spend all their twenties getting higher qualifications to show they are clever which, after all those years, finally enables them to get good jobs at banks or in the government.

'But surely it's crazy!' I exclaim. 'Think of the time spent studying subjects completely irrelevant to the work they ultimately do! And ordinary, poorer people have to pay tax to fund this! Also the working lives of these students are cut short by studying until they are thirty and then probably taking early retirement at fifty-five or sixty! They only work twenty-five or thirty years out of seventy-five or eighty years of life. Isn't that ridiculous?'

My companion agrees. He says the government is trying to rein it back. But, from his tone, it sounds like he doesn't expect much to come of this. I subsequently discover that a big effort was made to cut the years of study back in 2000 but it would seem that this may not have been altogether successful.[1]

Naturally, most of us assume that training and qualifications are 'good things'. We all want the surgeon who is about to operate on us to be suitably trained. But can there be too much in the way of training and qualifications? Do these ostensibly good things have a dark side? What could possibly be wrong with them?

1. The motives behind the creation of qualifications are not always pure

Dick Carpenter has organised the purchase of fifty floral arrangements. Half are from Louisiana and half from neighbouring Texas.[2] He has arranged for these arrangements to be judged by ten florists from Louisiana and eight from Texas. The judges are not told which display is from which state or even the purpose of the experiment. Which state comes out better? The displays from Texas are judged to be slightly better than those from Louisiana but Carpenter, being a scrupulous academic, says that the difference is not 'statistically significant'.

Why has Carpenter done this experiment? What is it all about?

He is testing whether a requirement for florists to be qualified results in higher-quality products. In Louisiana, florists have to be qualified. They have to pass an exam. In Texas, they don't. The answer, based on this little experiment, seems to be that a qualification makes no difference.

If that is right, why does Louisiana legally require new florists to be qualified?

Have there been demonstrations by angry consumers demanding that they should be protected from displays made by unqualified florists?

No.

Have Louisiana newspapers and government offices been swamped with customer complaints about inferior displays?

No. The people who demanded a legal requirement for new florists to obtain qualifications were ... florists. You don't need to be a cynic to suppose that the reason they called for this was probably in order to reduce competition.

The story of the florists of Louisiana is a gentle introduction to the idea that we should not take it for granted that qualifications always exist for good and honourable reasons. It suggests that requirements for qualifications can, in some cases at least, be excessive and provide no benefit.

In the USA, many occupations require qualifications or 'licensing' as Americans call it. In 2003, the Council of State Governments estimated that more than 800 occupations required a licence in at least one state.[3] Adam Summers did a survey of them.[4] Some occupations failed what he called 'the laugh test'. Try these: you are not allowed to be an upholsterer in California without a licence. You are not allowed to be an interior decorator there either.

The fact that you need a licence to be an interior decorator is part of the plot of a Woody Allen film, *Blue Jasmine*.[5] Jasmine, played by Cate Blanchett, needs a job and wants to work as an interior decorator. But she is not allowed to. She does not have a licence.

Summers found that many occupations required a licence in some states but not others. One might wonder why, if the public needs protection from, say, an unlicensed upholsterer in California, they don't need the same protection in Oregon. The difference suggests that this is not a matter of public interest but merely that lobby groups have got their way in some states but not others.

Jasmine wants to work as an interior decorator but it is against the law.

Licences for floristry, upholstery and interior decorating may seem merely funny and of no importance. But this introduction is only to suggest that we should not assume all licensing requirements are for a good reason. The same can apply in other fields, and the consequences can be surprisingly serious.

Prior to the Second World War, black Americans were increasingly successful in becoming plumbers, barbers and electricians.[6] Trade unions convinced state legislatures to pass laws which made it difficult for them to gain licences. A law proposed in Virginia provided that only barbers who had been to an approved barbers' school, had been registered apprentices for eighteen months and had passed an exam could get a licence. But black people could not even start on this path. There were no licensed barber schools that would admit them.[7] An African-American weekly publication, the *Norfolk Journal and Guide*, denounced the bill in 1929 as a 'pernicious measure, masquerading as a public health effort, but obviously an organized labor union project drawn in the special interest of white organized labour'.[8]

Licensing laws were used to obstruct black people from becoming barbers.

Licensing rules of this sort were proposed every year from 1928 to 1940. That is why we have good records of what happened. Happily they were defeated each time. But Virginia was exceptional. By 1941, all the states of America except Virginia and New York had passed licensing laws obstructing black men who wanted to become plumbers, barbers and/or electricians. The laws exploited the fact that black people tended to be less well educated and poorer in order to exclude them from this trade. Simply by being required to pass written exams and pay for courses, they were obstructed.

Consequently in the plumbing trade, there were substantial reductions in black employment. A 1953 investigation discovered that out of 3,200 licensed plumbers in Maryland, only two were African American. The purpose of such licensing laws may have been to discriminate against blacks or to reduce competition or both. Whichever it was, it was certainly against the public interest.

If we accept that qualifications are not always created for good and honourable reasons, we might look afresh at some professions that are particularly important in welfare states.

At first sight, the medical profession might seem one where the qualifications would surely not be polluted by

'When the NHS being planned BMA's [British Med Association] host was decisiv ensuring that no at all was permitted medical institu

David Green, 'Medical Care With State'.[10] Medical institutes provide competition to members of the selfish motives. Unfortunately, the history of medical qualifications tells a different story. Going all the way back to the fifteenth century, it involves different kinds of doctors repeatedly attempting to create monopolies. Practitioners have variously called themselves surgeons, physicians or apothecaries. Competition has been unwelcome.

In 1902, a doctor distributed leaflets in a poor area of Birmingham, England, announcing that he would see the poor for free. He was inundated with work. To try to reduce the flow, he issued a revised handbill saying he would now charge the poor threepence per consultation. His motive was obviously philanthropic. But what was the reaction of the General Medical Council? To ban 'advertising' such as he had done. The council characterised his behaviour as an attempt to take patients away from other medical men. The year before, the council also banned canvassing for patients. As a historian of the episode has written, 'the decisions of 1901 and 1902 were the first occasions on which the powers of the General Medical Council had been openly used to further the pecuniary interests of doctors at the expense of patients'.[9]

> 'In both the American and English cases, state involvement in the profession's institutions represented a solution to the failure of the profession to eliminate competitors adequately ... Unlike the profession, the state had the resources and administrative mechanisms for shaping the medical market in a monopolistic direction.'
>
> Jeffrey Lionel Berlant, *Profession and Monopoly*[12]

There was still competition among doctors over price, however, at this time. This annoyed the British Medical Association which, despite its professional gloss, acted like a trade union trying to keep prices up. The association was politically active, seeking to promote the interests of its members as laws regarding medical practice were developed. Through the General Medical Council and then the government itself, it eventually succeeded in quelling competition. It only started to cooperate with the major changes introduced in 1911 and 1946 in return for government compliance.[11] Competition was almost totally snuffed out. New doctors could not move into an area to compete with the existing ones if provision there was officially considered adequate. Though doctors may have been different in various ways, they were not allowed to compete with each other. Competition, which pushes good performance

> he US system of
> edical education
> like putting all
> s drivers through
> tronauts' training.'
>
> ment repeated among critics of
> ical training. It is unknown who said
> st.[14]

in so many other parts of life, was eliminated. That remains the position in Britain today.

Something similar took place in the USA and elsewhere, too. It emerges that even the medical profession, despite the fact that many doctors feel it is a vocation, is capable of seeking to frame regulations for the advantage of practitioners rather than patients. Bearing this in mind, let's look at medical training.

'An average e[...] exam and eyegla[...] prescription is 35 p[...] cent more expensi[...] in cities with mo[...] restrictive optomet[...] regulations.[...]

In the USA, a young person who wishes to become a doctor does a university course for four years. Then he or she goes to medical school for a further four years. Finally he or she does a 'residency' – which includes some medical work on a kind of trainee basis – for a further four years. If the budding doctor wants to become a specialist, the training takes even longer. It is not uncommon for people to have reached thirty before they are full doctors, by which point they are burdened with heavy debt unless their parents are rich and have paid for it. As Clayton Christensen put it, 'counting college, tomorrow's doctors will have spent 10 to 18 of the most productive years of their lives just training for their careers'.[13] We will see later that it may be doubted that this decade or more of preparation is truly necessary. But we know for sure that the training and qualification requirements are extremely time-consuming and expensive. This suits the existing practitioners. The drawn-out training keeps down competition and maintains high prices. This raises the prices and taxes paid by others.

'One of the many sources of high medical costs in the United States is the de facto monopoly of the American Medical Association in the distribution of licences to practice medicine.'

Free Exchange blog, *The Economist*[18]

2. Excessive training increases costs

The academic research into licensing suggests that it increases wages and prices by between 10 and 18 per cent.[16] One study found that strict licensing laws increased the wages of clinical laboratory staff by 16 per cent. In a study which added in the effect of licensing along with non-recognition of qualifications of one state by another and restrictions on advertising, it was found that the combined effect was to increase wages in more highly paid jobs, such as dentistry, by about 27 per cent.[17]

But even that figure may not capture the full effect. These studies compared people of similar knowledge and ability. They did not capture therefore the way people can spend months or years studying areas which are not necessary for the work that they will do. A doctor may study genetics without any improvement to the quality of his work if his actual work does not involve genetics. The cost of the extra training, which is an extra barrier to entry to the profession and causes a higher price, is not captured.

e American Medical Association ... renders
ortant services to its members and to the
dical profession as a whole. However it is also a
our union and, in our judgment, has been one of
 most successful ... For decades it kept down
 number of physicians, kept up the costs of
dical care, and prevented competition ... all, of
rse, in the name of helping the patient ... The
ders of the medicine have been sincere in their
ief that restricting entry into medicine would
p the patient. By this time we are familiar with
 capacity that all of us have to believe that what
n our interest is in the social interest.'

n and Rose Friedman, *Free to Choose*[19]

The large number of eternal students in Italy means that ordinary people there have to pay more in taxes. Excessive training and qualifications increase wages and thus the prices of the professions and trades concerned. People are made poorer because they have to pay for this. And specifically in the services which are often part of welfare states – education and healthcare – everybody has to pay more.

Some people may be thinking, 'Very well. So some prices may be somewhat higher but at least the demanding qualifications mean we can be sure the quality of our services is good.' Is that right?

3. Excessive training and the quality of services

It is a date unknown sometime between 2005 and 2009. We are in the accident and emergency department of Stafford Hospital. A stream of people is coming in. Most have minor injuries but some are in a life-threatening condition – perhaps suffering chest pain and about to suffer a heart attack. Which ones are which?

A triage nurse is supposed to see each patient and rush through anyone who is in imminent danger. But no triage nurse is present. The receptionist – who has no medical training – is deciding from a distance whether anyone looks in a bad enough state for her to call someone.[20]

In a ward in the same hospital, a woman is pressing a buzzer for a nurse.[21] The woman wants to relieve herself but she in not able to get out of bed. Nobody comes. She buzzes again and again. Still nobody comes. She calls out. Eventually a nurse arrives. But it is too late. The nurse belatedly moves the woman onto a commode and goes away. Now the woman is left on the commode for half an hour. She wants to go back to bed. But again, nobody comes. Finally she tries to make it by herself from the commode to the bed. She falls onto the floor. A concerned visitor nearby goes searching for a nurse. She can't find one.

'People of the same trade seldom meet together, even for merriment and diversion, but the conversation ends in a conspiracy against the public, or in some contrivance to raise prices.'

Adam Smith, *The Wealth of Nations* (1776)

Elsewhere in the hospital, many of the patients are developing bed sores. They should be turned regularly so that the pressure on particular parts of their bodies is relieved. But this does not happen frequently enough.

All this is in the official government report into the hundreds of unnecessary deaths and incidents of bad care that took place at this hospital over four years (see also Chapter 10).[22]

What was the root cause of the problem? The chairman of the inquiry unveiled his first report at a press conference in 2010. At that conference he said, 'A chronic shortage of staff, particularly nursing staff, was largely responsible for the sub-standard care.'[23]

Why was there a shortage of staff? In fact why is there often a shortage of staff in the British National Health Service? The immediate and obvious reason is that the government was trying to save money. Another reason may be the huge amounts of money spent on administrators rather than front-line medical staff. But there is another reason worth considering: nurses are more expensive than they used to be.

In the 1950s and 1960s, a nurse was like an apprentice. She started straight from school aged seventeen. She did three years training at a college attached to a hospital but most of her time was spent working on the wards. She was junior but she was a useful member of the team from the beginning. For the hospital, her work was relatively cheap. So she could be afforded more easily. That, in turn, meant it was less likely that there would be a shortage of nurses.

Then came demands that nursing should be more prestigious and recognised as a profession. The training was transformed into a three-year degree course. Practical work was still done but there was far less of it. Subjects like sociology were added that were not of direct relevance. In the 1950s and 1960s, a trainee who started at seventeen was a registered nurse at twenty. Now the average age at which a nurse registers is twenty-nine.[25] Even by that age, she or he has done precious little nursing work. But she or he has already cost £40,000 in tuition fees and more in bursaries and other costs (these figures date back to 2007 and now are surely higher).[26] It has even been suggested that the total cost of a trained nurse could be £100,000.[27] Finally, after all that time and cost, it is quite possible that she or he will leave the profession. In an ideal world, perhaps, every nurse would have a degree in sociology and many other desirable qualifications. But it means more expense. This helps to lead to the situation where a receptionist is doing triage in the emergency department and nobody comes when an elderly patient calls 'nurse'.

Higher requirements for training and qualifications mean fewer practitioners. In healthcare, fewer practitioners mean less attention for patients, which amounts to lower-quality care.

Morris Kleiner compared how various trades and professions have developed in different American states. He found that the requirements for a qualification reduced the growth rate of these occupations by 20 per cent.[28] Excessive and unnecessary qualifications in all cases reduce the number of practitioners. Where the requirements to become a doctor or nurse are excessive, there will be fewer of them.

Training and qualification requirements can also damage education. In a number of countries and most states in the USA, people are not permitted to teach without an officially recognised qualification. Some may think, 'Well, that sounds reasonable. I would like my child to be taught by someone who is qualified.' But the certification rule means, as Andrew Coulson has pointed out, that 'Bill Gates could not teach computer science'. Come to that, Einstein could not teach physics if he were alive today and Churchill and Caesar could not teach history. Maybe they would be no good as teachers. But most heads would be willing to give them a try.

> 'America presently suffers from a severe shortage of nurses of every type. The American Hospital Association reported in July 2007 that US hospitals faced a shortage of 116,000 nurses.'[24]

There is also the problem that the teacher training is sometimes of dubious value. 'The ed school establishment is more concerned with politics – both academic and ideological – than with learning,' according to Rita Kramer, who visited many 'ed schools' and wrote a book about what she found.[29] Teacher-training schools have one particular well-known blot on their records. For decades they taught a disastrously bad way of teaching children how to read (see Chapter 4). This took place in France, America, Britain and elsewhere. The training resulted in lower-quality teaching than would have taken place without it.

So there are several ways in which training – or excessive requirements for training – can damage the quality of services.

4. Monopoly control over training and qualifications reduces competition and innovation

Typically one institution – the government or an organisation approved by the government – decides what qualifications are needed in medicine and teaching. This can lead to a lack of flexibility and innovation in the kinds of training and qualifications. It can inhibit the creation of new kinds of jobs.

Take physician assistants in the USA. The category was invented because they take less long to train than full doctors but are able to do at least 73 per cent of what general practitioners do and they do it just as well.[31] The training takes two and a half years instead of seven.[32] The benefit of this category of jobs has been shown by the way demand for physician assistants has subsequently grown. Their numbers have increased from 13,000 to 83,000 in three decades.[33] It seems likely that other categories of medical staff would also have been created if it were not for the fact that there is monopoly control over qualifications and little incentive for the profession or government to create new rules or qualifications.

'The licensing of occupations is a continually expanding frontier, ev upgrading old trades and new servic to the mantle of professional statu and always justified in service the public good. On and on it roll "professionalising" the workforce it goes with layers of new regulati and board certification, all the w systematically redistributing ren from those outside the licensi system to those inside … inhibiti experimentation in new busine models and stifling innovatio

Jason Pot

Fulfilling a need

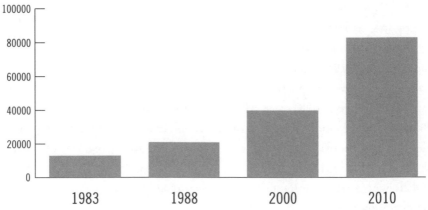

Number of physician assistants in the USA.[34]

5. Training and qualification requirements can stop the poor improving their lives or getting a job at all

A wide variety of people find it more difficult to get jobs because of licensing laws. Would-be florists in Louisiana have to spend money on training and an exam. Training and qualification requirements stopped black Americans becoming plumbers and hairdressers before the Second World War. Young people who might be excellent nurses find that they must navigate a degree course and years of training before they are allowed to contribute.

Tough licensing laws can make it difficult for those in the lower half of society to get jobs. Jestina Clayton grew up in a village in Sierra Leone where all girls learned African hair-braiding. She was an expert. It was a job she could do well in the USA. Except that when she went to Utah, she found that she needed a cosmetology license to do hair-braiding. Getting the licence required two years' schooling on completely irrelevant subjects at a cost of $16,000.[35] The licensing requirement prevented her from working.

Many government schools have failed to teach children to read and write well (see Chapter 4) so there are millions of people in the advanced world who have been left functionally illiterate. In this situation, it is verging on the inhumane to insist on written exams and licensing requirements for jobs or trades where they are not absolutely necessary.

na Clayton was prevented from working as a hair-braider by law.

If this were a matter of a few professions here and there, it might not be so important. But the requirement for qualifications has grown alarmingly. During the 1950s, about 4.5 per cent of the workforce in America had to get a licence to do their jobs. That figure had risen to 29 per cent by 2008.[36] There are now more than twice as many people whose job is affected by licensing requirements than are members of a union.[37]

You can't do that without a licence!

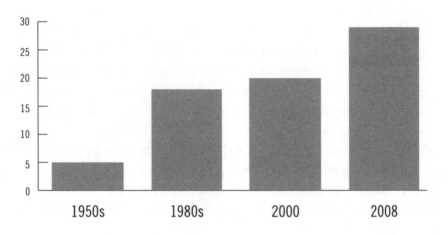

Proportion of the US workforce needing a licence to do their jobs.

Source: Morris M. Kleiner and Alan B. Krueger, 'Analysing the Extent and Influence of Occupational Licensing on the Labor Market'[38]

What can be done to reduce the damage inflicted by unnecessary or excessive requirements for training and qualifications?

In many cases, like floristry, there should be no requirement for any qualifications at all. But training and qualifications are obviously important in medicine, for example. What can be done here?

One idea comes from an unexpected place. We're in Liverpool in 1870 and there is criticism of accountants who do poor work. A group of accountants agree to band together as the Incorporated Society of Liverpool Accountants to try and establish themselves as well-qualified, honest professionals. Later the same year, a similar institute starts in London. The two institutes and several others decide to join together. Members are required to demonstrate their knowledge and expertise. The combined institute naturally puts about the idea that, if you want a good accountant, you had better make sure he – it is certainly be a 'he' at this time – is a member of what is soon known as the Institute of Chartered Accountants in England and Wales. This seems perfectly reasonable and sensible.

The institute grows in power and importance and towards the end of the century, it is close to establishing itself as the sole body through which someone can qualify as an accountant – in other words, it is close to making itself a monopoly. But just before this happens, it faces opposition. Some of it comes from men who have recently returned to Britain after fighting in the Boer War. As with other wars, the Boer War has helped make ordinary people aware of their own abilities and realise they are no less capable than men with advantages of birth and position. Men of this sort who have previously worked in accountancy are annoyed by the suggestion that only those who have the money and higher education enabling them to become members of the Institute of Chartered Accountants should be recognised as professionals.

On 30 November 1904, one of these men, Henry Lewis, convenes a meeting with seven colleagues at Balfour House in the City of London.[39] Henry Lewis is a formidable character – 'a born fighter … brusque, overbearing often to the point of rudeness'. The eight men create the London Association of Accountants. They aim to combat the attempts of the 'older established bodies to render the accountancy profession a closed one … shutting out many capable and qualified men'. They set their own standards for membership. They do not require people to pay to be 'articled' to a firm of accountants, which costs between 50 and 200 guineas. New members do not need to have family connections to enable them to get 'articles'. They do not need to have had a higher education. They only need to have expertise and experience in accountancy. Women are also admitted.

The fight for recognition takes years. The Institute of Chartered Accountants hoped for the 'obliteration' of this and other upstart bodies. But in the 1930s, the London Association of Accountants, by now joined with other bodies to become the Association of Chartered Certified Accountants (ACCA), is fully recognised. Bringing the story up to date, the ACCA now has 154,000 members and is so successful that it has become an international organisation with students from 170 countries. It has won a British government award for 'enterprise in international trade'.

Because of the struggle of these eight men joined by others of a similar kind, there are now six bodies in Britain which can grant qualifications in accountancy. There are also other bodies offering accreditation in related fields such as book-keeping.

The lesson of this is that if there are rival bodies with different criteria for saying 'you are qualified', you can create qualifications that are varied and suit different people. Rivalry between authorising bodies means they are more likely to be enterprising and innovative.

The conclusion, I suggest, is that monopoly licensing should not be permitted.

Unfortunately it is no easy matter to abolish an established licensing requirement or to give permission to new licensing bodies. In Florida, the government wanted to pass legislation removing licensing requirements for twenty trades including hair-braiding, teaching ballroom dancing and interior decorating. At first it seemed easy. The legislators were generally in favour. But the interior decorators and others lobbied hard. Some of their arguments were ludicrous. It was claimed that unlicensed interior designers might use fabrics which would spread disease and cause the deaths of 88,000 people a year.[41] One claimed that clashing colour schemes might adversely affect 'salivation'. Yet they won. The people who cared most about the continuation of such licences – practitioners who gained financially – lobbied hardest. If the evidently ridiculous arguments of decorators can win, imagine how much more difficult it would be to prevail against organisations of teachers or doctors. They would certainly claim that infringement of their monopolies would damage children or put lives at risk. Nevertheless, such battles must be fought if the damage done by monopoly authorising bodies is to be reduced.

> 'This is probably controversial to say but what the heck. Law schools would probably be wise to think about being two years instead of three.'
>
> Barack Obama, August 2013.[40] It is unusual for a politician to suggest that training might be excessive. President Obama once taught constitutional law so he is in a good position to know whether excessive time is spent obtaining legal qualifications.

•   •   •

The issue of training and qualification profoundly affects welfare states. The eternal students of Italy, Germany and elsewhere are subsidised by taxpayers, many of whom are poor. Excessive requirements for qualifications of medical professionals and teachers increase costs for taxpayers and reduce the quantity and quality of the welfare services they provide. The qualifications required trap less well-educated people in unemployment or in lower-skill jobs than they could otherwise do. So they damage social mobility and cohesion. Monopoly control over qualifications can also damage innovation and progress in medical care and education.

It may be difficult to make progress but the aim should be to achieve something like this:

- Many licensing requirements – especially in the USA – should be abolished altogether.

- Governments should ensure that they are not directly responsible for licensing. Instead they should confine themselves to recognising privately created licensing bodies.

- Governments should allow and encourage rival licensing bodies.

- Since practitioners who are already licensed have little incentive to create new bodies, governments should allow consumers of services such as hospitals and schools to establish licensing bodies.

- Eternal students should not be indulged at public expense. As in Switzerland students should choose vocational or purely academic study at the age of seventeen or eighteen, leading to an exam at twenty or twenty-one.

- Most study beyond that age should be financed by students doing productive and useful work in the field.

- Public subsidy for further study should be granted only to a small proportion of people for, say, another two or three years.

- There should be no opportunity to re-take years in which a student has failed to meet the required standard.

There are doubtless other measures that could be taken. But progress depends on a wider understanding that excessive requirements for training and qualification cause damage and that the people who are hurt include patients, students, taxpayers and the low-paid.

12.

Democracy is like a drunk husband

The trouble with representative democracies

THE SCANDALS SURROUNDING PUBLIUS CLODIUS Pulcher were remarkable even by Roman standards. Among many other things, he was accused of incest with all his sisters. There were four or five of them; historians are not completely sure which. But the biggest scandal involved a special religious ceremony reserved exclusively for women – the Bona Dea. No men were allowed. On this occasion, the ceremony took place at the home of Julius Caesar himself. It was hosted by his wife, Pompeia. Clodius went to the ceremony disguised as a woman. Some said he wanted to seduce Pompeia although there was no proof of it. In any event, he was discovered and tried for sac-

rilege. Caesar divorced Pompeia partly because of this incident. When it was suggested to him that his wife had surely not been seduced by Clodius, he made the famous reply, 'Caesar's wife must be above suspicion.'[1]

Clodius was highly ambitious. Despite all the scandals surrounding him, he sought high office. He was a patrician – a member of the high aristocracy. But he broke all the rules – getting himself adopted into a plebeian family so he could achieve power as a tribune of the plebs.[2] He succeeded at this and, in 58 BC, tried to increase his popularity by offering people free corn.[3] 'Corn' here means grain from

Publius Clodius Pulcher was ambitious.

which people could make a kind of gruel.⁴ For some years previously, corn had been sold to the less well off at a subsidised price. But Clodius took it a step further by making it free. To put it cynically – and in Clodius's case, a drop of cynicism seems a minimum – he bought popularity with taxpayers' money.

He was not around long enough to see the results. Along with so many other ambitious Romans, he was murdered. But the policy remained. No one dared remove it. It became ruinously expensive and unsustainable. The rural poor, who were already moving into Rome, arrived in even greater numbers. The policy was subject to fraud. Many people who were not genuinely poor collected free corn including well-to-do officials and high-ranking military officers.⁵ The numbers claiming the corn dole swelled to 350,000, an extraordinary figure considering the population of Rome was only of the order of 600,000, excluding foreigners and slaves.

'In the mid-eighteenth century, "democracy" was a word ... associated primarily with the ancient world and had negative connotations: democracies were conceived to be unstable, warlike, and prone to mutate into despotisms.'⁶

As one historian puts it, once the dole was established, 'the proletariat claimed this as a right which no politician who needed their votes could refuse'.⁷ The Republic, the semi-democratic government of ancient Rome, could not deal with the problem. Only when Caesar became dictator was the government able to make major inroads into the huge cost. Caesar halved the number entitled to it, saying

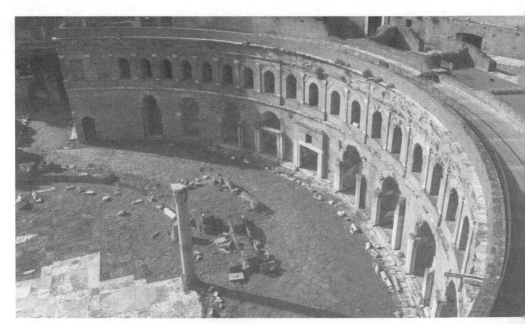

The remains of Trajan's Market can still be seen in Rome today.

he was making a different kind of provision by obtaining new colonies for the sur-plus city population.[8] But not even Caesar tried to abolish it.

The dole remained a feature of Roman life for centuries. You can still see rem-nants of it today. On the site of the forum in Rome there remain some parts of Trajan's Market, a building which was once so massive that it was described at the time as a wonder of the world. It was from here that the dole was administered.

Some Romans were opposed to the dole and even suggested it reflected a decline in the greatness of Rome. Juvenal famously remarked, 'The people that once bestowed commands, consulships, legions and all else, now meddles no more and eagerly longs for just two things: bread and circuses.'[9] The 'bread' he refers to is the corn dole. This corn dole started with Clodius, a politician seeking popu-larity and power.

The parallels with modern times are striking. Food stamps in the USA are the contemporary corn dole. They and many other provisions of welfare states have, like the corn dole, proved hard or impossible to remove by any politician wishing to hold on to power. No government minister in Britain has ever dared call for the abolition of the National Health Service, for example, any more than Caesar dared abolish the corn dole. No politician would dare suggest that parents should be charged fees for the schooling of their children in France, Germany or any of the countries where 'free' schooling has become normal.

In democracies, welfare states are like one-way ratchets. 'Free' things are promised and given by politicians seeking or holding on to power. Almost never are they removed. It does happen occasionally, but it takes years and usually decades of abuse, expense and scandal before a problem becomes so widely recognised that even modest reform takes place. Benefits for the incapacitated were increased substantially in Britain in the 1970s. The numbers claiming them soared beyond any idea of how many could gen-uinely be incapacitated. But the problem only began to be tackled seriously around 2009 or 2010, more than three decades later.

Most of us are committed to democracy, me included. But that should not stop us admit-ting that it is not perfect. Democracy is like a drunk husband – self-indulgent, stupid and with a tendency to knock things over and break them. Like a loyal wife, we continue to love democracy. But, also like a loyal wife, we have a right to name its faults.

> '**It has been said that democracy is the worst form of government except all those other forms which have been tried from time to time.**'
>
> Winston Churchill[10]

1. Politicians in democracies get elected by promising 'free' services and benefits, ignoring the long-term effects.

2. Politicians get elected and receive sponsorship by favouring interest groups at the expense of the general public. Advantages are concentrated in the hands of these interest groups – such as trade unions or businesses – while bad effects are diffused among everyone else. This is known as 'the tyranny of the minority'.

    > 'The government consi of a gang of men exac like you and me ... Th principal device ... is search out groups who p; or pine for something t can't get, and to promise give it to them. Nine tin out of ten that promis worth nothing. The te time is made good looting A to satisfy
    >
    > H. L. Menck

3. Politicians seeking power encourage the poorer half of society to believe they can become better off by taxing the rich. This may be modestly true in the short term but can make them worse off in the long term. Politicians readily blame the rich for problems because they know the rich have few votes. The rich increasingly tend to be regarded as having no right to consideration. This is a prime example of 'the tyranny of the majority'.

4. Representative democracy is a blunt instrument. Politicians and parties seek election offering a mix of policies. The electorate might approve of their policies A and B and not C, D or E. But, once in power, governments claim they have a 'mandate' to introduce any or all of them. They are also in a position to impose new policies F and G which were not mentioned in their manifestos at all.

    > 'A democracy is a st which recognises subjection of the mino to majority, that is, organisation for systematic use of viole by one class against other, by one part of population against anoth
    >
    > Lenin, *The State and Revolut*

5. Politicians make deals behind the scenes with each other. They support some of each other's policies even though they do not genuinely agree with them. A deal is made so that each politician can get through what he or she wants. In America, this is known as 'logrolling'.[14] In the European Union, it is routine.

    > Half of EU citizens do not h confidence in the democracy of t country. Slightly more than half do have confidence in the democrac the European Un
    >
    > Eurobarom

6. 'Checks and balances' and 'pork-barrel'[15] politics can make good government almost impossible. The 'checks and balances' may

be divisions of power – between the House of Representatives and the Senate in the United States for example – or overlapping authority between national and regional governments. In Australia, the states are responsible for healthcare but the national government provides the cash. In a sense, the states have responsibility without the power to fulfil it while the national government has power without the responsibility. Pork-barrel politics interferes with good government when a law can be passed only if it is adjusted or distorted to suit the short-term interests of a particular locality. Even the constitution can interfere with good government when it is applied in a way that its creators never imagined.

> **'What he got is a God-awful mess because that is all you can get past Congress!'**
>
> Professor Terry Moe on Obamacare[16]

7. There is a fundamental internal contradiction in representative democracy: a politician is meant to represent the wishes and interests of the electorate but he or she is also meant to have individual ideas about what should be done. In the midst of this contradiction, politicians can often pick and choose, sometimes representing the electorate and sometimes themselves. To put it another way, elected representatives can choose not to be representative.

8. Politicians often feel under pressure to talk and act on the basis of what people are supposed to think rather than what they genuinely think. From time to time, there is a difference.[17]

9. Politicians tend to come from a self-regarding, well-educated elite. They tend to become frustrated at the behaviour of ordinary people and feel it is their prerogative to boss them around.

> **'While democracy means a government accountable to the electorate, our rulers now make us accountable to them.'**
>
> Kenneth Minogue[18]

10. Electorates are highly susceptible to 'magic thinking', whereby they expect an end to be achieved simply because a politician says it is his policy to achieve it. A politician may say he intends to raise wages for the low-paid, for example, even though he has no plan which will actually achieve this aim.[19] Politicians are attracted to magic thinking, too, because they know it will please voters and increase their chances of getting elected. Phrases such as 'Yes we can!' and 'the Third Way' may be considered by some as examples of magic thinking.

11. Voters have little reason to consider the pros and cons of any issue in any depth

because the only power they can exercise is to vote for a party. This is one reason why they are so susceptible to magic thinking, described above. You could almost say they have been infantilised.

12. Since democracies ostensibly reflect the will of the people, individuals and the public generally feel less entitled to object to ever greater intrusions and instruction by government. So we arrive at a kind of democratic totalitarianism.

B.A. 'The government treat people like babies!

J.B. 'Maybe they are babies

B.A. 'They want to be!

Conversation with Professor Benito Arruñada

'Democracy encourages the fantasy despot in us all. Had we but cash enough, and power, what wrong would we not put right … Fantasy does corrupt, and this particular one has eroded the basic assumption that a man's property is his own business.'

Kenneth Minogue[21]

Criticisms such as these have been made since democracy first appeared. In ancient Greece, Plato caustically remarked, 'In politics we presume that everyone who knows how to get votes knows how to administer a city or a state. When we are ill … we do not ask for the handsomest physician, or the most eloquent one.'[22] Frédéric Bastiat, the French nineteenth-century economist, said, 'The state is that great fictitious entity by which everyone seeks to live at the expense of everyone else.'[23] You could say that the sentence is the appeal of the welfare state in a nutshell. More recently, Thomas Sowell, the American economist, commented, 'The first lesson in economics is scarcity. There is never enough of anything to satisfy all those who want it. The first lesson in politics is to disregard the first lesson of economics.'[24]

The flaws of democracy have been particularly dangerous in relation to welfare states. All twelve of the flaws listed above have played a part. Neither politicians nor the electorate have had an incentive to think things through. Both have been subject to magic thinking. Politicians have got elected by offering things to the population for free – ignoring long-term effects or unintended consequences. And so on.

The way that democracies come to demand that the state should put every problem right regardless of expense or other consequences was brilliantly described by Bastiat:

> Sir, I do not have the honour of knowing you, but I will bet ten to one that for the last six months you have been constructing utopias; and if you have been doing so, I will bet ten to one that you are making the state responsible for bringing them into existence. And you, Madam, I am certain that in your heart of hearts you would like to cure all the suffering of humanity and that you would not be in the slightest put out if the state just wanted to help in this.
>
> But alas! The unfortunate being, like Figaro, does not know whom to listen to nor which way to turn. The hundred thousand voices of the press and the tribune are all calling out to this being at once: 'Organize work and the workers. Root out selfishness. Repress the insolence and tyranny of capital. Carry out experiments on manure and eggs. Criss-cross the country with railways. Educate the young. Succour the elderly. Lend money interest free to those who want it. Encourage art and train musicians and dancers for us. Prohibit trade and at the same time create a merchant navy. Enlighten, develop, expand, fortify, spiritualize and sanctify the souls of peoples [etc.]'
>
> 'Oh, Sirs, have a little patience,' the state replies pitifully. 'I will try to satisfy you, but I need some resources to do this. I have prepared some projects relating to five or six bright, new taxes that are the most benign the world has ever seen. You will see how pleased you will be to pay them.'[25]

'What if there are limits to what governments can do?'

Jason L. Riley, *Please Stop Helping Us*[27]

Bastiat was satirising the tendency of democracies to call upon the state to make everything perfect in 1848 when welfare states had hardly got into first gear. Since then, we have seen an explosion of demands upon governments to provide. I suspect quite a few items on Bastiat's list were meant to be extreme or absurd. Some are now normal parts of welfare states: 'succour the elderly', for example.[26]

There is always going to be more childcare

Bastiat: 'everyone seeks to live at the expense of everyone else'.

that people want, more care for the elderly, more expensive medicines, more teachers, more nurses, bigger pensions and so on. That, in short, is why, in America for example, government spending has gone from a mere 7 per cent of GDP in 1900 to 41 per cent in 2011.[28] The rise in spending has been continuously upwards apart from the spikes caused by the two world wars. It seemed for a while as though a plateau had been reached in the 1980s and 1990s at around 35 per cent of GDP. But that has turned out to be merely a base camp from which spending has made a further assault on a new peacetime peak.

France was ahead of America. Following its revolutions in 1789 and 1870, the government was already spending 11 per cent of GDP by 1872.[29] The rise since then has continued relentlessly since then so France has maintained its lead. Its spending reached a new record of 57 per cent of GDP in 2012.

Marianne spends more and more

French government expenditure as a percentage of GDP.[30] These figures omit the spending spikes during the two world wars.

In Britain, the twentieth century began with government spending at an even higher level than France: 14 per cent.[31] It soared to 48 per cent in the mid-1970s but then fell back for a couple of decades before recovering to 45 per cent in 2011/12.[32]

Looking at the big picture, government spending as a proportion of GDP in these three countries rose six times, five times and three times respectively over 112, 141 and 112 years. It has been typical of advanced countries to triple their spending or more over the past century. More than all of the increase in spending has been focused on welfare. Other kinds of spending have been reduced to make way. Defence expenditure in Britain, for example, fell from 3.7 to 2.9 per cent of GDP between 1900 and 2010.[33] In the USA, defence spending fell from 10.1 per cent in 1960 to 5.6 per cent in 2012.[34]

Welfare state spending accounts for 69 per cent of the budget in Germany and 71 per cent in France.[35] Comparable figures are not easily available for all countries but four major advanced countries – France, Germany, Italy and Japan – all allocate remarkably similar proportions to welfare – between 66 per cent and 71 per cent. Even this is probably an underestimate because other areas of spending such as 'General Public Services' often include elements of welfare state expenditure.

How much is spent on the welfare state?

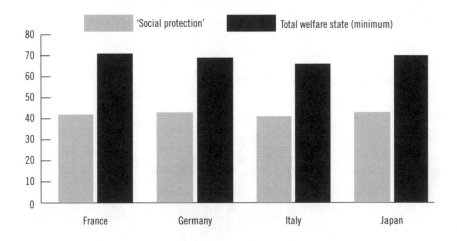

Minimum percentage of government spending devoted to 'social protection' and the welfare state more broadly including healthcare, education and housing in 2011.

Source: OECD[36]

Between 1980 and 2012, nearly all of the thirty-five countries studied by the OECD increased their social spending as a proportion of GDP.[37] The fastest increases were in those which previously had the smallest social provision. Japan's social spending doubled. Greece's more than doubled. Portugal's rose two and half times. Turkey's tripled. In democratic states, there is a kind of irresistible drive towards high welfare spending.

There were only two exceptions. One was the Netherlands. It changed tack as described in Chapter 2. The other was Sweden.

It is striking that Sweden, the country often regarded as the ultimate welfare state, is one of the few countries to have cut social spending over the past thirty years. How did this happen?

In the 1980s, it was business as usual. Swedish welfare spending was high and rising. At both the beginning and end of the decade, Sweden was spending more on welfare than any other country covered by the OECD.[38] Then came the recession of the early 1990s. Demand for welfare spending continued increasing but tax receipts fell. Sweden found that raising the money needed for more welfare spending had gone from hard to impossible. The budget deficit soared to 10 per cent.[39] There were only two options: go bust or cut back.[40]

So Sweden cut back. Welfare benefits were reduced and conditions for getting them were made tougher. These and other economy measures were taken to bring the welfare budget back to sustainability. The shock of this crisis also led to some modest re-thinking about how welfare should be delivered and some measures against unwelcome unintended consequences – like abuse of the system.

The Swedish welfare state hits the ceiling

Public social expenditure in Sweden as a percentage of GDP.

Source: OECD[41]

It might be tempting to conclude from Sweden's example, 'You see! Democracies can be sensible and draw back from disaster. They can reform their welfare states.'

Indeed they can. But what we can see in Sweden is that even in a particularly mature and level-headed democracy, the electorate needed to go right to the edge of a cliff before deciding to turn back. And subsequently, nineteen years after this moment, welfare spending in Sweden, while significantly down from its peak, remains well above average.

Let's take another country where reforms and obstacles have been implemented. America, in the 1990s, had a crisis of conscience about welfare spending. There was publicity about the cost, the unemployment that had been created and the fraud. The growing welfare dependency seemed contrary to the centuries-old national culture of rugged self-reliance. This culminated in President Clinton signing the Personal Responsibility and Work Opportunity Reconciliation Act in 1996, enabling and encouraging states to move away from cash entitlements towards workfare. Here it looked as if a nation was offended by the idea of people getting used to living on welfare and was acting to stop it. The pioneering spirit of the USA seemed to rise up in revolt. Major reforms took place and many people were taken off welfare rolls.

But within a decade, there was a slide back towards more welfare spending. The numbers receiving food stamps soared, partly because the eligibility criteria were loosened. The time during which people could receive unemployment benefits was increased. The semi-compulsory healthcare insurance scheme known as 'Obamacare' was introduced.

Sweden and America illustrate typical patterns: a country perceives there is a welfare state problem and pulls back. But the first flaw of democracy – the way politicians get elected by promising 'generous' things – sooner or later re-asserts itself. So despite occasional retreats, a Utopian idea of the welfare state is never defeated. It rallies and then makes further advances. The tendency is for more and more to be spent until, as in Sweden, the money simply runs out. It is arguable that Greece and Spain faced their recent financial crises, which necessitated sudden, painful cutbacks, because of welfare state spending.

Welfare states in democracies resemble people who can't swim paddling out into the sea. To begin with they are fine. They walk through the shallow water. Gradually progress gets more difficult but it is still possible. The water gets higher and higher up their bodies – past their knees, then their chests. Occasionally one turns back, saying, 'This is silly. I'm getting into danger!' But most continue on into the sea, because

> 'It is a kind of insanity, this uncontrollable inflation of the state... Regulations pile higher and new benefits accumulate ... In Sigmund Freud's *Civilisation and Its Discontents*, he pictures the mind as an ancient city, where nothing is ever demolished but new buildings are continually added. He would have recognised the sick, social democratic states of the twenty-first century, bulging with ever more good intentions, incapable of shedding those past their sell-by date.'
>
> Marc Sidwell, *City AM* [42]

the dynamic of politicians trying to get elected leads to more promises and bigger welfare states. Eventually the water rises up over the mouths of one or two of them and they are in imminent danger of drowning. Suddenly they have to be rescued – like Sweden or Greece. But does anyone say, 'This is crazy! We need to get back well within our depth – where we were only up to our knees'? No. They keep flirting with the maximum depth at which survival is possible.

But well before they are at this maximum depth, so much money needs to be raised to pay for the welfare states that it is no longer a matter of the government acting as Robin Hood, taking from the rich and giving to the poor. That does not raise enough. So cash is taken from those on average wages and then it is taken from the poor. Effectively, money is taken from the poor and then given back to them after a deduction has been granted to bureaucrats, who have charged them for the administration and sometimes added in instructions on where they must live, which doctor they should go to, what school their children must attend and what training course they must do.

One of the problems in representative democracies is that those who point out the drawbacks of big welfare states tend to get a hearing only when things are going badly wrong or disaster is afoot. It is hard to persuade people otherwise that a big welfare state has plenty of bad, unintended consequences. Such arguments count for little against the rallying cry of a politician who declares, 'It is wrong that in this great nation of ours anyone should go without decent childcare / decent care in old age [or whatever it might be]'. Of course it is always assumed that what the state provides will be 'decent' or 'high quality' regardless of any previous experience that suggests it will be nothing of the kind. Potential undesirable consequences are ignored or dismissed.

This, at least, is the tendency. Is it an absolute rule? Is every single country that goes towards democracy, from Sweden to India and Brazil to China, bound to end up with a welfare state that keeps growing until the harm is overwhelmingly obvious or the money runs out? Is there any way of stopping the self-harming tendency of democratic countries?

Frankly, it is hard to be confident that there is. Maybe we are headed for a world where – quite unnecessarily – mass unemployment is permanent, where education fails often and badly, where healthcare is not as good as it could be and millions die needless, early deaths. Maybe it will be a world where the spirit of independence, self-reliance and freedom continues to fade away, a large minority of children never learn to read and many people feel alienated from society.

Of course, it is conceivable that the downside of massive welfare states will become better recognised. The generation that believed that more welfare must always be better welfare may be replaced by another which perceives that it is not so simple. Unfortunately I am doubtful that this will happen – at least within representative democracies. We tend to take this form of democracy for granted as the natural, normal one. In point of fact, it has not existed for very long. It first took shape in the modern world in seventeenth-century Britain, emerging out of a war between king and parliament. The parliament, up to that point, had not been powerful. For a long while it had been merely a way in which powerful land-owners could make their voices heard by the monarch. But after the Civil War, it became much more than that. If this is, indeed, the origin or model for modern parliamentary or representative democracy let us recognise where it came from: it was an adjustment to a medieval system originally created for a feudal society. Viewed this way, it seems absurd to assume that it is ideal for modern times.

In America, the democratic system was influenced by both the British and Roman examples. But again, it was formed in circumstances very different from those of the present. The same applies to other democracies, except for some such as Japan where a new democratic system was recently and suddenly accepted. But even in these cases, the constitutions were designed to mimic the representative democracies which derived from seventeenth- or eighteenth-century models. In those times, of course, it took days or even weeks for information to travel from one part of a country to another. Representative democracy was the only democracy practicable.

But we have seen that representative democracy has a plethora of faults. Is there any better form of democracy? In particular, is there any form which would manage a welfare state better?

If one looks around the world, there are two kinds of state which

In 1660, the monarchy was restored and Charles II became king but parliament had asserted its power and increasingly became the real source of authority.

have successfully resisted the siren call of 'more welfare'. One consists of countries which are not full democracies: dictatorships, oligarchies or semi-democracies. In modern times, they have included the communist countries of Europe and Asia; Hong Kong when it was a colony; and Singapore, which is a democracy but where the same party has been in power for a generation and which makes life very difficult for the opposition. Most of us would not want a democracy with limits. We want government by clear consent.

The other kind of democracy that has kept a lid on welfare takes a different shape. Here is a flavour of how it works in one country.

In May 2013, the smallest region of this country had to take a decision about a proposed railway project costing the equivalent of US$7.5 million.[43] As with all such projects, you can imagine that some argued that it would be good for the economy and for access to the rest of the country while others maintained it would cause too much damage.

'If liberty and equality, as is thought by some, are chiefly to be found in democracy, they will be best attained when all persons alike share in government to the utmost.'

Aristotle, *Politics*

In most advanced countries, the decision would have been taken by a small group of politicians or civil servants. Such decisions are sometimes taken by people who have never even been to the place concerned. They are

True democracy: voting in the Swiss canton of Appenzell Innerhoden.

following the orders of their political party or the rules of a system. But in this region, the decision was taken by the local population of 15,717 souls.

The voters assembled in the town square. Following ancient tradition, men showed they were entitled to vote by carrying a sword. Women carried a voting card. The motion – whether or not to accept the railway project – was put and they voted by raising their hands. This is 'direct' democracy.

The decision, incidentally, was to approve the railway project. The region in question was the smallest canton in Switzerland, Appenzell Innerrhoden.

Not all referenda in Switzerland take place in town squares. The Appenzell Innerrhoden system is a rare, charming relic of old traditions. Most votes, of course, are done in the same way as votes in representative democracies.

Switzerland has national, cantonal and local referenda. They take place about three or four times a year. Typically there are two or three national issues, two cantonal and two local. The total number of issues varies between three and seven but it all depends on how many petitions have succeeded in obtaining the required number of signatures. Once the signatures are obtained, it can take as much as three years for a national issue to reach the ballot box. First, it is studied and debated by the parliament.

Switzerland's form of democracy is more thorough-going and complete than any other in the world. Switzerland also has a welfare state which is generally smaller and suffers fewer unintended consequences than elsewhere. Of course there are criticisms that could be made but Switzerland gets more things right in welfare than most other countries. One consequence is that unemployment there is significantly below average, for example.

Switzerland's social spending is lower than average. It absorbs 18.5 per cent of GDP compared to the average 22.1 per cent, according to the OECD definition. Switzerland also has lower-than-average total government spending (34.1 per cent versus 42.0 per cent) and therefore needs to take less in taxes (28.5 per cent versus 33.8 per cent).[44] This has been achieved despite the fact that Switzerland is surrounded by countries which mostly have above-average spending. The lower welfare spending and taxation are probably part of the reason Switzerland has achieved higher growth than other countries and has made its citizens into some of the most prosperous in the world apart from those in oil-rich and very small countries.[45]

Would you trust people to vote on whether they should have six weeks' holiday a year?

On 11 March 2012, the Swiss voted on the proposition that everyone should be legally entitled to six weeks' holiday a year. It is the sort of promise that a politician might use to gain popularity – as though he or she were making a gift. But when the Swiss had a referendum on the issue, evidently they seriously considered the drawbacks as well as the attractions. They voted the idea down by 1,531,986 votes to 771,717.[46]

You could argue that the fact that Switzerland has direct democracy and a welfare state under better control could be just a coincidence. It is a sample of only one so it is not conclusive. Is there any supporting evidence?

Some. There are twenty-six cantons in Switzerland and each has its own rules. Each one allows referenda to a different degree. So academics have been able to study how the amount of democracy in each of these cantons has affected the way it has been governed. This makes for a bigger sample size. At least three studies have found that the cantons with higher levels of direct democracy spend less on welfare than the rest.[47] These papers also looked at truly local governments – towns and villages – as well as cantons. So the sample size was bigger still and the results more robust. The most recent of these studies found that the correlation between direct democracy and lower welfare spending was 'highly statistically significant'.[48]

The governments of some cantons are obliged to have referenda to approve or reject major spending proposals. A couple of academics studied these cantons and compared them to the others.[49] They found that those with mandatory spending referenda spent 19 per cent less. It's a huge difference.

It is ironic. Some politicians and civil servants dismiss direct democracy, arguing that they, with their superior education and intellect, are sure to be better than ordinary people at running a country. Yet the evidence from Switzerland is the opposite. Ordinary people appear to be better and more sober in the exercise of power – when they have it – than elected, elite representatives. One Swiss study goes so far as to suggest that the 'representatives' in 'representative democracies' frequently do not represent. In Switzerland, 39 per cent of referenda, over a period of 140 years, turned down the proposals of politicians.[50]

Ballot for a referendum on 26th November 2006: 'Do you want to accept the federal law of 24th March 2006 on collaboration with the countries of East Europe?' and 'Do you want to accept the federal law of 24th March 2006 on family subsidies (Family Subsidies Law)?' The voter writes 'Yes' or 'No' in the box marked 'Antwort' (answer).

Do referenda make people happier?

PROFESSOR BRUNO FREY OF THE University of Zurich found a clear correlation between democracy and happiness. He used measures of the amount of democracy in cantons and the level of happiness people in them reported.[51] The canton of Basel Land had the highest democracy rating of 5.69 out of 6.00 and was notably happier than the canton of Geneva, with the lowest democracy rating of only 1.75. All the results were adjusted for demographic variables such as age and income. After such adjustments and a barrage of statistical tests, the results were found to be robust. Direct democracy really does appear to make people happier.

How big is the effect?
It was found to be as powerful as moving someone up from a low income to the next level up (out of five). It applies to everybody, too. The happiness effect of direct democracy reaches people of all social and educational classes.

What causes it?
One possible cause is that people get better government or, perhaps, government more in accordance with their views. But another and, it turns out, more significant cause is that people gain a sense of well-being from the feeling that they have the capacity to influence events. It is true that people may not always vote but they do so in big numbers when an issue is particularly important or is one on which they have strong views. Having a little power and a truly democratic decision makes people feel better.

So is direct democracy the answer? It appears to overcome at least seven of the twelve problems of representative democracy listed earlier – numbers 1, 4, 5, 7, 8, 9 and 11 – and to moderate another three or four of them. Unfortunately there are a couple of reasons to hesitate. Although Switzerland has one of the lowest rates of expenditure on its welfare state it has not wholly resisted the international trend. The proportion spent on 'public social expenditure' rose by a third between 1980 and 2012.[52] Its total expenditure, including non-welfare spending, as a proportion of GDP has been stable in recent years but the current level of 34.1 per cent is still up on the 27.9 per cent of 1970.[53] This is a country which has resisted the trend towards massive welfare states better than others but has not blocked it entirely.

A second worry is what we could call 'the California problem'. California is the most prominent American state where referenda are a regular part of political life. Unfortunately it is far from being a model of sensible, controlled government. On the contrary, it increased welfare expenditure to the point where it got itself into a financial crisis and was obliged to cut spending suddenly. As one report put it, California 'thrashed' its welfare programmes.[54] The state's budget crisis of 2008–12 even has its own Wikipedia entry.[55]

However, it can be argued that California has a system of direct democracy that is particularly badly designed. A San Francisco resident on 6 November 2013 had to face votes on seven city issues and eleven state ones.[56] There were separate documents for the city and the state. One was 147 pages long and the other 144. Voting conscientiously on so many referenda would be a massive undertaking, requiring days of reading and study. Only well-educated pensioners could attempt it. Moreover, California has all these votes on one day in the year.

Things are much easier for a voter in Switzerland, who has far fewer ballots to consider at any one time. The Swiss voter is more likely to want to and be able to look at the issues and vote. The exact design of direct democracy matters.

If we accept that direct democracy has something to offer, is there any other or additional strategy that a country might adopt to keep its welfare state under control?

One possibility is to create a binding obligation on governments to limit the level of debt. In Poland, a national debt limit of 60 per cent of GDP was introduced in 1997.[57] Despite all Poland's problems, this may well have helped it avoid getting anywhere near the sort of debt crisis experienced in Greece and, to a lesser extent, Italy and Spain. Poland enshrined the idea that no political party should be able – during its few years in government – to burden future generations with heavy debt.

Singapore has a similar but different law: a self-imposed obligation to maintain a balanced budget.[58] Each administration must balance the budget over its five-year period in office. It is only allowed to break this rule in exceptional circumstances and even then it must write to the President to ask permission. Whether such a rigorous system of budget discipline will be maintained if or when Singapore becomes a more fully free and democratic nation remains to be seen. But the rule has certainly served Singapore well, leading to great stability. Singapore has been more successful than any other advanced country in not imposing a debt burden on the next generation.

Other countries have made similar moves: Germany and Switzerland have introduced or enhanced their constitutions – in 2009 and 1999 respectively – to oblige governments to balance their budgets, as variously defined. Countries which have imposed these rules on themselves certainly appear to have done better than the rest.

A third possible strategy is to 'go local'. When everyone in a locality has to bear the costs as well as feel the benefits of decisions, they probably make better decisions. It seems to work for Switzerland. Local pride and a sense of identity are very strong there. I was once in Sils Maria, a little village 6 miles from the world-famous skiing resort of St Moritz. I asked if they had any mementoes for sale relating to St Moritz.

'No,' replied the shopkeeper firmly. 'We have mementoes of Sils Maria.'

There is no sure-fire answer to 'the problem of democracy'. But there do appear to be things that can be done to improve matters. A well-designed direct democracy, constitutional limits on budget deficits or debt and 'going local' have all shown that they can help.

13.

And the winner is…
~~communism~~ ~~capitalism~~
welfare statism!

Overview

A GREAT BATTLE OF IDEAS was played out in the twentieth century between communism and capitalism. Revolutions were followed by wars, famines, terror and millions of deaths. The communist cause was advanced by the Russian Revolution, the take-over of eastern Europe and communist revolutions and civil wars in China, Korea, Vietnam and Cambodia. Millions died from starvation in the Soviet Union and China. In Russia, Korea, Vietnam and elsewhere, the USA and other capitalist countries tried to resist communism. The Berlin Wall was a physical symbol of the divide between two ideas of how societies should be. As a child, I remember the tension and fear when the USA and the USSR squared up to each other during the Cuban missile crisis. The world waited nervously to see whether a nuclear war would erupt, potentially resulting in the deaths of many more millions.

But then the conflict ebbed. A critical mass of people in the communist countries became disillusioned by the economic underperformance and political oppression. In China in the 1980s, Deng Xiaoping led the country towards capitalism. In 1989, the Berlin Wall came down and all eastern Europe forsook communism. Communism was discredited. But capitalism did not completely win either. In much of the world, a constrained version of capitalism was tolerated without being loved. As memories of the poverty and terror resulting from communism faded, capitalism became subject to more distrust and criticism. And while all this was going on, quietly running past both these concepts – without a single shot fired – was the ultimate victor of the turmoil of the twentieth century: the welfare state.

It was as if two loud, clever politicians contended for leadership of the world but, in the end, people chose the quiet, boring one at the back. As a political or economic idea, it has not even got a name. What shall we call it? Welfare statism?

There was no great theoretician who came up with the idea or argued for it. No political thinker is famous for saying what a marvellous thing it is or could be. Welfare statism has no Karl Marx or Adam Smith. The father of the idea – if anyone deserves the title – was a vain, crusty, rather cynical old conservative: Otto von Bismarck. He thought a welfare state – or his modest, early version of it – would be a good way to keep the common people from revolting. He thought of it as a sop to the masses – a bone to be thrown on the floor for dogs to chew on.

From such an inglorious beginning, state welfare grew and conquered the world.

Welfare statism won because it was not an obvious failure like communism and appeared kinder than capitalism. Historians have barely noticed it. Sociologists are only beginning to catch up. But welfare states have been established in every single advanced democratic country in the world. If you say this to people they tend to be surprised. They have not thought of the world this way. But there are no exceptions. Welfare states cover the globe more extensively than any empire ever has. It is a fundamental change in the nature of world civilisation. Nor is it merely something half way between capitalism and communism.

'He who does not work shall not eat'

Lenin (clearly not a welfare statist).[1]

In communist countries, unemployment benefits were small on the basis that work was compulsory. Housing was a reward for a job, not compensation for being poor. Lenin said, 'He who does not work shall not eat' – hardly the words of a welfare statist. No, the welfare states of the world are a distinct form.

What has been their effect?

In 1934, Oxford University Press started publishing an ambitious series of books covering English history from the earliest beginnings. The original volumes went up to 1914. Then an additional, fifteenth volume was commissioned covering 1914 to 1945. It was written by one of the leading historians of the time, Professor A. J. P. Taylor. The opening words were striking:

> Until August 1914 a sensible, law-abiding Englishman could pass through life and hardly notice the existence of the state, beyond the post office and the policeman. He could live where he liked and as he liked. He had no official number or identity card. He could travel abroad or leave his country for ever without a passport or any sort of official permission. He could exchange his money for any other currency without restriction or limit. He could buy goods from any country in the world on the same terms as he bought goods at home. For that matter, a foreigner could spend his life in this country without permit and without informing the police...
>
> [During the First World War] the state established a hold over its citizens which, though relaxed in peacetime, was never to be removed and which the Second World War was again to increase. The history of the English state and of the English people merged for the first time.[3]

Like most traditional historians, Taylor noted the impact of the world wars but underestimated the quieter, less spectacular progress of the welfare state. But the picture he paints of a citizen before 1914 with untrammelled freedom and independence from state interference is, to modern eyes, almost incomprehensible.

The freedom Taylor describes might have been dismissed by Marx as 'bourgeois' – only affordable by the rich. But the poor exercised some of this freedom too. Think of the millions who poured across from Ireland, Great Britain, Italy, Poland, Germany and elsewhere to the United States in the nineteenth and early twentieth centuries. They, too, were free and unconstrained by state control or paperwork. They took risks and were obliged to work to survive. They had freedom and responsibility for themselves. What a huge contrast compared to how we live now.

'The Great Switch'

Phrase used by Jacques Barzun to describe 'the reversal of liberalism into its opposite'. Liberals originally believed in minimal government but came to favour welfare benefits and thus big government.[2]

Take Kate. She was born in a government hospital. Not long after birth, she was visited by a government health visitor. If her mother wanted – or was obliged – to work, Kate was deposited in day care, a nursery or a school run or paid for by the government. Then she went to government schools run in accordance with rules, regulations and guidance laid down by the government. The government specified or approved the nature and timing of her exams. This was followed by a university or technical college mostly financed by the government and under its control. Kate paid part of the cost of the course with a loan from the state, to be repaid during her adult life.

When Kate finished her education but was unemployed, the government gave her money on certain terms and conditions. When she had a child but no husband she was given a flat by the government. Now she has got a job, she is taxed by the government. She is obliged to make compulsory contributions to government social insurance, much of which goes to pay the pensions of her grandparents' generation. When she becomes ill she goes to a state-approved doctor who is paid, one way or another, by the government and who works in accordance with government rules and targets. She probably has a government identity card. She obviously needs a passport to travel, which is scanned at ports of entry, enabling her government to have a record of when she comes and goes.

'This is the main danger that today threatens civilisation: the nationalisation of life.'

José Ortega y Gasset[4]

While in government housing, Kate has to qualify for it and continue to qualify. Official forms have to be filled in. If she starts a business, she will be required to hire and fire staff in accordance with thousands of pages of government rules. She will be obliged to pay social insurance to the government in respect of each employee and pay tax on any profit her company might make. She would need government permission to start a school, build a home or create a hospital. She would need to obtain a government-approved licence to do a wide variety of occupations including, in many countries, teaching.

When she becomes older, Kate will receive a government pension. She may have to prove that she has made the required contributions. If she moves abroad, her country of origin may, in some cases, reduce this pension. If she becomes frail, she may be admitted to a government-financed and regulated home. She is quite likely to die in a government hospital and be cremated in a government crematorium.

All – or nearly all – the interventions in her life are for her own good. The idea is to protect her from harm. But one effect of all this state-organised, compulsory welfare is to guide and control her at every stage. This imaginary woman is monitored, guided, nudged and provided for 'from the cradle to the grave'. Financial incentives are imposed on her to push her to do what the government approves of or not to do what it disapproves of. Governments effectively prescribe how she ought to live. The process is limiting and controlling – almost domineering. There is something of Big Brother about it.[5] Orwell may have turned out to be a better forecaster of present times than Marx. But, of course, Orwell was not forecasting. He was warning.

In raising all the money needed to run welfare states and in trying to care for people and guide our behaviour, welfare states have caused myriad unintended consequences. They have downgraded the concepts of individual freedom and property rights. Welfare states are giving so much in some situations while taking so much in others and making conditions that it is inevitable that the ideal of liberty – once so important in the advanced world – has declined. As for property, it has become something to be re-distributed rather than respected.

Other effects have been less abstract. In the nineteenth century, there were outbreaks of widespread unemployment from time to time but they did not last. People priced themselves into work or moved to find it. Now we have great countries where an unemployment rate of 10 per cent is considered normal. In Spain, unemployment reached 27 per cent in 2013.[6] Among the young and certain racial groups, unem-

With few exceptions, welfare states have made mass unemployment permanent.

ployment is usually considerably higher than for the rest of the population. With few exceptions, welfare states have made mass unemployment permanent, which in turn has caused a pandemic of unhappiness.

Even the high official unemployment figures of recent times understate the full extent of it. Many people described as incapacitated, disabled or in 'early retirement' should more accurately be described as unemployed. Tens of millions of people around the world have been left living on welfare benefits, creating the bizarre paradox of societies which are richer than ever yet which have more people out of work and more who are dependent on government hand-outs.

It has become particularly difficult for those with a low educational level or who are truly disabled or from a racial minority to get work. State schooling has left a large minority of people unable to read and write properly. This has reduced their ability to earn or has led to them being unemployed. The widespread inadequacy of state education has been one of the most shameful aspects of welfare states. It has helped to create a division between the elite at the top and the poorly educated unemployed at the bottom. It is, perhaps, the greatest cause of modern inequality. This is a terrible irony: welfare states intended to help the poor instead have sealed many of them in a state of hopelessness.

Welfare states have also had a tendency to increase the amount of lone parenting and the number of couples who break up. This has caused millions more children to endure the unhappiness of an unstable home. It has made many women more vulnerable and many men less socialised and satisfied.

'In their efforts to cure specific evils, legislators have continually caused collateral evils they never looked for ... Though their production is explicable enough after it has occurred, it is never anticipated.'

Herbert Spencer, 'Over-legislation'[7]

There has been a large amount of fraud in the claiming of welfare benefits. Welfare states have given rise to the persistently high taxes that have encouraged fraud and substantial hidden economies. High levels of social insurance have similarly encouraged hidden economies.

Government housing has created ghettos of crime and fear. The illusion has been fostered that every effort is being made to house the poor whereas, in reality, their needs would be more effectively met simply by allowing more housing to be built. Government controls on housing have raised the cost for everyone but the most devastating effect has been on the poor. They have often been denied the home ownership that could improve their financial security and their sense of being part of society. Housing welfare benefits have trapped many poor people out of work, since by getting a job they would lose those benefits.

Welfare states take care of many frail, elderly people but they have often become extremely miserable through being looked after by strangers, away from their homes or relatives. Their children have often ceased to feel they have any responsibility for them and have neglected them. This – and the boom in lone parenting and in institutional care for infants – is part of a 'defamilisation' that many welfare states have brought about, causing people to be both less happy and less connected to society. Children, mothers and fathers have all become more isolated. As Emile Durkheim, one of the founders of sociology, wrote, 'the more weakened the groups to which [a man] belongs, the less he depends on them, the more he consequently depends only on himself and recognises no other rules of conduct than what are founded on his private interests'.[8] In Stockholm now, 60 per cent of all dwellings are occupied by someone who lives alone.[9]

Welfare states are administered by bureaucracies which may mean well but cannot help but appear to those who must apply to them as faceless authorities telling them what to do – pagan gods to be appeased with forms and applications. Inevitably, in some cases, the bureaucracies are inefficient and slow, leading to a sense of frustration and powerlessness among those who depend on them.

Welfare states divide us into authorities and supplicants. We ask for government housing. We try to get our children into good government schools instead of terrible ones. We plead with overworked nurses to make sure our elderly mothers are given the food and water they need. It is not as if the bureaucrats – or exhausted nurses or much-criticised teachers – are made happy by the arrangement. They feel stressed because of the complaints and limited by the many rules they must submit to. Supplicants and authorities… it is a civilisation in which personal dignity and responsibility are in retreat.

There are times and occasions when governments – for all that they may be democratic – act with a dogmatism reminiscent of fascist or communist regimes. Some welfare states decree which school a child must go to. They order that children with learning difficulties must be in classes alongside the brightest children regardless of the impact on the clever

'Cupcake compliance'

Phrase in a headline above an article about how the US government insisted that 'food sold at school fundraising bake sales must, with some exceptions, conform to federal standards'.[10]

ones. Some forbid home schooling, making it explicit that the family has been usurped by the state. There are places where children have literally been taken by police from their homes to prevent home schooling.[11] The logic of a welfare state can lead to such totalitarianism being considered right and proper.

'**FOR, TODAY AS IN THE** past, each of us, more or less, would like to profit from the labour of others. One does not dare to proclaim this feeling publicly, one conceals it from oneself, and then what does one do? One imagines an intermediary; one addresses the state, and each class proceeds in turn to say to it: "You, who can take fairly and honourably, take from the public and share with us." Alas! The state is only too ready to follow such diabolical advice; for it is composed of cabinet ministers, of bureaucrats, of men, in short, who, like all men, carry in their hearts the desire, and always enthusiastically seize the opportunity, to see their wealth and influence grow. The state understands, then, very quickly the use it can make of the role the public entrusts to it. It will be the arbiter, the master, of all destinies. It will take a great deal; hence, a great deal will remain for itself. It will multiply the number of its agents; it will enlarge the scope of its prerogatives; it will end by acquiring overwhelming proportions.'

Frédéric Bastiat, 'The State' (1848)[12]

The large number of people of working age who live on welfare benefits could be working and adding to economic output. Instead, taxes must be levied to pay for them and for other aspects of the welfare state. The resulting high rates discourage work, enterprise and saving, all of which contribute to economic growth. Many studies give evidence of the relation between taxation and diminished growth. Meanwhile, the bureaucrats who administer welfare states could otherwise have contributed to actual production or services.

Regulations and licensing add to the downward pressure which welfare states apply to economic growth. The growth rate of the advanced world has slowed in recent years. The root cause could well be our enveloping welfare states and regulations. The advanced world could have enjoyed far more economic growth and prosperity without welfare states.

It is the poor who have been hurt most. They are the ones going to the inferior schools and receiving a second-rate education. They are the ones whose families are most frequently fractured by the perverse incentives which some welfare states have created. They are more likely to be on welfare benefits, so they are the ones most tempted to lie and cheat to continue to qualify for them. They are the ones most likely to be unemployed. All these things have been profoundly damaging to their happiness.

'If you want to predict how happy someone is, or how long she will live ... you should find out about her social relationships ... Even people who think they don't want a lot of social contact still benefit from it.'

Jonathan Haidt, *The Happiness Hypothesis.*[13]

All human beings like to feel they are worthwhile – that they have a role in life. If you take away a person's work, you take away what most powerfully creates a sense of purpose and place in society. The unemployed often feel worthless. Nor does anybody genuinely feel proud and happy about being dishonest. Lives are poorer, too, if people cannot read and their knowledge and experience of culture are cramped. These are lives that have been downgraded by welfare states.

The better-off half of society, while less damaged, has not escaped unscathed. Most have sent their children to schools of a lower quality than they would otherwise have had. Their housing has been more limited than it could have been, their healthcare is of lower quality, and their income after tax smaller. At the top end, they find they are often taxed aggressively as though they were to blame for all the ills of the world. It is as if anger is being taken out on them. They feel defensive. Unsurprisingly, they try to find ways – legal and illegal – to avoid the heavy taxes. Their honesty has been undermined, too. No one feels good about themselves when they knowingly avoid tax. As with welfare benefits, the temptation has been too big for too long. The idea that one should always be honest has come to seem impossibly idealistic – even foolish.

The better-off often watch the same television programmes that have been dumbed down to reach those who have been failed by their schools. They see how births outside marriage have become normal. They would consider it unkind to condemn the behaviour of those who are poorer than themselves. So judgement of such behaviour is suspended and affects how they themselves live, too. The sense of adults having a duty to give their children a stable family upbringing has thus been gradually undermined across society even though it has affected the poor much more than the rich. The concept of right and wrong has withered and become focused on just a few kinds of behaviour such as racist comments. Few would now dare say that it is 'wrong' for a husband or wife to divorce and go off with someone else, leaving a broken family.

The ideals of philanthropy and charity still exist but they are not as important as before. Charitable giving in Britain is a fraction of what it was a century ago. Personal virtue has been contracted out to the welfare state. Indeed some people appear to believe they have asserted their virtue merely by voting for a party which favours more state welfare.

Welfare states have helped create a grievance culture. There is almost competition to be one of the hard done by who can demand 'support' from the welfare state. Even the relatively well off have decided to get into the act. There has been talk of the 'squeezed middle' – people who cannot claim to be low paid, unemployed, female, discriminated against or disabled but who realise that the only way to preserve their interests is by joining the ranks of clamouring 'victims'. This is often now the way to stake a claim on the beneficence of the all-powerful welfare state.

The other side of the coin is that the concepts of self-reliance, duty, responsibility, courage and independence have all dwindled. What use are they when a call on the welfare state may bring benefits which do not need to be worked for but only demanded? But the psychology of victimhood makes no one happy. It is like becoming a permanent teenager – confused, angry and outraged.

Overall, the picture of our world that emerges

> 'Politicians, agitators and lobbyists … have articulated modern societies as a collection of suffering classes, technically called "minorities". The political consequences of this status are such that minorities now constitute the vast majority of our population: women, racial groups, the handicapped, the inhabitants of the Third World, the aged, the mentally handicapped and many others are exploiters of egalitarian sentiments and claimants of advantages to be supplied by the government and enshrined in law. In this way, egalitarianism entrenches a form of mean-spirited competitiveness about grievances at the heart of the political process.'
>
> Kenneth Minogue[14]

is of a diminished civilisation – one that is less dynamic and impressive than it would otherwise have been, populated by citizens who are less admirable and less content.

The Servile Mind

Title of book by Kenneth Minogue about how the modern world is changing the mentality of people[15]

Some might react to this critique by saying, 'But at least welfare states have provided for the poor, cared for the ill and educated everyone. They have helped those who fall on hard times. And even people who are not poor have felt a sense of security.' There is truth in this and, in so far as it is true, it is good. But there are three ways in which this is less than a justification.

First, there are the unintended consequences described above, which have been so remarkably bad. Second, we should not compare the provision of welfare states against zero. We should compare them against what would otherwise have been provided by individuals for themselves, by families, mutual organisations, insurance, friendly societies, local government and charities. Third, we should bear in mind how often welfare states have not provided the services they promised. A large proportion of people have not been properly educated. They are functionally illiterate. The ill have not always been cared for. Some have died waiting for operations or for lack of up-to-date drugs. Some have not even been cared for properly in hospital. Some have been allocated housing which is mean and where they are terrified.

There is a tendency to apply a double standard. Private or independent provision of welfare is judged by its imperfections. A welfare state is judged by its aspirations. Both should be judged on their performance and outcomes, shouldn't they?

Despite all the above, let us remember some things which are good and some reasons for hope. Let's recall that the modern world is built on the history, culture and economic growth of previous centuries. 'There is a great deal of ruin in a nation,' as Adam Smith said. Major cultural and financial wealth has been established and remains. One might even regard welfare states as a kind of self-harming drug which only the richest countries can afford.

Also human beings are capable of seeing what has gone wrong and reacting. We take a long time to understand and even longer to do anything. But we humans are capable – eventually and after enough disasters – of doing the right thing.

What is the 'right thing'?

An absolutely minimal welfare state would probably achieve the best possible outcome. But even if democratic societies are not willing to be so radical, there are plenty of things which could make welfare states better. The detailed prescriptions are in each of the previous chapters of this book. But some themes keep cropping up:

The more that government monopoly power can be broken down, the better. Competition between private providers leads to better results at a lower cost.

Contracting out by governments is not as good as putting purchasing power in the hands of consumers.

Monopoly power in professions, trades and services is undesirable. Monopoly power of any kind tends to lead to inefficiency, waste, arrogance, poor service and rationing.

Democratic power is better when more truly and precisely democratic with referenda and local power. People also feel better for having the ability to take part in deciding how the country is run.

We should give up the idea of government as a giant insurance and pension company – a role in which it has proved incompetent and untrustworthy. We could move towards personal savings accounts with each of us having assets of which we are the legal owners. Such accounts can certainly be used for healthcare and pension and may also play a role for unemployment benefits or schooling. People do not readily waste their own money. Such savings can be backed up with insurance.

We should try to stop welfare states placing themselves in opposition to the family. Couples have often been discriminated against compared to lone parents with respect to welfare benefits and the allocation of housing. Family care of children and of the elderly has been discriminated against in favour of care by strangers.

Welfare states should, above all, think about what can go wrong when they are being 'generous'. Politicians delight in the idea that they are changing the world. Rarely do they stop to consider how their measures may have perverse consequences. If welfare benefits are high and easy to obtain, for example, one should consider whether more people may decide not to seek work seriously. There is no need to be cynical about human nature. We just should not treat people as though they were saints. Political discourse sometimes takes place in a parallel world where no one was ever influenced by money.

Measures such as these might help lead towards better welfare states. They might even lead to happier and more fulfilled people with greater wealth, better education and improved healthcare. But there is one problem with such a programme which cannot be wished away: the issue of freedom. Welfare states envelop us – particularly the poorest – in a system of government-imposed rules, regulations, schemes, insurance policies and so on. It is not just the chore of filling in the forms or the expense of paying social insurance and suchlike. There is a loss of personal independence and choice – the

'Social programs that undermine the work ethic and displace fathers keep poor people poor.'

Jason L. Riley, *Please Stop Helping Us*[16]

idea that, 'My life is my own. I go where I like and, provided I do not commit a crime, I do what I like.'

Yes, we may be able to make better welfare states. It is certainly possible that unemployment can be reduced and housing improved, more children may have their natural fathers with them and more of the elderly may be in close touch with their families. There can be a reduction in dishonesty and a greater sense of responsibility. It is certainly possible though not inevitable that better welfare states will be created. This would be of huge benefit to the happiness of mankind. Yet we must admit that freedom will not be as great as it once was. Minor things can be done to salvage some freedom – like allowing people to opt out of this or that government-approved action. But overall, some diminution of personal freedom is the unavoidable price we pay for welfare states.

Ten tips for better welfare states

1. Make housing cheaper by allowing supply to increase through an improved planning system. Social housing is a failed policy and is already being downgraded around the world.

2. Enable everyone to choose between competing private schools.

3. Create compulsory health savings accounts and health insurance provided by competing organisations. Allow patients to choose between competing doctors and hospitals.

4. Social insurance is preferable to means-tested benefits. Allow private companies and mutual societies to offer it.

5. Means-tested benefits should be a last resort and set at significantly lower levels than social insurance benefits. Both means-tested and social insurance benefits should be backed up by active demands that beneficiaries work, coupled with provision of help in getting it.

6. Minimise benefits or accommodation given to lone parents that is not also given to married parents.

7. Make financial support for care for the elderly as even-handed as possible between those in institutions and those cared for by their children.

8. Replace unfunded government pensions with compulsory, individual, funded schemes.

9. Introduce regular referenda for national, regional and local issues.

10. Introduce constitutional limits on budget deficits and total debt.

Best and worst welfare states

Unemployment

Best: South Korea, Switzerland, Singapore, Japan and Austria have consistently had the lowest rates over the past decade. Germany has significantly reduced its rate since 2005.

Worst: The countries with the highest, persistent mass unemployment in the recent past have been France, Italy, Spain, Greece and Poland.

Hidden Unemployed

Best: The highest rates of working-age men in work or seeking work are in Singapore, Switzerland, New Zealand and Japan.[1] (The figure for men is used to exclude varying cultural factors that influence employment rates for women in different countries.)

Worst: In Sweden, over 10 per cent of the working age population claim disability benefits. The lowest rates of working-age males in work or seeking work are in Belgium, France and Poland.

Healthcare

Best: Japan, the USA, Switzerland and Germany have some of the best results but US healthcare is very expensive. Singaporean healthcare, for which comparable results are not available, appears to be outstandingly good value.

Worst: The UK, Ireland and Denmark appear to have the worst outcomes.

Education

Best: Rates of functional illiteracy in Shanghai, Hong Kong, South Korea, Ireland, Japan and Singapore are less bad than elsewhere. However, this may reflect the cultures of east Asia rather than its education systems. In all the east Asian countries, parents supplement the government schooling with large amounts of 'shadow' private education.

Worst: The highest functional illiteracy figures among advanced countries are those for Sweden, Greece, Austria, Italy and France.[2]

Lone parenting

Best: Greece, Spain, Italy and Poland have the lowest rates among those countries surveyed.

Worst: America has the highest rate followed by Ireland, New Zealand, Canada and the UK.

Crime

Best: Japan, Italy, Portugal, Spain and Austria have relatively low levels of assaults and threats. Switzerland, the USA and Japan have relatively small black economies.

Worst: The worst countries are England & Wales, Ireland, New Zealand, the Netherlands and the USA (for assaults and threats). Note the overlap with countries that have high rates of lone parenting. Italy, Greece and Poland have the largest black economies. These are all countries where a great deal of money is taken out of legitimate wages to pay for the pensions of those already retired.

Pensions

Best: New Zealand, the Netherlands and Sweden have the lowest proportions of old people who are poor compared to the general population. The Netherlands, Australia and South Korea have the lowest government pension costs as a proportion of GDP. The Netherlands, Canada and Sweden have the lowest unfunded public sector pension liabilities. Singapore would come top on the latter two measures if it had been included in the relevant surveys. Overall, Singapore and the Netherlands come out best.

Worst: Ireland and Australia have a high proportion of relatively poor old people. Italy, France and Greece have the highest government pension costs as a proportion of GDP. France and Finland have the biggest unfunded public sector pension liabilities. Overall, the overhanging liabilities of France, Italy, Greece and Finland suggest that they have had the least successful pension systems.

Income

Best: Singapore, the USA and Switzerland have easily the highest levels of average per capita income.[3] These are all countries where the overall cost of their welfare states, including social security contributions, is below average or, in the case of Singapore, where deductions from pay go into personal funded accounts.

Worst: Greece, Portugal and Spain.

This summary excludes less advanced countries.

Groundhog Day –
but not everywhere:
themes and contrasts

AROUND THE WELFARE STATES OF the world, the same problems and phenomena appear again and again. But there are also huge contrasts. Every country that is economically advanced and democratic has a welfare state. There are no exceptions.

Many governments have a problem paying for pensions which are not funded. Only a few have avoided the trap, notably Singapore.

Many countries have semi-permanent high levels of unemployment. But there are exceptions such as Switzerland and Singapore.

Most countries have more births outside marriage than in previous generations. In Sweden, well over half children are born out of wedlock and, in Iceland, two out of three. But in Japan only one out of fifty is and, in South Korea, one in sixty-six.

Social housing is a big feature of the welfare states of Austria, France and the Netherlands. But it is minor in Norway and Germany.

All welfare states have government schooling but, in some east Asian countries, massive private education systems have grown up alongside.

All the welfare states of the advanced world have some government healthcare. But some, like Australia and France, have big private healthcare sectors, too.

Many welfare states embraced care for the elderly in institutions but then found it was getting too expensive and have started encouraging more of the elderly to stay at home. In Spain and Portugal it is commonplace for widowed elderly parents to live with their children as in earlier generations. In other countries, like Denmark, it has almost completely died out.

Appendix

Inequality – do bigger welfare states create more equal, happier people?

W HEN I VISITED THE OECD in Paris, I spent two days interviewing experts there on a wide range of subjects. But even by
the end of the first day, I had got a strong impression that most
of the staff had a shared belief in greater equality.

The following day, the press officer who had kindly arranged all the interviews
told me that a talk would be given to the staff that morning. It seems that the
OECD has visiting speakers and on this occasion it would be Professor Richard
Wilkinson, one of the two authors of *The Spirit Level*. In this book, he argues that
the more unequal a country is, the more likely its inhabitants are to suffer in a wide
variety of ways. The press officer invited me to join the OECD staff to hear the talk.
I won't repeat what Wilkinson said since I went as a guest rather than as a journalist. But he was very persuasive. Chart after chart indicated a correlation between
inequality and bad outcomes such as homicides. The case seemed overwhelming.
Any neutral who heard his talk would have come away at least three-quarters convinced. Most of the OECD staff – though perhaps not all – surely welcomed it as
authoritative confirmation of what they already believed.

Wilkinson is part of a worldwide intellectual movement focusing on inequality. Thomas Piketty and Emmanuel Saez have argued that the top 1 per cent in
the USA have greatly increased their share of income since the Second World
War. Since then, Piketty has gone on to write *Capital in the Twenty-First Century*,
in which he argues that modern capitalism necessarily means that inequality will
increase. Joseph E. Stiglitz, a Nobel Prize winner for economics, has written *The
Price of Inequality*, in which he argues that the level of inequality in the world is
due to the capitalist system not working as it should.

Each person who writes about inequality has his or her own ideas. But out of
it all emerges a kind of logic that goes like this: inequality causes unhappiness;

inequality has increased and therefore unhappiness has increased; the way to put this right is by taxing the rich and giving more money to the poor. In short, the people of the advanced world would be happier with bigger welfare states. More simply still: welfare states make people happier.

If this is true, it should affect what we do. So is it? Let's look at Professor Wilkinson's book since it addresses the issue most directly.

The Spirit Level has similar charts to the ones he showed in his talk in Paris. These repeatedly suggest that the more unequal a society is, the more it suffers. Such a society has more health and social problems and more murders. The children experience more conflict and more people suffer mental illness. There is no actual chart showing levels of happiness plotted against inequality. But it is implicit that all these various measures together amount to evidence that greater equality causes greater well-being. The evidence is buttressed with arguments from psychology and anthropology suggesting that people are hardwired to be happier in more equal societies. Inequality, it is argued, produces a sense of failure in those at the lower end.

Let's take the correlation between inequality and homicides. It is one of many illustrated with a chart. A scattergraph of dots representing countries shows their level of inequality plotted against the incidence of homicides. Superimposed on the dots is a straight line indicating a trend calculated by a computer from the data. The straight line gently rises, suggesting that the more inequality there is, the more homicides take place.

Inequality and homicides

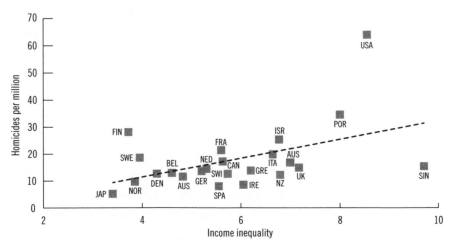

The point is clearly made. And there are plenty of charts like this with measure after measure showing similar results.

At first sight, it looks like game, set and match. But in statistics, there are certain tests that are done to establish how good correlations are. One standard procedure is to remove 'outliers' – individual cases which seem far removed from the others. In the case of homicides, Portugal is an 'outlier'. The dot representing the United States is so distant from the other countries that it is an 'extreme outlier'. Professor Peter Saunders tested what would happen to the correlation if the United States was removed but Portugal retained. There was still a correlation.[1] Then he applied a measure of the strength of this correlation, known as 'R squared'. R2 indicates in this case how much of the variance in homicide rates can be explained by inequality. It was very low – only 0.1, indicating that only 10 per cent of the variance in homicides was associated with levels of inequality.

He then tried another calculation of the statistical significance of the correlation called the p-value. A correlation that is really significant would have a p-value of 0.05 or less. The p-value in this case was 0.159. Professional social scientists simply would not regard the correlation as being of statistical significance. In other words, the correlation between inequality and homicides is not established at all. And if there is not a statistically significant correlation, we are a very long way indeed from proving causation.

Many of the other charts in *The Spirit Level* fail to survive these and other standard procedures such as testing for third variables.

A few correlations in *The Spirit Level* do stand up to the routine tests of social science. But very few. One is infant mortality.[2] But even in this case we should recall that correlation does not necessarily mean causation. There may be a third factor at work.[3]

Meanwhile, some charts which could have been created relating inequality to certain measures of well-being are notably absent. They would have shown correlations that are actually contrary to the ideas of Wilkinson and Piketty.

> 'In the United States ... those who consider themselves left-wingers exhibit a marked distaste for inequality, whereas those who consider themselves right-wingers are not affected by it. This effect is so strong in the United States that only rich left-wingers are negatively affected by inequality.'
>
> Professor Bruno Frey[4]

The more equal a society, the more racial intolerance there is, the greater the incidence of suicides and the larger the alcohol consumption. These correlations are not particularly big but they are slightly bigger than most of the associations that go the other way and they are statistically significant.[5] This is not to claim that any causation is involved, let alone proved. But the evidence that inequality improves outcomes for a society, though small, is just as good or better than the other way round.

It appears that the argument that inequality causes bad social effects is not backed by good evidence. Indeed there is some evidence that the only people whose happiness is truly disturbed by inequality are relatively rich left-wingers, according to Professor Frey (see quotation on previous page). But there is an even more fundamental problem with the theory. The measure of inequality used in *The Spirit Level* is called the Gini coefficient. It is named after Corrado Gini, the Italian statistician and sociologist who devised it. The Gini coefficient figures are usually assumed to be authoritative. But there is reason to doubt them.

Sweden has a low Gini coefficient with respect to income, which means that it is less unequal than most countries. However, there is a Gini coefficient of wealth as well as income, and according to the Gini figures, Sweden is one of the most *unequal* countries in terms of wealth. This is strange. It seems improbable that a country with notably equal incomes should have dramatically unequal wealth.

One possible explanation is that rich people in Sweden have reacted to high income tax rates there by minimising their declared income. Where possible, they may receive their income in less taxable ways. If this is true, the Gini coefficient of income for Sweden is unreliable. It is not measuring real income but merely declared and taxable income. It is measuring an illusion, not the reality.

One of the richest Swedes ever born

RUBEN RAUSING CREATED THE FIRST packaging company in Sweden. He made wax-coated cartons in the shape of a tetrahedron – a pyramid with a triangular base – hence the ultimate name of the company: Tetra Pak. It became the largest food packaging company in the world and at his death, Rausing was the richest Swede in the world. But his income and wealth did not appear in the statistics for Sweden. Rausing left Sweden for Rome in 1969 to avoid high taxes.

Hans, one of his three sons, is credited as a key figure in the success of Tetra Pak. In 2011 he was eighty-third in the Forbes listing of the richest people in the world. But he left Sweden too, in 1982, and moved to England. Naturally his large income has also not affected the Gini coefficient of his native country. The inequality of income in a country can appear lower than it would otherwise would be as a result of the richest people leaving.

The figures supposedly representing the incomes of the poor are unreliable, too. Chapter 1 of this book describes the in-depth research done by Kathryn Edin and Laura Lein in the USA interviewing single mothers about their income. They discovered that the majority of single mothers on benefits in the USA receive income which is not declared and about 40 per cent earn money from 'unreported' or 'underground' work. Of course, this income is not recorded in the Gini coefficient or most other measures of inequality. So the Gini figures for the poor are sure to be wrong. On top of that, the extent to which the figures for the poor are wrong is likely to vary from one country to another. Britain, America and Australia have welfare benefits based mainly on an assessment of 'means'. The more 'means' one appears to have, the less one receives on benefits. People on means-tested benefits in these countries have more incentive to lie about their means than people in countries where most welfare recipients receive insurance-based benefits. Therefore the inequality of Britain, America and Australia might well appear greater than it really is compared to other countries.

As if this were not enough, the Gini coefficient can be influenced by an influx of immigrants. For a long time, Sweden had a very low immigrant population. But then in the 1990s and 2000s, it allowed in more immigrants, who unsurprisingly received low incomes. The Gini coefficient of Sweden soon changed to indicate a more unequal society.[6] So the Gini coefficient can, in part, be merely a reflection of whether or not a country has accepted poor immigrants in the fairly recent past.[7]

Yet another difficulty is that some measures of inequality fail to take into account non-cash benefits such as health insurance and pensions. These may not appear as taxable income even though they have value to the person concerned.[8] Similarly, some studies do not include the value to poorer people of benefits such as food stamps, housing subsidies and Medicaid.[9]

So the Gini coefficient and other similar measures of inequality are unreliable. Of course it is possible to try to overcome the difficulties with various statistical techniques and where this is attempted, the process should be analysed closely to see if it is convincing and rigorously conducted. Such attempts have been thin on the ground. Most people are happy just to use the unreliable Gini coefficient.

It seems, therefore, that the idea that unequal societies cause unhappiness is thoroughly unproven. It is based on correlations that do not stand up to normal academic tests. It is also based usually on Gini calculations of inequality, which are unreliable. The evidence for the inequality idea is therefore about as dependable as a grainy zoom-lens photo of the Loch Ness monster taken on a misty day as night falls.

You might reasonably wonder: why have I spent so much time on it? It is because the theory has gained influence and credibility. It is sometimes talked of as a well-established fact. If the idea were justified by evidence, it would be very important. But it isn't.

Is that the end of the matter? No, of course, there will be further attempts to 'prove' the idea and they will have to be examined. But let's note that part of this issue that is currently much talked about has now been left hanging in the air: happiness. If equality does not bring it about, what does?

The study of happiness and, of course, its opposite – unhappiness – has been a growth industry in academia. In the USA, Europe and elsewhere, surveys have been done asking people just how happy or how satisfied they are with their lives. One of the biggest of these exercises took place in Britain in 2012 because the government wanted to start measuring and analysing 'general well-being'. The sample was particularly large: 165,000 adults aged sixteen and over.[10]

The key question was, 'Overall, how satisfied are you with your life nowadays?' People were asked to give a number from 0 to 10 where 0 is 'not at all' and 10 is 'completely'.

Three results were dramatically clear: among those in work, only a fifth gave an answer below 7. But among the unemployed, more than twice as many (45 per cent) did. The unemployed were also 3.6 times more likely than those with jobs to give an answer suggesting serious unhappiness.

Who is unhappy?

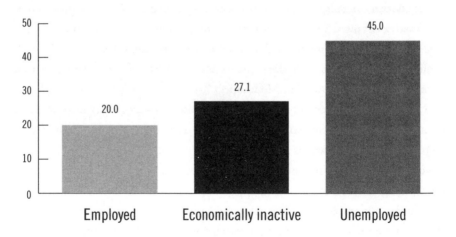

Percentage of people giving a life satisfaction score of below 7 out of 10. The 'economically inactive' are people not in work but not seeking work.

Source: Office for National Statistics[11]

A second dramatic finding related to marriage. Among married people only 18 per cent rated their level of satisfaction below 7. But among the divorced, more than twice as many (39.3 per cent) did so. Also more than three times as many of the divorced rated their satisfaction at a very low level – between 4 and 0.

Who else is unhappy?

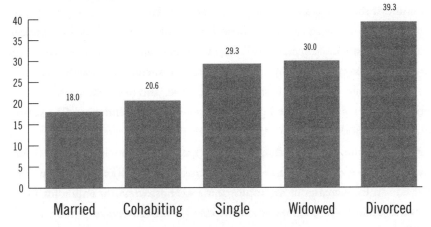

Percentages of people giving a life satisfaction score of below 7 out of 10.

Source: Office for National Statistics[12]

A third, powerful contrast emerged between the healthy and the unwell. Among the very healthy, only 2 per cent rated their level of satisfaction at between 4 and 0. The number soared to 35.2 per cent among those in very bad health.

The numbers I have reported are the bare figures without disentangling how the different factors interact with each other. It is obviously likely that those in very bad health are also unemployed, for example, so there are several factors involved. But I cite the bare figures because they are so dramatic regarding unemployment and marriage. And they are supported by more sophisticated academic analysis.

Professors Bruno Frey and Alois Stuzer, in Switzerland, summarise: 'Many ... studies have ... found, in many countries and many time periods that personally experiencing unemployment makes people very unhappy.'[13] Professors Andrew Clark and Andrew Oswald, in a 1994 study, concluded, 'Joblessness depressed well-being more than any other single characteristic, including important negative ones such as divorce and separation.'[14] Looking at figures for the USA, Oswald, this time with Professor David Blanchflower, similarly concluded, 'Joblessness is associated here with a huge amount of unhappiness,' adding, 'The other particularly large coefficient is on marriage,' which had a positive impact on happiness.'[15]

Some may object that asking people whether or not they are happy is only one measure of well-being. It could be misleading. So it is worth trying another measure. If someone commits suicide, it is surely evidence of severe unhappiness.

There are different kinds of studies and the results vary between them.[16] But among the so-called 'individual-level' studies, there seems to be near unanimity in finding a very strong association between unemployment and suicide.[17] Typically, one of them suggests that 'those who are unemployed are two or three times more likely to die by suicide than those who are in work'.[18] In one extreme case, Professor Dr Barbara Schneider and her colleagues looked at suicides in the Frankfurt-am-Main area of Germany and found that the unemployed were sixteen times more likely to die by suicide than the control group and that this was not changed substantially by adjusting the figures to allow for mental illness and personality disorder. In another study, Alfonso Ceccherini-Nelli and Stefan Priebe tried to discover whether it was possible to associate changes in suicide rates in Britain, America, France and Italy with levels of unemployment.[19] They found that 'in all four countries, increases in unemployment were associated with higher suicide rates and decreases of unemployment with lower suicide rates'.

What about marital status? There appears to be a difference in the reactions of men and women. One study found that divorced or separated women were 50 per cent more likely to commit suicide than their married counterparts while the men were almost three times more likely to do so.[20] On top of this, there is the damage to the happiness of the children when parents divorce or separate, as described in Chapter 6 of this book. It is also notable that suicide rates are generally lower in the Mediterranean countries such as Spain and Italy where defamilisation has not taken place as much as in most other countries.[21]

Male suicide rates across the world

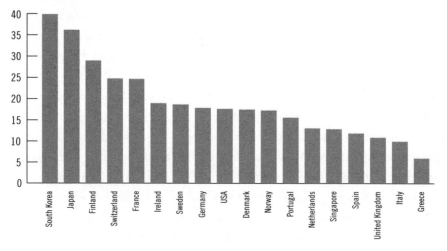

Suicide rates per 100,000. In most countries, male suicides far exceed female ones.

Source: World Health Organization

From all this evidence, it is clear that unemployment and family breakdown create huge amounts of unhappiness. It also suggests something else. If divorce leads to unhappiness, it might also be the case that living alone – or, more precisely, loneliness – may be an important influence on happiness.

When Esther Rantzen admitted she was lonely...

I AM HAVING TO FACE THE realities of a life spent largely alone ... I can't adjust. From the moment I was born I have been surrounded by people. Family. School friends. University friends. The teams I worked with. Best of all, my husband, two daughters and a son ... My weekdays are still full of activity. But my evenings and weekends are empty.

'You can find widows wherever you look ... we come home to an empty house. Statistics tell us that three out of five women over seventy-five live alone. That's most of us. No wonder so many of us buy a dog or talk to our TVs ... But they don't care if the day has been tough or rewarding.'

Esther Rantzen admitted that she had rung her daughter and told her that God wanted her to move in with her. She confessed she was only thinking of herself – 'of walking around an empty flat with no one to talk to'. Of all the articles and books that Rantzen, a British television presenter and journalist, has written in her long career, this article about her loneliness provoked by far the greatest response. Mostly it came from lonely people, particularly widows, 'because, alas, we women tend to outlive the men we love ... But we don't talk about it because loneliness bears its own stigma. Many correspondents wrote about the "shame" they felt and how "brave" and "honest" I had been, and in their letters they revealed just how much of a taboo there is in admitting you feel lonely.'[22]

John Cacioppo of the University of Chicago has studied loneliness and living alone, discovering some remarkable effects.[23] Loneliness raises blood pressure and levels of stress hormones, leading to a greater risk of illness and death.[24] It damages the quality of sleep so that it restores us less well both physically and mentally. He also found evidence that loneliness increases the risk of suicide.[25] Meanwhile research in Denmark indicates that those aged between thirty and sixty who live alone are more than seven times more likely to say they are not happy than those living with others.[26]

> 'Western societies have demoted human gregariousness from a necessity to an incidental ... The experience of isolation threatens our sense of purpose.'
>
> John Cacioppo and William Patrick[27]

I do not want to exaggerate the reliability of this evidence. Compared to unemployment and marital status, the significance of loneliness and living alone (which are not the same) has been much less studied. But it does seem likely that living alone or loneliness reduces levels of happiness.

How is the above related to a book about welfare states?

'People aged 25 to 44 are now five times more like to be living alone than they were in 1973.'

Daily Telegraph[30]

In the previous chapters I have argued that all these apparent causes of unhappiness – unemployment, divorce and living alone – have been made more common by welfare states. The way welfare states have increased unemployment is described in Chapter 3. The way they have increased divorce and lone parenting is outlined in Chapter 6. And the way they have increased the incidence of living alone has been described in the chapters on parenting (Chapter 6 again) and care of the elderly (Chapter 9).

The proportion of people living alone in different countries (see box) varies considerably. For example there is a marked contrast between the Mediterranean countries – Italy, Spain, Greece and Portugal – and the Nordic countries – Norway, Finland and Denmark (the figure for Sweden was not given). Living alone is far more common in the Nordic countries than in the Mediterranean ones, and so is suicide.[29]

More Nordics live alone than Mediterraneans

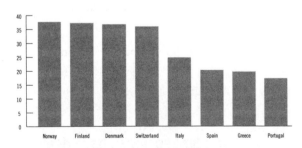

Percentage of single-person households. Countries selected from the OECD Family Database (last updated 1 July 2010)[28]

In sum, welfare states have tended to bring about circumstances which have caused unhappiness. There is much better evidence that welfare states cause unhappiness than there is of inequality doing so.

Against this it can be argued that welfare states reduce the fear of unemployment or incapacity and increase happiness in this way. That is possible. But there are other means of mitigating such fears which people have used in the past and could use again now –

such as insurance, friendly societies and mutual societies. Moreover, as described in the relevant chapters, it is possible to reform welfare states in ways that can reduce their tendency to cause unemployment, broken families and loneliness. Up until the present moment, however, the rises in unemployment, divorce and living alone encouraged by welfare states have been massive and have significantly diminished the sum of human happiness.

Welfare jargon explained

HERE ARE SOME TERMS YOU do not hear very often over a drink in a bar. Some are so unintuitive that even after hearing them many times, you may struggle to recall what they mean. 'Rent-seeking' has nothing to do with rent. 'Moral hazard' looks like a misspelt street sign. There are unnecessary, pretentious words like 'eudemonic'. And just very occasionally when you are least expecting it, there are phrases that are useful or even witty.

ACTIVE LABOUR MARKET PROGRAMME A government effort to get the unemployed into work through things such as training, workfare and sanctions for not seeking work. Distinct from 'passive' labour market programmes, where governments hand out money to the unemployed without doing very much to encourage or help them into work.

ACTIVITIES OF DAILY LIVING Activities which people need to be able to do to live independently. If you need help with them, you are deemed to be in need of long-term care. The activities include bathing, eating, dressing, walking across a room and getting in and out of bed. See also *instrumental activities of daily living*.

THE ALZIRA MODEL System of healthcare pioneered in Alzira, Spain. A company is paid a sum by the regional government based on the population of an area to provide both hospitals and primary healthcare.

BARRIERS TO ENTRY Obstacles that make it more difficult for new companies to compete in a business or for individuals to work in a particular craft or profession. For companies, barriers include onerous government regulations which cost new, small companies a disproportionate amount. For individuals, excessive government requirements for qualifications ('licensing') can hinder them from entering trades or professions. In both case, reduced competition means those already in the market can charge higher prices for inferior performance.

BEVERIDGE SYSTEM Welfare benefits system designed by Sir William Beveridge in a British coalition government paper in 1942. It is distinct from the *Bismarckian system* in that everyone is meant to pay the same contribution and be entitled to the same benefits. In Britain, the welfare system has moved far away from Beveridge's concept. Means-tested social assistance, which Beveridge intended to be of small importance, has come to dominate.

BISMARCKIAN SYSTEM Welfare system based on social insurance and pioneered by Otto von Bismarck in Germany. In contrast to the *Beveridge system*, contributions vary according to the income of the payer. The benefits vary similarly.

BROKEN WINDOW FALLACY See *seen and unseen*.

CHAPUZAS Ad hoc small jobs paid for in cash (Spain).

COMPETITION EFFECT Competition between workers for jobs is said to lower wages and thus increase the number of jobs created, reducing unemployment. Some argue that competition is encouraged if outsiders (the unemployed) are given a subsidy to make them better able to compete with insiders (those already in work).

CORPORATIST WELFARE STATE A welfare state in which corporate bodies such as trade unions, business associations and the church (usually the Catholic Church) play a significant role.[1]

COUNTERFACTUAL How things might have turned out if something had been different, such as a government policy. For example, someone might say, 'Many would starve if it were not for food stamps.' But a thorough counterfactual considers whether people would act differently in such circumstances. Some might work longer hours to earn more money. Some might buy cheaper food or spend less on other things. Government money saved on food stamps might mean lower taxes and thus higher net incomes for those who work. Other people might create charities to offer food for free and so on.

CROSS-SECTIONAL STUDY A study of lots of people at one moment in time. (Compare with *longitudinal study*.)

DEADWEIGHT EFFECT or **DEADWEIGHT COST** Some of the cost of a government programme may be 'wasted' because much of what it is intended to achieve would take place anyway.

DECOMMODIFICATION The idea that people are made into commodities by the requirement of capitalism that they work to earn money is known as 'commodification'. It is argued that they can be released from this oppression by a welfare state which makes them just as well off without working. They are thus 'decommodified'. Unfortunately, in countries where this has been tried, so many people have taken up the offer to be decommodified that a shortage of money to pay them has emerged. Consequently governments have adopted active labour market programmes and insisted that they work after all. Possibly they have been 'recommodified'.[2]

DEFAMILISATION The process by which families become less mutually dependent and connected. It has been encouraged by welfare state subsidies and services such as financial support specifically to lone parents, free or heavily subsidised childcare provided it is by strangers and free or subsidised care for the elderly – again, provided it is by strangers. It is perceived as a 'good thing' by some – particularly in parts of Scandinavia – but as undesirable by others, particularly in Mediterranean countries such as Spain, Italy and Greece.

DIAGNOSTIC-RELATED GROUP Classification of medical cases for the purpose of payment to hospitals or clinics. This is considered better than paying hospitals simply for medical procedures, which can lead to excessive use of the procedures and high cost. Payment by diagnostic-related group means hospitals have an incentive to be economical and innovative in their treatment. See also *diagnostic treatment combination*.

DIAGNOSTIC TREATMENT COMBINATION A more sophisticated version of a *diagnostic-related group*, introduced in the Netherlands in 2005. Each kind of medical case is defined more exactly and an assessment is made of what would be the normal procedures for dealing with it.

DISPLACEMENT EFFECT Sometimes governments provide subsidies to companies to employ particular kinds of workers such as the young or old. This can increase employment of that kind of person but reduce employment of other kinds of people. The overall net gain in employment might be little or nothing.

DOING BETTER FOR FAMILIES Title of an OECD publication. When politicians and think tanks say they are going to 'do better for families', they usually mean that taxpayers' money will replace the need for families to look after their own. The title might be more accurately re-phrased as 'Doing Away with Families'.

DROPOUT FACTORIES High schools in the USA where more than 60 per cent of students leave before completing their studies.

EFFECTIVE MARGINAL TAX RATE Measure of how worthwhile it is for someone to work longer hours or get a promotion or a pay rise. It is the rate of tax plus the welfare benefit withdrawal rate if someone has a small increase in earnings. So if someone would lose 30p in tax and 55p in benefits for an extra pound earned, the effective marginal tax rate would be 0.85. A high rate for low earners is sometimes called the 'poverty trap'.

ENDOGENOUS Coming from within. Compare with *exogenous*.

EUDEMONIC Something that makes people feel good or happy.

EXCEPTIONALISM The idea that something, usually a country, is special in a way that makes it unlike others. So 'American exceptionalism' is the belief that America is unique in having certain (good!) characteristics.

EXOGENOUS Coming from outside. Compare with *endogenous*.

EXPRESS FIRING Spanish expression meaning firing someone quickly without argument but at a high cost. In Spain, the alternative is 'justified' firing. The employer pays less compensation to the worker when a firing is 'justified'; however, the courts, at least up until 2012, were reluctant to accept any redundancies as 'justified'. So rather than waste time and money, some companies would just pay the extra cost of 'express firing'.

FAMILY POLICY In reality, most measures given this name consist of policies which tend to make the traditional family redundant. They are aimed primarily at getting women to take full-time, paid employment. The taxes used to finance this inevitably come, on balance, from families where a woman looks after her children at home or works part time.

THE FATAL CONCEIT Title of a book by Friedrich Hayek. He criticises the idea that an elite group in government of clever people can successfully organise the affairs of the whole population.

FUNCTIONAL ILLITERACY A level of illiteracy that does not amount to total illiteracy but means a person is unable to make use of simple written information such as understanding a poster advertising a pop concert.

GATEKEEPERS General practitioners are called 'gatekeepers' when only they can grant patients access to a specialist. Patients are prohibited from approaching specialists directly.

HLM French social housing. The initials stand for *Habitations à loyer modéré* (literally 'housing at a moderate rent').

HUD Housing and Urban Development. US federal government department created by President Lyndon Johnson. It directs social housing in America.

INSTRUMENTAL ACTIVITIES OF DAILY LIVING Activities which help people to live independently such as using a telephone, taking medication, handling money, shopping and preparing meals. The ability to do these things is important but not as fundamental as the ability to do *activities of daily living*.

LOS LIBERADOS Trade unionists in Spain who do nothing but union work while on the payroll of a company. They are free (or 'liberated') not to work for the company.

LIBERAL 'left wing' in North America, 'right wing' in continental Europe and confusion in Britain.

LOCKING-IN EFFECT or **RETENTION EFFECT** Reduction in the likelihood that a worker will seek another – possibly better – job as a result of receiving a government wage subsidy in his or her existing job.

LONGITUDINAL STUDIES Repeated observations of the same people or items over a period of time, sometimes stretching into decades. These studies are commonly regarded as superior to *cross-sectional studies* but they obviously take longer and are usually more expensive.

MEANS-TESTED BENEFITS Welfare benefits that are dependent on the 'means' (income and/or wealth) of the claimant. Similar to *social assistance* and *needs-based benefits*.

META-ANALYSIS Study combining the results of previous studies. The hope is that this produces a particularly authoritative result. But there is a risk that the academics who do it may find pretexts to rule out studies they do not like in order to get the result they prefer.

MORAL HAZARD Danger that people may act in an undesirable way because government policy has reduced the costs or risks of such behaviour. For example, a young woman may be encouraged to become pregnant outside marriage if the government provides single mothers with free accommodation and benefits.[3] See also *perverse incentives* and *unintended consequences*.

MULTIVARIATE ANALYSIS Any statistical method that helps evaluate the relative impact of a number of different variables on a given result. For example, it might establish whether loneliness is more highly correlated with living alone, being old or being a man.

NAMAPO Japanese word used on the internet meaning 'welfare' but with a pejorative overtone. Struck from the list of top 10 buzzwords in Japan 'for fear that it promoted discrimination against the poor'.[4] Supposedly derived from *seikatsu hogo*, meaning 'welfare'.

NATIONAL INSURANCE Social insurance in Britain.

NEEDS-BASED BENEFITS Benefits based on a person's needs rather than his or her entitlement through, say, unemployment insurance. The phrase captures the way in which someone who has more 'needs' – as a result of having, say, more children – gets higher benefits under this system. Similar to *means-tested benefits* and *social assistance*.

OBASUTEYAMA Legendary Japanese mountain where eldest sons, who were responsible for their aged parents, left them to die of starvation and exposure. Can be translated as 'Granny-dump Mountain'. The word has been used to describe public residential care in Japan and reflects disapproval of families which have resorted to such care.

PARTICIPATION TAX RATE A measure of how worthwhile it is for someone on welfare benefits to work at all. It is calculated as tax plus welfare benefits forgone as a proportion of gross earnings. So if someone earns £300 week gross but their taxes and welfare benefits forgone amount to £270, then the participation tax rate is 0.9. The equation is (tax + benefits foregone) ÷ gross earnings. See also *replacement rate* and *effective marginal tax rate*.

PERVERSE INCENTIVE An incentive or reward that unintentionally encourages behaviour or results that are undesirable or even the opposite of what was intended. See also *moral hazard* and *unintended consequences*.[5]

PREFERENCE FALSIFICATION The way people declare different views in public from the ones they express when they know they are going to be anonymous.[6]

THE PRODUCER INTEREST or **PRODUCER CAPTURE** The phenomenon of people who provide a service coming to think of their own interest rather than that of the consumer or the taxpayer they are supposed to serve. This can damage the quality and/or raise the cost of the service they provide. For example, teachers or policemen who try to get shorter working hours and early retirement for themselves may increase the cost of education or policing.

PUBLIC CHOICE THEORY The idea that governments often do not act for the good of the people or in accordance with democratic ideals. For example, a politician might accede to the wishes of a lobby group because it would bring more support than it would lose him or her. Civil servants and ministers may pursue ideas and interests which involve increasing the size of their departments. The same people might be benevolent but make rules or laws based on inadequate information. Their decisions can be biased by a desire to feel active or important.

PUBLIC HOUSING American term for what is called *social housing* in the UK.

PUBLIC SCHOOLS In Britain: private, fee-charging schools. In America: schools paid for by state governments. In this book I have tried not to use the term at all to avoid confusion but with regard to America I occasionally use the American meaning of the term.

RAMPING Practice in Australian hospital emergency departments of requiring ambulances to wait outside hospitals (presumably, in some cases, on a ramp) with their patients because there is not sufficient capacity to admit them without breaching a government target for the maximum permissible wait between admission and being seen by a doctor.

REGULATORY CAPTURE Influence over regulations by an interested party to gain advantages. For example, taxi drivers or doctors may influence the regulations concerning their own trade or profession and use this power to reduce competition.

RENTS Advantage or extra income derived by self-interested manipulation of a job, industry or system. Where there is perfect competition, it should be hard to obtain such rents.

RENT-SEEKING Gaining an advantage – financial or otherwise – by manipulating a system rather than creating new wealth or a better system. For example nurses might demand higher qualifications for future nurses to increase their own prestige or to limit the number of entrants to the profession, ensuring higher pay and greater job security for themselves.

REPLACEMENT RATE A measure of how worthwhile it is for someone to work as opposed to living on benefits. It is the net amount that someone would receive in welfare benefits compared to what he or she would get in work after tax. So if someone who got £220 per week in benefits would receive £250 after tax in work, the replacement rate would be 0.88. It is similar to the *participation tax rate* but the equation is arranged differently so one gets a slightly different result. The equation is: benefits ÷ (gross earnings – tax).

RESIDENTIAL HOME OR CARE HOME Place for the elderly to live which is not, in fact, their home. Services such as meals are prepared and some personal care and activities may be provided.

RETENTION EFFECT See *locking-in effect*.

SCREENING EFFECT The way subsidised, short-term employment may enable an employer to discover whether an unemployed person is productive enough to employ long term.

'SEEN AND UNSEEN' The effects of actions can be divided into those that are obvious (seen) and those that are not (unseen). The French economist Frédéric Bastiat gave the example of a boy who broke his father's window. A glazier was paid 6 francs to replace it. The seen effect is that work was created for the glazier and that he got income. The unseen effect is that otherwise the father would have used that money to buy a book or to get his shoes repaired. The cobbler or the bookseller would have benefited. Overall, no economic benefit is obtained through the breaking of the window. This is sometimes known as the 'broken window fallacy'.[7]

Bastiat: the 'seen and unseen'.

SELECTION BIAS The way a study may be misleading because the people who are selected for it – or who select themselves – affect the result. For example, a study might show that married people are less likely to be seriously depressed than single people. But it could be that people who are not seriously depressed 'select' themselves to be married. Superior studies attempt to deal with this problem.

SHADOW EDUCATION Private education that supplements government-provided education. It is widespread in Asia and exists in many other countries, too. The term includes private tutors and *Kumon* after-school centres.

'SIT-DOWN MONEY' Australian native term for welfare benefits.

SOCIAL ASSISTANCE Phrase used in continental Europe and, in earlier years, in Britain. Welfare benefits given when entitlement to unemployment insurance benefit has run out. The amount depends on the means and needs of the claimant. Very similar to *means-tested benefits* and *needs-based benefits*.

SOCIAL HOUSING British term for what Americans call *public housing*.

SOCIAL INSURANCE Compulsory government insurance which covers unemployment or disability. In many European countries, it also covers healthcare.

SOCIAL TRANSFERS Welfare benefits and services. Money is 'transferred' from some to others. The phrase is used by academics and some think tanks to make it sound like an innocuous business. Note how there is no mention of tax.

SUBSTITUTION EFFECT The way in which government incentives to an employer to take on workers with a particular ability can cause the employer to reduce the hiring of workers with a different ability. Similar to *displacement effect*.

THE THIRD SECTOR Charities and other voluntary organisations.

THREAT EFFECT Incentive to search for work created when continuation of unemployment benefit is dependent on something such as participation in a workfare programme.

THE TRAGEDY OF THE COMMONS The way assets can be abused if everyone owns them rather than just one person or company. Fishing stocks, for example, may get run down if everyone is allowed to fish in an area whereas, if a company owns the area, it would have a long-term interest in preserving the stocks.

TRANSITION EFFECT Gain in the employability of a long-term unemployed person that comes from doing work in, for example, workfare or public works.

UNINTENDED CONSEQUENCES Results of a policy which are far away from what the politicians or civil servants wanted. All policies – but particularly ones thought of as kind and beneficent – should be vetted for their possible unintended consequences. See also perverse incentives and moral hazard.

WAGE EFFECT The way a government subsidy for wages may be channelled into higher wages rather than higher employment.

It would be marvellous if some of these concepts could be described by phrases which are more self-explanatory: instead of 'public choice theory', for example, 'public corruption theory'? Unfortunately, once these terms are established, they are difficult to budge.

Acknowledgements

THE DEDICATION PAGE AT THE front of this book mentions some of the people I would like to thank. But there are so many others. I want to thank all who agreed to be interviewed, visited or photographed or who helped in any way. I cannot name them all but I will nevertheless mention a random collection of them and pray forgiveness from those I do not thank individually.

In England, I must mention George Currie, who has been a regular visitor to my home. He has helped me with all manner of things, stimulated me with thoughts and information and brought me good cheer. Martin Durkin should be mentioned because, despite contributing no content whatever, he stiffened my sinews and bolstered morale. Mark Littlewood, director general of the Institute of Economic Affairs, has given me encouragement and support, particularly with regard to launching the book. Peter Saunders gave me advice and information about statistical methods. His book *When Prophecy Fails* is not easy to get hold of but it is an outstanding critique of *The Spirit Level*, an influential book about inequality.[1] I would love to see him write a critique of Piketty's *Capital*. Alan Gibbs kindly made a contribution to the considerable costs of producing the book.

Some people who helped me have views that are very different from mine but I am still grateful for their input. Peter Whiteford, in Australia, was notable as someone who sees things differently but to whom I am grateful because he gave me the benefit of his considerable knowledge and thoughtfulness.

It was extraordinarily kind of Tharman Shanmugaratnam, the finance minister and deputy Prime Minister of Singapore, to give me some of his time. I have great respect for his insightfulness and for the welfare systems in Singapore, which are unique and generally far better than those in other advanced countries. I only hope that my remarks about democracy in that country will not mean I am barred from ever visiting again.

In America, I raise a glass of cheer and thanks to the anonymous friendly lady at the Job Center in Madison, Wisconsin, who allowed me to photograph her.

Then there were the two joyful girls who let me photograph them near the public housing of the Lower East Side in New York. I loved it when they mimicked my English accent and laughed with glee.

Two joyful girls striking a pose on the Lower East Side.

I am grateful to the schools in and near San Francisco which allowed me to visit, including the American Indian Public Charter School, which has been highly controversial but where I saw the most effective lessons I have ever witnessed. I also visited the Mayo Clinic in Minnesota, where at first I had a wholly inadequate tour but then a member of staff took pity on me and agreed to give me an impromptu, fuller and more informative tour. In Washington I enjoyed meeting Anne Montgomery, who is an expert on care for the elderly. I was comforted that the supremely knowledgeable Michael Tanner of the Cato Institute did not think I was completely off the mark in my thoughts on healthcare around the world. It was a pleasure to have lunch with Robert Lerman of the Urban Institute.

In Holland, it was a delight to meet Dr Eric Sijbrands, who told me about his innovative efforts to improve care for diabetic patients. In Poland, I had great pleasure interviewing Aleksandra Wiktorow and Zofia Czepulis-Rutkowska in the Blikle café. I also enjoyed meeting Ewelina Nojszewka. And, on the train from Amsterdam to Warsaw, I shared a sleeping compartment with an amiable Polish diplomat – name unknown – who warned me that I would find it difficult talking to Leszek Balcerowicz, the former deputy Prime Minister. The diplomat was charming but wrong. In fact, one of the happy memories of my trips is of taking an underground train with Balcerowicz after our interview. I was surprised that he travelled by public transport despite being so well known and controversial in Poland. I asked whether he was still unpopular with some people. He drily remarked that he had become less unpopular since he had been out of power.

I visited eleven countries: Sweden, France, Switzerland, Spain, Italy, the Netherlands, Poland, Australia, New Zealand, Singapore and the USA. It was a great pleasure to travel around the world and meet so many people who kindly gave their time. I thank all of them and sincerely apologise to the many I have not mentioned.

Notes

THE WORLD QUIZ

1   47 per cent of households are people living alone. The rate is higher in Stockholm. Eric Klinenberg, 'I want to be alone: the rise and rise of solo living', *The Guardian*, 30 March 2012, http://www.theguardian.com/lifeandstyle/2012/mar/30/the-rise-of-solo-living (accessed 18 November 2014).

2   'Employment Situation, First Quarter 2014', Ministry of Manpower, Singapore Government press release, 30 April 2014, http://www.mom.gov.sg/newsroom/Pages/PressReleasesDetail.aspx?listid=561 (accessed 18 November 2014); 'OECD unemployment increases to 7.6% in February 2014', OECD press release, 9 April 2014, http://www.oecd.org/std/labour-stats/HUR-Apr14.pdf (accessed 18 November 2014).

3   OECD, *Health at a Glance 2013: OECD Indicators* (Paris: OECD Publishing, 2013), p. 127, http://www.oecd.org/els/health-systems/Health-at-a-Glance-2013.pdf (accessed 18 November 2014).

4   F. A. McDougall, F. E. Matthews, K. Kvaal, M. E. Dewey and C. Brayne, 'Prevalence and Symptomatology of Depression in Older People Living in Institutions in England and Wales', *Age and Ageing* 36:5 (2007), 562–8, http://ageing.oxfordjournals.org/content/36/5/562.full (accessed 18 November 2014).

5   'OECD unemployment increases to 7.6% in February 2014'.

6   Jan van Dijk, John van Kesteren and Paul Smit, *Criminal Victimisation in International Perspective* (The Hague: Boom Juridische Uitgevers, 2007), Table 13: Assaults and threats, one-year prevalence rates 2003-04, available at http://unicri.it/services/library_documentation/publications/icvs/publications/ICVS2004_05report.pdf (accessed 18 November 2014). This is an old survey but has the virtue of being an international victimisation study which is likely to be more reliable than police figures compared across countries.

7   *OECD Health Data 2011*, cited in OECD, *Health at a Glance 2011* (Paris: OECD Publishing, 2011), pp. 91, 93, http://www.oecd.org/els/health-systems/49105858.pdf (accessed 18 November 2014).

8   Franklin Delano Roosevelt, message to Congress on unemployment relief, Washington DC, 21 March 1933.

9   See Chapter 6 on parenting.

10   See Chapter 8 on pensions.

11   See Chapter 9 on care for the elderly.

12   See Chapter 11 on training and qualifications.

CHAPTER 1: WHY ARE SO MANY SWEDISH PEOPLE DISABLED?

1   'Unemployment statistics during the Great Depression', United States History website,
       http://www.u-s-history.com/pages/h1528.html (accessed 18 November 2014).

2   Doris Kearns Goodwin, *Lyndon Johnson and the American Dream* (New York: St Martin's
       Press, 1991).

3   Frederic B. M. Hollyday (ed.), *Bismarck* (Englewood Cliffs, NJ: Prentice-Hall, 1970);
       Moritz Busch, *Bismarck: Some Secret Pages of His History*, vol. 2 (New York: Macmillan,
       1898).

4   Hollyday, *Bismarck*, p. 57; Busch, *Bismarck*, p. 258.

5   Hollyday, *Bismarck*, p. 58.

6   Polybius, *Histories*, Book 20. The third century BC seems implied but it is not stated.

7   Paul Spicker (ed.), *The Origins of Modern Welfare* (Oxford: Peter Lang).

8   Sources include *Plutarch's Lives*, tr. Bernadotte Perrin (London: Heinemann 1914);
       Diogenes Laertius, *The Lives and Opinions of Eminent Philosophers*, tr. C. D. Yonge
       (London, 1853); H. H. Scullard, *From the Gracchi to Nero: A History of Rome from 133 BC
       to AD 68* (Abingdon: Routledge [1959] 2011); Karl de Schweinitz, *England's Road to Social
       Security* (London: Oxford University Press, 1943).

9   The total enrolment in the food stamp programme, as of January 2014, was 46,542,005
       ('Supplemental Nutrition Assistance Program (SNAP)', US Department of Agriculture,
       Food & Nutrition Service website, http://www.fns.usda.gov/pd/29snapcurrpp.htm
       (accessed 18 November 2014).)

10   The population of the United States, as of 31 December 2013, was 317,292,487, according
       to the US Census Bureau Population Clock, http://www.census.gov/popclock (accessed
       18 November 2014).

11   'Fiscal Year 2014 in $ billion', usgovernmentspending website, http://www.
       usgovernmentspending.com/year_spending_2014USbn_15bs2n_40#usgs302 (accessed 18
       November 2014).

12   Nicole Liguori quoted in Isabelle Pouey-Sanchou, 'Très populaire, la soupe', *Sud Ouest*, 8
       December 2010, http://www.sudouest.fr/2010/12/08/tres-populaire-la-soupe-261516-1391.
       php?reagir=true (accessed 19 November 2014).

13   French unemployment averaged 1.5 per cent in the 1950s, 1.7 per cent in the 1960s, 3.8
      per cent in the 1970s, 9.0 per cent in the 1980s and 8.9 per cent in the 1990s. (John P.
      Martin, 'The Extent of High Unemployment in OECD Countries', Table 1, available
      at http://www.kansascityfed.com/publicat/sympos/1994/S94MARTI.PDF (accessed
      19 November 2014).) The latest figure for unemployment is the OECD Harmonised
      Unemployment figure for April 2014 from OECD.StatExtracts, http://stats.oecd.org/
      index.aspx?queryid=36324# (accessed 19 November 2014).

14   France GDP expenditure on welfare: 12.5 per cent in 1960, 15 per cent in 1970, 21
      per cent in 1980, 25 per cent in 1990, 29 per cent in 2000, 32.5 per cent in 2010
      (OECD, 'Social Spending During the Crisis', 2012, http://www.oecd.org/els/soc/
      OECD2012SocialSpendingDuringTheCrisis8pages.pdf (accessed 19 November 2014).)

15   From 4 per cent of those of working age to 5 per cent. The figure is likely to have risen
      further in the following years of rising unemployment (OECD, 'Sickness, Disability and
      Work: Keeping on Track in the Economic Downturn', 2009, Figure A2.7, http://www.
      oecd.org/employment/emp/42699911.pdf (accessed 19 November 2014).)

16   Walter Galenson and Arnold Zellner, 'International Comparison of Unemployment
      Rates', in National Bureau of Economic Research, *The Measurement and Behavior of
      Unemployment* (Princeton, NJ: Princeton University Press, 1957), available at http://www.
      nber.org/chapters/c2649.pdf (accessed 19 November 2014).

17   OECD figures for harmonised unemployment rates from OECD.StatExtracts, http://
      stats.oecd.org/index.aspx?queryid=36324# (accessed 19 November 2014).

18   OECD, 'Trends in Retirement and in Working at Older Ages', in *Pensions at a Glance
      2011: Retirement-income Systems in OECD and G20 Countries* (Paris: OECD Publishing,
      2011), available at http://dx.doi.org/10.1787/pension_glance-2011-6-en (accessed 19
      November 2014).

19   'Employment and Labour Markets: Key Tables from OECD, Table 6: Employment
      rate of older workers % of population aged 55–64', OECD iLibrary, http://www.oecd-
      ilibrary.org/employment/employment-rate-of-older-workers_20752342-table6 (accessed
      19 November 2014).

20   Schweinitz, *England's Road to Social Security*.

21   OECD, *OECD Employment Outlook 2009: Tackling the Jobs Crisis*, Chapter 4: 'Pathways
      onto (and off) Disability Benefits' (Paris: OECD, 2009), http://www.oecd.org/els/
      employmentpoliciesanddata/45219540.pdf (accessed 19 November 2014).

22   Michael R. Strain, 'A Jobs Agenda for the Right', *National Affairs* 18 (2014), http://
      www.nationalaffairs.com/publications/detail/a-jobs-agenda-for-the-right (accessed 19
      November 2014).

23   Ben Gersten, '5 charts show alarming trend in number of Americans collecting social
      security', *Money Morning*, 10 April 2013, http://moneymorning.com/2013/04/10/5-charts-
      show-alarming-trend-in-number-of-americans-collecting-social-security/ (accessed 19
      November 2014). This article asserts that the percentage of Americans of working age

on social security disability insurance more than tripled from 1.7 per cent to 5.8 per cent between 1970 and the time when the article was written.

24   *The Sun*, 20 December 2011, p. 33.

25   Kathryn Edin and Laura Lein, *Making Ends Meet: How Single Mothers Survive Welfare and Low-wage Work* (New York: Russell Sage Foundation, 1997), Table 2-6.

26   Ibid. 'Earned income tax credits' are for wages earned the previous year.

27   For example France (56.5%), Austria (55.1%), Italy (53.6%) (OECD.StatExtracts, http://stats.oecd.org/Index.aspx?DataSetCode=SOCX_AGG (accessed 19 November 2014).)

28   Ibid. OECD figure for 2013, up from 15.5 per cent in 1980 and surely far greater than in the 1950s.

29   I first saw these excerpts in Paul Tough, 'What does Obama really believe in?', *New York Times Magazine*, 15 August 2012.

CHAPTER 2: HEART OF THE DARKNESS

1   *Men, Suicide and Society: Why Disadvantaged Men in Mid-life Die by Suicide* (Samaritans, 2012), http://www.samaritans.org/sites/default/files/kcfinder/files/press/ Men%20Suicide%20and%20Society%20Research%20Report%20151112.pdf (accessed 19 November 2014). 'Phil' is one of six case studies provided by the Samaritans to the press on request and is available at http://www.samaritans.org/caller-case-study-phil (accessed 19 November 2014).

2   Rafael DiTella, Robert MacCulloch and Andrew J. Oswald (1999), 'The Macroeconomics of Happiness', ZEI working paper B 03-1999, http://www.econstor.eu/ bitstream/10419/39619/1/269376186.pdf (accessed 19 November 2014).

3   Ibid.

4   David Bell and David Blanchflower, *Youth Unemployment: Déjà Vu?* (2009), IZA discussion paper 4705, available at http://ssrn.com/abstract=1545132 (accessed 19 November 2014).

5   Arthur H. Goldsmith, Jonathan R. Veum and William Darity Jr, 'Unemployment, Joblessness, Psychological Well-being and Self-esteem: Theory and Evidence', *Journal of Socio-economics* 26:2 (1997), 133–58; Arthur H. Goldsmith, Jonathan R. Veum and William Darity Jr, 'The Psychological Impact of Unemployment and Joblessness', *Journal of Socio-economics* 25:3 (1996), 333–58.

6   T. A. Blakely, S. C. D. Collings and J. Atkinson, 'Unemployment and Suicide: Evidence for a Causal Association?', *Journal of Epidemiology and Community Health* 57 (2003), 594–600, http://jech.bmj.com/content/57/8/594.full (accessed 19 November 2014). This suggests that the unemployed are two to three times more likely to commit suicide even after various controls. 'About half of this association might be attributable

to confounding by mental illness', but even so, the association remains and I guess that it is possible that the mental illness is itself made worse by being unemployed. Regarding life expectancy, the way that unemployment reduces it is well established in many papers. See M. Harvey Brenner, 'Major Factors in the Prediction of National Life Expectancy: GDP and Unemployment' (2011), http://www.epw.senate.gov/public/index.cfm?FuseAction=Files.View&FileStore_id=37188bea-2c5f-4100-a767-f264f1a1ced2 (accessed 19 November 2014).

7 I say 'at least four' because the table below shows four years. However, another source shows six: Walter Galenson and Arnold Zellner, 'International Comparison of Unemployment Rates', in National Bureau of Economic Research, *The Measurement and Behavior of Unemployment* (Princeton, NJ: Princeton University Press, 1957), Table 1, available at http://www.nber.org/chapters/c2649.pdf (accessed 19 November 2014). This is the source for the Germany figures.

8 Catherine Guillemineau and Lucrezia Reichlin, 'Chômage et croissance en France et aux États-Unis: une analyse de longue période', *Observations et diagnostics économiques: revue de l'OFCE* 29 (1989), 161–184, chart at 164, http://www.persee.fr/web/revues/home/prescript/article/ofce_0751-6614_1989_num_29_1_1192 (accessed 19 November 2014).

9 'Labour market', Destatis website, https://www.destatis.de/EN/FactsFigures/Indicators/LongTermSeries/LabourMarket/lrarb003.html (accessed 19 November 2014).

10 Jerome Fahrer and Alexandra Heath, 'The Evolution of Employment and Unemployment in Australia', Reserve Bank of Australia, December 1992, http://www.rba.gov.au/publications/rdp/1992/pdf/rdp9215.pdf (accessed 19 November 2014).

11 James Denman and Paul McDonald, 'Unemployment Statistics from 1881 to the Present Day', *Labour Market Trends*, January 1996, http://www.ons.gov.uk/ons/rel/lms/labour-market-trends--discontinued-/january-1996/unemployment-since-1881.pdf (accessed 19 November 2014). The UK government did not keep official figures until 1911, when employment exchanges were established. The figures prior to that are from the records kept by trade unions. In fact in most countries, it seems, it is quite difficult for statisticians to create a series of figures which is reliable and consistent. The unemployment rate jumped up to 16.9 per cent in 1921 and stayed high until the outbreak of the Second World War. One possible reason for this is that unemployment benefits were made more generous at this time: see *The Welfare State We're In*. It is extraordinary that unemployment remained so high through the 1920s as well as the 1930s. One reason it is extraordinary is that the same thing does not seem to have happened in France.

12 2012 figures: Switzerland $78,928, Bermuda $84,460, Qatar $93,825, Norway $99,636, Luxembourg $103,925, Monaco $163,026 ('GDP per capita (current US$)', World Bank website, http://data.worldbank.org/indicator/NY.GDP.PCAP.CD/countries/1W?order=wbapi_data_value_2012%20wbapi_data_value%20wbapi_data_value-last&sort=asc&display=default (accessed 19 November 2014).)

13 Those employed for up to a year must be given a month's notice. Those who have worked for between one and nine years must get two months' notice. Beyond that, it is three months. These minima are far less than in some countries.

14   There have been union campaigns for one but they have not been successful. In 2014 there was a referendum which rejected its introduction.

15   OECD.StatExtracts for April 2014 or most recent available, http://stats.oecd.org/ index.aspx?queryid=36324 (accessed 24 June 2014). Singapore government figure for Singapore. Countries with no minimum wages: various sources including OECD. Some articles refer to Austria as having no minimum wage but it does appear to have one: see 'Real minimum wages', OECD.StatExtracts, http://stats.oecd.org/Index. aspx?DataSetCode=RMW# (accessed 19 November 2014). Germany had none in 2014 but one was due to start in January 2015.

   In Italy, although there is no national minimum wage, the unions negotiate minimum wages by sector. See Wageindicator.org http://www.wageindicator.org/main/salary/ minimum-wage/italy/minimum-wages-faq/minimum-wages-in-italy-frequently-asked-questions The same is true in some of the other countries mentioned but of course the impact and coverage of such agreements vary from country to country. That is why it is difficult or impossible to relate official statutory minimum wages to unemployment. In some countries they are rendered irrelevant by union negotiated rates.

16   Jean-Michel Bonvin and Eric Moachon, 'Reframing the Issue of Legitimacy in Workfare Policies', in Helena Blomberg and Nanna Kildal (eds), *Workfare and Welfare State Legitimacy* (Helsinki: NordWel, 2011), pp. 62–95, https://helda.helsinki.fi/bitstream/ handle/10138/41875/nordwel1.pdf?sequence=1 (accessed 19 November 2014), at pp. 80–1.

17   'Social Welfare', Migraweb website, http://www.migraweb.ch/en/themen/sociale-sicherheit/sozialhilfe/ (accessed 19 November 2014).

18   Bonvin and Moachon, 'Reframing the Issue of Legitimacy in Workfare Policies', pp. 77–8.

19   Nicola Duell, Peter Tergeist, Ursula Bazant and Sylvie Cimper, 'Activation Policies in Switzerland', OECD Social Employment and Migration Working Papers (2010), http:// www.oecd.org/berlin/46224109.pdf (accessed 19 November 2014). 'Studies from several countries have shown that strong job-search controls can have a considerable impact on re-employment rates. Switzerland stands out as *one of the countries with the strongest job-search requirements in the OECD. Even at initial registration for placement, Swiss jobseekers are liable to be sanctioned if they cannot present evidence of recent job-search actions.* During the subsequent monthly face-to-face meeting with their counsellors, jobseekers need to present proof of their job applications during the past period. The approximate number of job-search actions they need to report is often as high as 10 per month. Even during participation in an active measure, job-search efforts (as well as placement efforts by counsellors) need to be continued, albeit to a more limited extent' [emphasis added].

20   Ralph Howell, *Why Unemployment?* (London: Adam Smith Institute, 1985).

21   8.4 per cent in 2012 compared to 16.3 per cent for the OECD. See 'Employment and Labour Markets: Key Tables from OECD', Table 2: youth unemployment rate, OECD iLibrary, http://www.oecd-ilibrary.org/employment/youth-unemployment-rate_20752342-table2 (accessed 19 November 2014).

22   'Young and restless: the ratio of youth to adult unemployment worsens', *The Economist*,
     16 December 2010.

23   At the time I was in Spain, the national minimum wage came out at €640 a month. One
     source told me that less than 3 per cent of workers are on it.

24   Speech in the Reichstag, 20 March 1884, quoted in Frederic B. M. Hollyday (ed.),
     Bismarck (Englewood Cliffs, NJ: Prentice-Hall, 1970), p. 65.

25   In such circumstances, the longer-serving workers were so expensive to fire that they
     were practically unsackable. This, it is said, has led to such workers not working very
     hard, which, if it is true, will have damaged Spanish productivity.
         Inevitably the cost of significant lay-offs has been extremely expensive. I say 'has been'
     because while I was in Spain (March 2012) the new government had changed the law. It
     was made easier for lay-offs to be justified and people were waiting to see if the change
     would make any difference or whether the labour court judges would argue that the
     change was unconstitutional.
         When unemployment soared to 20% in 1984, a new law was passed permitting
     employers to hire people on temporary contracts. (See http://www.indexmundi.com/
     spain/unemployment_rate.html for unemployment rate and section 1.4 of http://www.
     eurofound.europa.eu/emcc/erm/studies/tn1304017s/es1304011q.htm for introduction
     of temporary contracts.) There was thus an implicit acknowledgement that the high
     security of long term employment has been bought at the expense of those who were not
     employed at all. This, however, still has not solved the problem. The majority of workers
     remain on the long-term contracts and those who are on the new short-term ones are the
     people who have been fired.

26   Andrés Torres and Enrique Morales, 'Las ETT colocan hasta seis veces más
     desempleados que el antiguo Inem', 24 June 1014, Teinteresa.es, http://www.teinteresa.
     es/empleo/ETT-colocan-desempleados-antiguo-Inem_0_1162686123.html (accessed 19
     November 2014).

27   'Consecuencias de rechazar una colocación adecuada en el paro', Citapreviainem.es, http://
     www.citapreviainem.es/rechazar-colocacion-adecuada-paro/ (accessed 19 November 2014).

28   Susana Serrano Davey, 'Employing Staff in Spain', Andalucia.com, http://www.
     andalucia.com/spain/business/employing-staff-spain2.htm (accessed 19 November
     2014).

29   'Spanish Income Tax 2014', SpainAccountants website, http://www.spainaccountants.
     com/it.html; 'Rates and Allowances 2014', SpainAccountants website, http://www.
     spainaccountants.com/rates.html (both accessed 19 November 2014).

30   The employer pays about 11.45 per cent of the wage and the employee about 7.7 per
     cent. As for income tax, it depends on the individual canton but in Geneva, which has
     relatively high taxes, it is less than 11 per cent for someone on a modest income. Federal
     income tax is well under 1 per cent ('Swiss rental income tax is high', Global Property
     Guide website, 8 April 2013 http://www.globalpropertyguide.com/Europe/Switzerland/
     Taxes-and-Costs (accessed 19 November 2014).)

The position could be something like this:

Cost to employer	
Wage	€1,500
plus social security	171.75
Total	**€1,671.75**

The money in the pocket of the employee could be:

Received by worker		
Wage		€1,500
less		
Social insurance @7.7pc	115.5	
Tax @about 11pc	165	
Net		**€1,219.5**

31 Farell E. Block, *Unemployment: Causes and Cures*, Cato Institute Policy Analysis, 10 October 1981.

32 The OECD publishes an index of 'employment protection' for each country. Ones with high employment protection tend to have high unemployment – like Spain, France, Greece and Portugal. But having low protection is not a guarantee of low unemployment.

33 Gregory Viscusi and Mark Deen, 'Why France has so many 49-employee companies', *Bloomberg Businessweek*, 3 May 2012, http://www.businessweek.com/articles/2012-05-03/why-france-has-so-many-49-employee-companies (accessed 1 December 2014).

34 Available at http://www.keepeek.com/Digital-Asset-Management/oecd/taxation/taxing-wages-2014/income-taxes-social-security-contributions-and-cash-benefits_tax_wages-2014-9-en#page4 (accessed 19 November 2014).

35 See chapter on education for table with rates of functional illiteracy.

36 Thomas Sowell, *Basic Economics: A Common Sense Guide to the Economy*, 4th ed. (New York: Basic, 2011), p. 250.

37 Mark Wilson, 'The Negative Effects of Minimum Wage Laws', *Policy Analysis* 701 (2012), http://object.cato.org/sites/cato.org/files/pubs/pdf/PA701.pdf (accessed 19 November 2014).

38 'Parents of 10 who won't get a job… because they're better off with £49,000 benefits', *Daily Mail*, 30 May 2012, p. 25.

39 This could be expressed as a kind of equation: Factors that increase the cost of employing people OR Factors that reduce the net pay of workers + High minimum wage/welfare benefits supplemented, perhaps, with cash jobs = Unemployment. Or to put it more simply: F + H = U.

40 Op. cit.

41   W. S. Siebert, 'The UK's Minimum Wage: a Bad Policy Implemented Well?', 3 February
      2013, paper obtained through the Institute of Economic Affairs, London. The increase
      in the minimum wage took place over a slightly longer period (1999 to 2012). The
      slightly longer period is used because there are figures available for that period from
      the Low Pay Commission's 2013 report. The national minimum wage rose by 71.9 per
      cent while average weekly earnings rose by 58.5 per cent and the consumer price index
      by 34.4 per cent. The retail prices index rose by 48.7 per cent (*National Minimum
      Wage: Low Pay Commission Report 2013*, Cm 8565, https://www.gov.uk/government/
      uploads/system/uploads/attachment_data/file/226822/National_minimum_wage_
      Low_Pay_Commission_report_2013.pdf (accessed 19 November 2014), p. 26). There
      were particularly big rises in the minimum wage in 2001 2003 and 2004: see *National
      Minimum Wage: Low Pay Commission Report 2012*, Cm 8302, https://www.gov.uk/
      government/uploads/system/uploads/attachment_data/file/32574/8302.pdf (accessed 19
      November 2014).

          The jump in low-skilled unemployment was clearly not just because the economy was
      in a worse state in 2011. Over the same period, the rise in overall unemployment was
      far more modest, going from 6.3 per cent to 8.1 per cent. Meanwhile in France, youth
      unemployment went down.

42   Jochen Kluve, '*Fördern und Fordern*: The Principle of "Help and Hassle" in German
      Labour Market Policy', in Lawrence Kay and Oliver Marc Hartwich (eds), *When Hassle
      Means Help: The International Lessons of Conditional Welfare* (London: Policy Exchange,
      2008), p. 59, http://www.policyexchange.org.uk/images/publications/when%20hassle%20
      means%20help%20-%20oct%2008.pdf (accessed 19 November 2014).

43   Ibid.

44   Ibid.

45   Caitlin Kenney, 'Germany's painful unemployment fix', Planet Money blog, 23
      September 2011, http://www.npr.org/blogs/money/2011/09/23/140707524/germanys-
      painful-unemployment-fix (accessed 19 November 2014).

46   The summary of the Hartz reforms is derived from Kluve, '*Fördern und Fordern*' (see
      above).

47   'In 2004, small businesses with fewer than ten employees were made exempt
      from dismissal protection for employees' (Ryan Bourne, 'Economic lessons from
      Germany', Spectator Coffee House blog, 12 June 2012, http://blogs.spectator.co.uk/
      coffeehouse/2012/06/economic-lessons-from-germany/ (accessed 19 November 2014).)

48   Klara Stovicek and Alessandro Turrini, *Benchmarking Unemployment Benefit Systems*
      (Brussels: European Commission Directorate General for Economic and Financial
      Affairs, 2012), p. 17 footnote, http://ec.europa.eu/economy_finance/publications/
      economic_paper/2012/pdf/ecb454_en.pdf (accessed 19 November 2014); Jelle Visser and
      Anton Hemerijck, *A Dutch Miracle: Job Growth, Welfare Reform and Corporatism in the
      Netherlands* (Amsterdam: Amsterdam University Press, 1997).

49   Stovicek and Turrini, *Benchmarking Unemployment Benefit Systems*.

50   William Beveridge recommended an insurance-based system in which means-testing
      would be a residual part. But the insurance element was reduced because it was more
      costly in the short term. The number on means-tested benefits grew enormously.

51   For the 2000–11 figures see http://epp.eurostat.ec.europa.eu/statistics_explained/index.
      php?title=File:Unemployment_rate,_2000-2011_(%25).png&filetimestamp=20120502
      100338#filelinks; for the 2012 figures see http://appsso.eurostat.ec.europa.eu/nui/show.
      do?dataset=une_rt_a&lang=en (both accessed 19 November 2014).

52   Chile, Israel and Turkey were the others.

53   The Netherlands had a deliberately low-wage economy after the Second World War.
      The welfare system was cautious and there was full employment. In the early 1960s,
      the jobless rate fell to a mere 0.9 per cent, which is likely to represent people moving
      from one job to another (Stephen Nickell, Luca Nunziata and Wolfgang Ochel,
      'Unemployment in the OECD since the 1960s. What Do We Know?', *Economic Journal*
      115 (2005), 1–27, available at https://wwz.unibas.ch/fileadmin/wwz/redaktion/fai/EIB_
      Arbeitsmarkt_HS08/NickellNunziataOchel.pdf (accessed 19 November 2014).) But
      gradually it became 'one of the most generous and extensive welfare states in the world'
      (Visser and Hemerijck, *A Dutch Miracle*, p. 119). The proportion of GDP raised in taxes
      and social security contributions jumped from 38.2 per cent to 52.2 per cent between
      1968 and 1980. In 1977, the *Financial Times* declared that the Dutch had succeeded in
      establishing 'one of the most prosperous and enlightened welfare states with minimum
      wages higher than in any other industrial society, high labour productivity, remarkably
      few strikes, and a widely developed social security network' (ibid., p. 120).
          Disaster followed. Nine years later, a sociologist working in the Netherlands referred
      to the country as 'perhaps the most spectacular employment failure in the advanced
      world' (Goran Therborn, *Why Some Peoples Are More Unemployed than Others*, cited in
      Visser and Hemerijck, *A Dutch Miracle*, p. 9). Two years before, unemployment had
      reached nearly 14 per cent of the workforce (Visser and Hemerijck, *A Dutch Miracle*,
      p. 9). Almost as many were on disability benefits or had taken early retirement.
      According to the OECD, broadly defined – or you might say 'real' – unemployment
      had reached an astonishing 27 per cent of the workforce. The expression 'the Dutch
      disease' began to be used in textbooks. The number on disability benefits multiplied
      from 200,000 to 700,000 between 1970 and 1985 (ibid., p. 128). The cost of paying
      disability benefits amounted to no less than 7.6 per cent of all the nation's economic
      activity (OECD, 'Sickness, Disability and Work', Table A2.1). For those aged between
      fifty-five and sixty-four, the proportion claiming disability benefit in 1987 was more than
      three times that of Germany: 980 per 10,000 workers as against 262, and 434 in Belgium
      (Visser and Hemerijck, *A Dutch Miracle*, p. 138). The proportion of people working in
      comparison to those on benefits collapsed from 14.9:1 in 1970 to 2.9:1 in 1985. (If you
      added in unpaid housewives there was a mere 1.2 people working to one dependant. And
      that is leaving the retired and children out of the equation (ibid., p. 128).)
          Governments tried to combat the problem, of course. In the early 1970s, they tried
      public works programmes focused on labour-intensive industries such as construction.
      That did not work. The government tried giving subsidies to companies in difficulty to
      keep them going. That did not work either (ibid., p. 159). Unions and employers agreed
      to restrain wages in 1982. But progress was minimal. Gradually the changes became more

radical because the situation was so bad. But the process was still agonisingly slow. The minimum wage was steadily reduced from 80 per cent of average wages in 1983 to 67 per cent in 1994 (ibid, p. 135, Figure 10).

In 1987, unemployment benefit was cut from 80 per cent to 70 per cent of previous earnings (ibid., p. 136). Many younger people who in the past would have been entitled to full benefits now only got 'partial' benefits and these did not last as long as before. The changes mostly affected the young. The value of disability benefits was significantly reduced for younger workers although not for older ones. They fell from 70 per cent of the person's previous wage to 70 per cent of the minimum wage. The disabled were required to have new, more objective medical examinations and their obligation to seek work was ratcheted up. They had to accept all 'normal' jobs instead of all 'appropriate' jobs.

Finally from the mid-1990s the government embarked on 'labour activation policies' – nudging people into work. Private companies were allowed to place people in jobs (ibid., p. 184). (Improving the 'nudging' was something that the Netherlands had previously attempted only in a very minor way (ibid., p. 161). There had long been a bureaucratic and ineffective government-run employment service.) The government embarked on what looked very much like 'workfare' programmes for the long-term unemployed and young people (ibid., p. 173). There was also a programme of re-training followed by work experience and then job placement. The government also tried to reduce the size of wedge for those who had been unemployed for a long time, provided the jobs were low wage.

Eventually all these reforms had an impact. The rate of unemployment fell from 14 per cent in 1983 to just over 6 per cent in 1997. The Netherlands went from having one of the worst levels of unemployment in Europe to one of the best. But the process took a long time and at the end, the Netherlands still had not fully managed to reverse the effect of having been 'one of the most … enlightened welfare states'.

54   Peter Saunders, *Re-moralising the Welfare State* (St Leonards, NSW: Centre for Independent Studies, 2013), p, 20 after citing OECD, British and Australian research.

55   Jason DeParle, *American Dream: Three Women, Ten Kids, and a Nation's Drive to End Welfare* (New York: Penguin, 2005).

56   John Stossel, 'We fund dependency', townhall.com, 3 October 2012, http://townhall. com/columnists/johnstossel/2012/10/03/we_fund_dependency/page/full (accessed 19 November 2014).

57   Version sent to me by email by Jennifer Noyes.

58   Jocelyn Bourgon, *A New Synthesis of Public Administration: Serving in the 21st Century* (Montreal : School of Policy Studies, Queen's University, 2011), p. 222.

59   For the fiscal year 2014 the caseload of TANF (Temporary Assistance for Needy Families) single parents was averaging 14,186 (email from Maura Taggart, DFES/BWF/Research and Statistics Section Chief, Department of Children and Families, 25 June 2014). See 'TANF Caseload Data 2014', Office of Family Assistance website, http://www.acf.hhs. gov/programs/ofa/resource/caseload-data-2014 (accessed 19 November 2014).

60   US Department of Health and Human Services, 'Indicators of Welfare Dependence: Twelfth Report to Congress', Table IND 4a, http://aspe.hhs.gov/hsp/13/Indicators/rpt. pdf (accessed 19 November 2014).

61   'National Level Annual Summary: Participation and Costs, 1969–2013', US Department of Agriculture, Food and Nutrition Service, Supplementary Nutrition Assistance Program, http://www.fns.usda.gov/sites/default/files/pd/SNAPsummary.pdf (accessed 20 November 2014).

62   Sources: Annual Statistical Supplement to the Social Security Bulletin, 2004, Table 4.C1; Annual Statistical Report on the Social Security Disability Insurance Program, 2003, Table 1, cited in 'Trends in the Social Security and Supplemental Security Income Disability Programs', Table equivalent for Chart 3, US Social Security Administration Office of Policy website, http://www.socialsecurity.gov/policy/docs/chartbooks/ disability_trends/sect01-text.html#chart3 (accessed 20 November 2014). The benefits concerned are called SSI and SSDI. The proportion of US workers receiving disability benefits has risen from about 25 per 1,000 in 1970 to 73 in 2011. This is nearly a tripling in the proportion (see Tad de Haven, 'The Rising Cost of Social Security Disability Insurance' (August 2013), Figure 3, http://www.downsizinggovernment.org/ssa/social-security-disability-insurance (accessed 20 November 2014).)

63   From 205 million in 1970 to 290 million in 2003; see https:// www.google.co.uk/publicdata/explore?ds=kf7tgg1uo9ude_&met_y=population&hl=en& dl=en&idim=country:US (accessed 20 November 2014).

64   Ben Gersten, '5 charts show alarming trend in number of Americans collecting social security', *Money Morning*, 10 April 2013, http://moneymorning.com/2013/04/10/5-charts-show-alarming-trend-in-number-of-americans-collecting-social-security/ (accessed 20 November 2014).

65   'Trends in the Social Security and Supplemental Security Income Disability Programs', Table equivalent for Chart 27, http://www.socialsecurity.gov/policy/docs/chartbooks/ disability_trends/sect02-text.html#chart27 (accessed 20 November 2014).

66   'IMF World Economic Outlook, April 2014', Knoema website, http://knoema.com/ IMFWEO2014Apr/imf-world-economic-outlook-april-2014 (accessed 20 November 2014). See also 'Unemployment', Singapore Ministry of Manpower website, http://stats. mom.gov.sg/Pages/Unemployment-Summary-Table.aspx (accessed 20 November 2014).

67   The applicant gets none of the sense of entitlement that is so common elsewhere. Each case is treated individually and the applicant is obliged to think in terms of his or her own resources and those of the family. If someone comes in with a sense of entitlement, this is immediately confronted.
      There are a few other aspects to the Singapore approach:

      •   A prized government rental flat is not allocated just because someone is poor and wants to leave the family home. Getting such a flat may be a reward for getting work but not a reward for being unemployed. The whole organisation is very conscious that it must avoid creating perverse incentives – rewards for 'bad' behaviour.

- There is absolutely no minimum wage.

- As in Switzerland and Germany, there is a strong emphasis on vocational education from the age of sixteen. About 65 per cent of students at that age attend polytechnics or technical schools. Only 30 per cent go to university initially, and a further 15 per cent go on to university after attending a polytechnic.

68 Lee Kuan Yew, *From Third World to First: The Singapore Story 1965–2000* (New York: HarperCollins, 2000).

69 The 4.2 per cent rate applies to earnings below S$80,000 (£39,000 at November 2014 exchange rates). From 2012, earnings up to $20,000 are not taxed. The next $10,000 is taxed at 2 per cent ('Income tax rates', Inland Revenue Authority of Singapore website, http://www.iras.gov.sg/irasHome/page04.aspx?id=1190 (accessed 20 November 2014).)

70 People are obliged to make payments to the Central Provident Fund at a rate of 20 per cent and their employer pays a further 15.5 per cent. Employees do not contribute if they earn less than $500 a month. Employers contribute to CPF for employees earning more than $50 a month. The full employer contribution rate of 15.5 per cent is payable for all employees aged under thirty-five. ('About the Central Provident Fund', OECD, http://www.oecd.org/finance/private-pensions/46260911.pdf (accessed 20 November 2014).)

71 Alessio J. G. Brown and Johannes Koettl, 'Active Labor Market Programs: Employment Gain or Fiscal Drain?', Institute for the Study of Labour Discussion Paper 680, September 2012, http://ftp.iza.org/dp6880.pdf (accessed 20 November 2014).

72 I am grateful to Peter Whiteford in Sydney for talking to me about this. He is knowledgeable on the subject and I have benefited from some of his insights. However, the summary is my own, not his.

CHAPTER 3: IN SEARCH OF THE BEST HEALTHCARE SYSTEM IN THE WORLD

1 Much of the information about the history of the system came from an interview with Tom Groot and Yvonne Krabbe at VU University Amsterdam.

2 My information came from an interview but there is information on the Dekker Commission in Kieke G. H. Okma, 'Recent Changes in Dutch Health Insurance: Individual Mandate or Social Insurance?' (January 2009), available at http://www.nasi.org/usr_doc/Recent_Changes_in_Dutch_Health_Insurance.pdf (accessed 20 November 2014). Dekker had been chief executive of Philips Electronics (1982–6).

3 When I was there in 2011, I was told they were about to bring the numbers down from 30,000 DTCs to 4,400. They were using the list produced by the World Health Organization. This was not based on the specifications of the specialists but on the diagnosis.

4 And indeed I have obtained and looked at several of the relevant papers and publications: Isabelle Joumard, 'Health Care Systems: Getting More Value for Money',

Economics Department Policy Note No. 2 (OECD, 2010); Isabelle Joumard, Christophe André and Chantal Nicq, 'Healthcare Systems: Efficiency and Institutions', Economics Department Working Papers No. 769 (OECD, 2010); Valérie Paris, Marion Devaux and Lihan Wei, 'Health Systems Institutional Characteristics: A Survey of 29 OECD Countries', OECD Health Working Papers No. 50 (OECD, 2010); OECD, *Value for Money in Health Spending* (Paris: OECD, 2010).

5   Jeremy Sammut is a research fellow at the Centre for Independent Studies in Sydney. His paper 'Why Public Hospitals are Overcrowded' cites a 2007 report saying that more than a third of emergency patients requiring admission to a public hospital waited over eight hours for a bed.

6   American Association of Port Authorities world port rankings 2011. Tianjin comes third and Rotterdam fourth. See http://aapa.files.cms-plus.com/PDFs/WORLD%20 PORT%20RANKINGS%202011.pdf (accessed 20 November 2014).

7   'Health expenditure, total (% of GDP)', World Bank website, http://data.worldbank.org/ indicator/SH.XPD.TOTL.ZS?order=wbapi_data_value_2012+wbapi_data_value+wbapi_ data_value-last&sort=desc (accessed 20 November 2014).

8   John C. Goodman, *Priceless: Curing the Healthcare Crisis* (Oakland, CA: Independent Institute, 2012).

9   Lee Kuan Yew, *From Third World to First: The Singapore Story 1965–2000* (New York: HarperCollins, 2000).

10 Readers familiar with American healthcare may be thinking, 'Wait a minute. This sounds like managed care. We have that in the States.' Yes, it does seem to have a lot in common with 'managed care'. People pay a company which provides health insurance and much of the medical care too. One of the biggest managed care companies is Kaiser Permanente. I visited its offices in Oakland, California and it was clear that Kaiser, too, puts a lot of effort into keeping its customers healthy. And for the same reason. It saves them money.

11 I met Alberto de Rosa, director general of a company which has a stake in private hospitals. He was the first manager of the Ribera Hospital so he has seen the story from the beginning. I asked whether the innovations of the Ribera and its successors have affected how the public hospitals perform.

  'The Ribera Hospital was the first hospital in Valencia to make epidurals available on a routine basis,' he tells me. 'Because of this, many mothers came to the Ribera Hospital to have their babies.' The public hospitals elsewhere in the region saw this happening so to prevent a deluge of births going to the Ribera, they started offering epidurals, too. And now? 'Now *all* the hospitals offer epidurals.'

  The Ribera Hospital also offered private rooms to mothers giving birth. In the public hospitals, women gave birth in wards of two or three. Again, to prevent an exodus to the Ribera, the other hospitals improved what they offer.

  It is a classic story of how a little competition can buck up standards. It tells us something about monopoly public provision. It can be full of people working for the public good yet nonetheless be well below a good standard.

De Rosa put it more bluntly. He said that the public hospitals put the interests of the professionals above those of the patients. The thought is contrary to what many assume. But when hospital professionals stop work at 3 p.m. and decline to offer epidurals to mothers, it is hard to conclude anything else.

12   OECD, *Health at a Glance 2013* (Paris: OECD Publishing, 2013), http://www.oecd.org/els/health-systems/Health-at-a-Glance-2013.pdf (accessed 20 November 2014). I am only including advanced countries, although one could argue that economically some of the eastern European countries are much less advanced than the others. I have left out the smaller ones such as Slovakia and Slovenia. I have also omitted Israel and Iceland. They are advanced but they are relatively small and I have not studied or mentioned them otherwise so they do not help disentangle the relative merits of the others.

13   Ibid.

14   Ibid.

15   Ibid.

16   OECD, *Value for Money in Health Spending*, p. 130, citing 2008 Commonwealth Fund International Health Policy Survey of Sicker Adults.

17   OECD Health Data 2011, cited in OECD, *Health at a Glance 2011* (Paris: OECD Publishing, 2011), p. 91, http://www.oecd.org/els/health-systems/49105858.pdf (accessed 20 November 2014).

18   Ibid., p. 93.

19   Ibid., p. 93.

20   Joumard, 'Health Care Systems'.

21   OECD Science, Technology and Industry Scoreboard 2009, cited in Sally C. Pipes in *The Pipes Plan: The Top Ten Ways to Dismantle and Replace Obamacare* (Washington: Regnery, 2012).

22   Shannon Brownlee, *Overtreated: Why Too Much Medicine Is Making Us Sicker and Poorer* (New York: Bloomsbury, 2007).

23   This story was told me by the father in 2012. He wishes to remain anonymous and the boy's name has been changed because he has been in dispute with the hospital.

24   Thomas C. Buchmueller and Alan C. Monheit, 'Employer-sponsored Health Insurance and the Promise of Health Insurance Reform', National Bureau of Economic Research Working Paper 14839, April 2009, http://www.nber.org/papers/w14839.pdf?new_window=1 (accessed 21 November 2014).

25   Ibid. This was confirmed in 1954. See also Alex Blumberg and Adam Davidson, 'Accidents of history created US health system', NPR website, 22 October 2009, http://www.npr.org/templates/story/story.php?storyId=114045132 (accessed 21 November 2014), which says that corporate health insurance initially became tax free in 1943.

26   If you have to pay your own insurance premiums and medical expenses, they are
     generally only tax deductible to the extent they exceed 10 per cent of your adjusted gross
     income (roughly speaking your annual income from all sources). So, if you have income
     of $60,000 per year, you would have to meet the first $6,000 of premiums and medical
     expenses out of after-tax dollars. So the tax system favours being an employee rather than
     independent. Source: email from Christian Wignall in California; John Waggoner, 'Tax
     Q&A: Are health insurance premiums deductible?', *USA Today*, 26 March 2014, http://
     www.usatoday.com/story/money/personalfinance/2014/03/26/tax-qa-health-insurance-
     deductible/6878171/ (accessed 21 November 2014).

27   For long-term growth in private health insurance see David McDaid, Miriam Wiley,
     Anna Maresso and Elias Mossialos, 'Ireland: Health Systems Review', *Health Systems
     in Transition* 11:4 (2009), Fig. 3.6, http://www.euro.who.int/__data/assets/pdf_
     file/0004/85306/E92928.pdf (accessed 21 November 2014). For material on waiting times,
     see Elliot Bidgood, 'Healthcare Systems: Ireland and "Universal Health Insurance" – An
     Emerging Model for the UK?', Civitas, 17 December 2013, http://www.civitas.org.uk/
     nhs/download/IrelandBrief2013 (accessed 21 November 2014).

28   OECD, *Health at a Glance 2011*, citing Commonwealth Fund International Health
     Policy surveys. Figures are for 2010.

29   Can we really expect that this would save money? In addition to the experience
     of Singapore, which has achieved low-cost healthcare, using this idea there have
     been a number of studies of health savings accounts in the USA. One of the most
     comprehensive – conducted by RAND – concluded that people with health savings
     accounts and insurance policies where they had to pay out of their own pocket until a
     certain level of spending was reached spent about 30 per cent less on their healthcare
     than those with conventional, full-coverage insurance. Did this result in them going
     without treatment that was important for their health? No. The policy had no adverse
     effect on their health outcomes. See Goodman, *Priceless*, pp. 161, 162, citing Amelia M.
     Haviland, Neeraj Sood, Roland McDevitt and M. Susan Marquis, 'How Do Consumer-
     directed Health Plans Affect Vulnerable Populations?', *Forum for Health Economics and
     Policy* 14:2 (2011).

30   Goodman, *Priceless*, citing Devon M. Herrick, 'Consumer Driven Health Care: The
     Changing Role of the Patient', National Center for Policy Analysis Policy Report No.
     276, May 2005; Devon M. Herrick, 'Shopping for Drugs: 2007', National Center for
     Policy Analysis Policy Report No. 293, November 2006.

31   Op. cit.

CHAPTER 4: 'DAISY, CROSS YOUR FINGERS.'

1   Marc Le Bris, *Et vos enfants ne sauront pas lire, ni compter ! La faillite obstinée de l'école
     française* (Paris: Stock, 2004).

2   Ibid.

3   Alexandra Topping, 'Germany's middle class happy with rampant inequality in schools',

The Guardian, 15 March 2011, http://www.theguardian.com/world/2011/mar/15/germany-middle-class-inequality-schools (accessed 21 November 2014).

4   Steve Gibbons, 'The link between schools and house prices is now an established fact', LSE blog, 25 September 2012, http://blogs.lse.ac.uk/politicsandpolicy/archives/27103 (accessed 21 November 2014). 'A link between better schools and higher house prices has emerged as one of the most stable empirical regularities, with studies worldwide reporting effects of a similar order of magnitude.'

5   Quoted in Amanda Constance, 'By Any Means...', *Absolutely Kensington*, February 2014, http://issuu.com/zestmedialondon/docs/abs_kensington_feb_2014/65 (accessed 21 November 2014). Professor Francis is one of the authors of a Sutton Trust report, 'Parent Power'.

6   Ibid.

7   Rita Kramer, *Ed School Follies: The Miseducation of America's Teachers* (New York: Free Press, 1991).

8   I was speaking to Schleicher before the PISA 2012 study came out so he was referring to PISA 2009. In PISA 2012, all the figures were different to a greater or lesser extent. The OECD functional illiteracy rate fell from 18.8 per cent to 18.0 per cent. However, reading was not the main focus of the later study whereas it was the main focus of the 2009 study. So the 2009 results are worth considering also. It is also conceivable, at least, that some countries are learning how to 'game' the PISA tests so that they look better. If this has been happening, then the earlier results may be more reliable. The 2009 results were as follows:

Shanghai	4.1%
South Korea	5.8%
Finland	8.1%
Hong Kong	8.3%
Canada	10.3%
Singapore	12.4%
Japan	13.6%
Australia	14.3%
New Zealand	14.3%
Netherlands	14.4%
Norway	14.9%
Poland	15.0%
Denmark	15.2%
Switzerland	16.9%
Sweden	17.5%
Portugal	17.6%
Belgium	17.7%
USA	17.7%
Germany	18.5%
UK	18.5%
OECD average	**18.8%**

Spain	19.5%
France	19.7%
Italy	21.0%
Greece	21.3%
Czech Republic	23.1%
Turkey	24.5%
Israel	26.6%
Russia	27.4%
Austria	27.5%
Mexico	40.1%

Source: OECD, *PISA 2009 Results, vol. 1: What Students Know and Can Do* (Paris: OECD Publishing, 2010), p. 194.

9   Detroit Regional Workforce Fund, 'Addressing Detroit's Basic Skills Crisis'.

10   Michael H. Cottman, 'Analysis: Illiteracy in Detroit a National Shame', New America Media website, 11 May 2011, http://newamericamedia.org/2011/05/analysis-illiteracy-in-detroit-a-national-shame.php (accessed 21 November 2014). The obvious answer to Manley's question is that the tests applied by his school were not rigorous. The school was letting children graduate who had not even learned to read. 'In 1989 … Dexter Manley, the All-Pro former defensive end for the Washington Redskins, offered a startling and embarrassing confession to Congress, saying he almost made it to the age of 30 without being able to read. Manley was embarrassed to say that he was illiterate and that he had memorized words and faked his way through life for years. "I broke down and started crying," Manley said in 1989. "How did I get through school when I couldn't read?" Manley told Congress that at the age of 28, he entered The Lab School of Washington with a second grade reading level. He would eventually earn as much as $350,000 a year playing for the Redskins – and keeping his closely-guarded secret from his fellow players for years.'

11   OECD, *PISA 2009 Results, vol. 1*, p. 102.

12   OECD, *PISA 2012 Results, vol. 1: What Students Know and Can Do*, rev. ed., Table I.4.1b (Paris: OECD Publishing, 2014), http://dx.doi.org/10.1787/888932935705 (accessed 21 November 2014). The figure of 18.0 per cent for the overall OECD average for functional literacy appears on page 196 in the text; see http://www.oecd.org/PISA/keyfindings/PISA-2012-results-volume-I.pdf (accessed 21 November 2014). The OECD average of 18.8% referred to by Andreas Schleicher was from PISA 2009, the most recently published report at that time.

13   Detroit Regional Workforce Fund, 'Addressing Detroit's Basic Skills Crisis', http://cbsdetroit.files.wordpress.com/2011/05/basicskillsreport_final.pdf (accessed 21 November 2014). GED (General Educational Development) tests are a group of five subject tests which, if passed, certify that someone has high-school-level academic skills.

14   Andrew J. Coulson, *Market Education: The Unknown History* (New Brunswick, NJ: Transaction, 1999).

15 Ibid.

16 Harriet Sergeant, *Among the Hoods: My Years with a Teenage Gang* (London: Faber and Faber, 2012). Further details appear in 'Wasted – The Betrayal of White and Black Caribbean Boys' (London: Centre for Policy Studies, 2009), http://www.cps.org.uk/files/reports/original/111027122608-20091127SocialPolicyWasted.pdf (accessed 29 January 2015).

17 Ibid., p. 8.

18 Ibid., p. 9.

19 Presentation by Dr Susan Sclafani, April 2005, cited by Literacy Texas, Literacy Facts. The statistic is also cited in Hans Meeder, 'Preparing America's Future: Enhancing the Quality of Adult Education and Family Literacy', May 2003, www2.ed.gov/about/offices/list/ovae/pi/AdultEd/ncfl.doc (accessed 21 November 2014).

20 Sergeant, *Among the Hoods*, p. 12.

21 Ibid., p. 10.

22 Ibid., p. 8.

23 Geoffrey Canada, 'Bringing Change to Scale: The Next Big Reform Challenge', in Karl Weber (ed.), *Waiting for 'Superman': How We Can Save America's Failing Public Schools* (New York: Public Affairs, 2010), p. 191.

24 All sorts of statistics are bandied about relating to illiteracy and juvenile offenders and prisoners, and some are more dramatic than the ones I have used; see for example Statistic Brain (http://www.statisticbrain.com/number-of-american-adults-who-cant-read/ (accessed 21 November 2014).) However, often I have not been able to trace the figures back to their original sources. The figures I have used come from National Center for Education Statistics, 'Literacy behind Prison Walls', October 1994, Table 2.3, http://nces.ed.gov/pubs94/94102.pdf (accessed 21 November 2014). The figures are clearly based on the National Adult Literacy Survey. This has various measures and levels of literacy. I have used the so-called 'quantitative' scale. According to this, 40 per cent of prison inmates are at the lowest level of literacy compared to 22 per cent of the general population.

25 Again, more dramatic figures are cited by some. The British Home Office archives carries details of the What Works initiative from the first years of this century, which refers to research by Lipton (1999) (http://webarchive.nationalarchives.gov.uk/20100413151441/http:/www.crimereduction.homeoffice.gov.uk/workingoffenders/workingoffenders1.htm (accessed 21 November 2014).)

26 Michael Brunner, *Reduced Recidivism and Increased Employment Opportunity through Research-based Reading Instruction* (US Department of Justice, 1993), https://www.ncjrs.gov/pdffiles1/Digitization/141324NCJRS.pdf (accessed 21 November 2014).

27 Cited in 'Literary Statistics', Begin to Read website, www.begintoread.com/research/

literacystatistics.com.html (accessed 21 November 2014).

28 Ibid.

29 Ibid.

30 Ibid.

31 Ibid.

32 In Britain, the phrase 'public school' means a fee-charging independent school. According to *Encyclopaedia Britannica* online, 'The term *public school* emerged in the 18th century when the reputation of certain grammar schools spread beyond their immediate environs. They began taking students whose parents could afford residential fees and thus became known as public, in contrast to local, schools' (http://library.eb.co.uk/levels/adult/article/61798 (accessed 21 November 2014).)

33 See Chapter 10 for more on the difficulties of firing teachers in the US.

34 Karl Weber, Introduction, in Weber, *Waiting for 'Superman'*, p. 20.

35 Peter Sacks, *Generation X Goes to College: An Eye-opening Account of Teaching in Postmodern America* (Chicago: Open Court, 1996). The author's name was a nom de plume because he was continuing to work as a teacher.

36 Op. cit., p. 7.

37 Op. cit., p. 195.

38 Mark Bray and Chad Lykins, *Shadow Education: Private Supplementary Tutoring and Its Implications for Policy Makers in Asia* (Manila: Asian Development Bank, 2012), p. 5, http://www.adb.org/sites/default/files/publication/29777/shadow-education.pdf (accessed 21 November 2014). The actual sentence in this report is: 'In addition, 6.8 per cent of junior secondary 3 pupils received tutoring at home, and 15.0 per cent followed correspondence courses.' It is not clear whether there might be overlap – and, if so, how much – between those at the *juku*, those with private tutors and those taking correspondence courses. The figures come from a Japanese government report in 2008 which is written in Japanese. I am tempted to think, however, that the overlap is unlikely to be very great. Any children following two kinds of shadow education would be extraordinarily exhausted. In which case, it seems likely that a minimum of 80 per cent of the children have private supplementary schooling at this age.

39 Ibid.

40 'Testing times', *The Economist*, 31 December 2011.

41 Email to the author, November 2012.

42 Michael B. Horn, 'What Koreans wish Obama understood about their schools', EducationNext website, 9 April 2014, http://educationnext.org/koreans-wish-obama-understood-schools/ (accessed 21 November 2014).

43 Bray and Lykins, *Shadow Education*.

44 Ibid.

45 Ibid.

46 Aristides Hatzis, 'Greece as a Precautionary Tale of the Welfare State', in Tom G. Palmer (ed.), *After the Welfare State: Politicians Stole Your Future … You Can Get It Back* (Arlington, VA: Students for Liberty, 2012), p30.

47 There is also supplementary education in other countries but it is less widespread. In Britain, the Sutton Trust, an education charity, did a survey of 11–16-year-olds and found that 20 per cent of white pupils received some kind of private tuition and 45 per cent of south Asian children ('On the road', *The Economist*, 16 November 2013, http://www. economist.com/news/britain/21589874-ethnic-minority-pupils-are-storming-ahead-thanks-partly-tutors-road (accessed 21 November 2014).)

48 'List of countries by foreign-born population', Wikipedia, http://en.wikipedia.org/wiki/ List_of_countries_by_foreign-born_population_in_2005 (accessed 21 November 2014), citing United Nations figures.

49 Andrew Coulson is the director of the Center for Educational Freedom at the Cato Institute in Washington DC. He argues that, wholly by chance, the Finnish curriculum happens to be more closely aligned with the method of testing in the PISA test than that of other countries since it concentrates on 'everyday' maths and science rather than higher-level skills (see Andrew Coulson, 'Being a Policy Specialist', in *Creating Your Path to a Policy Career*, Institute for Humane Studies at George Mason University, http://www.theihs.org/academic/wp-content/uploads/2014/08/ CreatingYourPathToAPolicyCareer.pdf (accessed 21 November 2014).) He draws attention to the fact that Finland did not do so well in another international assessment, the TIMSS (Trends in International Maths and Science Study) test. It came eighth in maths at the eighth-grade level – with a score only fractionally higher than those of the USA and England. (TIMSS study 2011. Finland scored 514 while the United States scored 509 and England 507. This compares with 613 for top-scoring Korea. It should also be noted that the Finnish result in the TIMSS study may be flattered by the fact that many European countries did not take part at all such as Germany, the Netherlands and France.) Coulson also notes that 'over 200 Finnish mathematics professors signed a letter in 2005 lamenting the poor and declining mathematics skills of their entering freshmen, and warning against generalizations based on misleading PISA results' (citing Kari Astala et al., 'The PISA survey tells only a partial truth of Finnish children's mathematical skills', Matematiikkalehti Solmu website, 31 August 2005, http://solmu.math.helsinki.fi/2005/ erik/PISAEng.html (accessed 21 November 2014).)

50 Winton appears to be 101 miles away so it is surprising that this was an alternative for his mother but this is what I believe he said.

51 http://www.kipp.org/about-kipp (accessed 21 November 2014).

52 From a conversation with Pierre Garello.

53   Caroline M. Hoxby, Sonali Murarka and Jenny Kang, 'How New York City's Charter
      Schools Affect Achievement', New York City Charter Schools Evaluation Project,
      September 2009 report, http://users.nber.org/~schools/charterschoolseval/how_NYC_
      charter_schools_affect_achievement_sept2009.pdf (accessed 21 November 2014).

54   Ibid., p. IV-13.

55   According to the company website it has thirty-six schools in Sweden and its educational
      programme operates in five schools in the UK, one in New York and one in India
      (http://www.kunskapsskolan.com/aboutus.4.52570e4b127643a7eac80001100.html
      (accessed 21 November 2014).)

56   There are a number of disadvantages. One is that a school may not be able to afford to
      offer all that the teacher and the parents would like. That could include, say, classes in
      another language or a music teacher or the creation of a language laboratory.

57   See OECD, *PISA 2009 Results, vol. iv: What Makes a School Successful?* (Paris: OECD
      Publishing, 2010), pp. 224, 225, http://www.oecd.org/PISA/PISAproducts/48852721.pdf
      (accessed 24 November 2014).

58   Matthew M. Chingos and Paul E. Peterson, *The Effects of School Vouchers on College
      Enrollment: Experimental Evidence from New York City*, Brown Center on Education
      Policy at Brookings / Harvard Kennedy School, August 2012, p. iv, http://www.hks.
      harvard.edu/pepg/PDF/Impacts_of_School_Vouchers_FINAL.pdf (accessed 24
      November 2014). It should be noted that the big effect seen among African Americans
      was not replicated among the Hispanics who were also part of the study. The paper
      offers various thoughts on this. One idea is that Hispanic parents get their children into
      college more frequently than African-American parents so the Hispanic parents in this
      study were less powerfully motivated to use the chance to send their children to private
      schools, which might increase their children's chances. Separately, private schools made
      the biggest difference with regard to getting into selective colleges – an indication of
      reaching a higher academic standard. The proportion of African Americans going into
      the selective colleges more than doubled when they were offered private schools. See
      also Alan B. Krueger and Pei Zhu, 'Another Look at the New York City School Voucher
      Experiment', *American Behavioral Scientist* 47:5 (2004), 658–98, which argues that the
      original study understated the effects.

59   I have omitted Japan because the exceptional circumstances there make the data
      misleading as an indicator of the quality of private education. The rated of functional
      illiteracy at the government schools is lower, at 12.3 per cent, than at the private schools
      (16.7 per cent). There are several reasons for this. The vast majority of all the students
      covered by the study, including most of those at private schools, were in state schools
      the year before. The PISA study takes in children who in Japan have just competed to
      get one of the limited places in the government secondary schools. The most able get
      places. Some of those who do not succeed – obviously the less able ones – go to private
      schools, presumably in order to be able to continue their education. So the sample of
      those at private schools is skewed towards the less able. Moreover the private schools
      have not at this stage had the children for long enough to make any difference. It should
      be added that there are some elite private schools where those who are able do go. I am

grateful to Miyako Ikeda at the OECD for explaining these circumstances to me. Any misunderstanding is my fault. If the figures from Japan had been included, the average figure for government schools would have been 17.8 per cent and that for private schools 6.5 per cent.

60 Taken from a table kindly extracted from PISA 2009 by Miyako Ikeda and emailed to the author.

61 Andrew J. Coulson, 'Comparing Public, Private, and Market Schools: The International Evidence', *Journal of School Choice* 3:1 (2009), 31–54.

62 Mark J. Perry, 'Why do public school teachers send their own children to private schools at a rate 2x the national average?', Carpe Diem blog, 9 October 2013, quoting Professor Walter E. Williams of George Mason University, http://www.aei.org/publication/why-do-public-school-teachers-send-their-own-children-to-private-schools-at-a-rate-2x-the-national-average (accessed 24 November 2014).

63 Cited in the education chapter of James Bartholomew, *The Welfare State We're In*, rev. ed. (London: Biteback, 2014). One of the papers concerned was titled 'The Relative Effectiveness of Private and Public Schools: Evidence from Two Developing Countries' (1989). The countries in question were Colombia and Tanzania.

64 Ibid.

65 Frédéric Bastiat, 'Freedom', in *The Collected Works of Frédéric Bastiat, vol. 1: The Man and the Statesman – The Correspondence and Articles on Politics*, tr. Jane and Michel Willems (Indianapolis: Liberty Fund, 2011), http://oll.libertyfund.org/titles/2393#Bastiat_1573-01_2277 (accessed 24 November 2014).

66 Funding was made available for private schools as well as government ones to enable different religious denominations to have their own schools ('Overview of the Dutch Secondary Education System', Fulbright Center). But over time, regulation of the schools increased (Andrew Coulson, 'On the Way to School: Why and How to Make a Market in Education', in Greg Forster and C. Bradley Thompson (eds), *Freedom and School Choice in American Education* (New York: Palgrave Macmillan, 2011).) The schools' control over the use of their buildings was removed. The government specified how decision-making powers were to be allocated between management, teachers and parents. A common curriculum was introduced and then extended. Schools were required to teach certain combinations of subjects. Particular tests were specified and even the way in which teaching was done. This erosion of independence discouraged the creation of new independent schools and barriers were erected to new schools such as minimum sizes. As the creation of new schools dwindled, the element of competition was eroded, too.

67 Coulson, 'On the Way to School'.

68 'Fast Facts on Private School Choice', Friedman Foundation for Educational Choice, June 2014, http://www.edchoice.org/Newsroom/Fast-Facts-on-Private-School-Choice.pdf (accessed 24 November 2014).

69 Op. cit.

CHAPTER 5: 'DO I HAVE "STUPID" TATTOOED ON MY FOREHEAD?'

1   He was appointed Prime Minister in March 2014.

2   The spelling and French in some of these comments was variable, which makes exact
      translation difficult. These are the original words in French: '*repaire de malfrats*'; '*ça
      ressemblait un peu à un camp de concentration (un ancien d'AFN)*' and '*cité tres grande avec
      10 batiments, plusieurs dealeurs associé avec les flaments et les iris, tous armée*'.

3   OECD, *Economic Policy Reforms 2011: Going for Growth* (Paris: OECD Publishing, 2011),
      Table 4.4.

4   Netherlands 32 per cent; Austria 23 per cent; Czech Republic, UK 20 per cent; Denmark
      19 per cent; France, Sweden 17 per cent; Finland 16 per cent; Ireland 8 per cent; Belgium
      7 per cent; Slovenia 6 per cent; Germany 5 per cent; Estonia, Greece, Hungary, Italy,
      Latvia, Slovakia <5 per cent (Kristian Niemietz, 'Abundance of Land, Shortage of
      Housing', Institute of Economic Affairs Discussion Paper No. 38, April 2012, http://
      www.iea.org.uk/sites/default/files/publications/files/Abundance%20of%20Land%20
      Shortage%20of%20Housing.pdf (accessed 25 November 2014).)

5   Rebecca Tunstall et al., 'The Links between Housing and Poverty: An Evidence Review',
      Joseph Rowntree Foundation, April 2013, http://www.jrf.org.uk/sites/files/jrf/poverty-
      housing-options-full.pdf (accessed 25 November 2014).

6   *The Economist*, 27 April 2013.

7   Stuart Adam, Mike Brewer and Andrew Shephard, 'Financial Work Incentives in Britain:
      Comparisons over Time and between Family Types',WP06/20, Institute of Fiscal Studies,
      October 2006, Table 2.1, http://www.ifs.org.uk/wps/wp0620.pdf (accessed 25 November
      2014).

8   Rebecca Tunstall, 'How housing traps people in unemployment', Business blog, *New
      Statesman*, 8 March 2013, http://www.newstatesman.com/business/2013/03/how-housing-
      traps-people-unemployment (accessed 25 November 2014). Tunstall is professor of
      housing policy at the University of York.

9   Tunstall et al., 'The Links between Housing and Poverty', p. 51.

10   In the long term, it depends whether the better incentive to work for those already
      getting the benefit has a bigger effect on unemployment levels than the reduced incentive
      to work for those who would become newly entitled to the benefit.

11   There is probably some damage in continental countries. It could come from reducing
      the mobility of those with favoured low rents who are reluctant to move to another part
      of the town or country to take up a better job (or any job).

12   John Hills, 'Ends and Means: The Future Roles of Social Housing in England', ESRC
      Research Centre for Analysis of Social Exclusion, CASEreport 34, February 2007,
      pp. 101, 102, http://sticerd.lse.ac.uk/dps/case/cr/CASEreport34.pdf (accessed 25
      November 2014). Note also Hills's observation: 'The proportion of social tenant

householders in paid employment fell from 47 per cent to 32 per cent between 1981 and 2006' (p. 2).

13 The waiting lists can be very long. In Stockholm they have been as long as eight years ('Sweden's housing queues "getting worse"', *The Local* (Sweden), 11 March 2013, http://www.thelocal.se/20130311/46672 (accessed 25 November 2014).)

14 To those of us in Britain and America who have seen the damage done by rents adjusted for income, the Swedish example might seem like a refreshing example of how this damage might be avoided. But there is some indication that the European Union does not see things this way and has clashed with Sweden because it wants social housing only to be made available for the poor. This is opposed to the Swedish idea that social housing should be available for everybody. ('Worrying development concerning social housing at EU level', AK Europa website, 8 November 2012, http://www.akeuropa.eu/en/worrying-development-concerning-social-housing-at-eu-level.html?cmp_id=7&news_id=1432&vID=9 (accessed 25 November 2014).)

Similarly in Denmark, 'the majority of vacant units are assigned by the respective housing associations on the basis of time on the waiting list and household size. There are no restrictions on who may join a waiting list, apart from a minimum age of 15 years ... Municipalities have the right to assign tenants to at least 25 per cent of vacant housing-association units. They (and the housing associations) do not necessarily do so on the basis of need. Many local authorities give priority on troubled estates to people working in the local area in order to improve their social composition by introducing residents with jobs' (Christine Whitehead and Kathleen Scanlon, *Social Housing in Europe* (London: London School of Economics and Political Science, 2007), available at http://vbn.aau.dk/files/13671493/SocialHousingInEurope.pdf (accessed 25 November 2014).)

15 Howard Husock, 'The Myths of *The Pruitt-Igoe Myth*', *City Journal*, 17 February 2012, http://www.city-journal.org/2012/bc0217hh.html (accessed 25 November 2014).

16 Whitehead and Scanlon, *Social Housing in Europe*, p. 65.

17 Ibid. Table 4 on page 154 shows that there is an over-representation of single parent households in Swedish public housing but this is on a relatively minor scale compared to, say, Britain. It shows 9.4 per cent of tenants are single-parent households compared to 5.5 per cent for all households combined. 12 per cent of the tenants are couples with children. So in Sweden, there are more couples with children in social housing than lone parents. In Britain, it is very much the other way round.

18 Associated Press, 'In Fla. housing project, rape just another crime', NBC News online, 11 July 2007, http://www.nbcnews.com/id/19698132/ns/us_news-crime_and_courts/t/fla-housing-project-rape-just-another-crime/#.UY07h7Vtggs (accessed 25 November 2014).

19 Ibid.

20 Ibid.

21 'Valls: "C'est une guerre contre la barbarie"', *Journal du dimanche*, 17 March 2013, http://

www.lejdd.fr/Politique/Actualite/Manuel-Valls-C-est-une-guerre-contre-la-barbarie-interview-596711 (accessed 25 November 2014).

22   British Crime Survey 2008/09, cited in 'Burglary risk: how much crime is there?', The Crime Prevention Website, http://thecrimepreventionwebsite.com/home-security-assessment/470/burglary-risk/ (accessed 25 November 2014).

23   Amelia Hill, 'Council estate decline spawns new underclass', The Observer, 30 November 2003, http://www.guardian.co.uk/society/2003/nov/30/housing.uknews (accessed 25 November 2014).

24   Howard Husock, 'Public housing developments bring Hope but history says projects call for caution', Manhattan Institute for Policy Research website, 15 February 2004, http://www.manhattan-institute.org/html/miarticle.htm?id=4374#.VHRstNKsX9U (accessed 25 November 2014).

25   Hills, 'Ends and Means', p. 4.

26   Barbara Sard and Will Fischer, 'Preserving Safe, High Quality Public Housing Should Be a Priority of Federal Housing Policy', Center on Budget and Policy Priorities, 8 October 2008, http://www.cbpp.org/files/9-18-08hous.pdf (accessed 25 November 2014).

27   'Demolished housing estates', UK Housing Wiki, http://ukhousing.wikia.com/wiki/Category:Demolished_housing_estates (accessed 25 November 2014).

28   Aline Leclerc and Elodie Ratsimbazafy, 'La démolition d'une nouvelle barre s'annonce à la cité des 4000', La Courneuve: urbains sensibles blog, Le Monde, 22 May 2012, http://lacourneuve.blog.lemonde.fr/2012/05/22/la-demolition-dune-nouvelle-barre-sannonce-a-la-cite-des-4000. See also 'Cité des 4000', Wikipédia (French), http://fr.wikipedia.org/wiki/Cité_des_4000 (both accessed 25 November 2014).

29   Aline Leclerc and Elodie Ratsimbazafy, 'Des faits divers et des politiques', La Courneuve: urbains sensibles blog, Le Monde, 20 June 2010, http://lacourneuve.blog.lemonde.fr/2010/06/20/des-faits-divers-et-des-politiques (accessed 25 November 2014).

30   See for example 'Implosion Capendeguy Beziers', http://www.youtube.com/watch?v=rydT54QYX50 (accessed 25 November 2014).

31   'La barre d'immeuble explosée en 8 secondes', LaDepeche.fr, http://www.ladepeche.fr/article/2008/01/28/429638-la-barre-d-immeuble-explosee-en-8-secondes.html (accessed 25 November 2014).

32   Hugh Schofield, 'Interview sealed minister's fate', BBC News online, 25 February 2005, http://news.bbc.co.uk/1/hi/world/europe/4299003.stm; 'Les 600m2 du couple Gaymard', Le Parisien, 16 February 2005, http://www.leparisien.fr/politique/les-600-m-2-du-couple-gaymard-16-02-2005-2005707104.php (both accessed 25 November 2014).

33   Schofield, 'Interview sealed minister's fate'.

34   Ibid.

35   'Comment expliquer qu'on trouve davantage de ménages aisés dans le
     parc locatif public que dans le parc locative privé', interview with Nicolas
     Lecaussin, *Atlantico*, 27 January 2014, http://www.atlantico.fr/decryptage/
     comment-expliquer-qu-on-trouve-davantage-menages-aises-dans-parc-locatif-public-que-
     dans-parc-locatif-prive-charles-beigbeder-964545.html (accessed 25 November 2014). It
     is said that the assertion was made by Charles Beigbeder, a candidate for mayor of Paris,
     citing Vincent Benard. Lecaussin makes the point that affluent families get both social
     housing (HLM) and housing under the auspices of various institutions such as the state
     railway – but still paid for by the public.

36   'Department of Housing: allegations of corrupt conduct in allocation of public
     housing (Operation Greenway)', Independent Commission against Corruption (New
     South Wales) website, http://www.icac.nsw.gov.au/investigations/past-investigations/
     investigationdetail/19 (accessed 25 November 2014).

37   See Les Kennedy, 'Housing bribes official faces jail', *Sydney Morning Herald*, 13
     September 2007, http://www.smh.com.au/news/national/housing-bribes-official-faces-
     jail/2007/09/12/1189276810256.html and 'Recommendations for prosecutions and
     updates', Independent Commission against Corruption (New South Wales) website,
     http://www.icac.nsw.gov.au/investigations/past-investigations/article/3119 for more details
     of the case (both accessed 25 November 2014). Norris was sentenced in 2011 but only
     given concurrent suspended sentences for his crimes.

38   Figure for 2014; see http://parliamentarystandards.org.uk/payandpensions/Pages/
     default.aspx. Average earnings were £27,017 in 2013; see http://www.ons.gov.uk/ons/
     publications/re-reference-tables.html?edition=tcm%3A77-332352 (both accessed 25
     November 2014).

39   *Daily Mail*, 7 February 2012.

40   *Sunday Telegraph*, 1 January 2012.

41   Ibid.

42   According to a 'Whitehall analysis' that was 'leaked to the *Daily Mail*'.

43   Ibid.

44   Howard Husock, 'Puffing the projects', *New York Post*, 8 June 2009, http://nypost.
     com/2009/06/08/puffing-the-projects (accessed 25 November 2014).

45   Alex Morton, *Ending Expensive Social Tenancies: Fairness, Higher Growth and More
     Homes* (London: Policy Exchange, 2012), http://www.policyexchange.org.uk/images/
     publications/ending%20expensive%20social%20tenancies.pdf (accessed 25 November
     2014).

46   Alice Pittini, 'Housing Affordability in the EU: Current Situation and Recent Trends',
     CECODHAS European Social Housing Observatory Research Briefing 5:1 (2012), available
     at http://www.iut.nu/Literature/2012/CECODHAS_HousingAffordability2012.pdf
     (accessed 25 November 2014).

47 'Policy Basics: Introduction to Public Housing', Center on Budget and Policy Priorities website, http://www.cbpp.org/cms/index.cfm?fa=view&id=2528 (accessed 25 November 2014).

48 Peter King, *Choice and the End of Social Housing* (London: Institute of Economic Affairs, 2006), http://www.iea.org.uk/sites/default/files/publications/files/upldbook327pdf.pdf (accessed 25 November 2014).

49 Ibid.

50 Douglas Rice, 'Sequestration could deny rental assistance to 140,000 low-income families', Center on Budget and Policy Priorities website, 2 April 2013, http://www.cbpp.org/cms/?fa=view&id=3945. See also 'Budget Authority by Program', Department of Housing and Urban Development, http://portal.hud.gov/hudportal/documents/huddoc?id=2012budgetauthbyprog.pdf, p. 83 (both accessed 25 November 2014).

51 'Budget Authority by Program'.

52 Rice, 'Sequestration could deny rental assistance to 140,000 low-income families'.

53 'Worrying development concerning social housing at EU level'. See also Florence Martin, 'Sweden: social housing under "businesslike principle"', in *EU Rethinks Role of Social Housing*, *Europolitics* supplement, 16 December 2011, p. 23 for further insights into the Swedish system and how the European Union has put pressure on it to change.

54 For 1979, the peak year, there were 5,187,000 dwellings rented from local authorities and 353,000 rented from 'private registered providers' (mostly housing associations), giving a combined total of 5,540,000. This represented 31 per cent of the total 17,882,000 dwellings in England. By 2012, the number rented from local authorities had fallen to 1,689,000 while the number rented from private registered providers had increased to 2,304,000, giving a combined total of 3,993,000. This represented 17 per cent of the total 23,111,000 dwellings in England. Data taken from 'Live tables on dwelling stock (including vacants)', Gov.uk, Table 104, https://www.gov.uk/government/statistical-data-sets/live-tables-on-dwelling-stock-including-vacants (accessed 25 November 2014).

55 'Facts about public housing', CLPHA website, http://www.clpha.org/facts_about_public_housing#_edn3 (accessed 25 November 2014). The figures given here are a fall from 1,329,000 to 1,191,110. This is slightly different from the figures and source quoted earlier in the chapter but the proportionate change is similar.

56 'Housing Assistance in Australia 2011', Australian Institute of Health and Welfare, June 2011, http://www.aihw.gov.au/WorkArea/DownloadAsset.aspx?id=10737419156 (accessed 25 November 2014). See 'Australia: housing tenure', .id website, http://profile.id.com.au/australia/tenure (accessed 25 November 2014), which shows a modest decline in the proportion of Australian social housing in 'greater capital cities' between 2006 and 2011.

57 Kathleen Scanlon and Christine Whitehead, *International Trends in Housing Tenure and Mortgage Finance* (London: London School of Economics and Political Science), Table 4, available at http://www.iut.nu/Literature/2004/InternTrends_Whitehead_etal_2004.pdf (accessed 25 November 2014). A draft paper by Björn Egner, 'Housing Policy in

Germany, 1945–2010: Continuity and Change', http://www.academia.edu/2963591/
Housing_Policy_in_Germany_1945-2010_Continuity_and_Change (accessed
25 November 2014), shows the dramatic decline in the volume of social housing
constructed, from 450,000 a year at the peak in the 1950s to less than 50,000 a year in
the late 1990s. The author says 'do not quote' so I apologise to him for doing so. If I had
unlimited time and resources, I would have tried to find another source.

58   Housing Act 1980. For a longer perspective see Sarah Heath, 'The Historical Context of
Rent Control in the Private Rented Sector', House of Commons Library Standard Note
SN/SP/6747, October 2013, www.parliament.uk/briefing-papers/sn06747.pdf (accessed
25 November 2014).

59   'Dwelling Stock by Tenure', www.communities.gov.uk/documents/housing/xls/table-
104.xls (accessed 25 November 2014). Immediately after rent controls were lifted and
landlords were permitted to charge market rents and had the secure ability to evict
tenants at the end of tenancies, the supply radically increased. The numbers rose to 2,086
in 1999, 3,182 in 2007 and 4,286 in 2012.

60   Steven A. Holmes, 'Fannie Mae eases credit to aid mortgage lending', *New York Times*, 30
September 1999, http://www.nytimes.com/1999/09/30/business/fannie-mae-eases-credit-
to-aid-mortgage-lending.html (accessed 25 November 2014).

61   As at 2013; see 'Households and Housing', Department of Statistics Singapore, http://
www.singstat.gov.sg/statistics/latest_data.html#20 (accessed 25 November 2014).

62   Howard Husock, 'Reinventing public housing', *Washington Times*, 8 November 2010,
http://www.washingtontimes.com/news/2010/nov/8/reinventing-public-housing;
Howard Husock, 'Reinventing public housing: is the Atlanta model right for your city?',
Cities on a Hill, 7 December 2009, available at http://www.manhattan-institute.org/
html/miarticle.htm?id=5702#.UYVA4bVtggs (both accessed 25 November 2014).

63   Author interview with Stanislawa Golinowska, November 2011.

64   Liu Shengjun, 'Showdown stage for housing controls', CaixinOnline, 13 June 2012,
p. 3, http://english.caixin.com/2012-06-13/100400466.html (accessed 25 November 2014).
See also Stuart Jackson, 'The door is not shut to those looking to develop in the Middle
Kingdom', *The Times*, 25 August 2011: 'The local government now requires that we and
other developers apply for consent to sell completed residential units at a pre-determined
price.'

65   Liu, 'Showdown stage for housing controls'.

66   Matthew Yglesias, *The Rent Is Too Damn High: What to Do about It, and Why It Matters
More than You Think* (New York: Simon and Schuster, 2012).

67   Percentage weightings in the British Retail Price Index. The raw figures can be found by
going to 'Consumer Price Indices – Series', Office for National Statistics website, http://
www.ons.gov.uk/ons/datasets-and-tables/data-selector.html?table-id=2.5&dataset=mm23
(accessed 25 November 2014), and selecting the category of food.

68 'Reflections', p. 66, http://www.bls.gov/opub/uscs/reflections.pdf (accessed 25 November 2014), citing the US Bureau of Labor Statistics Consumer Expenditure Survey. See also Chart 42, p. 69.

69 Food as a percentage of household expenditure was 15 per cent and 16 per cent for the lowest deciles of income in 2010 in the UK compared to an average of 11 per cent for the overall population and only 8 per cent for the highest-earning decile. So food expenditure is a more significant item for the least well off. See Giles Horsfield (ed.), 'Family Spending: A Report on the 2010 Living Costs and Food Survey', Office for National Statistics, 2011, Table 3.3, http://www.ons.gov.uk/ons/rel/family-spending/family-spending/family-spending-2011-edition/family-spending-2011-pdf.pdf (accessed 25 November 2014).

70 'Communications Market Report', Ofcom, July 2012, p. 350, http://stakeholders.ofcom.org.uk/binaries/research/cmr/cmr12/CMR_UK_2012.pdf (accessed 25 November 2014).

71 Percentage weightings in the British Retail Price Index. The raw figures can be found by going to 'Consumer Price Indices – Series', Office for National Statistics website, http://www.ons.gov.uk/ons/datasets-and-tables/data-selector.html?table-id=2.5&dataset=mm23 (accessed 25 November 2014), and selecting the category of housing (CZHF).

72 The raw figures can be found by going to http://www.ons.gov.uk/ons/datasets-and-tables/data-selector.html?table-id=2.5&dataset=mm23 (accessed 26 November 2014) and selecting the categories Food and Housing.

73 Oliver Marc Hartwich, 'The cult of Australian property', Centre for Independent Studies website, 3 February 2011, http://www.cis.org.au/media-information/opinion-pieces/article/2343-the-cult-of-australian-property (accessed 26 November 2014).

74 Ibid.

75 World Bank online data for 2011, http://data.worldbank.org/indicator/EN.POP.DNST (accessed 26 November 2014).

76 'International House Price Database', Federal Reserve Bank of Dallas website, http://www.dallasfed.org/institute/houseprice/index.cfm (accessed 26 November 2014). Click on 'First quarter 2014' to download data and then click RHPI (Real House Price Index) tab. The *Economist* interactive guide to the world's housing markets shows a much more modest rise in the price of UK housing of only 100 per cent in real terms over an almost identical timescale. There are of course many different ways to calculate average house prices. One could take a single dwelling and see how it changes in value. Or one could take an average of prices and see how they change. The latter could be misleading because the average dwelling might become bigger or smaller over the period in question. I have found the Dallas index more credible. The *Economist* index shows real house prices actually lower in 1997 than in 1975. Having lived through that time and owned housing, this is frankly hard to believe. A given dwelling in any part of London, certainly, rose in real terms. In any case, for those who prefer the *Economist* version, the rise is still very dramatic and a marked contrast to what happened in Germany. *The Economist* agrees that German prices fell in real terms. The *Economist* data is here: http://www.economist.

com/blogs/dailychart/2011/11/global-house-prices (accessed 26 November 2014). *The Economist* says that prices in Switzerland rose 35.5 per cent in real terms. See also Halifax House Price Index at http://www.lloydsbankinggroup.com/media1/economic_insight/halifax_house_price_index_page.asp (accessed 26 November 2014) and click on 'Historical house price data'.

77   'International House Price Database'.

78   'House prices versus earning', *Monevator*, 15 March 2012, using figures from the Halifax and from national average full-time earnings for men, http://monevator.com/house-price-to-earnings-ratio-2012 (accessed 26 November 2014).

79   Table A32: Household Expenditure by Tenure, 2011, in 'Family Spending, 2012 Edition', Office for National Statistics website, 4 December 2012, http://www.ons.gov.uk/ons/publications/re-reference-tables.html?newquery=*&newoffset=50&pageSize=25&edition=tcm%3A77-267317 (accessed 26 November 2014).

80   Different measures of similar things can come up with some markedly different figures. Earlier in the chapter there is reference to housing accounting for over a quarter of the Retail Price Index. But in another table produced by the Office for National Statistics, housing, fuel and power together amount to 22 per cent of the expenditure of the lowest decile in Britain in 2011 and 8 per cent for the highest. The figures are lower than the weighting in the RPI but the way that the poor have to spend much more of their income on housing is dramatically made. See ONS Family Spending 2012 edition release, Appendix A, Table A8, http://www.ons.gov.uk/ons/rel/family-spending/family-spending/family-spending-2012-edition/family-spending---list-of-tables-appendix-a--2012-edition.html#tab-List-of-tables--Appendix-A (accessed 26 November 2014).

81   Unfortunately I have not got the directly comparable figure for Germany. *The Economist* uses OECD and other figures to make a useful chart of house prices measured in different ways. Unfortunately the measure of housing price compared to earnings is re-based to a supposed long-term average of 100. The raw figures, which would be more useful, are not shown. The fact that the OECD thinks that there is a long-term average to which such figures, implicitly, are likely to return, shows how it has misunderstood what has been happening in different housing markets most strongly affected by planning controls (http://www.economist.com/blogs/dailychart/2011/11/global-house-prices (accessed 26 November 2014).)

82   Figures from Prof. Dr Tobias Just, managing director of the International Real Estate Business School at the University of Regensburg, in an email to the author. The figures are for average apartment prices in euros per square metre compared to 'local purchasing power parity'. For Germany overall, the cost fell from 0.159 to 0.140. Prof. Just included the year-by-year series for Germany overall and some of the major cities. It is fair to say that the picture for the cities is more varied. In four, the cost went up and in three it went down. It seems likely that the cost of apartments in the cities rose relative to those elsewhere. But even in Berlin, which saw the biggest uplift following the re-unification of Germany and the move of the government there from Bonn, the uplift was not huge (from 0.165 to 0.19). I am grateful to Oliver Hartwich for putting me in touch with Prof. Just.

83   'House price to income ratio, Germany compared to Continent', Global Property
     Guide, http://www.globalpropertyguide.com/Europe/germany/price-gdp-per-cap
     (accessed 26 November 2014).

84   'Cost of living in Germany', InterNations website, http://www.internations.org/
     germany-expats/guide/16008-economy-finance/cost-of-living-in-germany-15974 (accessed
     26 November 2014).

85   Cologne Institute for Economic Research, cited in Hartwich, 'The cult of Australian
     property'.

86   Hartwich, 'The cult of Australian property'.

87   Alan W. Evans and Oliver Marc Hartwich, *Unaffordable Housing: Fables and Myths*
     (London: Policy Exchange, 2005), p. 24, citing 'European Union, Housing Statistics in
     the EU 2002', http://www.policyexchange.org.uk/images/publications/unaffordable%20
     housing%20-%20jun%2005.pdf (accessed 26 November 2014).

88   From 98.8 square metres to 96.8 (Becky Barrow, 'The big squeeze: Average British home
     has shrunk by two square metres in just a decade forcing families to split bedrooms
     and even store their shopping in their car', Mail Online, 7 January 2014, http://www.
     dailymail.co.uk/news/article-2535136/Average-British-family-home-size-shrinks-two-
     square-metres-decade-increasing-numbers-forced-live-flats.html (accessed 26 November
     2014).)

89   Sources: For house prices, US Census Bureau and US Department of Housing and
     Urban Development, as quoted in US Census Bureau, *Statistical Abstract of the United
     States 2012*, Table 975, http://www.census.gov/compendia/statab (accessed 26 November
     2014), and the equivalent table in various previous years. For income, US Census Bureau
     Survey of Median Household Income, Table H-6.

90   Anne Baxendale, 'Fitting the bill', Shelter policy blog, 30 April 2013, http://blog.shelter.
     org.uk/2013/04/fitting-the-bill (accessed 26 November 2014). Shelter is a housing charity
     in Britain.

91   *Property Market Report 2011*, Valuation Office Agency, 2011, http://www.voa.gov.uk/dvs/_
     downloads/pmr_2011.pdf (accessed 26 November 2014). In the north-west, the value of
     unequipped dairy land in Cheshire was £14,820 and of land for residential development
     in Liverpool £1.5m. In both cases, I have taken the more valuable kind of agricultural
     land in the area concerned.

92   Email to author from Patrick Law of Barratt plc, 14 July 2014.

93   Government data on 'average valuations of residential building land with outline
     planning permission: weighted average valuation per hectare', in England, taken from
     'Live tables on dwelling stock (including vacants)', Gov.uk., Table 104.

94   In London, the price rose from £1.9m/ha to £6.5m/ha in the same period, having peaked
     at £10.5m in 2008.

95   Kerry McQueeney, 'Revealed: How the poor, middle class and rich spend their money in America … and the 1% aren't so different after all', *Daily Mail*, 2 August 2012 (accessed 17 December 2014), citing the Consumer Expenditure Survey. http://www.dailymail. co.uk/news/article-2182646/Spending-America-How-poor-middle-class-rich-divided-incomes.html and see for more detail http://www.bls.gov/cex/22012/midyear/income. pdf.

96   OECD, *Economic Policy Reforms 2011: Going for Growth*, Table 4.1.

97   Niemietz, 'Abundance of Land, Shortage of Housing'.

98   Randall O'Toole, *American Nightmare: How Government Undermines the Dream of Homeownership* (Washington, DC: Cato Institute, 2012), Table 9.1.

99   Ibid., p. 148.

100 O'Toole, *American Nightmare*, p. 149. California: Environmental Quality Act 1969, housing unaffordable by 1979. Oregon: legislation 1973, housing unaffordable by 1979. King County, WA: urban growth boundary in 1985, housing unaffordable by 1989.

101 Price of second-hand dwellings by INSEE using first-quarter figures: http://www. bdm.insee.fr/bdm2/affichageSeries.action?idbank=000817678&bouton=OK&code Groupe=23. Average annual full-time wages from INSEE: http://www.bdm.insee.fr/ bdm2/affichageSeries.action?idbank=001665118&codeGroupe=1475 (both accessed 26 November 2014).

102 Cost of construction index using first-quarter figures from INSEE: http://www.insee.fr/ en/bases-de-donnees/bsweb/serie.asp?idbank=000008630 (accessed 26 November 2014).

103 I was alerted to the startling contrast between the rise in construction costs and the rise in the cost of land with permission to build by Vincent Bénard, 'Libres! Foncier réglementé, familles mal logées', *Contrepoints*, 1 October 2012, http://www.contrepoints. org/2012/10/01/98977-libres-foncier-reglemente-familles-mal-logees (accessed 26 November 2014). I have since researched all the figures except one independently and from official sources. They are slightly different from those cited by Bénard but not significantly so. However, the figure that was most difficult to confirm was the increase in the price of land with permission to build over that period. I spent some hours on this and so did a researcher who speaks French better than me but without complete success. Bénard writes that such land rose seven times in value. I have no reason to doubt it but neither have I been able to confirm it. However, I found another source which refers to a 3.6-times increase in real terms over the period 1997–2011: 'Augmentation du prix des terrains à bâtir', SeLoger website, http://financer.seloger.com/160465/225429/ cnt.htm (accessed 26 November 2014). That figure, with inflation added back in, would mean a rise of 4.4 times given that the general price level rose from 82 to 100 according to OECD statistics. But the official sources show that land with permission to build rose 7.6 per cent between 2010 and 2011 so I have taken that off, which brings the increase to 2010 to 4.06 times. I have then quoted this as a percentage rise of 306 per cent – or 300 per cent to use a round number. This is used as a minimum that is as reliable as possible in the circumstances. The actual figure may be a great deal bigger, as Bénard asserts. We

do have official figures from 2007 which show a rise from €51 to €64 per square metre between 2007 and 2011. That rise of 25 per cent may look modest at first glance but it is actually remarkably strong considering that this was a period of worldwide financial crisis and rising unemployment in France. Here are links to some of the statistics available: http://www.statistiques.developpement-durable.gouv.fr/donnees-ligne/r/enquete-prix-terrains-batir-eptb.html; http://www.statistiques.developpement-durable.gouv.fr/fileadmin/documents/Produits_editoriaux/Publications/Chiffres_et_statistiques/2013/chiffres-stats473-eptb2012-decembre2013-v2.pdf (both accessed 26 November 2014).

CHAPTER 6: 'IN OUR LIBERAL SOCIETY...'

1   John Stuart Mill, *On Liberty* (London: Penguin, [1859] 1985), p. 176.

2   Ekaterina Hertog, '"The Worst Abuse against a Child Is the Absence of a Parent": How Japanese Unwed Mothers Evaluate Their Decision to Have a Child outside Wedlock', *Japan Forum* 20:2 (2008), 193–217.

3   OECD Family Database, 'Share of Births outside Marriage and Teenage Births', http://www.oecd.org/social/family/SF2_4_Births_outside_marriage_and_teenage_births_Jan2013.pdf (accessed 26 November 2014).

4   At the time of writing he is an associate professor at the Research Institute of Industrial Economics in Stockholm and at the University of Lund.

5   OECD, *Doing Better for Families* (Paris: OECD Publications, 2011), p. 27.

6   Andrea Cianini, interview at the University of Rome.

7   'Birth summary tables, England and Wales, 2012', Office for National Statistics website, http://www.ons.gov.uk/ons/publications/re-reference-tables.html?edition=tcm%3A77-314475 (accessed 26 November 2014).

8   Op. cit.

9   US Census Bureau, *Statistical Abstract of the United States 2012*, Table 1335, http://www.census.gov/compendia/statab/2012/tables/12s1335.pdf (accessed 26 November 2014). I have combined this with Eurostat figures which do not go so far back but which go further forward, to 2012. ('Live births outside marriage', Eurostat, http://epp.eurostat.ec.europa.eu/tgm/table.do?tab=table&plugin=1&language=en&pcode=tps00018 (accessed 26 November 2014).)

10   These figures from Eurostat are markedly and surprisingly lower than that supplied by the US Census Bureau (*Statistical Abstract of the United States 2012*, Table 1336, http://www.census.gov/compendia/statab/2012/tables/12s1336.pdf (accessed 26 November 2014).) The link to the Eurostat figures is here: http://ec.europa.eu/eurostat/tgm/table.do?tab=table&init=1&plugin=1&pcode=tps00012&language=en (accessed 17 December 2014). I guess they have different ways of measurement but they tell the same story of a rally in the rate of marriage in Sweden.

11 Gundi Knies, 'Life Satisfaction and Material Well-being of Children in the UK', Institute for Social and Economic Research Working Paper No. 2012-15, July 2012, https://www.iser.essex.ac.uk/publications/working-papers/iser/2012-15.pdf (accessed 26 November 2014).

12 Ibid.

13 OECD, *Doing Better for Families*, p. 28.

14 Paul R. Amato, 'The Impact of Family Formation Change on the Cognitive, Social, and Emotional Well-being of the Next Generation', *Marriage and Child Wellbeing* 15:2 (2005), 75–96. It would appear that Amato is referring to studies which generally did not control for socio-economic status. If so, it is a pity. However in my book *The Welfare State We're In*, rev. ed. (London: Biteback 2014), the chapter on parenting refers to numerous studies which did control for socio-economic status and still found that lone parenting and divorce are associated with an increased incidence of the same sort of disadvantages. It can also be argued that lone parenting generally results in the child living in a poorer household so, to this extent, the effect of being poorer should be included as an effect of lone parenting.

15 Quoted in Adam Sage, '"God's nutcase" Frigide Barjot confronts Hollande on same-sex marriage', *The Times*, 27 December 2012.

16 Judith S. Wallerstein and Joan B. Kelly, *Surviving the Breakup: How Children and Parents Cope with Divorce* (New York: Basic, 1996 reprint), p. 73.

17 Ibid. p. 73.

18 Penelope Leach, *Family Breakdown: Helping Children Hang On to Both Their Parents* (London: Unbound, 2014). Quotation taken from the serialisation in the *Daily Mail*, 19 June 2014, http://www.dailymail.co.uk/femail/article-2661981/The-toxic-truth-DIVORCE-parents-confront-Dont-kid-Separation-harms-children-And-devastating-new-series-Penelope-Leach-explains-why.html (accessed 26 November 2014).

19 Amato, 'The Impact of Family Formation Change on the Cognitive, Social, and Emotional Well-being of the Next Generation', p. 79.

20 Asta Leppä, 'The mysteries of divorce, Finnish style', *Helsingin Sanomat*, 8 February 2013.

21 Email to the author. 21 per cent marry and stay married. 14 per cent remain living together unmarried. One drawback of this study is that it is based on official figures which count parents who jointly register the birth of a child but who live at separate addresses as 'cohabiting'. This may obviously not be cohabiting. There seems to be a lack of authoritative and reliable research on this subject.

22 B. Rodgers and J. Prior, *Divorce and Separation: The Outcomes for Children* (York: Joseph Rowntree Foundation, 1998), p. 25, cited in Heather Juby and David F. Farrington, 'Disentangling the Link between Disrupted Families and Delinquency', *British Journal of Criminology* 41 (2001), 22–40, available at http://troublesofyouth.pbworks.com/f/Ruby+and+Farrington.pdf (accessed 26 November 2014).

23   I. Kolvin et al., 'Social and Parenting Factors Affecting Criminal Offence Rates: Findings
      from the Newcastle Thousand Family Study (1947–80)', *British Journal of Psychiatry* 152
      (1988), 80–90, cited in Juby and Farrington, 'Disentangling the Link between Disrupted
      Families and Delinquency'.

24   Juby and Farrington, 'Disentangling the Link between Disrupted Families and
      Delinquency'. One should add that in this study the boys who stayed with their mothers
      and where there was no step-father did as well as intact families.

25   March 2012. Quoted in, 'Were a quarter of prisoners in care as children?', Fullfact.org,
      22nd October 2012, https://fullfact.org/factchecks/were_quarter_prisoners_in_care_as_
      children-28547 (accessed 26 November 2014).

26   Linda J. Waite and Maggie Gallagher, *The Case for Marriage: Why Married People
      Are Happier, Healthier, and Better Off Financially* (New York: Doubleday, 2000), p.
      77, cited in Kelly Musick and Larry Bumpass, 'Re-examining the Case for Marriage:
      Union Formation and Changes in Well-being', *Journal of Marriage and Family* 72:1
      (2012), 1–18.

27   John Cairney et al., cited in the introduction to 'Stress, Social Support and Depression in
      Single and Married Mothers', *Social Psychiatry and Psychiatric Epidemiology* 38:8 (2003),
      442–9.

28   L. E. Young, S. L. Cunningham and D. S. Buist, 'Lone Mothers Are at Higher Risk for
      Cardiovascular Disease Compared with Partnered Mothers: Data from the National
      Health and Nutrition Examination Survey III (NHANES III)', *Health Care for Women
      International* 26:7 (2005), 604–21.

29   Hara Estroff Marano, 'Debunking the marriage myth: it works for women too', *New
      York Times*, 4 August 1998, available at http://smartmarriages.com/debunking.html
      (accessed 26 November 2014). The article cites research quoted by Dr Linda J. Waite, a
      professor of sociology. Dr Waite's book *The Case for Marriage* (op. cit.) includes research
      of these issues.

30   Source: Andrew Steptoe, Panayotes Demakakos and Cesar de Oliveira, 'The
      Psychological Well-being, Health and Functioning of Older People in England', in James
      Banks, James Nazroo and Andrew Steptoe (eds), *The Dynamics of Ageing: Evidence from
      the English Longitudinal Study of Ageing 2002–10 (Wave 5)* (London: Institute of Fiscal
      Studies, 2012), Chapter 4, http://www.ifs.org.uk/elsa/report12/ch4.pdf (accessed 26
      November 2014).

31   Ibid.

32   Marano, 'Debunking the marriage myth'.

33   S. M. Stanley, S. W. Whitton and H. J. Markman, 'Maybe I Do: Interpersonal
      Commitment and Premarital or Nonmarital Cohabitation' *Journal of Family Issues* 25
      (2004), 496–519.

34   The story of Jay Belsky is taken from his own account, 'The Politicized Science of

Day Care: A Personal and Professional Odyssey, *Family Policy Review* 1 (2003), 23–40, available at http://kidsfirstcanada.org/politicized-science.pdf (accessed 26 November 2014).

35 Ibid.

36 See Belsky's CV, available at http://www.psychology.sunysb.edu/attachment/vitae/belsky_cv.pdf (accessed 26 November 2014).

37 Belsky, 'The Politicised Science of Day Care'.

38 Ibid.

39 Jenet Jacob Ericson, 'The Effects of Day Care on the Socio-emotional Development of Children', FamilyFacts.org Report No. 2, April 2011, http://www.familyfacts.org/reports/2/the-effects-of-day-care-on-the-social-emotional-development-of-children (accessed 26 November 2014). This report summarises thirty years of research but concentrates on the NICHD study.

40 Ibid.

41 Ibid.

42 Ibid.

43 Cited in Lance T. Izumi, 'Universal school programs don't recognize the diversity of needs', *New York Times*, 25 February 2013, http://www.nytimes.com/roomfordebate/2013/02/25/is-public-preschool-a-smart-investment/universal-school-programs-dont-recognize-the-diversity-of-needs (accessed 17 December 2014).

44 Ibid.

45 Ibid.

46 Penelope Leach, *Children First: What Society Must Do – and Is Not Doing – for Our Children Today* (London: Penguin, 1994), pp. 77–9.

47 Jonas Himmelstrand, 'Universal daycare leaves Sweden's children less educated', *National Post*, 26 April 2011, http://fullcomment.nationalpost.com/2011/04/26/jonas-himmelstrand-two-generations-of-universal-daycare-have-left-sweden's-children-less-educated (accessed 26 November 2014).

48 Leach, *Children First*.

49 As described by Jonathan Haidt, *The Happiness Hypothesis: Putting Ancient Wisdom to the Test of Modern Science* (London: Arrow, 2006), p. 111.

50 Ibid., p. 114.

51 I know this from personal experience. When I was taken to nursery school by my father, I revolted and struggled against it to such a degree that the headmistress ended up holding my arms and my father my legs as I kicked and screamed. The story may,

of course, have gained in drama as my parents told it in later years but it is clear that I rebelled sufficiently against being left there to make a notable scene. I then spent a lot of time with the cooks in the kitchen because I did not want to accept going to the school. Meanwhile I have personal knowledge of a little girl who, deposited at a nursery school, refused to join the others and sat outside in the corridor for her first six months there.

52   Described in Haidt, *The Happiness Hypothesis*, p. 114.

53   Jill Kirby, 'Childcare policy should start with children', ConservativeHome, 17 October 2012, http://www.conservativehome.com/thecolumnists/2012/10/jill-kirby-childcare-policy-should-start-with-children.html (accessed 26 November 2014). Jill Kirby was director of the Centre for Policy Studies in London 2007–11.

54   Leach, *Children First*, pp. 77–8.

55   Karen Rowlingson and Stephen McKay, *Lone Parent Families: Gender, Class and State* (London: Prentice Hall, 2002).

56   Jeremy Sammut, 'Culturally deaf to causes of child abuse', Ideas@TheCentre, Centre for Independent Studies, 20 April 2012, http://www.cis.org.au/publications/ideasthecentre/article/4074-culturally-deaf-to-causes-of-child-abuse (accessed 26 November 2014).

57   In the USA, if a single mother were to marry a man with a job, the rent would more or less double since the rent in public housing is more or less 28 per cent of total household earnings. Additionally, the 'tax credit' received by the woman – really a wage subsidy – would disappear because she would be assessed on household income, not her own.

58   Figures from interview with Howard Husock.

59   Information for the UK from when I interviewed and accompanied welfare fraud inspectors in the 1990s. From the USA, email from Lisa Conyers, who talked with social workers on Indian reservations (also in the 1990s). These social workers were required to look for items of clothing stored by boyfriends. Hence the phrase they commonly used: 'shoes under the bed'.

60   Peter Saunders, *Re-moralising the Welfare State* (St Leonards, NSW: Centre for Independent Studies, 2013), p. 35.

61   Quoted in Heather Mac Donald, 'Chicago's Real Crime Story', *City Journal*, Winter 2010, http://www.city-journal.org/2010/20_1_chicago-crime.html (accessed 26 November 2014).

62   Saunders, *Re-moralising the Welfare State*, p. 30, citing Adele Horin, 'Generation IOU: parents fork out $22 billion a year to help their adult children', *The Age*, 26 July 2012.

CHAPTER 7: 'PEOPLE USED TO BE GRATEFUL AND EAGER…'

1   The information for this match is from 'Blackpool 4 Bolton 3: How the thrilling Matthews Final unfolded at Wembley', Mail Online, 11 May 2011, http://www.dailymail.co.uk/sport/football/article-1385690/

Blackpool-4-Bolton-3-How-Matthews-Final-unfolded-Wembley.html . This is an abridged version of the *Daily Mail*'s original report on the match. See also '1953 FA Cup Final', Wikipedia, http://en.wikipedia.org/wiki/1953_FA_Cup_Final; 'The Matthews Final', BBC Sport Online, 1 October 2000, http://news.bbc.co.uk/sport1/hi/in_depth/2000/wembley/936013.stm (all accessed 26 November 2014).

2   'Blackpool 4 Bolton 3'.

3   Simon Rice, 'The ten best acts of sportsmanship: Lutz Long', *The Independent* 20 November 2009, http://www.independent.co.uk/sport/football/news-and-comment/the-ten-best-acts-of-sportsmanship-1823706.html?action=gallery&ino=3. The Wikipedia entry for Luz Long differs slightly from the version in *The Independent* but is more detailed (http://en.wikipedia.org/wiki/Luz_Long). A Spiegel Online article casts doubt on the idea that they became friends but it confirms the help and the congratulations. It adds that Rudolf Hess was cross about the gesture of congratulations (Michael Wulzinger, 'Hitler's "Battle of the Colors": doubt cast on Olympic friendship between Owens and Long', 27 January 2012, http://www.spiegel.de/international/zeitgeist/hitler-s-battle-of-the-colors-doubt-cast-on-olympic-friendship-between-owens-and-long-a-811582.html (all accessed 26 November 2014).)

4   Rice, 'The ten best acts of sportsmanship'.

5   'Bradman, Sir Donald', Australian Inspiration, http://www.australianinspiration.com.au/Quotes/Authors/B/BradmanSirDonald.aspx (accessed 26 November 2014).

6   John Clark, 'Foxsports.com.au takes a look at the greatest sledges in cricket history as the India series approaches', Fox Sports online, 13 December 2011, http://www.foxsports.com.au/cricket/foxsportscomau-takes-a-look-at-the-greatest-sledges-in-cricket-history/story-e6frf3g3-1225975348816#.UhtHQBttimU (accessed 26 November 2014).

7   Sunil Gavaskar, Colin Cowdrey Lecture 2003. Text available at http://www.espncricinfo.com/wctimeline/content/story/129197.html (accessed 26 November 2014).

8   Shane Warne, 'It seemed my sledging had gone too far when McMillan stormed in wielding a gun', Mail Online, 26 August 2013, http://www.dailymail.co.uk/sport/article-63591/It-sledging-gone-far-McMillan-stormed-wielding-gun.html (accessed 26 November 2014).

9   Clark, 'Foxsports.com.au takes a look at the greatest sledges in cricket history as the India series approaches'.

10   Jason Epstein, 'A-Rod is not one of history's greatest monsters', National Review Online, 12 August 2013, http://www.nationalreview.com/article/355495/rod-not-one-historys-greatest-monsters-jason-epstein (accessed 26 November 2014).

11   Barbara Holland, *Gentlemen's Blood: A History of Dueling from Swords at Dawn to Pistols at Dusk* (New York: Bloomsbury, 2003).

12   Field Marshal Sir William Slim, *Defeat into Victory* (London: Cassell, 1956).

13　Marcus Aurelius, *The Emperor's Handbook: A New Translation of the Meditations*, tr. C. Scot Hicks and David V. Hicks (New York: Scribner's, 2002), IV.33.

14　The Book of Common Prayer has gone through a number of versions. I am not sure in which edition these words were first used but they were in the book by the time of the 1662 edition.

15　In parallel with the way that the words of confession have been revised over the years, so the words of the L'Oréal slogan have been revised. Originally they were 'Because I'm worth it'. Then they were changed to 'Because you're worth it' in the mid-2000s and again, in 2009, to 'Because we're worth it'. The slogan thus shifted to involve everybody – or at least every woman – in a sense of original worth, as opposed to original sin. L'Oréal also owns a hair and body products line for children called L'Oréal Kids, the slogan for which is 'Because we're worth it too'.

16　'At the movies with Margaret and David', ABC, http://www.abc.net.au/atthemovies/txt/s3235006.htm (accessed 27 November 2014).

17　I wrote a fuller note on this film on the website www.thewelfarestatewerein.com. Please use the search facility to find the entry.

18　*Reducing Re-offending by Ex-prisoners*, Social Exclusion Unit, July 2002, available at http://www.bristol.ac.uk/poverty/downloads/keyofficialdocuments/Reducing%20Reoffending.pdf (accessed 4 December 2014).

19　Ibid.

20　Denis Fougère, Francis Kramarz and Julien Pouget, 'Crime and Unemployment in France', March 2003, http://dev3.cepr.org/meets/wkcn/3/3519/papers/Kramarz.pdf (accessed 27 November 2014).

21　Povilas Lastauskas and Eirini Tatsi, 'Spatial Nexus in Crime and Unemployment in Times of Crisis: Evidence from Germany', Cambridge Working Papers in Economics CWPE 1359, December 2013, available at http://papers.ssrn.com/sol3/papers.cfm?abstract_id=2365267 (accessed 27 November 2014).

22　An Australian study in 1992 (admittedly rather out of date) asserts that cross-sectional and individual-level studies provide good evidence for the link but that studies over time do not. The evidence for studies over time is mixed. The paper tries to make sense of the paradox by suggesting that female work participation rates, given a 'patriarchal society', result in greater opportunities for crime due to such things as children being less supervised and women putting themselves in more vulnerable situations (John Braithwaite, Bruce Chapman and Cezary A, Kapuscinski, 'Unemployment and Crime: Resolving the Paradox', Australian National University, April 1992, http://crg.aic.gov.au/reports/50-89.pdf (accessed 27 November 2014).)

23　David Chazan, '"Only" 1,067 vehicles set ablaze on New Year's Eve in France', Telegraph Online, 1 January 2014, http://www.telegraph.co.uk/news/worldnews/10546263/Only-1067-vehicles-set-ablaze-on-New-Years-Eve-in-France.html (accessed 27 November 2014).

24 Fiona Brookman, *Understanding Homicide* (London: Sage, 2005).

25 This seems intuitively true. A boy who makes an insulting gesture at a teacher or someone in the street would seem more likely to commit a burglary than one who doesn't. But I admit I have not tracked down much academic study of this. One reference I can offer, however, is 'Violence and Discipline Problems in US Public Schools 1996–97', National Center for Education Statistics Statistical Analysis Report, March 1998, http://nces.ed.gov/pubs98/98030.pdf (accessed 27 November 2014).

26 Allen Beck et al., *Survey of State Prison Inmates, 1991*, US Department of Justice Bureau of Justice Studies, March 1993, http://www.bjs.gov/content/pub/pdf/SOSPI91.PDF (accessed 27 November 2014).

27 Steven D. Levitt and Lance Lochner, 'The Determinants of Juvenile Crime', in Jonathan Gruber (ed.), *Risky Behaviour among Youths: an Economic Analysis* (Chicago: University of Chicago Press 2001), available at http://www.nber.org/chapters/c10692.pdf (accessed 27 November 2014).

28 'Reducing re-offending by ex-prisoners' July 2002. See details above.

29 According to a 1987 survey, 'only one quarter were living with both parents' (Andrew Bebbington and John Miles, 'The Background of Children who Enter Local Authority Care', *British Journal of Social Work* 19:1 (1989), 349–68).

30 One useful study of this sort puts it this way: 'The influence of family structure is mediated by family processes,' which means, in lay language, that broken families come to be associated with higher adolescent crime through the way the parents tend to supervise the children less and, even more, the way the parents tend to have less close relationships with their children. But the study found that when it came to violent crime, even these and other 'processes' could not fully account for the lower rate among the children of married, natural parents. See Stephen Demuth and Susan L. Brown, 'Family Structure, Family Processes and Adolescent Delinquency: The Significance of Parental Absence versus Parental Gender', *Journal of Research in Crime and Delinquency* 41:1 (2004), 58–81, available at http://ejournal.narotama.ac.id/files/DeMuthandBrownJRCD%5B1%5D.pdf (accessed 27 November 2014).

31 'The per cent of female-headed households raised the level of social interactions for murder, serious crimes generally, burglary (at the 10 per cent level), and larceny' (Edward L. Glaeser, Bruce Sacerdote and José A. Scheinkman, 'Crime and Social Interactions', *Quarterly Journal of Economics* 111:2 (1996), 507–48). In this sentence, the phrase 'social interactions' appears to refer to interactions with people who may influence someone towards crime. They are therefore undesirable interactions. The authors quote from another study in which a young criminal says, 'That [the gang] is the only thing I'm connected to. That's my family.'

32 Jan van Dijk, John van Kesteren and Paul Smit, *Criminal Victimisation in International Perspective* (The Hague: Boom Juridische Uitgevers, 2007), p. 81. available at http://unicri.it/services/library_documentation/publications/icvs/publications/ICVS2004_05report.pdf (accessed 18 November 2014). This paper used crime prevalence figures for 2003/4 and

previous surveys. It also used, where marked with an asterisk, figures from European Survey of Crime and Safety (2005 EU ICS).

For out of wedlock births: OECD, *Doing Better for Families* (Paris: OECD Publications, 2011). Only advanced countries included. Scotland and Northern Ireland excluded so as not to overemphasise the United Kingdom.

33　　See for example, 'Study links crime with literacy skills', BBC News Online, 3 November 1998, http://news.bbc.co.uk/1/hi/uk/206732.stm; Christina Clark and George Dugdale, 'Literacy Changes Lives: The Role of Literacy in Offending Behaviour', National Literacy Trust, November 2008, p. 7, http://www.literacytrust.org.uk/assets/0000/0422/Literacy_changes_lives__prisons.pdf (both accessed 27 November 2014). It is also worth noting that an American study stated that black and Hispanic prisoners actually had better literacy than those of the same races who were not in prison. Overall, however, the prison population had lower literacy than the overall US population. See 'Literacy Behind Bars – Results from the 2003 National Assessment of Adult Literacy Prison Survey', National Center for Education Statistics, May 2007, http://nces.ed.gov/pubsearch/pubsinfo.asp?pubid=2007473 (accessed 27 November 2014).

34　　Mark Morgan and Mary Kett, 'The Prison Adult Literacy Survey: Results and Implications', Irish Prison Service, June 2003, http://www.epea.org/uploads/media/Adult_Literacy_Survey.pdf (accessed 27 November 2014).

35　　See Chapter 4 on education.

36　　Jonathan Haidt, *The Happiness Hypothesis: Putting Ancient Wisdom to the Test of Modern Science* (London: Arrow, 2006).

37　　First published in *Rewards and Fairies* (1910).

38　　*Bromley Briefings Prison Factfile June 2011*, Prison Reform Trust, June 2011, p. 52.

39　　Ibid.

40　　As a journalist, I interviewed fraud teams working for Customs and Excise and the Inland Revenue some years ago.

41　　Edgar L. Feige and Richard Cebula, 'America's Underground Economy: Measuring the Size, Growth and Determinants of Income Tax Evasion in the US', Munich Personal RePEc Archive Paper No. 2672, January 2011, http://mpra.ub.uni-muenchen.de/29672/1/MPRA_paper_29672.pdf (accessed 27 November 2014).

42　　http://en.wikipedia.org/wiki/Parson_Weems.

43　　'CBS2 investigation looks into use of disabled parking placards', CBS Los Angeles website, 31 January 2013, http://losangeles.cbslocal.com/2013/01/31/cbs2-investigation-reveals-rampant-fraud-in-use-of-disabled-parking-placards (accessed 27 November 2014).

44　　Available at http://www.mytimemachine.co.uk/trafalgar.htm (accessed 27 November 2014).

45　　Lee Kuan Yew, *From Third World to First: The Singapore Story 1965–2000* (New York: HarperCollins, 2000).

46   *The Economist*, 20 July 2013.

47   Ibid.

48   Kevin Drum, 'America's real criminal element: lead', *Mother Jones*, January/February 2013, http://www.motherjones.com/environment/2013/01/lead-crime-link-gasoline (accessed 27 November 2014).

49   David G. Green, 'Crime Reduction Factsheet. How Can We Reduce Reoffending by Known Criminals – the Overseas Evidence', available at http://www.civitas.org.uk/pdf/ CrimeReductionFactsheet.pdf (accessed 27 November 2014).

50   Gary C. Robb, 'Police Use of CCTV Surveillance: Constitutional Implications and Proposed Regulations', *University of Michigan Journal of Law Reform* 13 (1979), 571.

51   Tom Reeve, 'How many cameras in the UK? Only 1.85 million, claims ACPO lead on CCTV', *Security News Desk*, 1 March 2011, http://www.securitynewsdesk. com/2011/03/01/how-many-cctv-cameras-in-the-uk (accessed 27 November 2014). The effectiveness of cameras in reducing crime is a matter of dispute. It has been claimed that they can achieve a 51 per cent reduction in crime in car parks but that the improvement elsewhere is much more modest; see Brandon C. Welsh and David P. Farrington, 'Public Area CCTV and Crime Prevention: An Updated Systematic Review and Meta-analysis', *Justice Quarterly* 26:4 (2009), 716–45. These results appear unconvincing. It seems unlikely that so many cameras would be installed if there were not many people in security who have been convinced that they make a significant difference.

52   Geoffery Li, 'Private security and public policing', Statistics Canada, December 2008, http://www.statcan.gc.ca/pub/85-002-x/2008010/article/10730-eng.htm (accessed 27 November 2014).

53   Ronald van Steden and Rick Sarre, 'The Growth of Private Security: Trends in the European Union', *Security Journal* 20 (2007), 222–35.

54   Jan van Dijk, 'The International Crime Victims Survey: Latest Results and Prospects', *Criminology in Europe* 11:3 (2012), 24–33, available at http://www.esc-eurocrim.org/ newsletter/Dec12ESCnewsletter.pdf (accessed 22 December 2014).

55   'State-by-state and national crime estimates by year(s)', Uniform Crime Reporting Statistics, http://www.bjs.gov/ucrdata/Search/Crime/State/RunCrimeStatebyState.cfm (accessed 27 November 2014). These are 'offenses known to law enforcement' and not based on victim studies.

56   Ibid.

57   One quickly learns that in the business of levels of crime, there is no such thing as a wholly reliable statistic.

58   For more on this, see my book *The Welfare State We're In*, rev. ed. (London: Biteback, 2014).

59   Charles Murray, *Coming Apart: The State of White America 1960–2010* (New York: Crown Forum, 2012).

CHAPTER 8: NOT TO BE READ BY ANYONE UNDER THE AGE OF FORTY

1   I later discover that her title is Under-Secretary of State for Social Affairs in the
     Chancellery of the President.

2   OECD, *Pensions at a Glance 2011: Retirement-income Systems in OECD and G20 Countries*
     (Paris: OECD Publishing, 2011), table on p. 155, http://www.oecd-ilibrary.org/docserver/
     download/8111011e.pdf?expires=1417104070&id=id&accname=guest&checksum=471AAB
     11D6F95A1A98702650AB5CD443 (accessed 27 November 2014).

3   'Poland', OECD Better Life Index, http://www.oecdbetterlifeindex.org/countries/Poland
     (accessed 27 November 2014).

4   Friedrich Schneider, Andreas Buehn and Claudio E. Montenegro, 'Shadow Economies
     All over the World: New Estimates for 162 Countries from 1999 to 2007', World Bank
     Policy Research Working Paper 5356, July 2010, http://www-wds.worldbank.org/servlet/
     WDSContentServer/WDSP/IB/2010/10/14/000158349_20101014160704/Rendered/
     PDF/WPS5356.pdf (accessed 27 November 2014). See also Jacek Krawczyński, 'The
     Shadow Economy in Poland: How Payment Systems Help Limit the Shadow Economy',
     presentation given in Warsaw, 23 September 2009, http://www.konferencje.kmbase.pl/
     downloads/KrawczynskiEN.pdf accessed 27 November 2014.

5   OECD, *Pensions at a Glance 2011*, p. 155.

6   Ibid.

7   Rebecca Christie and Peter Woodifield, 'Europe's $39 trillion pension risk grows as
     economy falters', Bloomberg News, 11 January 2012, http://www.bloomberg.com/
     news/2012-01-11/europe-s-39-trillion-pension-threat-grows-as-regional-economies-sputter.
     html (accessed 27 November 2014).

8   Dr Oliver Hartwich, 'Fix the super roof while the sun is still shining', *Insights* (New
     Zealand Initiative), 15 June 2012, http://nzinitiative.org.nz/Media/Insights/June+2012/
     June+2012.html?uid=49 (accessed 27 November 2014).

9   'World Population Ageing 2009', United Nations Department of Economic and Social
     Affairs, December 2009, http://www.un.org/esa/population/publications/WPA2009/
     WPA2009_WorkingPaper.pdf (accessed 27 November 2014).

10   Christie and Woodifield, 'Europe's $39 trillion pension risk grows as economy falters'.

11   Johan de Deken, 'Pension Reforms in Germany: Can Occupational and Private Pensions
     Compensate for the Erosion of Social Insurance?', *Aegon Global Pensions View*, March
     2013.

12   OECD Ministerial Meeting on Social Policy, Paris, 2–3 May 2011, session 3: 'Paying for
     the past, providing for the future: intergenerational solidarity', http://www.oecd.org/els/
     public-pensions/47711990.pdf (accessed 27 November 2014).

13   Richard Jackson, *The Global Retirement Crisis: The Threat to World Stability and What to
     Do about It* (Washington, DC: Center for Strategic and International Studies, 2002),

p. 24, http://csis.org/files/media/csis/pubs/global_retirement.pdf (accessed 27 November 2014).

14   Testimony before the Commission on Security and Cooperation in Europe, 20 June 2011, http://csis.org/files/ts110620_Jackson.pdf (accessed 27 November 2014). Jackson is senior fellow at the Center for Strategic and International Studies.

15   Ibid.

16   Wataru Suzuki, 'Intergenerational Inequality Caused by the Social Security System', Cabinet Office, Government of Japan, ESRI Discussion Paper Series No. 281, January 2012, http://www.esri.go.jp/en/archive/e_dis/abstract/e_dis281-e.html (accessed 27 November 2014). 'Intergenerational inequality can be represented by the net benefit rate defined as the ratio of the net benefit by the social security system to the lifetime income.' I believe that here 'social security' refers to pensions. I am not sure whether 'lifetime income' refers to total earnings or total contributions to the pension system. If it is the latter, the change is very dramatic. But even if it is the former, the point remains that the later generations are going to do badly compared to the earlier generations.

17   Testimony before the Commission on Security and Cooperation in Europe, 20 June 2011.

18   Laurent Mauduit, 'La privatisation rampante de la Sécurite sociale', *Marianne*, 25 March 2013, http://www.marianne.net/La-privatisation-rampante-de-la-Securite-sociale_a227460.html (accessed 27 November 2014).

19   Cited in Christie and Woodifield, 'Europe's $39 trillion pension risk grows as economy falters'.

20   Greece is a dramatic example: 'Legislation passed in 2010 reduced state pension benefits, imposed penalties for early retirement and increased average retirement age so that workers must now work for at least 40 years, up from 37. Benefits can now no longer exceed 65 per cent of final salary (down from 70 per cent) and must be based on average career earnings instead of an average over the final five years of service' (David Adams, 'A Greek tragedy', *European Pensions*, November/December 2011, http://www.europeanpensions.net/ep/A-Greek-tragedy.php (accessed 27 November 2014).)

21   Michael Lewis, 'Beware of Greeks bearing bonds', *Vanity Fair*, 1 October 2010, http://www.vanityfair.com/business/features/2010/10/greeks-bearing-bonds-201010 (accessed 27 November 2014).

22   Figures calculated from C. Eugene Steuerle and Caleb Quakenbush, 'Social Security and Medicare Taxes and Benefits over a Lifetime: 2012 Update', Urban Institute 2012, http://www.urban.org/UploadedPDF/412660-Social-Security-and-Medicare-Taxes-and-Benefits-Over-a-Lifetime.pdf (accessed 27 November 2014). 'Present value' estimates are calculated using a 2 per cent discount rate. Why 2 per cent? The Urban Institute website explains, 'We used a 2 per cent real rate because it's as good a rate of return as one can expect from a private annuity and not far from a long-term real rate of return on a fairly protected mix of government securities.' And furthermore, 'you don't want a much lower rate of return because you want to take some account of economic growth. So 2 per cent

real return seems to us to be a reasonable compromise. The Congressional Budget Office has used a 3 per cent rate of return for some of its calculations – a bit high, but in the same ballpark' (http://www.urban.org/retirees/Estimating-Social-Security.cfm#Q2 (accessed 27 November 2014).)

23   Press release, 11 June 2012, quoting OECD, *Pensions Outlook 2012* (Paris: OECD Publishing, 2012).

24   The rates of income tax are relatively low especially for the low paid, which makes up for the higher social security payments; see http://www.expat.hsbc.com/1/PA_ES_Content_Mgmt/content/hsbc_expat/pdf/en/global_tax_navigator/going_to_japan.pdf (accessed 27 November 2014).

25   Op. cit.

26   Korea has 28.8 per cent self-employed workers compared to 7.0 per cent in the USA, 12.3 per cent in Japan and 13.9 per cent in Britain ('Underground economy amounts to 23% of national GDP in Korea', BusinessKorea, 5 March 2013, http://www.businesskorea. co.kr/article/767/underground-economy-amounts-23-national-gdp-korea (accessed 27 November 2014), citing report by the Hyundai Research Institute).

27   Schneider et al., 'Shadow Economies All over the World' (figures for 2006); OECD, *Pensions at a Glance 2011*, p. 155 (figures for 2007). In both cases, these seem to be the latest figures available. I have included all the advanced economies in the OECD list.

28   Schneider et al., 'Shadow Economies All over the World'.

29   Source for the pension burden: OECD, *Pensions at a Glance 2011*, p. 155. Source for the employment rate: 'Short-term Labour Market Statistics', OECD.StatExtracts, data for 2007, http://stats.oecd.org/Index.aspx?DatasetCode=STLABOUR (accessed 27 November 2014). The advantage of using the employment rate of working-age men is that it removes from the equation any cultural variations in the employment rates of women.

30   Nina Adam, 'Southern Europeans flock to Germany', *Wall Street Journal*, 7 May 2013, http://online.wsj.com/article/SB10001424127887323372504578468360472635932.html (accessed 27 November 2014).

31   Vivienne Walt, 'Forget Paris: stymied by socialist policies, the French start to quit France', *Time*, 21 May 2013, http://world.time.com/2013/05/21/forget-paris-stymied-by-socialist-policies-the-french-start-to-quit-france (accessed 27 November 2014).

32   James Bartholomew, *The Welfare State We're In*, rev. ed. (London: Politico's, 2006), p. 307. I have had to use this old data because, without doing a great deal of digging, I am not aware of a contemporary and reasonably advanced (thus comparable) country without either government pay-as-you-go pensions or compulsory private pension schemes. Hong Kong now has a compulsory private scheme. Countries like Singapore and Hong Kong with such schemes seem to have higher savings rates than those with government pay-as-you-go schemes. See 'Gross Savings (% of GDP)', World Bank website, http:// data.worldbank.org/indicator/NY.GNS.ICTR.ZS?page=1 (accessed 27 November 2014).

33 Kelly Greene and Vipal Monga, 'Workers saving too little to retire', *Wall Street Journal*, 19 March 2013, http://online.wsj.com/article/SB10001424127887323639604578368823406398606.html (accessed 27 November 2014).

34 Jill Insley, 'Half of UK not saving enough for retirement, says study', *The Guardian*, 7 June 2011, quoting figures given by Tom McPhail of Hargreaves Lansdown, http://www.guardian.co.uk/money/2011/jun/07/half-uk-not-saving-retirement (accessed 27 November 2014).

35 Assistant Professor, Department of Sociology, University of Amsterdam. 'Pension reforms in Germany: can occupational and private pensions compensate for the erosion of social insurance?', *Aegon Global Pensions View*, March 2013.

36 OECD, *Pensions at a Glance 2011*, p. 149.

37 Daniel Borenstein, 'Public employee pensions much higher than advertised', *Contra Costa Times*, 2 May 2011, http://www.contracostatimes.com/daniel-borenstein/ci_17299237?nclick_check=1 (accessed 27 November 2014).

38 See Steven Malanga, 'Pension propaganda: don't believe the public-sector unions when they say that worker pensions are modest', *City Journal*, Summer 2011, http://city-journal.org/mobile/story.php?s=7277#.VAtHG_ldXCo (accessed 27 November 2014).

39 The best possible figure for this does not seem to be easily available so I have had to use an estimate. The table referred to below shows full-time workers' median earnings of $36,378 for females and $47,127 for males. Weighting the average according to the different numbers creates a figure of $42,404 for both sexes. That figure was for 2009. Uplifting it by 4 per cent to get to a 2011 figure brings it to $44,098. I am grateful to Christian Wignall for his help with this. See US Census Bureau, *Statistical Abstract of the United States 2012*, Table 650, http://www.census.gov/compendia/statab/2012/tables/12s0650.pdf (accessed 27 November 2014).

40 Francis J. Lawall and Justin C. Esposito, 'Chapter 9 Bankruptcy of Stockton, Calif., moves forward', *Mondaq*, 24 May 2013, http://www.mondaq.com/unitedstates/x/241040/Insolvency+Bankruptcy/Chapter+9+Bankruptcy+Of+Stockton+Calif+Moves+Forward (accessed 27 November 2014).

41 Eduard Ponds, Clara Severinson and Juan Yermo, 'Funding in Public Sector Pension Plans: International Evidence', OECD Working Papers on Finance, Insurance and Private Pensions No. 8, May 2011, http://www.oecd.org/finance/private-pensions/47827915.pdf (accessed 27 November 2014).

42 Ibid.

43 Ibid.

44 James Bloodworth, 25 February 2013, http://www.leftfootforward.org/2013/02/how-best-to-support-an-ageing-population-more-immigration (accessed 27 November 2014).

45 The Turner Commission commented in 2004: 'Only high immigration can produce

more than a trivial reduction in the projected dependency ratio over the next 50 years.'
See '20 bogus arguments for mass immigration', Migration Watch UK website, http://
www.migrationwatchuk.co.uk/briefingPaper/document/269 (accessed 27 November
2014), item 12 and footnote 13.

46   OECD, *Pensions at a Glance 2011*, p. 149.

47   Ibid.

48   Ibid., p. 272

49   Richard Evans, 'Holland's pensions superiority called into question', *Daily Telegraph*,
12 May 2013, http://www.telegraph.co.uk/finance/personalfinance/pensions/10050061/
Superiority-of-Dutch-pensions-called-into-question.html (accessed 30 November 2014),

50   Oonagh McDonald, 'Holding back the flood', *Financial World*, November 2012.

51   See CPF website, http://mycpf.cpf.gov.sg/CPF/About-Us/HistoryofCPF.htm (accessed
30 November 2014).

52   Lee Kuan Yew, *From Third World to First: Singapore and the Asian Economic Boom* (New
York: HarperBusiness, 2011), p. 105.

53   See CPF website: http://mycpf.cpf.gov.sg/CPF/About-Us/Intro/Intro (accessed 30
November 2014). At fifty-five, the money goes into a Retirement Account, subject to
various provisions and choices.

54   These rates were new for 2014: see CPF website, http://mycpf.cpf.gov.sg/Employers/Gen-
Info/cpf-Contri/ContriRa.htm (accessed 30 November 2014). When I was in Singapore,
the rates were slightly different and the highest rate of contribution to the Special
Account was 8 per cent. The system is being constantly reviewed and revised.

55   See CPF website, http://mycpf.cpf.gov.sg/Members/Gen-Info/Int-Rates (accessed 30
November 2014).

56   The minima are S$20,000 in the Ordinary Account and S$40,000 in the Special
Account: see 'Instruments that can be invested under CPFIS', http://mycpf.
cpf.gov.sg/NR/rdonlyres/DCD118FF-473E-4A5C-8A0F-322687316646/0/INV_
InstrumentsunderCPFIS.pdf (accessed 30 November 2014).

57   In the Ordinary Account, people have a wider choice of investments than in the Special
Account. The rules are quite restrictive in terms of allowing people to choose shares for
themselves. See 'Instruments that can be invested under CPFIS'.
      Most of the money that is eligible to be invested in financial instruments such as unit
trusts is not invested in this way but remains on deposit. According to an advertisement
by the bank OCBC, in 2005, only S$29 billion out of a possible S$104 billion was
invested in financial instruments: http://www.ocbc.com/assets/PDF/Retirement_How_
to_invest_your_CPF_wisely.pdf.

58   'The Chilean Pension System', OECD Ageing Working Paper AWP5.6 1998. 'The report
was prepared by Mr. Joaquin Vial Ruiz-Tagle, Director of the Budget, and Ms. Francisca

Castro, Counsellor, Ministry of Finance, Chile.' http://www.oecd.org/els/public-pensions/2429310.pdf (accessed 30 November 2014).

59 While at the OECD, a senior and notably anti-capitalist employee was positively complacent in dismissing Chile as an idea that had flopped.

60 Edward Palmer, 'The Swedish Pension Reform Model: Framework and Issues', available at http://www.oecd.org/finance/financial-markets/2638200.pdf (accessed 30 November 2014). The report is undated but it appears to have been written in the first half of 2000.

61 Australia's superannuation system, started in 1992, is also worth considering. In the relatively short time since its creation, the assets rose to $1.5 trillion, equivalent to the national GDP in 2012 (see Dr Martin Parkinson, 'Future Challenges: Australia's Superannuation System', November 2012, http://www.treasury.gov.au/PublicationsAndMedia/Speeches/2012/Australias-Superannuation-System (accessed 22 December 2014).) It may be significant that Australia's gross savings rate rose from 21 per cent to 25 per cent between 2005 and 2012. This savings rate was above that of most comparable countries. For example, here are some rates in 2012: France 18 per cent, Germany 24 per cent, USA 17 per cent, UK 11 per cent ('Gross savings (% of GDP)', World Bank website, http://data.worldbank.org/indicator/NY.GNS.ICTR.ZS (accessed 30 November 2014).)

62 This is the case in Britain and America, at least. For the USA see Michael Tanner, 'Still a Better Deal: Private Investment vs. Social Security', *Policy Analysis* 692 (2012), pp. 6–7, http://object.cato.org/sites/cato.org/files/pubs/pdf/PA692.pdf (accessed 30 November 2014). For the UK, see the annual report produced by Barclays on equity returns over the long term. Access to the full report is not free but some relevant data is available at 'Your investment starts here', Barclays Stockbrokers website, https://www.barclaysstockbrokers.co.uk/get-started/investment-journey/Pages/your-investment-journey-starts-here.aspx (accessed 30 November 2014), showing superior returns for equities over the long term.

63 In New Zealand a person qualifies for a flat-rate benefit, varying according to living circumstances such as living alone or with a partner but not according to income. 'You must also have lived in New Zealand for at least 10 years since you turned 20. Five of those years must be since you turned 50' ('New Zealand superannuation overview', Work and Income (New Zealand) website, http://www.workandincome.govt.nz/individuals/65-years-or-older/superannuation/superanuation-overview.html (accessed 30 November 2014).) The rate for a single person living alone as at 1 April 2014 was NZ$421.76. Rates table is available at http://www.workandincome.govt.nz/manuals-and-procedures/deskfile/nz_superannuation_and_veterans_pension_tables/new_zealand_superannuation_tables.htm (accessed 30 November 2014).

CHAPTER 9: 'WHILE HER DEAR FATHER LIVED…'

1 Leonardo Fusè, *Parents, Children and Their Families: Living Arrangements of Old People in the XIX Century, Sundsvall Region, Sweden* (Umeå: Umeå University, 2008), http://umu.diva-portal.org/smash/get/diva2:141642/FULLTEXT01 (accessed 30 November 2014).

2 Ilona Ostner et al., 'Family Policies in Germany', available at http://www.york.ac.uk/

inst/spru/research/nordic/gerpoli.PDF (accessed 30 November 2014). The report is
undated but it appears to have been written in 2003 or 2004.

3   Maria Iacovou, 'The Living Arrangements of Elderly Europeans', Institute for Social and
      Economic Research, February 2000, https://www.iser.essex.ac.uk/research/publications/
      working-papers/iser/2000-09.pdf (accessed 30 November 2014).

4   Ibid. The author emphasises the 'inadequacy' of the north–south or Catholic–Protestant
      differences to explain the contrasts between the countries.

5   'Current conditions and challenges of Japanese senior citizens: aging of the elderly
      population', JARC website, 27 August 2008, http://www.jarc.net/int/?cat=23 (accessed 30
      November 2014). The figure is 61.7 per cent for 2005.

6   OECD, *Doing Better for Families* (Paris: OECD Publications, 2011), p. 28.

7   Klaus Haberkern and Marc Szydlik, 'State Care Provision, Societal Opinion and
      Children's Care of Older Parents in 11 European Countries', *Ageing and Society* 30 (2010),
      299–323, Table 1.

8   Marie-Eve Joël, Sandrine Dufour-Kippelen and Sanda Samitca, 'The Long-term Care
      System for the Elderly in Portugal', ENEPRI Research Report No. 84, June 2010, http://
      www.ceps.eu/book/long-term-care-system-elderly-portugal (accessed 30 November 2014);
      Norma K. Raffel and Marshall W. Raffel, 'Elderly Care: Similarities and Solutions in
      Denmark and the United States', *Public Health Reports* 102:5 (1987), 494–500.

9   Raffel and Raffel, 'Elderly Care'.

10   It is true that the proportion of elderly living with their children has fallen. 'The
      proportion living alone has increased steadily since 1960, at an estimated rate of about
      1 per cent a year' (Alberto Palloni, 'Living Arrangements of Older Persons', *Population
      Bulletin of the United Nations* 42–3 (2002), http://www.un.org/esa/population/
      publications/bulletin42_43/palloni.pdf (accessed 30 November 2014).) It is also true
      that government provision was increased and changed in 2000, although this was scaled
      back somewhat in 2005 because of the rising cost. Japan introduced a long-term care
      insurance programme, which involves means testing and assessment of the physical and
      other needs of the elderly person. I suspect the terms are quite strict and so, despite this
      extra provision, there is still more incentive in Japan than elsewhere for children to take
      responsibility for their parents. In any case, most of the statistics in this chapter pre-date
      the 2000 reform or were produced not very long after it.
         It used to be a matter of shame if a family failed to look after its elderly. There were
      scandals of families not looking after their elderly well which presumably encouraged the
      new government provision. But it must surely be difficult to know how widespread this
      truly was. See Mayumi Hayashi, 'The Care of Older People in Japan: Myths and Realities
      of Family "Care"', History and Policy website, 3 June 2011, http://www.historyandpolicy.
      org/papers/policy-paper-121.html (accessed 30 November 2014).
         'The number of elders receiving care at home – compared to institutions – is high.
      In total of 12.6 per cent of the population over the age of 65 received long-term care, of
      which 2.8 per cent in institutions (4 per cent OECD average) and 9.8 per cent at home

(OECD average 7.9 per cent) in 2011 (OECD Health Data 2012)' ('Japan: Highlights from *A Good Life in Old Age? Monitoring and Improving Quality in Long-term Care*, OECD Publishing, 2013', OECD website, http://www.oecd.org/els/health-systems/Japan-OECD-EC-Good-Time-in-Old-Age.pdf (accessed 30 November 2014).)

11 Gary V. Engelhardt and Nadia Greenhalgh-Stanley, 'Public Long-term Care Insurance and the Housing and Living Arrangements of the Elderly: Evidence from Medicare Home Health Benefits', Care for Retirement Research Working Papers, December 2008, http://crr.bc.edu/working-papers/public-long-term-care-insurance-and-the-housing-and-living-arrangements-of-the-elderly-evidence-from-medicare-home-health-benefits (accessed 30 November 2014).

12 'Statistical bulletin: 2011 Census: Key Statistics for England and Wales, March 2011', Office for National Statistics website, http://www.ons.gov.uk/ons/rel/census/2011-census/key-statistics-for-local-authorities-in-england-and-wales/stb-2011-census-key-statistics-for-england-and-wales.html (accessed 30 November 2014).

13 See ibid.

14 'The return of the multi-generational family household', Pew Research Social and Demographic Trends, 18 March 2010, http://www.pewsocialtrends.org/2010/03/18/the-return-of-the-multi-generational-family-household (accessed 30 November 2014). 'Multi-generational' here means 'at least two adult generations or a grandparent and at least one other generation'.

15 Ibid.

16 For example the EU treats publicly provided care for the elderly as a human right rather than merely a good thing and suggests that for the poor it should be free or low cost – see 'The future of health care and care for the elderly: guaranteeing accessibility, quality and financial viability', Europa website, http://europa.eu/legislation_summaries/employment_and_social_policy/disability_and_old_age/c11310_en.htm (accessed 30 November 2014). That is easy for a supranational organisation to say which does not have to raise the money and appears uninterested in the choice of individual elderly people or the fact that paying for one person's elderly care means taking money from another. The OECD, to be fair, takes a more realistic approach. However, it tends to take for granted the idea of government care and to call for more regulation and better statistics rather than to review the big picture and ask whether its dream system of highly regulated care by well-qualified people is either affordable or wholly desirable.

17 Survey by the Japanese Ministry of Health, Labour and Welfare's Health and Welfare Bureau for the Elderly. 46 per cent chose 'Receive long-term care at home if there are services that enable me to live at home independently of my family members'; 24 per cent chose 'Live at home receiving combination of external long term care services and care by my family'; 4 per cent chose 'Live at home receiving care by mainly my family'. As for those who preferred institutional care, 12 per cent chose 'Move into fee charging home for the aged or house for the elderly with care to receive long-term care'; 7 per cent chose 'Stay in special nursing home or other facility for the elderly to receive long-term care'; 2 per cent chose 'Stay in the hospital to receive long-term care'. I do not know

what age group was asked this question or what the participants thought of as being 'long-term care', which might be somewhat different from what people have in mind in Britain or America or elsewhere. The figures appeared on the slides of a talk given by Masahiko Hayashi, Deputy Assistant Minister for International Affairs at the Ministry of Health, Labour and Welfare. The talk was given at the Daiwa Anglo-Japanese Foundation on 6 November 2013.

18   A blog for the *New York Times* refers to a study saying that money influences the decision (Paula Span, 'They don't want to live with you either', New Old Age blog, 24 March 2009, http://newoldage.blogs.nytimes.com/2009/03/24/they-dont-want-to-live-with-you-either/?_php=true&_type=blogs&_r=0 (accessed 30 November 2014).) I agree with that. But it does not refer to any research into what the elderly actually want. It is conceivable that some of the elderly do not want to impose on their children but that, in taking that view, they are condemning themselves to lonely isolation. Even if they do not want to live in the same household, they might well like to live close by so they can see their children and grandchildren easily and often.

19   'Go gentle into that good night', *The Economist*, 17 March 2012. The article is a review of Ira Byock, *The Best Care Possible: A Physician's Quest to Transform Care through the End of Life* (New York: Avery, 2012).

20   'The return of the multi-generational family household'. Unfortunately it is not immediately clear in the report whether Pew surveyed people in residential care homes and, if so, how they categorised them. Meanwhile in a footnote, the centre states that regression analysis models indicate that living arrangements have independent impact on health, depression and loneliness but not, rather strangely, on reported happiness.

21   'Having access to practical help from others was not related to happiness, but levels of loneliness and self-esteem were' (John T. Cacioppo and William Patrick, *Loneliness: Human Nature and the Need for Social Connection* (New York: W. W. Norton, 2008), p. 218), referring to evaluations of older people.

22   Ibid., p. 93, citing research covered by *Science* magazine.

23   Ibid., p. 94, citing research by psychologist Dan Russell and colleagues.

24   Joseph E. Gaugler et al., 'Predicting Nursing Home Admission in the US: A Meta-analysis', *BMC Geriatrics* 7 (2007), 13.

25   See Guido Kleinhubbert and Antje Windmann, 'Alone by the millions: isolation crisis threatens German seniors', Spiegel Online International, 10 January 2013, http://www.spiegel.de/international/germany/germany-faces-epidemic-of-lonely-and-isolated-seniors-a-876635.html (accessed 30 November 2014).

26   Cacioppo and Patrick, *Loneliness*, p. 94.

27   Kleinhubbert and Windmann, 'Alone by the millions'.

28   For example, 'An elderly person living alone increased his or her likelihood of institutionalization by 1.79 times compared to an elderly person living with his or her

spouse' (Ulrike Steinbach, 'Social Networks, Institutionalization, and Mortality among Elderly People in the United States', *Journal of Gerontology* 47:4 (1992), S183–S190.)

29 Judith D. Kasper, Liliana E. Pezzin and J. Bradford Rice, 'Stability and Changes in Living Arrangements: Relationship to Nursing Home Admission and Timing of Placement', *Journal of Gerontology: Social Sciences* 65 B:6 (2010), 783–91.

30 All the more so considering that the results are controlled for factors such as income.

31 Kasper et al., 'Stability and Changes in Living Arrangements'. Of those who started by living with a spouse or living alone and then lived with an adult child, 12.2 per cent went to a nursing home.

32 F. A. McDougall et al., 'Prevalence and Symptomatology of Depression in Older People Living in Institutions in England and Wales', *Age and Ageing* 36:5 (2007), 562–8. This study does not seem to state explicitly that those who are at home are both those living alone and those with family but it appears to be the case. The main focus of the study is the condition of people in institutions.

33 Ibid.

34 Ibid.

35 Christine Smoliner et al., 'Malnutrition and Depression in the Institutionalised Elderly', *British Journal of Nutrition* 102:11 (2009), 1663–7.

36 Ibid.

37 Ibid.

38 'The state of health care and adult social care in England in 2011/12' by the Care Quality Commission. Quite bizarrely, the report does not highlight this appalling finding and even reverses the emphasis by saying that 62 per cent of inpatients said they 'always' got enough help with feeding (Care Quality Commission, *The State of Health Care and Adult Social Care in England: An Overview of Key Themes in Care in 2011/12*, November 2012, HC 763, http://www.cqc.org.uk/sites/default/files/documents/cqc__soc_201112_final_tag.pdf (accessed 30 November 2014).)

39 Jenny Hope and Daniel Martin, 'Shameful! Damning report reveals the plight of neglected, malnourished elderly in hospitals and care homes', *Daily Mail*, 23 November 2012, http://www.dailymail.co.uk/news/article-2237126/Shameful-Damning-report-reveals-plight-neglected-malnourished-elderly-hospitals-care-homes.html (accessed 30 November 2014), reporting on Care Quality Commission, *The State of Health Care and Adult Social Care in England*. The figures relate to care of patients generally but it is widely accepted that it is those who are elderly, especially those with dementia, who tend to be treated with less respect. In any case, the elderly constitute a disproportionately large number of hospital patients. On looking more closely at the actual report, it seems that more precise figure for those not treated with proper respect was actually 9 per cent rather than 10 (p. 42). The report sometimes uses rounded up numbers and in other places shows more precise numbers. Some things are either not measured or the figures

are not revealed. For example, no patient survey figure of whether patients had enough help with feeding in private hospitals is given.

40   Chris Smyth, 'NHS care of elderly: the scandal gets worse', *The Times*, 13 October 2011, http://www.thetimes.co.uk/tto/health/news/article3192887.ece (accessed 30 November 2014).

41   Daniel Martin, 'Frail elderly patients "left to starve in hospitals", admit more than two-thirds of NHS nurses', *Daily Mail*, 31 August 2010, http://www.dailymail.co.uk/health/article-1307250/Frail-elderly-patients-left-hungry-hospitals-admit-thirds-NHS-nurses.html (accessed 30 November 2014).

42   Jane Kelly, 'It's time to admit it: the NHS is unable to look after our elderly', *The Spectator*, 18 May 2013, http://www.spectator.co.uk/features/8909201/among-the-bed-blockers (accessed 30 November 2014).

43   J. Kayser-Jones et al., 'Factors Contributing to Dehydration in Nursing Homes: Inadequate Staffing and Lack of Professional Supervision', *Journal of the American Geriatrics Society* 47:10 (1999), 1187–94.

44   Sandra F. Simmons, Cathy Alessi and John F. Schnelle, 'An Intervention to Increase Fluid Intake in Nursing Home Residents: Prompting and Preference Compliance', *Journal of the American Geriatrics Society* 49:7 (2001), 926–33.

45   Lani G. Gallagher, *The High Cost of Poor Care: The Financial Case for Prevention in American Nursing Homes*, National Consumer Voice for Quality Long-term Care, April 2011, http://theconsumervoice.org/uploads/files/issues/The-High-Cost-of-Poor-Care.pdf (accessed 30 November 2014).

46   Ibid.

47   Ibid., citing Vicky Lyman, 'Successful Heel Pressure Ulcer Prevention Program in a Long-term Care Setting', *Journal of Wound Ostomy and Continence Nursing* 36:6 (2009), 616–21.

48   Daniel R. Levinson, 'Medicare Atypical Antipsychotic Drug Claims for Elderly Nursing Home Residents', Department of Health and Human Services (United States), May 2011, http://oig.hhs.gov/oei/reports/oei-07-08-00150.pdf (accessed 30 November 2014).

49   Ibid.

50   Sophie Borland, 'One in four dementia sufferers prescribed dangerous "chemical cosh" drugs which are only meant as a last resort', *Daily Mail*, 21 February 2012 http://www.dailymail.co.uk/health/article-2103979/One-dementia-sufferers-prescribed-dangerous-chemical-cosh-drugs-meant-resort.html (accessed 30 November 2014).

51   'Toby Edelman statement to Senate Committee regarding anti-psychotic drugs in nursing facilities', Center for Medicare Advocacy website, 18 April 18 2012, http://www.medicareadvocacy.org/toby-edelman-testifies-regarding-antipsychotic-drugs-in-nursing-facilities (accessed 30 November 2014).

52   See for example Jane Worroll, '"I used a spy camera to catch a care home thug beating up my mother": How a daughter's suspicions lead to her uncovering harrowing abuse', *Daily Mail* 23 April 2012, http://www.dailymail.co.uk/news/article-2133673/BBC-One-Panorama-Undercover--Elderly-Care-Ash-Court-residents-daughter-uncovers-harrowing-abuse.html (accessed 30 November 2014).

53   James Slack and Ryan Kisiel, 'Profits before patients: care home residents subjected to horrific abuse went to A&E 76 times in three years – but private owner did nothing', *Daily Mail*, 8 August 2012, http://www.dailymail.co.uk/news/article-2184892/Winterbourne-View-abuse-report-Pinned-slapped-doused-water.html (accessed 30 November 2014).

54   '73 per cent of councils still commission 15 minute visits', press release, Unison website, 17 June 2013, http://www.unison.org.uk/news/73-of-councils-still-commission-15-minute-care-visits (accessed 30 November 2014). In theory this is the minimum but it is thought that it tends to become the norm.

55   'America's Long-term Care Crisis: Challenges in Financing and Delivery', Bipartisan Policy Center, April 2014, http://bipartisanpolicy.org/wp-content/uploads/2014/03/BPC-Long-Term-Care-Initiative.pdf (accessed 30 November 2014).

56   Pedro Olivares-Tirado et al., 'Predictors of the Highest Long-term Care Expenditures in Japan', *BMC Health Services Research* 11 (2011), 103, http://www.biomedcentral.com/1472-6963/11/103 (accessed 30 November 2014).

57   Christine de la Maisonneuve and Joaquim Oliveira Martins, 'Public Spending on Health and Long-term Care: a New Set of Projections', OECD Economic Policy Papers No. 6, June 2013, http://www.oecd.org/eco/growth/Health%20FINAL.pdf (accessed 30 November 2014).

58   Richard Cracknell, 'The Ageing Population', House of Commons Library Research, http://www.parliament.uk/documents/commons/lib/research/key_issues/Key-Issues-The-ageing-population2007.pdf (accessed 30 November 2014).

59   *Statistical Handbook of Japan 2014*, Statistics Japan website, Table 2.2, http://www.stat.go.jp/english/data/handbook/c0117.htm#c02 (accessed 30 November 2014). This table compares the proportion of population aged over sixty-five with that aged fifteen to sixty-four.

60   *Caring for Older Australians: Productivity Commission Inquiry Report*, June 2011, vol. 1, chapter 5: 'Assessment of the current aged care system', http://www.pc.gov.au/__data/assets/pdf_file/0004/110929/aged-care-volume1.pdf (accessed 30 November 2014).

61   Esther Mot is at the CPB Netherlands Bureau for Economic Policy Analysis.

62   I met Vic when he drove me to an appointment in Sydney.

63   Kelly, 'It's time to admit it'.

64   Ibid.

65 'Who needs care?', Longtermcare.gov, http://longtermcare.gov/the-basics/who-needs-care (accessed 30 November 2014).

66 'Man lay dead for three years', *Stockholm News*, 26 March 2011, http://stockholmnews.com.preview.binero.se/more.aspx?NID=6955 (accessed 30 November 2014).

67 'Stockholm man lay dead in flat for two years', *The Local* (Sweden), 22 May 2013, http://www.thelocal.se/20130522/48062 (accessed 30 November 2014).

68 Justin Nobel, 'Japan's lonely deaths: a business opportunity', *Time*, 6 April 2010, http://www.time.com/time/world/article/0,8599,1976952,00.html?xid=rss-topstories (accessed 30 November 2014).

69 'Current conditions and challenges of Japanese senior citizens'.

70 Kleinhubbert and Windmann, 'Alone by the millions'.

71 Rosemary Bennett, 'A friendly face and a cup of tea takes edge off loneliness', *The Times*, 11 December 2012, http://www.thetimes.co.uk/tto/public/timesappeal/article3626922.ece (accessed 30 November 2014). The Women's Royal Voluntary Service has since been re-named the Royal Voluntary Service.

72 A 1994 survey claimed that one in three acknowledge feelings of 'hatred', according to Hayashi, 'The Care of Older People in Japan'.

73 Conversation with Francesco Maietta of Censis, a socio-economic research institute in Rome; see also Daniel González, 'Italy grants special treatment to needed immigrants', AZCentral.com, http://www.azcentral.com/news/articles/global-immigration-italy-domestic.html (accessed 30 November 2014).

74 My informant was Francesco Maietta. The lower estimate comes from Claudia Villosio and Giulia Bizzotto, 'Once There Were Wives and Daughters, Now There Are *Badanti*', WALQING Social Partnership Series, September 2011, http://www.walqing.eu/fileadmin/download/external_website/WALQING_SocialPartnershipSeries_2011.14_ElderlyCare_ITA.pdf (accessed 30 November 2014). They suggest 684,000 immigrant carers.

75 'No room for mum and dad: less than 30% of adults would look after their parents', Care UK website, 30 July 2014. http://www.careuk.com/news/no-room-mum-and-dad-less-30-adults-would-look-after-their-parents (accessed 30 November 2014).

76 The comment was made on 15 March 2013: see Rosemary Bennett, 'Children in daycare "face mental health risk"', http://www.thetimes.co.uk/tto/health/child-health/article3712099.ece (accessed 30 November 2014). I have changed 'moving away from work' to 'moving away for work'.

CHAPTER 10: 'ALL ANIMALS ARE EQUAL…'

1 George Orwell, *Animal Farm* (London: Secker and Warburg 1945). *Animal Farm* was an allegory of Soviet communism. The political elite which took over the farm soon found ways to give themselves privileges.

2   Quoted in 'David Cameron's speech on public service', *The Guardian*, 6 June 2006, http://www.guardian.co.uk/politics/2006/jun/06/publicservices.conservatives (accessed 30 November 2014).

3   Eduardo Porter, 'Health care and profits, a poor mix', *New York Times*, 8 January 2013, http://www.nytimes.com/2013/01/09/business/health-care-and-pursuit-of-profit-make-a-poor-mix.html?pagewanted=all&_r=0 (accessed 30 November 2014).

4   *Italy Today: Social Picture and Trends 2010* (Milan: Censis, 2011), p. 55.

5   The description of the 'rubber rooms' and the statistics are taken from Terry M. Moe, *Special Interest: Teachers Unions and America's Public Schools* (Washington, DC: Brookings Institution, 2011).

6   Ibid.

7   Ibid.

8   Karl Weber, 'A Nation Still at Risk', in Karl Weber (ed.), *Waiting for 'Superman': How We Can Save America's Failing Public Schools* (New York: Public Affairs, 2010), p. 7.

9   Ibid. The figures have been changed into percentages.

10 'Michelle Apperson, Teacher of the Year, gets lay-off notice from Sacramento School District amid budget cuts', *HuffPost Education*, 15 June 2012, http://www.huffingtonpost.com/2012/06/15/michelle-apperson-teacher_n_1601015.html (accessed 30 November 2014).

11 Scott Reeder, 'Teachers get fired, but don't leave classroom', Hidden Violations website, http://hiddenviolations.com/stories/?prcss=display&id=358596 see also http://hiddenviolations.com/pdf/7.pdf (accessed 30 November 2014). The case was heard in 2002.

12 Ibid.

13 Op. cit.

14 Author interview with Lance Izumi, who works for the Pacific Research Institute in San Francisco.

15 Jason Song and Jason Felch, 'Union leader calls on LA teachers to boycott *Times*', *Los Angeles Times*, 15 August 2010, http://articles.latimes.com/2010/aug/15/local/la-me-teachers-react-20100816 (accessed 30 November 2014).

16 In the 1950s, teachers' unions had little power. Schools were dominated by administrators. Then in the 1960s, the unions began to establish themselves. States began to adopt laws that allowed, or even promoted, collective bargaining for public employees. Teacher unions could disrupt schooling. The public (government) schools were, in each state, a monopoly. The customers of the schools, the state and the parents, could not go elsewhere. So the unions got their way. The next stage came through the rising subscriptions from their members. They were able to use the money to buy political

influence. The teachers' unions have been the biggest contributors of all to politicians in federal elections. They have bought power and used it to protect their members and, in the process, damage the education of children.

17   Moe, *Special Interest*, pp. 36, 37.

18   Ibid., pp. 282, 283.

19   Neil O'Brien, 'Reform of teachers' pensions is fair. Unsurprisingly, the ultra-left don't see it that way', Telegraph Online blog, 28 June 2011, http://blogs.telegraph.co.uk/news/neilobrien1/100094388/reform-of-teachers-pensions-is-fair-unsurprisingly-the-ultra-left-dont-see-it-that-way (accessed 30 November 2014). O'Brien, then director of Policy Exchange, was commenting on the National Union of Teachers and its complaints about the reform of teachers' pensions.

20   The teacher unions have also opposed the creation of free schools and schools funded by tax credits – schools which have given choice to poor people, something which was previously only available to the rich. It is easy to suspect that their motivation for doing so is not, as they claim, the well-being of students but the maintenance of their own power and income.

21   Thomas Frank, 'States expand lucrative pensions to more jobs', *USA Today*, 9 December 2011, http://usatoday30.usatoday.com/news/nation/story/2011-12-08/state-pensions-workers/51750670/1?loc=interstitialskip (accessed 30 November 2014).

22   From 48, 188 to 75,135 (ibid.).

23   Ibid. Those eligible for enhanced or early retirement rose from 59,685 to 77,394.

24   See Richard Thomson, 'Attali runs out of credit: The EBRD president was finally forced to yield to calls for his head', *The Independent*, 27 June 2006, http://www.independent.co.uk/news/business/attali-runs-out-of-credit-the-ebrd-president-was-finally-forced-to-yield-to-calls-for-his-head-writes-richard-thomson-1494218.html (accessed 30 November 2014).

25   'Le public part toujours à la retraite beaucoup plus tôt que le privé', *Le Figaro*, 24 March 2013, http://www.lefigaro.fr/retraite/2013/03/23/05004-20130323ARTFIG00413-le-public-part-toujours-plus-tot-a-la-retraite-que-le-prive.php (accessed 30 November 2014). The article cites *Le Monde* as the original source.

26   'Government employees in Ontario earn 14 per cent more than private-sector workers', Fraser Institute website, 20 February 2013, http://www.fraserinstitute.org/research-news/news/news-releases/Government-employees-in-Ontario-earn-14-per-cent-more-than-private-sector-workers (accessed 30 November 2014). The exact figures are 97.3 per cent of public sector employees and 53.5 per cent of those in the private sector.

27   Ibid. In the public sector, 0.7 per cent lose their jobs compared to 3.9 per cent in the private sector.

28   Jason Clemens, Amela Karabegović and Milagros Palacios, 'Comparing Public and

Private Sector Compensation in Ontario', Fraser Institute, February 2013, http://www. fraserinstitute.org/uploadedFiles/fraser-ca/Content/research-news/research/publications/ comparing-public-and-private-sector-compensation-in-ontario.pdf (accessed 30 November 2014).

29 Maury Gittleman and Brooks Pierce, 'Compensation for State and Local Government Workers', *Journal of Economic Perspectives* 26:1 (2012), 217–42. The researchers admitted that the figures are not definitive for a number of reasons including gaps in the information they can obtain. But they added, 'The data suggest that public sector workers, especially local government ones, on average, receive greater remuneration than observably similar private sector workers. Overturning this result would require, we think, strong arguments for particular model specifications, or different data.'

30 Ed Holmes and Matt Oakley, 'Public and Private Sector Terms, Conditions and the Issue of Fairness', Policy Exchange, May 2011, http://www.policyexchange.org.uk/images/ publications/public%20and%20private%20sector%20terms%20conditions%20and%20 the%20issue%20of%20fairness%20-%20may%2011.pdf (accessed 30 November 2014).

31 Michael Lewis, 'Beware of Greeks bearing bonds', *Vanity Fair*, 1 October 2010, http:// www.vanityfair.com/business/features/2010/10/greeks-bearing-bonds-201010 (accessed 27 November 2014).

32 'Healthy Returns? Absence and Workplace Health Survey 2011', CBI, May 2011, http:// www.cbi.org.uk/media/955604/2011.05-healthy_returns_-_absence_and_workplace_ health_survey_2011.pdf (accessed 22 December 2014).

33 Zoé Shepard, *Absolument dé-bor-dée! Ou le paradox du fonctionnaire* (Paris: Albin Michel, 2010), pp. 23–4.

34 Andrew Malone, 'Will the Emperor of Excess bankrupt France?', *Daily Mail*, 27 October 2011, http://www.dailymail.co.uk/news/article-2053994/Nicolas-Sarkozy-Will-Emperor-Excess-bankrupt-France.html (accessed 30 November 2014).

35 Colin Robinson, 'Liberalisation of the Energy Market: A Favourable Supply-side Shock for the UK Economy?', Surrey Energy Economics Centre, June 1994, http://www.seec. surrey.ac.uk/research/SEEDS/SEEDS73.pdf (accessed 30 November 2014). The figure of 91,500 employees was for 1986.

36 Sunita Kikeri and John Nellis, 'An Assessment of Privatization', *World Bank Observer* 19:1 (2004), 87–118.

37 Robinson, 'Liberalisation of the Energy Market'.

38 Eliana Johnson, 'IRS paying over 200 employees to work full-time for labor union', National Review Online, 8 July 2014, http://www.nationalreview.com/ corner/352876/irs-paying-over-200-employees-work-full-time-labor-union-eliana-johnson (accessed 3 March 2015). In Spain, even private companies are obliged by law to pay for full-time trade union employees.

39 The number of *liberados* depends on the number of employees.

40 Adrian T. Moore, 'Private Prisons: Quality Corrections at a Lower Cost', Policy Study No. 240, Reason Foundation, April 1998, http://reason.org/files/d14ffa18290a9aeb969d1a6c1a9ff935.pdf (accessed 1 December 2014).

41 Ibid., p. 18.

42 'The Life Programme', Participle website, www.alifewewant.com/display/HOME/Our+Story (accessed 1 December 2014). The time spent in the family home might be thought to be the most useful but 'the majority of this time was spent collecting information and data to fulfil the reporting duties'.

43 Ibid.

44 'Getting IT', *The Economist*, 17 October 2002, http://www.economist.com/node/1394744 (accessed 1 December 2014).

45 Ibid.

46 Ibid.

47 Ted Ritter, 'Secret papers reveal Blair's rushed NPfIT plans', ComputerWeekly.com, 18 February 2008, http://www.computerweekly.com/blogs/public-sector/2008/02/secret-papers-reveal-blairs-ru.html (accessed 1 December 2014).

48 'A few responses to comments, misconceptions etc about my *Times* interview', Dominic Cummings's blog, 20 June 2014, http://dominiccummings.wordpress.com/2014/06/20/a-few-responses-to-comments-misconceptions-etc-about-my-times-interview (accessed 1 December 2014). He also remarked, 'Government departments are so dysfunctional that even the great officials who could manage things properly are seldom allowed to by the system.'

49 *Le Point*, 27 June 2013, http://boutique.lepoint.fr/produit/491/fonctionnaires-les-chouchous-du-pouvoir (accessed 1 December 2014).

50 Blake Hurst, 'An Imaginary Dustup? The Incalculable Harm of Regulation', *The American*, 8 January 2012, http://www.american.com/archive/2012/january/an-imaginary-dustup-the-incalculable-harm-of-regulation (accessed 1 December 2014).

51 Ibid.

52 Edward Cody, 'Seven peculiar rules imposed on the French', WorldViews blog, *Washington Post*, 16 April 2013, http://www.washingtonpost.com/blogs/worldviews/wp/2013/04/16/seven-peculiar-rules-imposed-on-the-french (accessed 1 December 2014).

53 'Ces bureaucrates qui nous tyrannisent', *Le Point*, 21 March 2013.

54 Ibid.

55 Ibid.

56 Ibid.

57　Ibid.

58　Graham Ruddick, 'UK planning laws "a living nightmare", says Redrow founder Steve Morgan', Telegraph Online, 9 September 2011, http://www.telegraph.co.uk/finance/newsbysector/constructionandproperty/8751013/UK-planning-laws-a-living-nightmare-says-Redrow-founder-Steve-Morgan.html (accessed 1 December 2014).

59　David Barrett, 'Police red tape revealed: reams of paperwork to look through a window', Telegraph Online, 16 October 2010, http://www.telegraph.co.uk/news/uknews/law-and-order/8068202/Police-red-tape-revealed-reams-of-paperwork-to-look-through-a-window.html (accessed 1 December 2014).

60　Gregory Viscusi and Mark Deen, 'Why France has so many 49-employee companies', *Bloomberg Businessweek*, 3May 2012, http://www.businessweek.com/articles/2012-05-03/why-france-has-so-many-49-employee-companies (accessed 1 December 2014).

61　Ross Clark, 'Why councils ask if you're transgender when you call about the wheelie bins', *Daily Mail*, 20 March 2013, http://www.dailymail.co.uk/news/article-2296107/Why-councils-ask-youre-transgender-wheelie-bins.html (accessed 1 December 2014).

62　Michael Howard, 'Keep the bureaucrats' hands off our hospices', *The Times*, 18 December 2012. Lord Howard, chairman of Help the Hospices, was previously a senior government minister and then leader of the Conservative Party.

63　Ibid.

64　The think tank was iFRAP, which stands for *Fondation pour la recherche sur les administrations et les politiques publiques*. Quoted in 'Ces bureaucrates qui nous tyrannisent'.

65　Edward L. Glaeser, 'Growth engines', *City Journal*, Special Issue 2013, http://www.city-journal.org/2013/special-issue_small-businesses.html (accessed 1 December 2014).

66　Giuseppe Nicoletti and Stefano Scarpetta, 'Regulation, Productivity, and Growth: OECD evidence', World Bank Policy Research Working Papers, January 2003, http://elibrary.worldbank.org/doi/pdf/10.1596/1813-9450-2944 (accessed 1 December 2014).

67　John Stossel, *No They Can't: Why Government Fails – but Individuals Succeed* (New York: Threshold, 2012).

68　John Dawson and John Seater, 'Federal Regulation and Aggregate Economic Growth', January 2013, available at http://www4.ncsu.edu/~jjseater/regulationandgrowth.pdf (accessed 1 December 2014).

69　'Ease of Doing Business Index'. World Bank website, http://data.worldbank.org/indicator/IC.BUS.EASE.XQ/countries/1W?display=default (accessed 1 December 2014).

70　'Gross Domestic Product', Geostat website, http://geostat.ge/index.php?action=page&p_id=119&lang=eng (accessed 1 December 2014).

71   'GDP per capita, PPP (current international $)', World Bank website, http://data.
     worldbank.org/indicator/NY.GDP.PCAP.PP.CD?order=wbapi_data_value_2011%20
     wbapi_data_value%20wbapi_data_value-last&sort=desc (accessed 1 December 2014).
     These are figures adjusted for purchasing power parity. They represent a standard of
     living equivalent to what a dollar could buy in the USA.

72   There will certainly be people who say, 'It is not fair to compare France and Hong Kong.
     Hong Kong has had special advantages. It has been an *entrepôt* for China for example.' I
     might find this objection more convincing if such people would identify any country with
     minimal restrictions on trade, commerce and free enterprise which had done badly and, at
     the same time, a country with high regulations and restrictions on trade which had done
     anything like as well. I would also point out that Hong Kong had its own manufacturing
     and service industries that did not depend on it being an *entrepôt*. Meanwhile there are
     other islands offshore from great continents which have not similarly developed into
     wonderfully successful economies: Sri Lanka, Malta, Cuba and Madagascar are examples.

73   Richard Fisher Speech at the Cato Institute, 10 October 2012, http://www.cato.org/
     events/europes-crisis-welfare-state-lessons-united-states (accessed 1 December 2014).

74   'The "progressive" IRS', *New York Post*, 28 June 2013, http://nypost.com/2013/06/28/the-
     progressive-irs (accessed 1 December 2014).

75   Quoted in 'Where's the special prosecutor? The IRS scandal demands an independent
     investigation', *Chicago Tribune*, 30 June 2013, http://articles.chicagotribune.com/2013-06-
     30/opinion/ct-edit-irs-20130630_1_new-irs-conservative-groups-irs-scandal (accessed 1
     December 2014).

76   Quoted in Dan Mitchell, 'More libertarian-leaning humor from Jay Leno', International
     Liberty blog, http://danieljmitchell.wordpress.com/2013/06/23/more-libertarian-leaning-
     humor-from-jay-leno/?utm_source=twitterfeed&utm_medium=twitter (accessed 1
     December 2014).

77   Timothy Hinks and Artjoms Ivlevs, 'Communist Party Membership and Bribe Paying in
     Transitional Economies', University of the West of England Economics Working Papers
     Series 1401, 2014, http://www2.uwe.ac.uk/faculties/BBS/BUS/Research/Economics%20
     Papers%202014/1401.pdf (accessed 1 December 2014).

78   In western Europe the probability of having to pay a bribe is 0.53 per cent, as against 4.55
     per cent in the 'transitional economies' (ibid., Table 1). 'Communism created structural
     incentives for engaging in corrupt behaviors, which became such a widespread fact of
     life that they became rooted in the culture in these societies' (Wayne Sandholtz and Rein
     Taagepera, 'Corruption, Culture, and Communism', *International Review of Sociology*
     15:1 (2005), 109–31). Note also a study of bribery in Uganda in which the author remarks,
     'Firms typically have to pay bribes when dealing with public officials whose actions
     directly affect the firms' business operations' (Jakob Svensson, 'Who Must Pay Bribes
     and How Much? Evidence from a Cross-section of Firms', Institute for International
     Economics Studies, Stockholm University, May 2012, available at http://www.diva-
     portal.org/smash/get/diva2:343782/FULLTEXT01.pdf (accessed 1 December 2014).)

79   Matt Chorley, 'Revealed: The health bosses who ordered cover-up at hospital unit where
      16 babies died are finally named and shamed', *Daily Mail* 20 June 2013, http://www.
      dailymail.co.uk/news/article-2345216/REVEALED-The-health-bosses-ordered-cover-
      hospital-unit-16-babies-died-finally-named-shamed.html (accessed 1 December 2014).

80   'Mid Staffordshire Trust inquiry: how the care scandal unfolded', *Daily Telegraph*,
      6 February 2013, http://www.telegraph.co.uk/health/healthnews/9851763/Mid-
      Staffordshire-Trust-inquiry-how-the-care-scandal-unfolded.html (accessed 1 December
      2014).

81   Andrew Gilligan, 'NHS bureaucrats care for themselves, not the patients', *Daily
      Telegraph*, 9 April 2010, http://www.telegraph.co.uk/health/7569995/NHS-bureaucrats-
      care-for-themselves-not-the-patients.html. See also the official report at http://www.
      midstaffspublicinquiry.com/report (both accessed 1 December 2014).

82   Sebastián Galiani, Paul Gertler and Ernesto Schargrodsky, 'Water for Life: The Impact of
      the Privatization of Water Services on Child Mortality', *Journal of Political Economy* 113:1
      (2005), 83–120.

83   Ibid.

84   Stuart Holder, 'Privatisation and Competition: The Evidence from Utility and
      Infrastructure Privatisation in the UK', twelfth plenary session of the OECD Advisory
      Group on Privatisation, Helsinki, 17–18 September 1998, p. 20, http://www.oecd.org/
      daf/ca/corporategovernanceofstate-ownedenterprises/1929658.pdf (accessed 1 December
      2014).

85   Ibid.

86   'El 82% de los funcionarios se decanta por la sanidad privada', *Libre Mercado* 11 February
      2014, http://www.libremercado.com/2014-02-11/el-82-de-los-funcionarios-se-decanta-
      por-la-sanidad-privada-1276510463 (accessed 1 December 2014).

87   I gave an example of this phenomenon in *The Welfare State We're In*. A baby died
      unnecessarily in a private hospital. It was front-page news and was commented on
      extensively. However at a similar time, there were cases of several unnecessary deaths of
      babies in NHS hospitals which barely got into the news at all.

88   Op. cit.

89   Sir Ernest Benn, *Why Freedom Works: Passages from Books 1924–53* (London: Benn, 1964).

90   For the pensions system in Australia see http://www.pensionfundsonline.co.uk/content/
      country-profiles/australia/80 and for Hong Kong see http://www.pensionfundsonline.
      co.uk/content/country-profiles/hong-kong/104 (both accessed 1 December 2014).

91   Karin Svanborg-Sjövall, 'Privatising the Swedish Welfare State', *Economic Affairs* 34:2
      (2014), 181–92. 'Welfare quasi-markets are increasingly subject to input-related regulation
      and control.'

CHAPTER 11: 'IT'S LIKE PUTTING ALL BUS DRIVERS THROUGH ASTRONAUTS' TRAINING.'

1   In theory, at least, a first degree or *laurea* takes three years. Then there is a *laurea magistrale*, equivalent to a master's degree, taking two more years, to be followed by a *dottorato di ricerca*, equivalent to a PhD, taking another 3–4 years. Since secondary school continues until a person is nineteen, this would easily take someone to the age of twenty-eight or even thirty, if one is allowed to progress more slowly. I am not sure how the attempt to reduce the years of study is currently working in practice but my informants clearly thought that for many people, things had not changed very much.

2   Dick M. Carpenter II, 'Blooming Nonsense', *Regulation*, Spring 2011, available at http://object.cato.org/sites/cato.org/files/serials/files/regulation/2011/4/regv34n1-8.pdf (accessed 1 December 2014). Carpenter is director of strategic research at the Institute for Justice and an associate professor at the University of Colorado.

3   Morris M. Kleiner and Alan B. Krueger, 'Analyzing the Extent and Influence of Occupational Licensing on the Labor Market', *Journal of Labor Economics*, 31:2 (2013), S173–S202, available at http://www.hhh.umn.edu/people/mkleiner/pdf/Final.occ.licensing.JOLE.pdf (accessed 1 December 2014).

4   Adam B. Summers, 'Occupational Licensing: Ranking the States and Exploring Alternatives', Policy Study 361, Reason Foundation, August 2007, http://reason.org/files/762c8fe96431b6fa5e27ca64eaa1818b.pdf (accessed 01 December 2014).

5   Perdido Productions, 2013.

6   David E. Bernstein, *Only One Place of Redress: African Americans, Labor Regulations, and the Courts from Reconstruction to the New Deal* (Durham, NC: Duke University Press, 2001).

7   Ibid., p. 38.

8   Ibid.

9   David Green, *Working-class Patients and the Medical Establishment: Self-help in Britain from the Mid-nineteenth Century to 1948* (Aldershot: Gower / Hounslow: Maurice Temple Smith, 1985), p. 46.

10   David Green, 'Medical Care without the State', in Arthur Seldon (ed.), *Re-privatising Welfare: After the Lost Century* (London: Institute of Economic Affairs, 1996).

11   'In 1911 and 1946 the government of the day needed professional cooperation, and paid their asking price' (ibid., p. 186).

12   Jeffrey Lionel Berlant, *Profession and Monopoly: A Study of Medicine in the United States and Britain* (Berkeley: University of California Press, 1975), pp. 303, 305.

13   Clayton Christensen, 'The Future of Medical Education', in Clayton M. Christensen, Jerome H. Grossman and Jason Hwang, *The Innovator's Prescription: A Disruptive Solution For Health Care* (New York: McGraw-Hill, 2009).

14   Comment mentioned in email to the author from James F. Cawley, professor at George
      Washington University.

15   Ibid.

16   Kleiner and Krueger, 'Analyzing the Extent and Influence of Occupational Licensing on
      the Labor Market'.

17   Ibid.

18   'A spoonful of monopoly helps the medicine go down', Free Exchange
      blog, *The Economist*, 21 September 2007, http://www.economist.com/blogs/
      freeexchange/2007/09/a_spoonful_of_monopoly_helps_t (accessed 1 December 2014).

19   Milton Friedman and Rose Friedman, *Free to Choose: A Personal Statement* (New York:
      Harcourt Brace Jovanovich, 1980).

20   *Report of the Mid Staffordshire NHS Foundation Trust Public Inquiry, vol. 1: Analysis of
      Evidence and Lessons Learned (Part 1)*, HC898-I, February 2013, p. 118, http://www.
      midstaffspublicinquiry.com/sites/default/files/report/Volume%201.pdf (accessed 1
      December 2014).

21   *Independent Inquiry into Care Provided by Mid Staffordshire NHS Foundation Trust
      January 2005 – March 2009, vol. 1*, HC 375-I, February 2010, p. 57, http://webarchive.
      nationalarchives.gov.uk/20130107105354/http://www.dh.gov.uk/prod_consum_dh/
      groups/dh_digitalassets/@dh/@en/@ps/documents/digitalasset/dh_113447.pdf (accessed 1
      December 2014).

22   Ibid.

23   'Patients "routinely neglected" at Stafford Hospital', *Daily Telegraph*, 24 February 2010,
      http://www.telegraph.co.uk/health/healthnews/7306347/Patients-routinely-neglected-
      at-Stafford-Hospital.html (accessed 1 December 2014). This newspaper report has it in
      indirect quotes but another report, which I now cannot find, had it in direct quotes.

24   Christensen et al., *The Innovator's Prescription*, p. 357.

25   Sophie Borland, 'Trainee nurses "spend too long in lecture halls and not enough time
      with patients"', *Daily Mail*, 23 September 2011, http://www.dailymail.co.uk/health/
      article-2040825/Trainee-nurses-spend-time-patients.html (accessed 1 December 2014).

26   'What a waste! The NHS spends millions on training, but we are recruiting from
      overseas', Mail Online, 22 January 2007, http://www.dailymail.co.uk/health/
      article-430676/What-waste-The-NHS-spends-millions-training-recruiting-overseas.html
      (accessed 1 December 2014).

27   Celia Hall, 'NHS cuts "leave new nurses without jobs"', *Daily Telegraph*, 26 April 2006.

28   Kleiner and Krueger, 'Analyzing the Extent and Influence of Occupational Licensing on
      the Labor Market'.

29   Rita Kramer, *Ed School Follies: The Miseducation of America's Teachers* (New York: Free Press, 1991).

30   Quoted in Carpenter, 'Blooming Nonsense'. Jason Potts is an economist at the Queensland University of Technology.

31   Roderick Hooker, James Cawley and David Aprey, 'Economic Assessment of Physician Assistants', in *Physician Assistants: Policy and Practice*, 3rd ed. (Philadelphia: F. A. Davis, 2010).

32   Email to author from James Cawley.

33   Victoria Stagg Elliott, 'Number of physician assistants doubles over past decade', amednews.com, 27 September 2011, http://www.amednews.com/article/20110927/ business/309279997/8 (accessed 1 December 2014).

34   Sources: ibid. for 2000 and 2010 figures; figures for 1983 and 1988 from Carol Kleiman, 'Physician assistants taking a larger care role', *Chicago Tribune*, 11 September 1988, http:// articles.chicagotribune.com/1988-09-11/news/8801290433_1_physician-assistants-order-laboratory-tests-patients-medical-histories (accessed 1 December 2014).

35   Jacob Goldstein, 'So you think you can be a hair-braider?', *New York Times Magazine*, 12 June 2012, http://www.nytimes.com/2012/06/17/magazine/so-you-think-you-can-be-a-hair-braider.html?pagewanted=all&_r=0 (accessed 1 December 2014).

36   Kleiner and Krueger, 'Analysing the Extent and Influence of Occupational Licensing on the Labor Market'.

37   Union membership in the USA stood at 12 per cent in 2008.

38   Op. cit. It should be mentioned that these statistics are not all exactly comparable with each other but they appear to be the best available.

39   'Our History', ACCA website, http://www.accaglobal.com/uk/en/discover/about/history. html (accessed 24 December 2014). Also conversation with and email from Colin Davis at the ACCA.

40   'For many, two years is plenty', *The Economist*, 31 August 2013, http://www.economist. com/news/united-states/21584392-president-suggests-scrapping-last-year-law-school-many-two-years-plenty (accessed 1 December 2014). The article asserts that law schools sprang up in the nineteenth century in two forms: elite universities teaching the subject for three years and night schools which catered to the sons of immigrants. The 'snootier' institutions 'convinced the American Bar Association to accredit only schools that required a costly three years' worth of courses'. It also claims that the average 2013 graduate will be $140,000 in debt 'according to one estimate'.

41   'Rules for fools', *The Economist*, 12 May 2011, http://www.economist.com/node/18678963 (accessed 1 December 2014).

CHAPTER 12: DEMOCRACY IS LIKE A DRUNK HUSBAND

1   Heritage History on Clodius, http://www.heritage-history.com/www/heritage.php?Dir=c haracters&FileName=clodius.php.

2   Ibid.

3   H. H. Scullard, *From the Gracchi to Nero: A History of Rome from 133 BC to AD 68* (Abingdon: Routledge [1959] 2011), p. 99.

4   'Roman society, Roman life', Roman Empire website, http://www.roman-empire.net/ society/society.html (accessed 1 December 2014). Bread only came into general use at the beginning of the second century.

5   Research notes by Fraser citing 'Veyne 1930/1990 244'.

6   From the publisher's description of Joanna Innes and Mark Philp (eds), *Re-imagining Democracy in the Age of Revolutions: America, France, Britain, Ireland 1750–1850* (Oxford: Oxford University Press, 2013), http://ukcatalogue.oup.com/product/9780199669158.do (accessed 1 December 2014).

7   Scullard, *From the Gracchi to Nero*, p. 152.

8   Ibid., pp. 287, 152, 122.

9   Ibid, p. 287. There are some who regard the corn dole as part of the reason for the decline of the Roman Empire: 'The dole became an integral part of the whole complex of economic causes that brought the eventual collapse of Roman civilization. It undermined the old Roman virtues of self-reliance. It schooled people to expect something for nothing … The necessity of feeding the soldiers and the idlers in the cities led to strangling and destructive taxation. Because of the lethargy of slaves and undernourished free workmen, industrial progress ceased.

     'There were periodic exactions from the rich and frequent confiscations of property. The better-off inhabitants of the towns were forced to provide food, lodging, and transport for the troops. Soldiers were allowed to loot the districts through which they passed. Production was everywhere discouraged and in some places brought to a halt. Ruinous taxation eventually destroyed the sources of revenue.' (From Henry Hazlitt, 'Poor Relief in Ancient Rome', in *The Conquest of Poverty* (New Rochelle, NY: Arlington House, 1973), available at http://www. fee.org/the_freeman/detail/poor-relief-in-ancient-rome (accessed 1 December 2014).)

10   Hansard, HC Deb, 11 November 1947, vol. 444, col. 207.

11   American journalist and satirist (1880–1956).

12   1917.

13   *Public Opinion in the European Union*, Standard Eurobarometer 78, Autumn 2012, pp. 52, 54, http://ec.europa.eu/public_opinion/archives/eb/eb78/eb78_publ_en.pdf (accessed 2 December 2014).

14   The origin of this word is the tradition in the USA that neighbours who had cut a lot of
      timber would find it sensible to join together to roll each other's logs (*Online Etymology
      Dictionary*, http://www.etymonline.com/index.php?allowed_in_frame=0&search=logroll
      ing&searchmode=none (accessed 2 December 2014).)

15   The term 'pork barrel' is 'used in reference to the use of government funds for projects
      designed to please voters or legislators and win votes. The term, which is recorded from
      the early 20th century in this sense, refers to the use of such a barrel by farmers, to keep
      a reserve supply of meat' (Elizabeth Knowles (ed.), *Oxford Dictionary of Phrase and Fable*,
      2nd ed. (Oxford: Oxford University Press, 2005).)

16   Conversation with Terry Moe. He was talking about the Affordable Care Act ('Obamacare')
      but the individual act is not as significant as the difficulty of getting coherent policy into law.

17   Timur Kuran, 'Now out of Never: The Element of Surprise in the East European
      Revolution of 1989', *World Politics* 44:1 (1991), pp. 7–48. This refers to the fall of
      communism but the same concepts apply to democratic states.

18   In conversation with Ed Feulner, as reported in email to author from John Blundell.
      Minogue (1930–2013) was Emeritus Professor of Political Science at the London School
      of Economics and Political Science.

19   I first heard of 'magic thinking' in conversation with Leszek Balcerowicz, the former
      deputy Prime Minister of Poland. The phrase has different meanings in different
      contexts. Its application to politics seems to me to be very useful and identifies an
      important part of the psychology of government and of voting.

20   Benito Arruñada is Professor of Business Organization at Pompeu Fabra University,
      Barcelona. We were talking about how governments trick people, how easy they are to
      trick and how they may even partly want everything decided for them.

21   Kenneth Minogue, *The Egalitarian Conceit: False and True Equalities* (London: Centre
      for Policy Studies, 1989), http://www.cps.org.uk/publications/reports/the-egalitarian-
      conceit (accessed 2 December 2014).

22   See http://thinkexist.com/quotes/plato/3.html (accessed 2 December 2014).

23   Frédéric Bastiat, *Selected Essays on Political Economy*, tr. Seymour Cain (Princeton, NJ:
      Van Nostrand, 1964).

24   Quoted in Geoffrey A. Plauché, 'Idealistic politics', *Libertarian Standard*, 21 April 2011,
      http://www.libertarianstandard.com/2011/04/21/idealistic-politics (accessed 2 December
      2014).

25   Frédéric Bastiat, 'The State', in *'The Law,' 'The State,' and Other Political Writings 1843–
      1850* (Indianapolis: Liberty Fund, 2012), pp. 93–5.

26   The story of St Jeanne of Jugan suggests there was little if any state support for the
      elderly in Bastiat's time (see 'Our History', Little Sisters of the Poor website, http://www.
      littlesistersofthepoor.org/ourlife/our-history (accessed 2 December 2014).) as does the

history of healthcare, which was dominated by voluntary mutual benefit societies (see Simone Sandier, Valérie Paris and Dominique Polton, *Health Care Systems in Transition: France* (Copenhagen: WHO Regional Office for Europe, 2004), p. 5, http://www.euro. who.int/__data/assets/pdf_file/0009/80694/E83126.pdf (accessed 2 December 2014).)

27 Jason L. Riley, *Please Stop Helping Us: How Liberals Make It Harder for Blacks to Succeed* (New York: Encounter, 2014).

28 See usgovernmentspending website, http://www.usgovernmentspending.com/us_20th_ century_chart.html (accessed 2 December 2014). This chart shows the rise in spending. However the precise figures for recent years are not shown. For the 2011 figure I have used the one used by Chris Edwards of the Cato Institute in testimony ('American government spending: 41% of GDP', Cato at Liberty blog, Cato Institute website, 19 October 2011, http://www.cato.org/blog/american-government-spending-41-gdp (accessed 2 December 2014).) The use of this figure was criticised as being an OECD figure but I prefer to use it as the OECD figures are more likely to be comparable internationally than national figures ('Is government spending really 41 per cent of GDP?', Off the Charts blog, 18 October 2011, http://www.offthechartsblog.org/ is-government-spending-really-41-percent-of-gdp (accessed 2 December 2014).)

29 'Les dépenses publiques depuis un siècle', Vie Publique website, 12 June 2013, http:// www.vie-publique.fr/decouverte-institutions/finances-publiques/approfondissements/ depenses-publiques-depuis-siecle.html (accessed 2 December 2014).

30 Sources: 1872–2000: ibid.; 2012: 'Total government expenditure', Eurostat, http://epp. eurostat.ec.europa.eu/tgm/table.do?tab=table&init=1&plugin=1&language=en&pcode= tec00023 (accessed 2 December 2014).

31 'UK public spending as per cent of GDP', ukpublicspending website, http://www. ukpublicspending.co.uk/total_spending_chart#copypaste (accessed 2 December 2014).

32 'UK Public Spending since 1963', *The Guardian*, http://www.theguardian.com/news/ datablog/2010/apr/25/uk-public-spending-1963#data (accessed 2 December 2014).

33 1900: GDP £1,885m and defence spending £71.3m. 2010: GDP £1,458bn and defence spending £42.5bn. ('Total public spending: expenditure – charts – GDP debt', ukpublicspending website. http://www.ukpublicspending.co.uk/ total_spending_2010UKmn.)

34 Defence spending in the USA was much lower in 1900 but all government spending then was much lower at that time. 1900: GDP $20,567m and defence spending $331.6m. 1960: GDP $526.4bn and defence spending $53.3bn. 2012: GDP $15.7trn and defence spending $0.88trn ('Government spending in the US', usgovernmentspending website, http://www. usgovernmentspending.com/total_spending_1960USmn (accessed 2 December 2014).) It is true that there has been a 'peace dividend' in that governments no longer need to spend so much on defence since there appears to be no imminent threat of world war. However, it is also true that this has created extra space for welfare state spending to move into.

35 'Government expenditure by function', OECD.StatExtracts, http://stats.oecd.org/Index. aspx?DatasetCode=SNA_TABLE11 (accessed 2 December 2014).

36   Ibid.

37   Willem Adema, Pauline Fron and Maxime Ladaique, 'Is the European Welfare State
     Really More Expensive?', OECD Social, Employment and Migration Working Papers
     No. 124, October 2011, p. 41, http://www.oecd-ilibrary.org/docserver/download/
     5kg2d2d4pbf0.pdf?expires=1380823120&id=id&accname=guest&checksum=22B3FED95
     63363089C574081F4670D99 (accessed 2 December 2014).

38   Ibid. In 1980 the figure for 'public social expenditure' was 27.2 per cent and in 1989 it
     was 29.3 per cent. The OECD averages were 15.7 per cent and 17.3 per cent respectively.

39   Goran Persson, 'The Swedish Experience in Reducing Budget Deficits and Debt',
     Federal Reserve Bank of Kansas City Economic Review, Q1 1996, pp. 7–9, http://www.
     kansascityfed.org/publicat/econrev/pdf/1q96pers.pdf (accessed 2 December 2014).

40   Government spending as a proportion of GDP reached 68 per cent in 1993. This is the
     highest figure I remember seeing and surely is at the upper limit for a non-communist
     society. The figure came down all the way to below 48 per cent in 2012. See 'The US
     and Europe: governments of equal size?', e21 website, 8 February 2012, http://www.
     economics21.org/commentary/us-and-europe-governments-equal-size (accessed 2
     December 2014).

41   Adema et al., 'Is the European Welfare State Really More Expensive?'

42   Marc Sidwell, 'The long view: behind the debt ceiling madness lurks the insanity
     of an uncontrollable state', *City AM*, 11 October 2013, http://www.cityam.com/
     article/1381452052/long-view-behind-debt-ceiling-madness-lurks-insanity-uncontrollable-
     state (accessed 2 December 2014).

43   'Appenzell Innerrhoden enjoys "pure democracy", *The Local* (Switzerland), 24 May 2013,
     http://www.thelocal.ch/20130524/appenzell-practices-democracy-in-its-purest-form
     (accessed 2 December 2014).

44   The government expenditure figures are from a table of OECD figures kindly extracted
     and sent to me by Chris Edwards of the Cato Institute. They are marked 'Annexe 25
     General Government Total Outlays – Per cent of Nominal GDP'. The figures go up to
     2013 but since those figures must be forecast ones, given that the table was published
     in that year, I have taken the figures for 2012. The tax statistics are OECD figures
     from OECD.Statextracts (http://stats.oecd.org/Index.aspx?QueryId=21699 (accessed 2
     December 2014).) I have used the latest figure (2011) for Switzerland but since there is no
     OECD figure for that year I have taken the one for 2010.

45   There are different estimates one could use. I have used the World Bank's GDP per
     capita on a purchasing power parity basis for 2013 (http://data.worldbank.org/indicator/
     NY.GDP.PCAP.PP.CD?order=wbapi_data_value_2011%20wbapi_data_value%20
     wbapi_data_value-last&sort=desc, accessed 2 December 2014). The countries ahead of
     Switzerland were Qatar, Macao, Luxembourg, Kuwait, Singapore, Brunei, Norway and
     the UAE. Close behind were Hong Kong and the USA.

46   'Bundesratsbeschluss über das Ergebnis der Volksabstimmung vom 11. März 2012',

p. 6624, http://www.admin.ch/opc/de/federal-gazette/2012/6623.pdf (accessed 2 December 2014).

47 Lars Feld, Justina Fischer and Gebhard Kirchgässner, 'The Effect of Direct Democracy on Income Redistribution: Evidence for Switzerland', London School of Economics and Political Science, October 2006, http://sticerd.lse.ac.uk/dps/pepp/pepp23.pdf (accessed 2 December 2014). This paper refers in the introduction to two previous studies: C. Schaltegger, 'The Effects of Federalism and Democracy on the Size of Government: Evidence from Swiss Sub-national Jurisdictions', *ifo Studien* 47 (2001), 145–62; A. Vatter and M. Freitag, 'Die Janusköpfigkeit von Verhandlungsdemokratien: Zur Wirkung von Konkordanz, direkter Demokratie und dezentraler Entscheidungsstrukturen auf den öffentlichen Sektor der Schweizer Kantone', *Swiss Political Science Review* 8 (2002), 53–80.

48 Feld et al., 'The Effect of Direct Democracy on Income Redistribution'. See Table 2.

49 Lars P. Feld and John G. Matsuka, 'Budget Referendums and Government Spending: Economic Evidence from Swiss Cantons', available at http://www.iandrinstitute.org/New%20IRI%20Website%20Info/I&R%20Research%20and%20History/I&R%20Studies/Feld%20and%20Matsusaka%20-%20Fiscal%20Evidence%20from%20Swiss%20Cantons%20IRI.pdf (accessed 2 December 2014).

50 Bruno Frey, 'The Role of Democracy in Securing Just and Prosperous Societies: Direct Democracy – Politico-economic Lessons From Swiss Experience', *American Economic Review* 84:2 (1994).

51 Bruno Frey and Alois Stutzer, 'Happiness, Economy and Institutions', *Economic Journal* 110:466 (2000), 918–38.

52 From 13.8 per cent to 18.5 per cent (OECD figures); see Adema et al., 'Is the European Welfare State Really More Expensive?', Table A.I.1.3.

53 For the current figure see ibid. The 1970 figure comes from *OECD Economic Surveys 1985–86: Switzerland* (Paris: OECD Publishing, 1986).

54 Patrick McGreevy and Melanie Mason, 'Spending impulse curbed in California', *Washington Post*, 26 September 2013, http://www.washingtonpost.com/national/spending-impulse-curbed-in-california/2013/09/26/7cb43b2c-1efa-11e3-8459-657e0c72fec8_story.html (accessed 2 December 2014).

55 See http://en.wikipedia.org/wiki/2008%E2%80%9312_California_budget_crisis (accessed 2 December 2014).

56 Emails from Christian Wignall to the author, October 2013.

57 In my interview with Leszek Balcerowicz in Warsaw, he said that he introduced this limit. I see that the limit was in line with but not identical to the European Union limits on spending. But Poland is different from other EU countries by having enshrined the rule in its constitution. See also Ian Lienert, 'Should Advanced Countries Adopt a Fiscal Responsibility Law?', IMF Working Paper WP/10/254, November 2010, p. 17, http://www.imf.org/external/pubs/ft/wp/2010/wp10254.pdf (accessed 2 December 2014).

58   See Lienert, 'Should Advanced Countries Adopt a Fiscal Responsibility Law?'; Jón R.
      Blöndal, 'Budgeting in Singapore', *OECD Journal on Budgeting* 6:1 (2006), p. 51, http://
      www.oecd.org/gov/budgeting/40140241.pdf (accessed 2 December 2014).

CHAPTER 13: AND THE WINNER IS… ~~COMMUNISM~~ ~~CAPITALISM~~ WELFARE STATISM!

1   Lenin, *The State and Revolution* (1917).

2   Jacques Barzun, *From Dawn to Decadence: 500 Years of Western Cultural Life* (London:
      HarperCollins, 2000), p. 688.

3   More of the quotation can be read here: http://www.heretical.com/British/mhistory.html
      (accessed 2 December 2014).

4   José Ortega y Gasset, *La rebelión de las masas* (1930).

5   Big Brother appears in George Orwell's novel *Nineteen Eighty-Four*. He is the dictator of
      a totalitarian state whose citizens are under constant surveillance by the authorities.

6   'Spain's jobless rate falls for first time in two years', BBC News online, 25 July 2013,
      http://www.bbc.co.uk/news/business-23447087 (accessed 2 December 2014).

7   Herbert Spencer, 'Over-legislation', *Westminster Review*, July 1853, available at Library
      of Economics and Liberty website, http://www.econlib.org/library/LFBooks/Spencer/
      spnMvS7.html (accessed 2 December 2014).

8   Quoted in Jonathan Haidt, *The Happiness Hypothesis: Putting Ancient Wisdom to the Test
      of Modern Science* (London: Arrow, 2006), p. 133.

9   Eric Klinenberg, *Going Solo: The Extraordinary Rise and Surprising Appeal of Living Alone*
      (New York: Penguin Press, 2012).

10   George F. Will, 'Cupcake compliance illustrates Washington's quest to control
      everything', *National Post*, 21 August 2014, http://fullcomment.nationalpost.
      com/2014/08/21/george-f-will-cupcake-compliance-illustrates-washingtons-quest-to-
      control-everything (accessed 2 December 2014).

11   Home schooling has been illegal in Germany since Hitler banned it in 1938. It is one of
      the few Nazi laws still on the books. Hitler introduced the ban to force all children to
      attend state-approved schools where they were to be indoctrinated with Nazi ideology.
      In one case 'the children, between 7 and 14 years old, were forcibly removed from
      their parents, Dirk and Petra Wunderlich, and taken into state custody at an unknown
      location' (Peter Martino, 'Europe: treating homeschoolers like terrorists', Gatestone
      Institute website, 10 September 2013, http://www.gatestoneinstitute.org/3969/europe-
      homeschoolers (accessed 2 December 2014).)

12   Frédéric Bastiat, *Selected Essays on Political Economy*, tr. Seymour Cain (Princeton, NJ:
      Van Nostrand, 1964), p. 144. I have changed one word from 'with' to 'will'.

13   Op. cit.

14   In pamphlet on egalitarianism for the Centre for Policy Studies, reported in an email to the author by John Blundell.

15   Kenneth Minogue, *The Servile Mind: How Democracy Erodes the Moral Life* (New York: Encounter, 2010).

16   Jason L. Riley, *Please Stop Helping Us: How Liberals Make It Harder for Blacks to Succeed* (New York: Encounter, 2014). The book argues that programmes ostensibly designed to help blacks have actually harmed them.

BEST AND WORST WELFARE STATES

1   'Labor force participation rate, male (% of male population ages 15+) (modeled ILO estimate)', World Bank website, http://data.worldbank.org/indicator/SL.TLF.CACT. MA.ZS (accessed 2 December 2014).

2   Sweden's functional illiteracy was worse in the 2012 PISA than it had been in previous studies. This could be an aberration or it might reflect deterioration.

3   World Bank gross national income per capita based on purchasing power parity converted to international dollar rates, meaning the purchasing power is the same as would be in the USA. Figures for 2013. High figures (excluding oil states and very small tax havens): Singapore $76,850, Switzerland $56,580, USA $53,960. Low figures: Portugal $25,350, Greece $25,650, Spain $31,850 (http://data.worldbank.org/indicator/NY.GNP. PCAP.PP.CD/countries (accessed 2 December 2014).

APPENDIX

1   Peter Saunders, *When Prophecy Fails* (St Leonards, NSW: Centre for Independent Studies, 2011), pp. 33–4.

2   Ibid., pp. 48–9.

3   Wilkinson and Piketty replied to Saunders and other critics in a revised edition of *The Spirit Level*. They argued that there were 'no hard and fast rules' about including outliers. They said that testing for third variables would have various drawbacks including creating 'unnecessary noise' and they did not address the criticism that they omitted to show the R2 figures and statistical significance or otherwise of their findings.

I asked a fellow of the Royal Statistical Society who also happens to be a qualified actuary whether these replies were satisfactory. He replied, 'If you really want to draw an inference, then it would be a good idea to test robustness by removing outliers.' He said that Wilkinson and Piketty's failure to address the issues of R2 and statistical significance was itself 'very significant'. He also suggested that 'addition of other variables does not add noise, it removes noise by providing alternative explanations and by explaining something more fully'.

4   Summarising Alberto Alesina, Rafael Di Tella and Robert MacCulloch, 'Inequality and
     Happiness: Are Europeans and Americans Different?', *Journal of Public Economics* 88:9–
     10 (2004), 2009–42.

5   It is fair to say that there has been an active and sometimes acrimonious disagreement
     between Wilkinson and Saunders. I have read and made use of the critique of
     Wilkinson's work but only after considering the responses to it contained in the later
     edition of *The Spirit Level*. The responses do not include any substantive reply to the
     criticism that he and Piketty failed to use standard tests used by social scientists. He
     could well say to me that this book is full of ideas and assertions that have not been
     subjected to the normal tests of social science. That is wholly true. However, this book is
     not offered by an academic social scientist as an academic piece of work.

6   'Sweden's Gini coefficient for disposable income is now 0.24, still a lot lower than the
     rich-world average of 0.31 but around 25% higher than it was a generation ago' ('The
     New Model', *The Economist*, 11 October 2012, http://www.economist.com/node/21564412
     (accessed 3 December 2014).) The article attributes the change to the less left-wing
     government and does not seem to consider the impact of immigration despite referring
     to it. In Malmö, in 2010, immigrants accounted for 80,000 out of 300,000 inhabitants
     according to *The Guardian* (Ian Traynor, 'Sweden joins Europe-wide backlash against
     immigration', *The Guardian*, 24 September 2010, http://www.theguardian.com/
     world/2010/sep/24/sweden-immigration-far-right-asylum (accessed 3 December 2014).)

7   Japan is one of the countries which has low inequality according to the World Bank.
     This is the information used by Wilkinson and Piketty. But the OECD does not agree,
     placing it as slightly more unequal than the median. The difference is accounted for by
     the fact that the World Bank does not include the incomes of self-employed farmers and
     single-person households but the OECD does. These people constitute 40 per cent of
     the population. It does seem, at the least, unreliable to describe Japan as a country of low
     inequality. Certainly it does not have a culture of equality. But if one was going to assert
     confidently that it has low inequality, one should perhaps then consider to what extent
     this might be because Japan has had less immigration than most countries.

8   Michael Tanner, 'The Income–Inequality Myth', National Review Online, 10 January
     2012, http://www.nationalreview.com/articles/287643/income-inequality-myth-michael-
     tanner (accessed 3 December 2014). 'A recent study by Mark Warshawsky of the Social
     Security Board suggests that nearly all of the recent increase in earnings inequality "can
     be explained by the rapid increase in the cost of health insurance employee benefits,
     and that therefore [there] has not been as significant increase, if any, in inequality of
     compensation."'

9   Ibid.

10   'First ONS Annual Experimental Subjective Well-being Results', Office for National
     Statistics, 24 July 2012, http://www.ons.gov.uk/ons/dcp171766_272294.pdf (accessed 3
     December 2014).

11   Ibid.

12 Ibid.

13 Bruno S. Frey and Alois Stutzer, 'The Economics of Happiness', *World Economics* 3:1 (2002).

14 Andrew E. Clark and Andrew J. Oswald, 'Unhappiness and Unemployment', *Economic Journal* 104:424 (1994), pp. 648–59.

15 David G. Blanchflower and Andrew J. Oswald, 'International Happiness: A New View on the Measure of Performance', *Academy of Management Perspectives*, February 2011, pp. 6–22, http://www.dartmouth.edu/~blnchflr/papers/int%20happiness.pdf.

16 *Men, Suicide and Society: Why Disadvantaged Men in Mid-life Die by Suicide*, Samaritans, September 2012, http://www.samaritans.org/sites/default/files/kcfinder/files/Men%20and%20Suicide%20Research%20Report%20210912.pdf (accessed 3 December 2014).

17 'Individual level studies ... are studies in which the units of analysis are individuals ... Individual level studies are most appropriate when investigators are interested in explaining variations between individuals.' (Anna V. Diez-Roux, 'Potentialities and Limitations of Multilevel Analysis in Public Health and Epidemiology', in Daniel Courgeau (ed.), *Methodology and Epistemology of Multilevel Analysis: Approaches from Different Social Sciences* (Dordrecht: Kluwer, 2003).) This kind of study is distinct from 'ecological' studies, which are nothing to do with the environment but in which different areas, like countries, are compared. Thus, it may be that a country with lots of unemployment does not have a high rate of suicide yet, within that country, the unemployed are nonetheless much more likely to commit suicide than the employed. One might guess that the explanation of this could be that the culture of a country and other country-specific factors also affect the incidence of suicide.

18 Kouichi Yoshimasu et al., 'Suicidal Risk Factors and Completed Suicide: Meta-analyses Based on Psychological Autopsy Studies', *Environmental Health and Preventive Medicine* 13:5 (2008), 243–56.

19 Alfonso Ceccherini-Nelli and Stefan Priebe, 'Economic Factors and Suicide Rates: Associations over Time in Four Countries', *Social Psychiatry and Psychiatric Epidemiology* 46:10 (2011), 975–82.

20 *Men, Suicide and Society*, p. 39.

21 Admittedly it is conceivable that some Catholic countries may under-report their suicides. Cross-country comparisons unfortunately have this problem of different rates of reporting and also varying accuracy in measurement.

22 Esther Rantzen, '"I never thought I would be so lonely": Esther Rantzen's aching emptiness', *Daily Mail*, 8 August 2011, http://www.dailymail.co.uk/femail/article-2023581/I-thought-I-lonely-Widowed-Esther-Rantzen-admits-aching-emptiness.html; and Esther Rantzen, 'Lonely Britain', *Daily Mail*, 13 October 2011, http://www.dailymail.co.uk/femail/article-2048488/Lonely-Britain-When-Esther-Rantzen-wrote-Mail-aching-loneliness-received-overwhelming-response-heartfelt-understanding.html (both accessed 3 December 2014).

23   Hara Estroff Marano, 'The Dangers of Loneliness', *Psychology Today*, 1 July 2003, http://
      www.psychologytoday.com/articles/200308/the-dangers-loneliness (accessed 3 December
      2014).

24   Louise Hawkley et al., 'Loneliness Is a Unique Predictor of Age-related Differences in
      Systolic Blood Pressure', *Psychology and Aging* 21:1 (2006), 152–64.

25   Ibid. The extent to which this is the case is not clear. At one extreme, a Swedish study
      found that loneliness among children aged 12–13 was associated with a threefold
      increase in risk of suicide at age 24–5 (Anne Lise Stranden, 'Suicide linked to loneliness
      in childhood', *ScienceNordic*, 29 May 2014, http://sciencenordic.com/suicide-linked-
      loneliness-childhood (accessed 3 December 2014).) At the other extreme, Cacioppo
      himself reported an increased risk of 'premature death' of seniors of 14 per cent. This
      would include suicide but would not comprise suicide alone (David McNamee,
      'Loneliness increases risk of early death in seniors', *MNT*, 17 February 2014, http://www.
      medicalnewstoday.com/articles/272705.php (accessed 3 December 2014).)

26   The pattern shown in this research is very clear. There has been a big rise in the
      proportion of people in this age group who are living alone. This is due to divorce,
      separation and some who never live with partners. Meanwhile there has also been a
      (more modest) increase in the proportion of those over sixty living alone. What is
      probably more significant here is that more people are living longer so the number of
      over-sixties living alone has increased significantly. This particularly affects women, who
      tend to outlive their husbands and partners. Among women aged sixty-one and above,
      47.9 per cent live alone – a frightening statistic. The proportion of women living alone
      passes 90 per cent by the time they reach eighty-five.

27   John T. Cacioppo and William Patrick, *Loneliness: Human Nature and the Need for Social
      Connection* (New York: W. W. Norton, 2008).

28   Strictly speaking, Portugal is not a Mediterranean country, but I include it with the
      Mediterranean countries as it has so much in common with them.

29   Suicide rates, like most statistics, are not always to be relied upon. The culture of
      one society may be such that it is particularly unwilling to admit that a person has
      committed suicide. There are also some strange changes in figures over time, with the
      rate in Denmark falling more than half in only eight years from 1990. The source for the
      latter is Diego De Leo and Russell Evans, *International Suicide Rates: Recent Trends and
      Implications for Australia*, Australian Institute for Suicide Research and Prevention, 2003.

30   Wesley Johnson, 'Britain "becoming lonelier place to live"', *Daily Telegraph*, 7 March
      2013, http://www.telegraph.co.uk/news/9916134/Britain-becoming-lonelier-place-to-live.
      html (accessed 24 December 2014).

WELFARE JARGON EXPLAINED

1   The phrase was popularised and perhaps invented by Gøsta Esping-Andersen in his
      influential book *The Three Worlds of Welfare Capitalism* (Cambridge: Polity Press,
      1989). See my blog on an extract from his book at http://www.thewelfarestatewerein.

com/general/2011/10/esping-andersen-and-his-three-worlds-of-welfare-capitalism.php (accessed 3 December 2014).

2   I hope Esping-Andersen, who used the idea of 'decommodification' in *The Three Worlds of Welfare Capitalism* (see above), will forgive this jocular account of how the concept comes up against reality.

3   Not everyone would agree with this definition, which is probably not the original one and certainly is not the one used in insurance and finance, where 'risk' is the key word.

4   Rebecca Milner, 'Japan's top buzzwords for 2012', Japan Pulse blog, *Japan Times*, 3 December 2012, http://blog.japantimes.co.jp/japan-pulse/japans-top-10-buzzwords-for-2012 (accessed 3 December 2014).

5   One example would be a law intended to conserve suitable habitats for endangered species by decreeing that no development should be allowed in such places. This could create an incentive to property owners to destroy anything that might be categorised as suitable for an endangered species otherwise the possibility of development might be removed. See Sean Masaki Flynn, 'In pictures: perverse incentives', *Forbes*, 19 February 2009, p. 8, http://www.forbes.com/2009/02/19/bonuses-incentives-pay-leadership-compensation_perverse_incentives_slide_8.html (accessed 3 December 2014).

6   Timur Kuran, 'Now out of Never: The Element of Surprise in the East European Revolution of 1989', *World Politics* 44:1 (1991), pp. 7–48.

7   Frédéric Bastiat, 'What Is Seen and What Is Not Seen', available at Library of Economics and Liberty website, http://www.econlib.org/library/Bastiat/basEss1.html (accessed 3 December 2014).

ACKNOWLEDGEMENTS

1   It is available from the Centre for Independent Studies website: http://www.cis.org.au/publications/cis-special-publications/article/3474-when-prophecy-fails (accessed 3 December 2014).

Index

Picture Credits